T0238696

Communications
in Computer and Information Science   986

Commenced Publication in 2007
Founding and Former Series Editors:
Phoebe Chen, Alfredo Cuzzocrea, Xiaoyong Du, Orhun Kara, Ting Liu,
Dominik Ślęzak, and Xiaokang Yang

Editorial Board

Simone Diniz Junqueira Barbosa
Pontifical Catholic University of Rio de Janeiro (PUC-Rio),
Rio de Janeiro, Brazil
Joaquim Filipe
Polytechnic Institute of Setúbal, Setúbal, Portugal
Ashish Ghosh
Indian Statistical Institute, Kolkata, India
Igor Kotenko
St. Petersburg Institute for Informatics and Automation of the Russian
Academy of Sciences, St. Petersburg, Russia
Krishna M. Sivalingam
Indian Institute of Technology Madras, Chennai, India
Takashi Washio
Osaka University, Osaka, Japan
Junsong Yuan
University at Buffalo, The State University of New York, Buffalo, USA
Lizhu Zhou
Tsinghua University, Beijing, China

More information about this series at http://www.springer.com/series/7899

Hu Peng · Changshou Deng
Zhijian Wu · Yong Liu (Eds.)

Computational Intelligence and Intelligent Systems

10th International Symposium, ISICA 2018
Jiujiang, China, October 13–14, 2018
Revised Selected Papers

Editors
Hu Peng
School of Information Science
and Technology
Jiujiang University
Jiujiang, China

Changshou Deng
School of Information Science
and Technology
Jiujiang University
Jiujiang, China

Zhijian Wu
School of Computer
Wuhan University
Wuhan, China

Yong Liu
School of Computer Science
and Engineering
The University of Aizu
Aizu-Wakamatsu, Fukushima, Japan

ISSN 1865-0929   ISSN 1865-0937   (electronic)
Communications in Computer and Information Science
ISBN 978-981-13-6472-3   ISBN 978-981-13-6473-0   (eBook)
https://doi.org/10.1007/978-981-13-6473-0

Library of Congress Control Number: 2019931955

© Springer Nature Singapore Pte Ltd. 2019
This work is subject to copyright. All rights are reserved by the Publisher, whether the whole or part of the material is concerned, specifically the rights of translation, reprinting, reuse of illustrations, recitation, broadcasting, reproduction on microfilms or in any other physical way, and transmission or information storage and retrieval, electronic adaptation, computer software, or by similar or dissimilar methodology now known or hereafter developed.
The use of general descriptive names, registered names, trademarks, service marks, etc. in this publication does not imply, even in the absence of a specific statement, that such names are exempt from the relevant protective laws and regulations and therefore free for general use.
The publisher, the authors and the editors are safe to assume that the advice and information in this book are believed to be true and accurate at the date of publication. Neither the publisher nor the authors or the editors give a warranty, express or implied, with respect to the material contained herein or for any errors or omissions that may have been made. The publisher remains neutral with regard to jurisdictional claims in published maps and institutional affiliations.

This Springer imprint is published by the registered company Springer Nature Singapore Pte Ltd.
The registered company address is: 152 Beach Road, #21-01/04 Gateway East, Singapore 189721, Singapore

Preface

The current volume of CCIS comprises the proceedings of the 10th International Symposium on Intelligence Computation and Applications (ISICA 2018) held in Jiujiang, China, during October 13–14, 2018. ISICA 2018 successfully attracted over 80 submissions. After rigorous reviews and plagiarism checking, 32 high-quality papers were selected for inclusion in CCIS 986. ISICA conferences are one of the first series of international conferences on computational intelligence that combine elements of learning, adaptation, evolution, and fuzzy logic to create programs as alternative solutions to artificial intelligence. The past ISICA proceedings including six volumes of CCIS and four volumes of LNCS have been indexed in DBLP, Google Scholar, EI-Compendex, Mathematical Reviews, SCImago, and Scopus.

ISICA 2018 featured the most up-to-date research in the analysis and theory of evolutionary computation, neural network architectures and learning, neuro-dynamics and neuro-engineering, fuzzy logic and control, collective intelligence and hybrid systems, deep learning, knowledge discovery, and reasoning. ISICA 2018 provided a venue to foster technical exchanges, renew everlasting friendships, and establish new connections. Prof. Yuanxiang Li, one of the pioneers in parallel and evolutionary computation at Wuhan University, wrote a beautiful poem in Chinese for the ISICA 2018 event. It is our pleasure to translate his poem with the title of "ISICA2018 in Jiujiang":

> Purple mist is rising on the top of Lu Mountain;
> Clear stream is lying in Lianxi;
> We are coming to the Xunyang river bank;
> Surrounded by the three rivers of Xiangjiang, Yangtze, and Ganjiang;
> For the meeting of intelligence applications.
> Both young talent and old friends;
> Gather at the ancient Zhu Xi's School;
> Admire how Zhu Xi advanced Confucianism, Buddhism and Taoism;
> Watch the stone in the stream where Zhu Xi had a nap;
> Look for creative inspiration for evolutionary computation.

Prof. Li's poem points out one of ISICA's missions of pursuing the truth that a complex system inherits the simple mechanism of evolution, while simple models may lead to the evolution of complex morphologies. Following the success of the past nine ISICA events, ISICA 2018 continued to explore the new problems emerging in the fields of computational intelligence.

On behalf of the Organizing Committee, we would like to thank warmly the sponsors, Jiujiang University and Wuhan University, who helped in one way or another to achieve our goals for the conference. We wish to express our appreciation to Springer for publishing the proceedings of ISICA 2018. We also wish to acknowledge the dedication and commitment of both the staff at the Springer Beijing Office and the

CCIS editorial staff. We would like to thank the authors for submitting their work, as well as the Program Committee members and reviewers for their enthusiasm, time, and expertise. The invaluable help of active members of the Organizing Committee, including Xiaogang Dong, Hui Wang, Xinyu Zhou, Peng Hu, Feipeng Wang, Juan Zhu, Yan Zhang, Yan Liu, Haiyan Huang, Xiaojing Wang, Youxue Zhou, and Jian-qiang Chen, in setting up and maintaining the online submission systems by EasyChair, assigning the papers to the reviewers, and preparing the camera-ready version of the proceedings is highly appreciated. We would like to thank them for helping to make ISICA 2018 a success.

November 2018

Hu Peng
Changshou Deng
Zhijian Wu
Yong Liu

Organization

ISICA 2018 was organized by Jiujiang University and sponsored by Wuhan University.

Honorary Chairs

Zhangxin Chen	University of Calgary, Canada
Qingfu Zhang	City University of Hong Kong, SAR China

General Chairs

Changshou Deng	Jiujiang University, China
Zhijian Wu	Wuhan University, China
Yong Liu	University of Aizu, Japan

Program Chairs

Yuanxiang Li	Wuhan University, China
Lixin Ding	Wuhan University, China
Kangshun Li	South China Agricultural University, China

Local Chair

Hu Peng	Jiujiang University, China

Publicity Chairs

Xiaogang Dong	Jiujiang University, China
Hui Wang	Nanchang Institute of Technology, China
Xinyu Zhou	Jiangxi Normal University, China

Contents

Nature-Inspired Computing

Bio-Inspired Computing

Knowledge-Based Artificial Intelligence

Predictive Data Mining

Nature-Inspired Computing

Solve the IRP Problem with an Improved PSO

Zelin Wang[1](✉), Shi Cheng[1], and Hu Peng[2]

[1] College of Computer Science and Technology, Nantong University,
Nantong 226009, China
whwzl@whu.edu.cn
[2] School of Information Science and Technology, Jiujiang University,
Jiujiang 332005, China

Abstract. It is difficult to solve the inventory-routing problem, because it is a NP hard problem. To find the optimal solution with polynomial time is very difficult. Many scholars have studied it for many years to find a good solving method. This paper analyzed the inventory-routing optimization problem. Then considered PSO has a good performance in solving combinatorial optimization problems. The PSO was improved to make it be suitable for solving discrete combination optimization problems. In order to improve the performance of the PSO algorithm to solve the inventory routing problem, this paper put forward dynamic adjustment of inertia weight and accelerator factor of the PSO, and introduced mutation operator in PSO. It is proved by numerical experiments that the proposed algorithm has certain performance advantages, and it also proves that the improved algorithm can improve the performance of the algorithm.

Keywords: Particle swarm optimization algorithm ·
Inventory routing problem · Inertia weight · Accelerated factor

1 Introduction

Inventory routing problem (IRP) is to determine the inventory strategy and distribution strategy. The inventory strategy aims to determine the distribution object and distribution number of goods in every planning period, and distribution strategy is to determine the commodity distribution route. IRP seeks to minimize the sum of inventory costs and distribution costs. The IRP problem is the combination of inventory problem and distribution problem, which is to solve these two problems on one platform at the same time. Because these two problems are the opposite problem, in the pursuit of the minimum inventory cost, it will inevitably bring the maximum distribution cost; On the contrary, if the pursuit of distribution cost is minimized, it will inevitably bring the maximum inventory cost. But at the same time solve the two problems is a very tough job, both the problem itself is N-P difficult problem. Especially when the customer number of distribution goods is more, and the customer's demand is stochastic demand conditions, the problem of IRP optimal strategy is often very complex. The solution of problem often makes delivery number, distribution interval and the distribution route lack of stability. This paper tries to +adopt the greedy algorithm and the improved discrete differential evolution algorithm to search IRP approximate optimal solution.

© Springer Nature Singapore Pte Ltd. 2019
H. Peng et al. (Eds.): ISICA 2018, CCIS 986, pp. 3–16, 2019.
https://doi.org/10.1007/978-981-13-6473-0_1

In the existing available literature, the literature [1] through theoretical analysis and proof, there is a 98.5% chance of getting the best of the problem with the strategy of fixed partition to solve the problem of inventory cost and distribution cost. The partition can effectively simplify the problem and reduce the difficulty of the problem. Therefore, this paper also adopts the idea of fixed partition, which does not need to cost a lot of cost for the low probability event. Literature [2] is the earliest IRP partition thought introduction. The author put the individual customer requirements decomposition, and allow multiple vehicles to serve a customer, so that in the actual operation of the problem there will be more difficult. Literature [3] improved the literature [2]. Each customer can only allow a vehicle to server in a delivery period, can't separate distribution, but the strategy is to seek the optimal solution, so that the scale of problem is relatively small size. Literature [4] adopts the classic Lagrangian relaxation algorithm to solve the IRP problem, which is complicated and not easy to implement. Moreover, with the increase of the size of the problem, the complexity of the algorithm increases exponentially.

In solving the questions of IRP, because of the complexity of the problem itself, when the problem scale is larger, to find the optimal solution is a very tricky question. Literature [5] to try using the variable neighborhood search heuristic intelligent methods to solve the problem of IRP. The IRP problem is solved in two phases. First using variable neighborhood search heuristic algorithm to solve the vehicle routing problem with limited capacity, and this stage is not considering the inventory cost, which purpose is to achieve a feasible initial solution. Then in the second stage the initial solution is optimized with iteration method, and the ideal results have been achieved. In literature [6], the author proposed a tabu search heuristic intelligent algorithm to solve the problem of the shortest path of the inventory, and compared the running effect of the algorithm with the effect of the original Lagrangian relaxation algorithm, and proved that this method proposed is far superior effect.

From literature [7–9], from one side we can see that the PSO, in recent years, has made significant effect, because of its global convergence and robustness in solving massive combinatorial optimization problems. In this paper, the problem of IRP is solved by using the greedy method and the improved discrete PSO algorithm.

2 Problem Model

2.1 Problem Description

For the logistics mode based on the supplier management inventory, a distribution center corresponds to multiple n customers scattered in different geographical locations, with $n = \{0, 1, 2, 3 \ldots N\}$ to represent the collection of customers, where 0 represents the distribution center. Assuming that the requirements of n customers for the product in the distribution center are random, but the needs of the customers are relatively independent, and the customers demand distribution is the same. Each customer's needs cannot be broken up. Assuming that the inventory cost of the distribution center is not considered, and the product assumption of the distribution center will not be out of stock. Assuming that the number of vehicles is unlimited and the driving ability is unlimited, and have the same loading capacity, and the demand of each customer will not exceed the load capacity of the vehicle. If the customer's order quantity exceeds the demand, the corresponding inventory cost will be increased. If the order quantity is less than the quantity demanded, it will cause the loss of goods. The vehicle starts from the distribution center and ends up at the distribution center. The goal of solving the problem is to seek inventory strategy and distribution strategy of the minimization sum of inventory cost and distribution cost.

2.2 Variable Definition and Problem Modeling

See Table 1.

Table 1. Variable definition

Variable	Implication
n	Customer number
u_i	Random quantity demand of customer i
x_i	Inventory of customer i
v	Vehicle number
C_v	Load capacity
c_{ij}	Delivery cost between the customer i and customer j
h_i	Unit inventory rate of customer i
P_i	Unit loss rate of customer i
d_i	Delivery quantity of customer i
c_i	Maximum inventory of customer i
$f_i(u_i)$	Density function of random demand of customer i
x_{ijv}	$x_{ijv} = \begin{cases} 1 & \text{delivery vehicle } v \text{ drive from customer } i \text{ to customer } j \\ 0 & \text{otherwise} \end{cases}$

Inventory cost:

$$H_i = h_i \int_0^{x_i+d_i} (x_i + d_i - u_i)f_i(u_i)du_i + p_i \int_{x_i+d_i}^{\infty} (u_i - (x_i + d_i))f_i(u_i)du_i \quad (1)$$

Delivery cost:

$$c_t = \sum_{i=0}^{n}\sum_{j=0}^{n}\sum_{v=1}^{v} c_{ij}x_{ijv} \quad (2)$$

IRP total cost model:

$$\min \ c_{all} = c_t + \sum_{i=1}^{n} H_i \tag{3}$$

s.t.

$$\sum_{v=1}^{v} \sum_{j=1}^{n} x_{ijv} = 1 \quad \forall i \in N \tag{4}$$

$$\sum_{v=1}^{v} \sum_{i=1}^{n} x_{ijv} = 1 \quad \forall j \in N \tag{5}$$

$$\sum_{i=1}^{n} x_{i0v} = 1 \quad v = 1, 2, \cdots v \tag{6}$$

$$\sum_{i=1}^{n} x_{0iv} = 1 \quad v = 1, 2, \cdots v \tag{7}$$

3   PSO Algorithm and Improvisation

3.1   PSO Algorithm Basic Idea

Assuming that the problem to be solved is a minimization problem, and the mathematical model of the problem is $min \ f \ (x_1, x_2, \ldots, x_n)$, where $x_j \in [L_j, U_j]$, and $1 \leq j \leq n$. The $X(0)$ is the initial population. Let $X_i(t) = (x_{i1}(t), x_{i2}(t), \ldots, x_{in}(t))$ is the ith individual in the t-generation population, and the population individual is n-dimensional spatial structure, and the population size is NP. The particle swarm optimization algorithm (PSO) [7], which is a kind of superior performance of intelligent algorithms, was put forward by the Eberhart and Kennedy in 1995. The algorithm requires cooperation between individual in the population, using the outstanding individuals in the population as well as the best individual in their own history for the evolution of individuals, so as to achieve the population individual information sharing, and excellent individual competitive learning each other, to realize swarm intelligence, and guidance optimization of population evolution in the process of the whole [8, 9]. PSO algorithm using speed position search model, form is as follows:

$$V_{id}(N+1) = W \times V_{id}(N) + c_1 \times rand() \times (P_{id} - V_{id}(N)) \\ + c_2 \times rand() \times (P_{gd} - X_{id}(N)) \tag{8}$$

$$X_{id}(N+1) = X_{id}(N) + V_{id}(N+1) \tag{9}$$

Equations (8) and (9) indicates that the position of the ith particle of n particles in the solution space of D dimension is $X_i = (X_{i1}, X_{i2}, \ldots, X_{id})$, the velocity is $V_i = (V_{i1}, V_{i2}, \ldots, V_{id})$, where $i = (1, 2, \ldots, n)$, and $d = (1, 2, \ldots, D)$. The fitness value is calculated by substituting Xi into the optimization objective function, and the optimal individual of the ith particle is $P_i = (P_{i1}, P_{i2}, \ldots, P_{id})$, called P_{best}, and the optimal individual of the whole particle swarm is $Pg = (P_{g1}, P_{g2}, \ldots, P_{gd})$, called Pgest. The particle swarm searches the entire solution space through velocity and position update. In [11], the W is the inertial weight, the c_1 and c_2 are acceleration factors, also known as individual and social learning factors, and a random number which is between 0 and 1 can gained by the rand() function, and N is the number of current iterations. The calculation ideas of individual optimal individuals and global optimal individuals are as follows:

$$P_{best}(t+1) = \begin{cases} P_{best}(t) \; if f\,(P_{best}(t)) < f(x_i(t+1)) \\ x_i(t+1), \; if f(x_i(t+1)) < \; = f(P_{best}(t)) \end{cases} \tag{10}$$

$$P_{gest}(t+1) = min\{P_1(t+1), P_2(t+1), \cdots, P_N(t+1)\} \tag{11}$$

Where, $f(.)$ is the objective function of the optimization problem, corresponding to the fitness function of PSO algorithm. The fitness function of different optimization problems is also different. When the algorithm updates the extreme, it is the priority to update the individual optimal value of the particles, and then to update the global optimal value according to the individual optimal value of all particles. Since the $Pgest$ in the entire particle swarm is taken as the optimal position. The PSO described above is also called global PSO. If the optimal location found in the fixed neighborhood of each particle is $Pgest$, this is the local version of PSO.

The PSO algorithm is simple and requires fewer parameters to be controlled. The specific algorithm is as follows:

Step 1: Initialize the algorithm and set the initial values of various basic parameters (such as the number of particles, maximum iteration times, acceleration factor, inertia weight, etc.).

Step 2: Randomly generate particles of the initial position and velocity sequences;

Step 3: Use the objective function to evaluate the particle, and calculate the $Pbest$ and $pgest$ initial value;

Step 4: Use formulation (8) to update the particle's velocity;

Step 5: Use formulation (9) to update the particle's position;

Step 6: Calculate the fitness value of particles, and use the formulation (10) to update the particle's individual $Pbest$ optimal position;

Step 7: Use formulation (11), according to the updated all particle $Pbest$ values, to update $Pgest$;

Step 8: Judge algorithm whether meets the termination conditions or not (reach the specified number of iterations or already get the optimal value or meet other conditions), if judgment result is to satisfy the condition, go to step 9, or return to step 4;

Step 9: Record and output pgest value and stop the algorithm.

3.2 Improvement of Particle Swarm Optimization Algorithm for IRP Problem

Discrete Particle Swarm Optimization Algorithm

PSO algorithm in solving large-scale, multidimensional problems has natural advantages which avoided the inefficiencies of exhaustive search, also avoids the random search without purpose. It has the direction, global search algorithm with a purpose. It had been proved by theory and practical application that it is an excellent algorithm in many intelligent algorithms for solving large-scale, multidimensional combinational optimal problems.

This paper is to solve the IRP problem by step method, and the first step is to operate partition and optimize partition.

The second step is to change the PSO algorithm into discrete PSO algorithm. First of all, the traditional PSO algorithm which can solving continuous optimization problems was improved, made him into can solve a discrete combination optimization problems.

Because each partition obtained by the first step optimization is an independent loop of Hamilton, and each individual solution is a Hamilton loop, therefore, need to use PSO to solve partition optimization. The classical PSO algorithm must be improved for the particle's position, speed, and operating in the following the corresponding improvement.

1. The position can be defined as a Hamilton circle with all nodes. Assuming that there are N nodes, and the arc between them exists. The position of the particle can be expressed as sequence $x = (n_1, n_2, \ldots, n_N, n_1)$.

2. The velocity can be defined as the exchange set of particle position, which can be described as an ordered list of permutation sequence, denoted as: $V = \{(i_k, j_k), i_k, j_k \in \{1, 2, \ldots, N\}, k \in \{1, 2, \ldots, m\}\}$, where m is the number of velocity transformation. In the exchange sequence, first, the first exchange subset is performed. Then, the second exchange is performed, and so on.

3. The addition operation Position and velocity
   The operation is that a group of permutation sequences were acted on the position of a particle, in turn. The operation result is a new position.

4. Subtraction of position and position
   The result of subtraction of the particle position and position is too a new permutation sequence. For example, if $x = (1, 3, 2, 5, 4, 1)$, $y = (1, 2, 4, 5, 3, 1)$, then $x + s_1 + s_2 = y$, $s_1 = (5, 2), s_2 = (3, 2), y - x = \{(5, 2), (3, 2)\}$.

5. The addition operation of the particle velocity and velocity
   The result of two permutation sequences combinations is a new permutation sequence. That is, a new velocity.

6. The multiplication of real numbers and particle velocity
   Assuming that c is a real number, which value is a random, in (0, 1), and the velocity is a permutation sequence. The essence of the multiplication is to intercept permutation sequence, where the intercept value is int(c * k).

Dynamic Adjustment of the PSO Parameters

Because the inertia weight W has a great influence on the global search ability and local search ability of the PSO algorithm, therefore, the specific setting method of its value is worth studying. In the process of the operation of the algorithm. We hope that the global convergence capability is getting weaker and weaker, while the local search capability is getting stronger and stronger, so that we can give consideration to the both convergence of the algorithm and avoiding premature phenomenon. Clearly setting a fixed value to it does not balance the two factors. According to the analysis of the problem, the inertia weight W should be in reverse relation with the number of evolution generation, that is, with the gradual advance of the evolution, it gradually decreases.

In addition, the choice method of the acceleration factor c_1, c_2 can adopt random choice or purposeful choice. Appropriate choice method of them will improve the convergence speed of algorithm and avoid be caught into the local extremum.

In view of the problem of IRP, this paper used the cauchy distribution to dynamic adjust the inertial weight W. Cauchy distribution flanks are widely distributed, which is suitable for research of IRP. The algorithm can expand in the evolution process of the evolution of the range, so as not to fall into local optimum. Dynamic adjustment is carried out according to the following formula.

$$F = \begin{cases} 1 - \left| \frac{f_{ave} - f}{f_{ave} - f_{best}} \right| & if \quad f_{ave} > f \\ Cauchy(-2, 0.4) & otherwise \end{cases} \tag{12}$$

Where f is the fitness value of $Xa(t)$ individual, and f_{ave} is the average fitness value of the current population, and f_{best} is the best fitness value of the current population.

The probability density function of cauchy distribution is

$$f(x) = \frac{1}{\pi} \left[\frac{0.4}{(x-2)^2 + 0.4} \right] \tag{13}$$

Where the dynamic adjustment of the inertial weight W is related to the fitness value, adjust dynamically according to the fitness value.

For C_1, C_2 acceleration factor dynamic adjustment, this paper adjusted it based on evolution generation. In the initial stages of the evolution. Let the C_1 smaller values, so that keep the diversity of population. Along with the evolution of advancing step by step, slowly increase the value of the C_1 to speed up the convergence speed of the algorithm. The C_1 is adjusted according to the following formula.

$$c1 = \begin{cases} \frac{g}{100-g} + 1 & c1 < 3 \\ 3 & otherwise \end{cases} \tag{14}$$

Where, g is the value of the current generation variable. Let C_1 value dynamic adjust tin the [1, 3]. In addition, $C_2 = 4 - C_1$.

Mutation Operation

Relative to the evolutionary algorithm, the particle swarm optimization has not crossover and mutation operations. Although the method is simple, it inevitably weakens algorithm's ability to control the global search and local search. In order to further improve the performance of particle swarm optimization algorithm, this paper introduced mutation operator into PSO algorithm.

In previous studies, random mutation and gaussian mutation are the most frequently used for mutation operator. The random mutations can significantly increase the algorithm's global search ability, but ignore the current solution, thereby reducing the performance of the PSO, and Gauss algorithm can enhance the local search ability of algorithm, also may let algorithm falls into local optimum, cause premature phenomenon.

The ability of particle swarm optimization algorithm has a lot to do with inertia weight W. The W Settings, in the last section, used cauchy distribution to dynamically adjust, so that in solving practical problems the performance of the algorithm was greatly improved. In order to increase the global searching ability in the early stage of evolution, random mutation operator is introduced into PSO algorithm. In order to increase the ability of local search, gaussian mutation operator is introduced into PSO algorithm. In order not to allow the algorithm to search everywhere aimlessly at the initial stage, random operators can be introduced in probability, and gaussian variation can be introduced in probability to avoid the algorithm falling into the local optimum. Formula (9) is improved as follows:

$$X_{id}(N+1) = \begin{cases} X_{id}(N) + V_{id}(N+1) & rand[0,1] < 0.5 \\ rand[x_{min}, x_{max}] & otherwise \end{cases} \tag{15}$$

$$X_{id}(N+1) = \begin{cases} X_{id}(N) + V_{id}(N+1) & rand[0,1] < 0.5 \\ P_{gest}(1 + Gauss(\sigma)) & otherwise \end{cases} \tag{16}$$

In the early evolution, using formula (15) instead of formula (9), and in the late evolution, using formula (16) to replace the formula (9). In this way, the algorithm not only considers the particularity of the individual, avoiding aimless global search, but, to some extent, enhances the global search ability of the algorithm. It is considered to avoid falling into the local optimum and to some extent enhance the local search capability in the later stage of the algorithm.

Therefore, this paper improves the standard PSO algorithm from three aspects, so as to guarantee the diversity of individual population and the convergence of the algorithm.

4   PSO Idea of Solving Stochastic Demand IRP Problem

4.1   The Client is Partitioned by Greedy Algorithm

First of all, according to the vehicle capacity and client demand quantity and the client's location coordinates, used a greedy algorithm to partition the customers, consequently get partition set, and then optimized the partition set by discrete differential evolution, consequently get S collection of partition.

IRP is a very complex problem of N-P. This article first to establish the coordinate system of coordinates dot with distribution center, and then sorted customer with location of abscissa x value from small to large, and then sorted customer with ordinate Y value from small to large. So we have a set of $X((Xm, y_1), (x_2, y_2), \ldots, (x_n, y_n))$. According to the initial demand quantity μ of each customer, algorithm partitioned customer. Partition started scanning from customer (Xm, y_1) in collection X, with the limit Cv vehicle capacity. The set X divided into M subset, respectively, the $XM((Xm, y_1), (x_2, y_2), \ldots, (x_i, y_i), X_2(), \ldots, Xm())$. The sum of customers demand quantity in each subset is not more than Cv. Let's say that this M subset is K_1.

Adjusted partitions, Surrounded each customer in a loop according to coordinate in the Fig. 1. The last element in the set Xm was transferred to the first element of the X_1 collection, and then checked whether the sum of all customers demand quantity in X_1 collection is more than vehicle capacity Cv, such as more than, transferred the last element of the X_1 set to X_2 set, become the first element in the X_2 set. Continued checking where the sum of all customers demand quantity in X_1 collection exceed the vehicle capacity, such as more than, continued to transfer the current last element of the X_1 to become the first element in the X_2. So repeatedly, until the sum demand quantity in the set X_1 did not exceed vehicle capacity. And then I was going to adjust X_2 as the method of adjustment X_1, and then I was going to check X_3 again, and I was going to do it again and again until M sets were checked out. Let's say that the set was K_2.

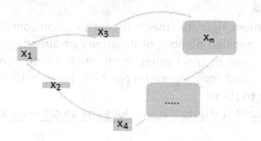

Fig. 1. Customer coordinate

Again to adjust set K_2 as the method of adjustment set K_1, and K_3 set was gotten, and so on, Ks sets were gotten. If the sum of demand of the last element in X_{m-1} and the demand of all the elements of X_m did not more than vehicle capacity, put this element to the X_m set. Let's go to consider the penultimate element of X_{m-1} until the sum of new elements demand which you consider and the all element demand of the new X_m set was more than vehicle capacity. No longer join, at this point, the number of elements in new X_m is S value.

4.2 The Improved Discrete PSO Algorithm is Used to Optimize the Partition

Through the first step processing, the S partition sets is obtained. The improved discrete difference evolution algorithm is adopted to optimize the path of s partition sets to find the optimal partition set of S partitions.

The algorithm step

The algorithm for looking for the optimal partition set
1 Initialization population number NP, generation number g
2 Initial position sequence and initial velocity sequence of population particles randomly or greedy
3 The particle was evaluated by using the objective function of the problem and the initial values of P_{best} and P_{gest} were calculated
4 According to formulation (12) (13) and (14), the W C_1 C_2 were calculated
5 Formulation (8) is used to update the particle velocity
6 Formulation (14) or (15) is used to update the particle position
7 Calculation the fitness value of particle and update individual optimal position of particle
8 Update the p_{gest} using the formulation (11),according to all the P_{best}
9 Judgment algorithm meets the termination conditions (reach the specified number of iterations or already get the optimal value or meet other conditions), if meets the termination conditions, algorithm reached the step 10, if not to return to step 4
10 Record and output p_{gest} values and stop the algorithm

5 Numerical Experiment

5.1 Set Relevant Parameters

1. Set population scale NP = 50
2. Set evolution generation g = 100
3. Set customer number n = 10
4. C_{ij} is proportional to the distance between customer i and customer j, which is set the line spacing between them.
5. Set inventory rate $h = 1$, and the loss rate $p = 10$
6. Set vehicle delivery capacity $Cv = 600$
7. Set customer requirement $\mu < 200$, which follow a poisson distribution

5.2   Numerical Experiment

The Experiment Designed According to of Hybrid Algorithm Proposed in this Paper

According to the greedy algorithm of Sect. 3.1, and according to the coordinate value, client ranked as follows (Table 2):

(3, 9, 4, 7, 5, 10, 2, 6, 8, 1)

And then, according to the greedy algorithm, we got the first partition set K1:

((3, 9, 4, 7), (5, 10, 2)(6, 8, 1))

Finally, according to the greedy algorithm, a series of partition sets are obtained:

K2: ((1, 3, 9, 4), (7, 5, 10), (2, 6, 8))

K3: ((8, 1, 3), (9, 4, 7, 5), (10, 2, 6))

Table 2. Client dataSet

Client	Client coordinates	Client requirement	Maximum inventory
0*	(0, 0)	150	200
1	(85, 29)	199	200
2	(50, 60)	180	200
3	(5, 40)	177	200
4	(18, 5)	140	200
5	(30, 88)	166	200
6	(60, 49)	88	200
7	(25, 48)	90	200
8	(72, 30)	199	200
9	(10, 39)	160	200
10	(45, 76)	197	200

*Client 0 is delivery center, which inventory is set infinity.

Through the greedy algorithm of Sect. 3, we end up with three partition sets, *K1*, *K2*, *K3*. Furthermore, the discrete PSO algorithm of Sect. 3.2 is used to optimize the three partitions, to find the optimal distribution path, to find the optimal partition.

K1: ((3, 9, 7, 4), (5, 10, 2), (61, 8)); total cost: 125.41 + 207.042 + 200.39 = 532.842

K2: ((3, 9, 1, 4), (7, 10, 5), (2, 6, 8)); total cost: 210.831 + 200.532 + 193.307 = 602.79

K3: ((1, 8, 3), (9, 5, 7, 4), (10, 6, 2)); total cost: 210.852 + 195.652 + 196.392 = 602.896

Thus, the optimal partition set is evolved: *K1*, and delivery routing is: (0-3-9-7-4-0) (0-5-10-2-0) (0-2-6-8-0), total cost was 532.842.

The Experiment was Carried out With the Previous Ideas

According to [5], the results of the experiment were also obtained by the optimal set K_1, but the experiment time was 2.0375e−4s, and the experiment time of the paper algorithm was 1.99041E−4s.

According to [6], the results of the experiment were also obtained by the optimal set K_1, and the experiment time was 2.0535E−4s.

Experiment adopted the discrete PSO algorithm, which was improved by standard PSO algorithm. but the inertial weight W and accelerated factor C_1, C_2 were not adjusted by dynamic adjustment mechanism, but a series of fixed values are used for the experiment.

Table 3. Experimental results of different W adjustment methods

W adjustment method	Optimal partition set	Time consumption	Minimum cost
0.4	((1, 8, 3), (9, 5, 7, 4), (10, 6, 2))	2.0037E−4	604.82
0.5	((3, 9, 1, 4), (7, 10, 5), (2, 6, 8))	2.001E−4	602.93
0.8	((3, 9, 7, 4), (5, 10, 2), (61, 8))	3.407E−4	533.064
Self-adjustment	((3, 9, 7, 4), (5, 10, 2), (61, 8))	1.99041E−4	532.842

Table 4. Experimental results of different C_1 adjustment methods

C_1 factor adjustment method	Optimal partition set	Time consumption	Minimum cost
0.4	((3, 9, 7, 4), (5, 10, 2), (61, 8))	2.382E−4	533.072
0.6	((3, 9, 1, 4), (7, 10, 5), (2, 6, 8))	2.0108E−4	603.076
0.9	((1, 8, 3), (9, 5, 7, 4), (10, 6, 2))	2.0039E−4	605.059
Self-adjustment	((3, 9, 7, 4), (5, 10, 2), (61, 8))	1.99041E−4	532.842

Table 5. Experiment results of differential $X_a(t)$ setting strategy

$X_a(t)$ setting strategy	Optimal partition set	Time consumption	Minimum cost
Formulation (9)	((3, 9, 7, 4), (5, 10, 2), (61, 8))	2.3189E−4	532.842
Random mutation	((3, 9, 1, 4), (7, 10, 5), (2, 6, 8))	1.8311E−4	603.10
Gaussian mutation	((3, 9, 1, 4), (7, 10, 5), (2, 6, 8))	1.8294E−4	603.07
Strategy proposed by this paper	((3, 9, 7, 4), (5, 10, 2), (61, 8))	1.99041E−4	532.842

6 Analysis

Through the analysis of Sect. 4.1 experiment, it can be concluded that the algorithm proposed in this paper is practical feasible, and can find the optimal solution in many feasible solutions.

Through the analysis of Sect. 4.2 experiment, it shows that the proposed algorithm has the advantages of real, although use [5, 6] thinking also can obtain the optimal partition set, but time consuming compared with the algorithm of this paper, a little less. [5] time consuming is 2.0375E−4, but the experiment by the algorithm proposed by this paper is 1.99041E−4. Compared with the algorithm in this paper, which is 2.2% slower. [6] it takes 2.0535e−4s, which is 3.0 points slower than the algorithm in this paper.

Through the analysis of Table 3 experiments, this paper puts forward the adjustment method of the W weight. When W is set to 0.4 and 0.5, the algorithm will go into local optimum algorithm, but W is set to 0.8, although can obtain the optimal partition set, but takes up a lot of 1.349e−6, increased by 0.67% than the dynamic adjustment idea proposed by this paper.

Through the analysis of Table 4 obtained by experiment, this paper proposed the adjustment of the crossover of differential evolution method is effective. When C_1 is set to 0.6 and 0.9, algorithm search the local optimum. When C_1 is set to 0.4. The algorithm time consumption will take longer. Compared with the algorithm of this paper, it takes 19.6% slower.

Through the analysis of Table 5, the method proposed in this paper has some advantages. Compared with the random mutation, the method is relatively time consumption shorter. Compared with Gaussian mutation, it is relatively not easy to get into local optimization.

7 Conclusion

Through the anatomy of the IRP problem, it is known that it is a NP hard problem, and it is hard to find an ideal solution in a reasonable time. Considering the particle swarm optimization algorithm outstanding performance in solving large-scale, multidimensional performance on combinatorial optimization problems, this paper tried to adopt the particle swarm optimization algorithm to solve the problem of IRP. given the standard particle swarm optimization algorithm is to solve the problem of continuous, and the IRP problem is discrete problems, thus in this paper, the particle swarm optimization algorithm was improved to make it is suitable for solving discrete combination optimization problems.

Additionally according to the particularity of the IRP, in this paper, the particle swarm optimization algorithm is carried on the dynamic adjustment inertial weight W and acceleration factor, to make them with the gradually development of evolution of dynamic adjustment. The purpose is in the early stages of the evolution, the algorithm has more diversity, and along with the advancement of evolution, the convergence of the algorithm was gradually strengthen, such not only ensure the convergence of the algorithm, and also helps the algorithm falls into local optimum.

The feasibility of the proposed algorithm is verified by numerical experiments, and compared with the latest algorithm, the optimal partition set obtained by this algorithm is proved to be optimal. Finally, the experimental results show that the proposed method had the advantage of adjusting the inertial weight and the acceleration factor, and can balance the convergence and the diversity of the population.

Acknowledgments. The authors would like to thank the doctoral fund provided by NanTong university. This work is supported by the Natural science foundation of China (No. 61763019).

References

1. Anily, S., Bramel, J.: An asymptotic 98.5% effective lower bound on fixed partition policies for the inventory-routing problem. Discrete Appl. Math. **145**(1), 22–39 (2004)
2. Anily, S., Federgruen, A.: One warehouse multiple retailer systems with vehicle routing costs. Manag. Sci. **36**(1), 92–114 (1990)
3. Chan, L., Federgruen, A., Simchi-Levi, D.: Probabilistic analyses and practical algorithms for inventory-routing models. Oper. Res. Int. J. **46**(1), 96–106 (1998)
4. Rafie-Majd, Z., Pasandideh, S.H.R., Naderi, B.: Modelling and solving the integrated inventory-location-routing problem in a multi-period and multi-perishable product supply chain with uncertainty: lagrangian relaxation algorithm. Comput. Chem. Eng. **109**, 9–22 (2017)
5. Mjirda, A., Jarboui, B., Macedo, R., Hanafi, S., Mladenovic, N.: A two phase variable neighborhood search for the multi-product inventory routing problem. Comput. Oper. Res. **52**, 291–299 (2014)
6. Li, K.P., Chen, B., Sivakumar, A.I., Wu, Y.: An inventory routing problem with the objective of travel time minimization. Eur. J. Oper. Res. **236**, 936–945 (2014)
7. Tang, R.: Decentralizing and coevolving differential evolution for large-scale global optimization problems. Appl. Intell. **4**, 1–16 (2017)
8. Ghasemishabankareh, B., Li, X., Ozlen, M.: Cooperative coevolutionary differential evolution with improved augmented Lagrangian to solve constrained optimisation problems. Inf. Sci. **369**, 441–456 (2016)
9. Salman, A.A., Ahmad, I., Omran, M.G.H.: A metaheuristic algorithm to solve satellite broadcast scheduling problem. Inf. Sci. **322**, 72–91 (2015)
10. Wang, Z., Wu, Z., Zhang, B.: Packet matching algorithm based on improving differential evolution. Wuhan Univ. J. Nat. Sci. **17**(5), 447–453 (2012)

Artificial Bee Colony Algorithm Based on Uniform Local Search

Yan Zhang[✉], Hu Peng, Changshou Deng, Xiaojing Wang,
Haiyan Huang, and Xujie Tan

School of Information Science and Technology, Jiujiang University,
Jiujiang, China
zy_xx_jju@163.com

Abstract. Although Artificial Bee Colony (ABC) algorithm is simple and efficient, it also has some disadvantages too. For example, the ABC is good at exploration but poor at exploitation and easily falls into local optimum. In order to overcome these shortcomings and improve the efficiency of the algorithm, the Uniform Local Search Artificial Bee Colony (UGABC) algorithm has been proposed in this paper. The algorithm greatly improves the exploitation ability. For the purpose of comparison, we used four algorithms to experiment. The experimental results show that the UGABC has the best accuracy and the fastest convergence rate among four algorithms.

Keywords: Artificial bee colony · Uniform design · Uniform local search · Gbest

1 Foreword

There are a large number of nonlinear, non-differentiable multi-peak complex optimization problems in the engineering technology and optimizations fields. Traditional optimization methods are difficult to solve these problems. In recent years, the intelligent algorithm proposed by scientists can effectively solve these complex problems. For example, Kenney et al. [1] proposed Particle Swarm Optimization (PSO) algorithm simulating birds predation behavior. Yang et al. [2] proposed Cuckoo Search (CS) algorithm simulating cuckoo parasitic brooding. In 2005, the Turkish scientist Karaboga [3] simulated the behavior of bee collecting honey proposed the Artificial Bee Colony (ABC) algorithm. Compared with some traditional evolutionary algorithms, ABC algorithm has the advantages of simplicity, high speed, strong performance, good robustness, etc. It has a very effect on continuous functions [4, 5], and has been widely supplied and developed.

It is crucial to strike a balance between local search and global search for algorithms to solve optimization problems. Emphasizing local search helps to improve the convergence speed of the algorithm, but it is easy to fall into local optimum. Emphasizing global search helps to find new optimal solutions and avoid premature convergence, but it will reduce the convergence speed of the algorithm. The ABC algorithm is better in global search, while the local search is slightly worse, which makes the algorithm easily fall into local optimum. Peng et al. [6] proposed a uniform

© Springer Nature Singapore Pte Ltd. 2019
H. Peng et al. (Eds.): ISICA 2018, CCIS 986, pp. 17–26, 2019.
https://doi.org/10.1007/978-981-13-6473-0_2

local search method, which randomly selecting two individuals in the population, and generating a new optimal individual through uniform design, which can significantly enhance the local search ability of the algorithm, thereby improving the overall optimization of the algorithm performance.

The ABC algorithm is sensitive to the search strategy, and different search strategies significantly affect the optimization performance of the algorithm. Therefore, scholars have made a lot of improvements to the ABC algorithm's search strategy to improve the optimization performance of the algorithm. Inspired by the PSO algorithm, Zhu and Kwong [7] proposed the GABC algorithm, which introduces a Gbest in the search strategy, which improves the performance of the algorithm. Because the GABC algorithm has small changes to the search strategy, the effect is good and has received extensive attention.

Inspired by the GABC algorithm and the uniform local search method, we proposed a new algorithm named Uniform Local Search Gbest Artificial Bee Colony (UGABC) to solve the optimization problem. The UGABC algorithm combines the strong local search ability of ULS and GABC algorithms in order to improve the optimizations of the algorithm and solve the optimization problems.

2   ABC Algorithm and GABC Algorithm

2.1   ABC Algorithm

In the ABC algorithm, a Food Source represents a feasible solution of the problem to be solved. We use the "Fitness" to measure the pros and cons of a food sources. All bees are divided into Employed Bees, Onlooker Bees and Scout Bees. Different bees guide the entire bee colony to find quality food sources by sharing information and role conversion. At the beginning of the algorithm, all food sources are found by scouts, and then the food source is exploited by employed bees and scout Bees. Continued development has exhausted the resources of the food source, and the employed bees of the food source that depleted the resources are converted into scout bees to find more food sources. For convenience, we take the minimization problem as an example. The steps of the algorithm are as follows.

(1) Initialization phase: Randomly generate SN initial food sources.
(2) Employed bees search for new food sources in their respective food source neighborhoods, and choose a food source with a large fitness value using greedy method. When all employed bees complete the search, they returned to the dance area and share the information of food sources to the onlooker bees by means of swing dance.
(3) Onlooker bees select food sources based on information shared by employed bees, the greater the fitness value, the greater the probability of being selected.
(4) A food source is abandoned if the food source has not been updated after the Limit cycle. The corresponding employed bee is converted into a scout bee. The scout bees use the initialization formula to start randomly looking for new food sources.
(5) Record the best solution so far.

(6) Determine if the termination condition is met. If the termination condition is met, the optimal solution is output and the algorithm ends. Otherwise, go to (2).

· In the step (2), use Eq. 1 to determine the neighbor food source.

$$v_{ij} = x_{ij} + \varphi_{ij}(x_{ij} - x_{kj}) \tag{1}$$

Here x_{ij} is a randomly selected food source, φ_{ij} is a random number between $[-1, 1]$, k is a randomly selected location index.

2.2 GABC Algorithm

The literature [7] proposed the GABC algorithm, which is based on the ABC algorithm to change the formula 1 into the formula 2. Although the changes are small, but the effect is good.

$$v_{ij} = x_{ij} + \varphi_{ij}(x_{ij} - x_{kj}) + \psi_{ij}(y_j - x_{ij}) \tag{2}$$

Here y_j is the Optimal solution of Column j, ψ_{ij} is a random number between $[0, C]$. C is a non-negative constant. C plays a very important role in balancing local search and global search. When C = 0, Eq. 2 becomes Eq. 1. From the literature [7] we know that when C = 1.5, the GABC algorithm works best.

3 Uniform Local Search Artificial Bee Colony Algorithm

3.1 Uniform Local Search

Uniform Design (UD) is an experimental design method jointly proposed by Professor Fang and mathematician Wang in 1978 [8]. The basic idea of UD is to use the number theory method to find some more uniform sets of points in the experimental area, and then use these points to arrange experiments. Such experimental results are representative and it can reduce the number of experiments. Literature [9] proved that if there are k factors, each factor has q levels, if a comprehensive experiment is performed; the number of experiments in the orthogonal design is q^2. The uniform design uses the uniform distribution theory to select q points to do experiments. So the number of experiments is q. When q is large, the superiority of uniform design is very prominent. Compared with the orthogonal design experimental method, the uniform design has the advantages of fewer experiments and better robustness.

Peng et al. proposed a Uniform Local Search (ULS) based on UD and applied it to the DE algorithm. The experimental results show that ULS can enhance the local search ability of the DE algorithm [6].

Like orthogonal design, uniform design also has a set of tables for building experiments. Generally, using $U_n(q^s)$ represent uniform design table. The table has n rows and s columns. Here n represents the number of experiments, s represents the maximum number of independent factors, and each factor contains n levels. Table 1 is a uniform design table. As you can see from Table 1, the maximum number of levels per factor is equal to the number of experiments. For ease of use, uniform design provides a number of experimental tables, and the specific construction of the tables and more experimental tables can be found in Ref. [9, 10].

Table 1. Uniform design table $U_7(7^6)$

No.	1	2	3	4	5	6
1	1	2	3	4	5	6
2	2	4	6	1	3	5
3	3	6	2	5	1	4
4	4	1	5	2	6	3
5	5	3	1	6	4	2
6	6	5	4	3	2	1
7	7	7	7	7	7	7

Literature [6] found that in the process of uniform local search optimization, the $U_6(6^6)$ uniform design table can be obtained by deleting the last row of $U_7(7^6)$. There are two reasons. First, the last line of $U_7(7^6)$ is the original individual, which is redundant. The second reason is that the experimental results obtained in advance show that the results of $U_6(6^6)$ is the best. In the experiment, each factor has six levels to get the best experimental results. If the number of levels of each factor is too large, it will take more evaluations to affect the performance of the algorithm [6].

The uniform local search step is as shown in Algorithm 1. In the ULS, if the problem dimension D is greater than six, we randomly decompose the D dimension into six groups. ULS requires six experimental individuals to be constructed. The total number of evaluations also needs to be six times.

Algorithm 1: Uniform local search

1: Input: Population SN, Function evaluation times FEs;

2: Randomly select two individuals $X_{i,G}$ and $X_{j,G}$ from SN;

3: Combining $X_{i,G}$ and $X_{j,G}$ construct six test individual $Y_1, ..., Y_6$ according to $U_6(6^6)$;

4: Calculating the objective function value $f(Y_1), ..., f(Y_6)$;

5: Choosing an optimal individual O from $Y_1, ..., Y_6$;

6: If $f(X_{i,G}) > f(O)$, replace $X_{i,G}$ with O;

7: $FEs = FEs + 6$;

8: Return and replace SN and FEs.

3.2   Uniform Local Search Artificial Bee Colony Algorithm Steps

The steps of UGABC are shown in Algorithm 2. We embedded the ULS into the loop of GABC in order to enhance the algorithm's local optimization ability. Although ULS can greatly improve the convergence speed, it is a greedy choice mechanism, so if the number of executions of ULS is too many, it may cause the algorithm to fall into local extreme. In order to strike a balance between convergence speed and population diversity, we only perform ULS once per cycle.

Algorithm 2: UGABC

1: Input the number of food sources SN, $Limit$ and Objective function evaluation times $MaxFEs$;

2: Randomly generate SN individuals;

3: Calculate the objective function value of each individual;

4: $FEs = SN$;

5: While $FEs < MaxFEs$

6: For $i = 1 : SN$

7: Eemployed bees to search for new food sources in the neighborhood according to formula (2) and record food sources with better fitness values;

8:   Onlooker bees choose the food source to collect honey according to the information shared by the employed bees. The better the fitness value, the better the probability that the food source is selected;

9: If a food source has not been updated after a limit of cycles, then the food source will be abandoned by the employed bee. The employed bee becomes a scout bee. The scout bee uses the formula (2) to start randomly searching for new solutions;

10: Recording the optimal values and optimal solutions so far;

11: EndFor

12: execution algorithm 1 to perform Uniform Local Search;

13: EndWhile

14: Returns the optimal solution and the optimal value.

---

4   Experimental Results and Analysis

4.1   Test Function and Experiment Setup

In order to verify the effectiveness and superiority of the UGABC algorithm, we selected 13 commonly used benchmark functions in literature [11] as test set. In the simulation experiment, four algorithms of ABC, UABC, GABC and UGABC were selected for comparison experiments. Based on the principle of fairness, the parameters of these four algorithms are: SN = 50, Dim = 30, Limit = 50, MaxFEs = Dim * 5000, where C = 1.5 in GABC algorithm and UGABC algorithm, each benchmark function is independent run 30 times. The hardware environment used in the experiment was Intel I7 processor, 8 GB memory, and the software environment was Windows 7 and MATLAB 7.

In order to objectively and fairly evaluate the experimental results, the results were analyzed using Wilcoxon rank sum test and Friedman test in statistics. The Wilcoxon rank sum test is based on the rank sum of the samples to determine whether the two samples are from the same population. The Wilcoxon rank sum test can analyze whether there is a significant difference between the algorithm participating in the comparison and the experimental result of the UGABC algorithm running independently 30 times on the benchmark functions. The Friedman test uses rank to analyze whether there is a significant difference in the population distribution of multiple independent samples. The Friedman test ranks the rank mean of each sample. The smaller the rank means, the better the test results [12].

4.2 UGABC Algorithm Quality Analysis

The average error and standard deviation of the UGABC algorithm and the other three algorithms are shown in Table 2. The significance level of the Wilcoxon rank sum test is 0.05. At the bottom of Table 2, the symbols "$-$", "$+$", and "$\approx$" are used to indicate that the corresponding algorithm is inferior, superior, and equivalent to the UGABC algorithm. The rank of Friedman test is in Table 4. Figure 1 plots the average convergence curve for each algorithm running independently for 30 times on 13 benchmark functions. It can be found from Table 2 that the UGABC algorithm has strong convergence ability and good convergence precision. From the results of the Wilcoxon rank sum test in the last three rows of Table 2, it can be seen visually that the UGABC algorithm is the best among the algorithms involved in the comparison.

Table 2. Mean error value and standard deviation of algorithms and comparison results based on Wilcoxon's rank sum test

F	MeanError ± StdDev			
	ABC	UABC	GABC	UGABC
f_1	1.54E−16 ± 2.15E−16−	3.67E−23 ± 5.00E−23−	4.43E−32 ± 3.80E−32−	6.17E−38 ± 4.42E−38
f_2	8.85E−11 ± 3.40E−11−	1.62E−13 ± 9.05E−14−	6.34E−18 ± 2.02E−18−	1.40E−20 ± 6.48E−21
f_3	8.24E+03 ± 1.55E+03−	9.06E+01 ± 4.91E+01≈	9.36E+03 ± 2.29E+03−	9.67E+01 ± 4.60E+01
f_4	4.73E+01 ± 4.30E+00−	2.74E+01 ± 3.79E+00−	3.72E+01 ± 4.48E+00−	1.89E+01 ± 1.96E+00
f_5	8.48E−01 ± 6.38E−01+	7.30E−01 ± 1.04E+00+	7.99E−01 ± 3.02E+00+	1.57E+01 ± 2.61E+01
f_6	1.67E−01 ± 3.723E−01−	0.00E+00 ± 0.00+00≈	0.00E+00 ± 0.00+00≈	0.00E+00 ± 0.00+00
f_7	3.08E−01 ± 5.08E−02−	8.66E−02 ± 1.57E−02−	1.37E−01 ± 2.18E−02−	4.44E−02 ± 1.28E−02
f_8	3.82E−04 ± 2.97E−09−	3.82E−04 ± 5.46E−11−	3.82E−04 ± 2.21E−08−	3.82E−04 ± 4.54E−13
f_9	4.07E−12 ± 1.90E−11−	8.70E−15 ± 1.73E−14−	4.14E−16 ± 1.09E−15−	0.00E+00 ± 0.00+00
f_{10}	3.95E−10 ± 1.83E−10−	6.04E−12 ± 2.92E−12−	5.02E−14 ± 7.21E−15−	3.19E−14 ± 3.61E−15
f_{11}	1.08E−07 ± 5.83E−07+	7.40E−18 ± 2.77E−17≈	4.77E−06 ± 2.57E−05+	4.92E−04 ± 2.65E−03
f_{12}	4.50E−19 ± 6.19E−19−	7.85E−25 ± 8.10E−25−	1.58E−32 ± 1.98E−34−	1.57E−32 ± 5.47E−48
f_{13}	1.36E−16 ± 2.91E−16−	2.69E−23 ± 3.81E−23−	3.47E−32 ± 1.63E−32−	1.35E−32 ± 5.47E−48
−	11	9	10	−
+	2	1	2	−
≈	0	3	1	−

As can be seen from Fig. 1, the UGABC algorithm has stronger convergence ability than other algorithms. The convergence speed of UGABC is slightly worse than other algorithms in f_5 and f_{11}. In addition to this, the UGABC algorithm has an absolute advantage. Table 3 gives the Friedman test rankings for the UGABC algorithm and the algorithms involved in the comparison. The GUABC algorithm ranks first, which illustrates the advantages of the UGABC algorithm from a statistical perspective.

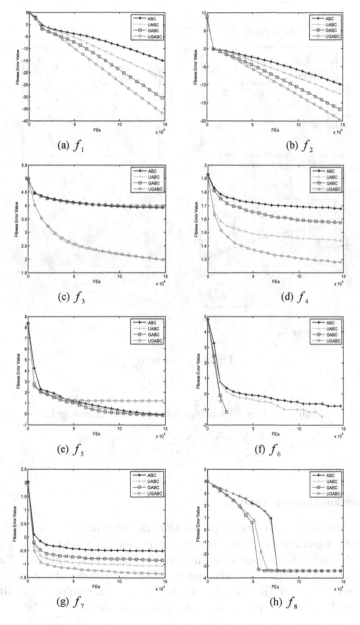

(a) f_1 (b) f_2

(c) f_3 (d) f_4

(e) f_5 (f) f_6

(g) f_7 (h) f_8

Fig. 1. Convergence curve on four algorithms on benchmark functions

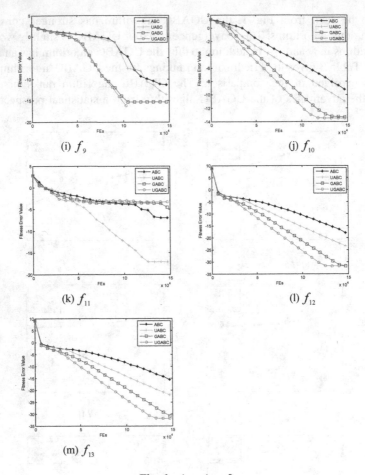

(i) f_9

(j) f_{10}

(k) f_{11}

(l) f_{12}

(m) f_{13}

Fig. 1. (*continued*)

Table 3. Average rankings achieved by Friedman test

ABC	UABC	GABC	UGABC
3.62	2.19	2.54	1.65

4.3   Dimension Change Analysis

To further illustrate the advantages of the UGABC algorithm, we selected different dimensions for experimentation and recorded experimental results. Table 4 gives the experimental results of the four algorithms in 50 dimensions. Similar to Table 2, in order to objectively compare the advantages and disadvantages of the algorithm, the last three lines of Table 4 gives the Wilcoxon rank sum test results of four algorithms. Table 5 gives the Friedman test results for the 50-dimensional.

From Table 4, we find that in the 50-dimensional problems, the UGABC algorithm is significantly better than the ABC algorithm in all benchmark functions. Compared with the UABC algorithm, UGABC has the comparable experimental results on both f_5 and f_{11}. UGABC algorithm is superior to UABC in the rest of the benchmark functions. Compared with the GABC, UGABC slightly worse than GABC in f_5. Both algorithms converge to 0 in f_6. UGABC's test results are better than GABC in other functions.

Table 4. Mean error value and standard deviation of algorithms at dim = 50 and comparison results based on Wilcoxon's rank sum test

F	MeanError ± StdDev			
	ABC	UABC	GABC	UGABC
f_1	2.75E−15 ± 4.37E−15−	4.19E−19 ± 7.77E−19−	1.40E−30 ± 1.82E−30−	3.08E−39 ± 2.07E−39
f_2	2.87E−10 ± 1.38E−10−	8.31E−12 ± 7.06E−12−	3.53E−17 ± 8.03E−18−	3.30E−21 ± 1.48E−21
f_3	3.03E+04 ± 2.84E+03−	5.48E+02 ± 1.80E+02≈	3.41E+04 ± 6.60E+03−	6.56E+02 ± 2.50E+02
f_4	7.04E+01 ± 3.15E+00−	4.14E+01 ± 2.27E+00−	6.61 E+01 ± 3.31E+00−	3.84E+01 ± 2.68E+00
f_5	1.48 E+01 ± 8.82E−01−	1.74E+01 ± 2.80E+01≈	5.61E+00 ± 1.54E+01+	2.81E+01 ± 3.55E+01
f_6	2.23E+00 ± 1.28E+00−	1.17E+00 ± 6.87E−01−	0.00E+00 ± 0.00+00≈	0.00E+00 ± 0.00+00
f_7	8.29 E−01 ± 1.14E−01−	2.09 E−01 ± 5.09E−02−	3.91 E−01 ± 7.16E−02−	1.06 E−01 ± 2.81E−02
f_8	6.37 E−04 ± 6.60E−08−	6.36 E−04 ± 3.49E−10−	6.36 E−04 ± 1.09E−08−	6.36 E−04 ± 2.24E−12
f_9	2.51E−08 ± 1.31E−07−	5.88E−13 ± 2.06E−12−	1.77E−14 ± 2.84E−14−	0.00E+00 ± 0.00E+00
f_{10}	6.47E−10 ± 2.23E−10−	1.11E−09 ± 8.89E−10−	1.29E−13 ± 1.45E−14−	6.56E−14 ± 6.72E−15
f_{11}	9.81E−12 ± 5.04E−11−	8.62E−05 ± 4.62 E−04−	1.97E−10 ± 1.05E−09−	0.00E+00 ± 0.00E+00
f_{12}	1.45E−18 ± 1.61E−18−	1.12E−20 ± 1.79E−20≈	1.17E−32 ± 3.52E−33−	9.42E−33 ± 8.69E−36
f_{13}	1.01E−15 ± 9.14E−16−	1.59E−19 ± 2.28E−19−	6.24E−31 ± 5.96E−31−	1.35E−32 ± 2.21E−34
−	13	11	11	−
+	0	0	1	−
≈	0	2	1	−

Table 5. Average rankings achieved at dim = 50 by Friedman test

Dim	ABC	UABC	GABC	UGABC
50	3.46	2.73	2.42	1.38

5   Conclusion

In order to improve the local search ability of the ABC algorithm, this paper proposes an artificial bee colony algorithm based on uniform local search. The algorithm introduces Gbest for neighborhood search in the stage of employed bees and onlooker bees, and embeds ULS after each cycle, which significantly improves the local search ability of the algorithm. It can be seen that the UGABC algorithm is superior to the comparison algorithm in solving accuracy, convergence speed and running time from the test results of different dimensions of 13 standard benchmark functions.

Acknowledgement. This work was supported by The National Science Foundation of China (No. 61763019), The Natural Science Foundation of Heilongjiang Province (General Program: F2017019), The Science and Technology Plan Projects of Jiangxi Province Education Department (No. GJJ161072, No. GJJ161076, No. GJJ170953), The Education Planning Project of Jiangxi Province (No. 15YB138, No. 17YB211).

References

1. Kennedy, J., Eberhart, R.: Particle swarm optimization. In: Proceedings of the 4th IEEE International Conference on Neural Networks, pp. 1942–1948. IEEE Service Center, Piscataway (1995)
2. Yang, X.S., Deb, S.: Cuckoo search via Levy flights. In: World Congress on IEEE Nature & Biologically Inspired Computing, pp. 210–214 (2009)
3. Karaboga, D.: An idea based on honey bee swarm for numerical optimization. TR06, Computers Engineering Department, Engineering Faculty, Erciyes University, Kayseri (2005)
4. Karaboga, D., Akay, B.: A comparative study of artificial bee colony algorithm. Appl. Math. Comput. **2**(14), 108–132 (2009)
5. Karaboga, D., Basturk, B.: On the performance of artificial bee colony (ABC) algorithm. Appl. Soft Comput. **8**(1), 687–697 (2008)
6. Peng, H., Wu, Z., Deng, C.: Enhancing differential evolution with communal learning and uniform local search. Chin. J. Electron. **26**(4), 725–733 (2017)
7. Zhu, G., Sam, K.: Gbest-guided artificial bee colony algorithm for numerical function optimization. Appl. Math. Comput. **217**(7), 3166–3173 (2010)
8. Wang, Y., Fang, K.: A note on uniform distribution and experimental design. Mon. J. Sci. **26** (6), 485–489 (1981)
9. Fang, K.: Uniform design-number theory method in the application of experimental design. Acta Math. Appl. Sinica **04**, 363–372 (1980)
10. Fang, K.: Uniform design. Tactical Missile Technol. **02**, 56–69 (1994)
11. Yao, X., Liu, Y., Lin, G.: Evolutionary programming made faster. IEEE Trans. Evol. Comput. **3**(2), 82–102 (1999)
12. Peng, H., Wu, Z., Zhou, X., et al.: Bare-bones differential evolution algorithm based on trigonometry. J. Comput. Res. Dev. **12**, 2776–2788 (2015)

An Improved Firefly Algorithm Hybrid with Fireworks

Xiaojing Wang[1(⊠)], Hu Peng[1], Changshou Deng[1], Lixian Li[1], and Likun Zheng[2]

[1] School of Information and Science, Jiujiang University, Jiangxi 332005, China
wxj31897574@qq.com
[2] School of Computer and Information Engineering,
Haerbin Commerce University, Haerbin 150028, Heilongjiang, China

Abstract. Firefly algorithm (FA) is a global optimization algorithm with simple, less parameter and faster convergence speed. However, the FA is easy to fall into local optimum, and the solution accuracy of the FA is lower. In order to overcome these problems. An improved Firefly algorithm hybrid with Fireworks (FWFA) is proposed in this paper. Because the local search ability of the fireworks algorithm's search strategy is strong, we introduce the fireworks algorithm neighborhood search operator of the fireworks algorithm into the firefly algorithm to improve the local search ability of the Firefly algorithm. Through the simulation and analysis of 28 benchmark functions, verify the effectiveness and reliability of the new algorithm. The experimental results show that the new algorithm has excellent search ability in solving unimodal functions and multimodal functions.

Keywords: Swarm intelligence · Firefly algorithm (FA) · Domain search · Fireworks algorithm (FWA) · Hybrid algorithm

1 Introduction

Firefly algorithm (FA) [1] is a new intelligent algorithm. It is proposed by Yang in 2008. Firefly algorithm simulates the biological characteristics of fireflies, such as luminosity, mutual attraction and movement, and searches for partners in a certain range. After several moves, the algorithm achieves the purpose of optimization. Firefly algorithm is simple, with few parameters and fast convergence speed. It is applied to optimal configuration of distributed power [2], train operation adjustment [3], no-wait flowshop scheduling [4], path planning [5], assessment of groundwater quality [6] and other problems, and successfully solved the production problem. It is an excellent intelligent stochastic algorithm.

The shortcomings of FA are slow convergence speed, easy to fall into local optimum, strong correlation between optimization results and parameters. Researchers have made various improvements to it. In 2014, Yu et al. proposed a step setting strategy based on individual best position and global best position [7], and in 2015, they proposed a nonlinear dynamic adjustment step strategy [8], which improved the search quality of the Firefly algorithm. In 2018, Wang [9] et al. proposed a new

© Springer Nature Singapore Pte Ltd. 2019
H. Peng et al. (Eds.): ISICA 2018, CCIS 986, pp. 27–37, 2019.
https://doi.org/10.1007/978-981-13-6473-0_3

algorithm based on local uniform search and variable step size (UVFA), which reduces the time complexity of the standard Firefly algorithm, improves the convergence accuracy and enhances the robustness of the algorithm.

Researchers have proposed many personalized hybrid algorithms for various swarm intelligence algorithms to obtain good performance of optimization problems. For example, A hybrid algorithm based on Firefly algorithm and Differential Evolution [10], A hybrid algorithm based on Particle Swarm and Fireworks [11], A hybrid swarm intelligence optimization for benchmark models by blending PSO with ABC [12], Obstacle avoidance path planning of intelligent mobile based on Improved Fireworks-Ant Colony hybrid algorithm [13], Glowworm-Particle Swarm hybrid Optimiza [14], A hybrid optimization algorithm of Cuckoo Search and DE [15], A Hybrid Optimization algorithm based on Artificial Swarm and Differential Evolution [16].

This paper optimizes the search process of standard FA by using the strong exploitation ability of Fireworks algorithm (FWA) [17], embeds the explosive search process into the standard FA. An improved Firefly algorithm hybrid with Fireworks is proposed. Although the mechanism of Firefly algorithm and Fireworks algorithm is different, but the algorithm is parameterized, the interface can be interoperable, and the unique parameters can be constant quantization.

2   Firefly Algorithm

The standard Firefly algorithm is a heuristic algorithm based on the glowing and courtship behavior of fireflies. It is used to solve the stochastic optimization problem. The algorithm handles the bioluminescence and photoluminescence behavior of firefly, making the algorithm simple, efficient and practical. Three hypotheses are proposed. Firstly, all fireflies are unisex. So, one firefly will be attracted to other fireflies regardless of their sex. Secondly, attractiveness is proportional to their brightness. Thus, for any two flashing fireflies, the less bright one will move toward the brighter one. The attractiveness is proportional to the brightness and they both decrease as their distance increases. If there is no brighter one than a particular firefly, it will move randomly. Thirdly, the brightness of a firefly is affected or determined by the landscape of the objective function. For a minimization problem, the brightness can be reciprocal of objective function. It means that a brighter firefly has a smaller objective function value.

In FA, the main formulas include relative luminance formula, relative attractiveness formula and position update formula [18].

The luminance formula is:

$$I(\mathrm{r}) = I_0 \mathrm{e}^{-\gamma r} \tag{1}$$

where is the maximum fluorescence brightness of fireflies, i.e. the fluorescence brightness at r = 0, which is related to the value of the objective function, the better the value of the objective function, the higher the brightness of the firefly itself; γ is the intensity absorption coefficient to reflect the weakening characteristics of light intensity, in most cases, $\gamma \in [0.01, 100]$; r is usually the Euclidean distance between fireflies i and j.

The attractiveness can be calculated as follows:

$$\beta(r) = \beta_0 e^{-\gamma r^2} \tag{2}$$

where β_0 is the attractiveness at $r = 0$, and γ is the absorption coefficient of light intensity.

The movement of a firefly X_j, which is attracted to another brighter firefly X_i, is determined by

$$x_j(t+1) = x_j(t) + \beta(x_i(t) - x_j(t)) + \alpha\varepsilon_j \tag{3}$$

where $x_j(t + 1)$ is the position of firefly x_j after the move of $t + 1$; α is a random value with the range of $[0, 1]$; and ε is a Gaussian random number with the range of $[0, 1]$.

FA steps are shown in Algorithm 1.

Algorithm 1: The Standard FA

---

1) Choose fitness function. $f(X), X= (x_1, x_2, ..., x_d)^T$
2) Randomly initialize the fireflies population.$X_i, (i=l, 2,...,n)$
3) Initialization algorithm basic parameters γ、 β_0、 *MaxFEs*
4) *FEs=n*
5) While (*FEs< MaxFEs*)
6)   For *i=1:n*
7)   For *j=1:n*
8)   If *(I_j>I_i)*
9)   Compute relative attraction. according to formula (2)
10)   Move x_i toward x_j according to formula (3)
11)   Compute the fitness value of *f(X)*
12)   *FEs= FEs+1*
13)   End if
14)   End for
15)   End for
16)   Rank all fireflies and determine the best location
17) End while

In the algorithm, individuals exchange information by fluorescence to form a positive feedback mechanism, which ensures that the whole population can find the optimal solution with a higher probability.

3 Proposed Approach

3.1 Domain Search Model

In the standard FA, the attraction between fireflies is random. If the number of attractions is too large, it will cause repeated oscillations and increase the time cost. If the number of attraction is too small, it will miss the best value and premature convergence. Therefore, attracting quantity and search scope has become an important factor. If the local optimal value is found first and then iterate, the performance of the optimization algorithm can be achieved by promoting the global optimization with the local optimal value. That is, by enhancing the local exploitation capacity to promote the overall exploration capability.

Based on the above considerations, an optimal solution is obtained in the domain with radius r_{i1}. After iteration, the optimal solution is regarded as the optimal individual in the population, which is regarded as the central point and searched radially with radius r_{i2}. The second optimal value is obtained, and then the solution is regarded as the individual of the population and the individual as the central point and the radius as the r_{i3} radiation search, and so on. This radial search is similar to the fireworks and sparks generated when the fireworks explode. The fireworks are the individual of the parent population and the sparks are the children of the iterated update population.

Domain search is performed in D-dimensional space, and the search process in two-dimensional space is shown in Figs. 1(a) to (d). Firefly individual F_{i1} is a better individual obtained for the first time. Based on this individual as a benchmark and radius r_{i1} as a domain, the better individual F_{j1} is obtained and F_{j1} as the next generation F_{i2}. After the iteration, F_{i2} is taken as the center and r_{i2} is taken as the radius to

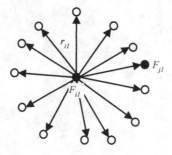

(a) Domain search produces better values F_{j1}

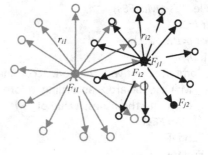

(b) Produce superior values F_{j2} with F_{j1} as a seed

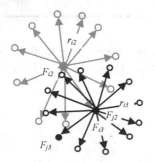

(c) Produce superior values F_{j3} with F_{j2} as a seed

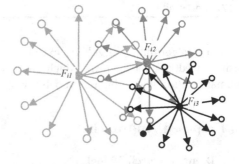

(d) The process of generating a better value for domain search

Fig. 1. The search model for 2D space domain

search the domain. The optimal value F_{j2} is obtained, and F_{j2} is taken as the F_{i3} after the iteration. F_{i3} as the center and r_{i3} as the radius of the domain search, get a better value of F_{j3}, so iterate on until the optimal or the maximum number of evaluations.

3.2 Fireworks Search Strategy

Based on the above model, the process of searching neighborhood by using Firefly algorithm is introduced, and the standard FA is improved. In the Firefly algorithm, the explosion radius and the number of sparks produced by each fireworks explosion are calculated according to their fitness values relative to other fireworks in the fireworks population. For the fireworks x_i, the Ai of the explosion radius is calculated as follows:

$$A_i = \hat{A} \times \frac{f(x_i) - y_{min} + \varepsilon}{\sum_{i=1}^{N} (f(x_i) - y_{min}) + \varepsilon} \tag{4}$$

where $y_{min} = \min(f(x_i)), (i = 1, 2, \ldots, N)$, it is the minimum fitness value of the current population. It is a constant used to adjust the size of the explosion radius.

The number of exploding sparks S_i of fireworks x_i is calculated as follows:

$$S_i = \hat{S} \times \frac{y_{max} - f(x_i) + \varepsilon}{\sum_{i=1}^{N} (y_{max} - f(x_i)) + \varepsilon} \tag{5}$$

where $y_{max} = \max(f(x_i)), (i = 1, 2, \ldots, N)$, it is the fitness maxima of the current population. $\hat{S}$ is a constant that adjusts the number of explosions. ε is the smallest part of a machine to avoid zero operation.

In the improvement of FA, formula (4) is used to calculate the radius of neighborhood search, and formula (5) is used to calculate the number of fireflies within the radius.

3.3 An Improved Firefly Algorithm Hybrid with Fireworks

Based on the idea of neighborhood search model, a firework-type neighborhood search operator is added to the standard FA. At the same time. An improved Firefly algorithm hybrid with Fireworks (FWFA) is proposed using the above population generation method. After each search of the standard FA, the number of fireflies within the search radius and radius is calculated, and then a firework search is conducted to generate new firefly individuals, and finally the population is updated to complete a search. The algorithm steps are shown in Algorithm 2. The difference between the algorithm and the standard FA is 13 to 16 rows.

Algorithm 2: The proposed FWFA

1) Choose fitness function. $f(X), X = (x_1, x_2, ..., x_d)^T$
2) Randomly initialize the fireflies population. $X_i, (i=l, 2, ..., n)$
3) Initialization algorithm basic parameters γ, β_0, $MaxFEs$
4) $FEs = n$
5) While $(FEs < MaxFEs)$
6) For $i = 1:n$
7)   For $j = 1:n$
8)   If $(I_j > I_i)$
9)   Compute relative attraction. according to formula (2)
10)   Move x_i toward x_j according to formula (3)
11)   Compute the fitness value of $f(X)$
12) $FEs = FEs + 1$
13)   Compute search radius according to formula (4)
14)   Calculate the number of fireflies in the radius according to formula (5)
15)   Fireworks search to create new fireflies
16)   Regeneration population
17)   End if
18)   End for
19) End for
20) Rank all fireflies and determine the best location.
21) End while

4   Simulation Experiments

4.1   Experimental Setup and Benchmark Function

In this paper, 28 standard test functions in CEC2013 are used to analyze and verify the convergence rate and the quality of the FWFA. The test functions are shown in Table 1. See Reference [19] for a detailed description. The function f_1–f_5 is a unimodal peak function, which is used to test the optimization accuracy of the algorithm and the performance of the algorithm. The function f_6–f_{20} is a basic multimodal function with multiple minimum values. The number of local optimum points increases exponentially with the increase of dimension, which is used to test the ability of the algorithm to jump out of local optimum. The function f_{21}–f_{28} is a composition function with both unimodal peak and multimodal functions.

The experimental hardware environment is Intel Core i7-4790 CPU@3.60 GHz processor, 8 GB memory, 64-bit operating system; the software environment is Windows 7 operating system, MATLAB R2016b version.

In the experiment, the dimension D of 28 test functions was set to 30, each function was run 30 times, the maximum number of iterations MaxFEs was set to D * 5000, and the population size was 50. The parameters of FA, WSSFA, VSSFA and FWFA are set in the same way. Among them, the attractiveness of firefly β0 is 1, the step factor α is 0.2, and the optical absorption factor γ is 1. The maximum number of sparks for standard FWA and FWFA is 40, the minimum spark number is 2, and the number of Gauss mutations is 5.

Table 1. The CEC'13 benchmark functions

	No.	Function name	Optimal value
Unimodal function	1	Sphere function	−1400
	2	Rotated high conditioned elliptic function	−1300
	3	Rotated bent cigar function	−1200
	4	Rotated discus function	−1100
	5	Different powers function	−1000
Basic multimodal function	6	Rotated Rosenbrock's function	−900
	7	Rotated Schaffers F7 function	−800
	8	Rotated Ackley's function	−700
	9	Rotated Weierstrass function	−600
	10	Rotated Griewank's function	−500
	11	Rastrigin's function	−400
	12	Rotated Rastrigin's function	−300
	13	Non-continuous rotated Rastrigin's function	−200
	14	Schwefel's function	−100
	15	Rotated Schwefel's function	100
	16	Rotated Katsuura function	200
	17	Lunacek Bi_Rastrigin function	300
	18	Rotated Lunacek Bi_Rastrigin function	400
	19	Expanded Griewank's plus Rosenbrock's function	500
	20	Expanded Scaffer's F6 function	600
Composition functions	21	Composition function 1 (n = 5, rotated)	700
	22	Composition function 2 (n = 3, unrotated)	800
	23	Composition function 3 (n = 3, rotated)	900
	24	Composition function 4 (n = 3, rotated)	1000
	25	Composition function 5 (n = 3, rotated)	1100
	26	Composition function 6 (n = 5, rotated)	1200
	27	Composition function 7 (n = 5, rotated)	1300
	28	Composition function 8 (n = 5, rotated)	1400

4.2   Results

In order to directly evaluate the performance of FWFA, the standard FA, the improved WSSFA [7], the improved VSSFA [8], the standard FA and the FWFA are compared, and the Wilcoxon rank sum test [20], the specific data as shown in Table 2. At the bottom of the table, the Wilcoxon's rank sum test results at a 0.05 significance level between FWFA and others are summarized, in which the symbol "−", "+", and "≈" represent that the performance of the related algorithm is worse than, better than and similar to that of FWFA, respectively. The rough part is the average error optimal value in the comparison algorithm.

Table 2. Experimental results of FA, WSSFA, VSSFA, FWA, and FWFA for all test functions at D = 30

Functions	FA Mean error	WSSFA Mean error	VSSFA Mean error	FWA Mean error	FWFA Mean error
f_1	9.40E + 04−	9.02E + 04−	9.04E + 04−	2.50E + 04−	**1.88E + 04**
f_2	2.31E + 09−	2.39E + 09−	2.20E + 09−	1.91E + 08−	**1.20E + 08**
f_3	4.30E + 20−	1.75E + 21−	2.76E + 21−	1.95E + 13−	**3.09E + 12**
f_4	4.70E + 05−	6.94E + 05−	1.65E + 05−	6.79E + 04−	**6.23E + 04**
f_5	5.59E + 04−	6.49E + 04−	5.99E + 04−	4.38E + 03−	**1.69E + 03**
f_6	2.38E + 04−	2.15E + 04−	2.14E + 04−	2.32E + 03−	**1.17E + 03**
f_7	2.60E + 07−	2.26E + 07−	1.18E + 07−	2.42E + 03≈	**1.85E + 03**
f_8	2.12E + 01−	2.12E + 01−	2.12E + 01−	2.10E + 01−	**2.10E + 01**
f_9	4.74E + 01−	4.75E + 01−	4.68E + 01−	3.82E + 01≈	**3.71E + 01**
f_{10}	1.43E + 04−	1.29E + 04−	1.30E + 04−	2.77E + 03−	**1.99E + 03**
f_{11}	1.44E + 03−	1.50E + 03−	1.40E + 03−	4.93E + 02−	**3.92E + 02**
f_{12}	1.41E + 03−	1.34E + 03−	1.33E + 03−	6.19E + 02−	**5.53E + 02**
f_{13}	1.39E + 03−	1.29E + 03−	1.32E + 03−	6.34E + 02≈	**6.26E + 02**
f_{14}	9.10E + 03−	9.12E + 03−	8.77E + 03−	4.01E + 03−	**2.65E + 03**
f_{15}	9.15E + 03−	9.08E + 03−	8.92E + 03−	7.08E + 03−	**5.51E + 03**
f_{16}	4.34E + 00−	4.37E + 00−	4.27E + 00−	2.15E + 00−	**1.53E + 00**
f_{17}	2.58E + 03−	2.58E + 03−	2.44E + 03−	6.22E + 02−	**5.36E + 02**
f_{18}	2.54E + 03−	2.47E + 03−	2.51E + 03−	8.02E + 02≈	**7.62E + 02**
f_{19}	1.10E + 07−	1.12E + 07−	8.30E + 06−	1.23E + 05−	**1.20E + 04**
f_{20}	1.50E + 01−	1.50E + 01−	1.50E + 01−	1.46E + 01≈	**1.46E + 01**
f_{21}	5.87E + 03−	5.85E + 03−	5.54E + 03−	2.29E + 03−	**2.08E + 03**
f_{22}	9.84E + 03−	9.75E + 03−	9.57E + 03−	4.94E + 03−	**3.37E + 03**
f_{23}	9.84E + 03−	9.58E + 03−	9.67E + 03−	7.94E + 03−	**6.62E + 03**
f_{24}	6.26E + 02−	5.86E + 02−	5.64E + 02−	3.33E + 02≈	**3.31E + 02**
f_{25}	4.53E + 02−	4.51E + 02−	4.56E + 02−	3.58E + 02≈	**3.55E + 02**
f_{26}	4.47E + 02−	4.45E + 02−	4.30E + 02−	2.29E + 02≈	**2.24E + 02**
f_{27}	1.87E + 03−	1.87E + 03−	1.84E + 03−	1.44E + 03−	**1.36E + 03**
f_{28}	9.51E + 03−	9.32E + 03−	9.49E + 03−	4.76E + 03−	**4.29E + 03**
±/≈	28/0/0	28/0/0	28/0/0	20/0/8	-

Comparing with standard FA, WSSFA and VSSFA, FWFA has absolute advantages over standard FA, WSSFA and VSSFA in 28 functions. Compared with standard FWA, FWFA achieves excellent results in 20 test functions, and the results of the other 8 functions are similar, and the average error values depend on. There is a slight advantage. Overall, the FWFA is ideal.

In order to analyze whether there are significant differences in the overall distribution of multiple independent samples, Friedman test is used to rank the rank mean of each sample. As shown in Table 3, the rank also reflects the performance of the algorithm. The smaller the rank mean, the better the performance of the algorithm [21].

Table 3. Average rankings based on the Friedman test

Algorithm	FA	WSSFA	VSSFA	FWA	FWFA
Ranking	4.46	4.07	3.46	1.96	1.04

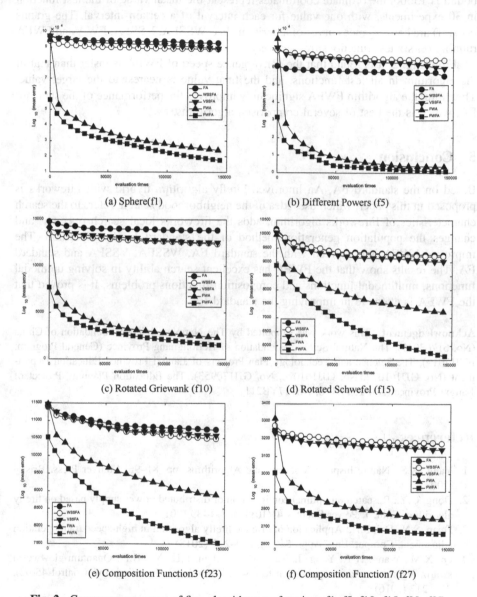

(a) Sphere(f1)

(b) Different Powers (f5)

(c) Rotated Griewank (f10)

(d) Rotated Schwefel (f15)

(e) Composition Function3 (f23)

(f) Composition Function7 (f27)

Fig. 2. Convergence curves of five algorithms on functions f1, f5, f10, f15, f23, f27

In order to intuitively reflect the convergence process of FWFA and other comparison algorithms, two functions are selected from single peak function, multi-peak function and composite function to display here, as shown in Fig. 2. The abscissa coordinates of the graph indicate the evaluation times of the function, and the upper bound is 15000; the ordinate coordinates represent the mean value of the test function in 30 experiments, with one value for each interval of a certain interval. The graphs (a) to (f) are convergence curves of algorithms FA, WSSFA, VSSFA, FWA and FWFA running on six test functions, respectively.

From Fig. 2, it is found that the convergence speed of FWFA is faster than that of the algorithm in all test functions, and the final value is nearest to the target value. Therefore, the algorithm FWFA significantly improves the performance of the standard FA, which is the best of several comparison algorithms.

5   Conclusion

Based on the standard FA, An improved Firefly algorithm hybrid with Fireworks is proposed in this paper, which uses idea of the neighborhood search, refers to the search characteristics of Fireworks algorithm, adds the fireworks local search operator, and changes the population generation method of the standard Firefly algorithm. The improved FWFA is compared with the standard FA, WSSFA, VSSFA and standard FA. The results show that the FWFA has excellent search ability in solving unimodal functions, multimodal functions and composition functions problems. It is proved that the FWFA is effective in improving the standard FA.

Acknowledgement. This work was supported by The National Science Foundation of China (No. 61763019), The Natural Science Foundation of Heilongjiang Province (General Program: F2017019), The Science and Technology Plan Projects of Jiangxi Province Education Department (No. GJJ161072, No. GJJ161076, No. GJJ170953), The Education Planning Project of Jiangxi Province (No. 15YB138, No. 17YB211).

References

1. Yang, X.S.: Nature-Inspired Metaheuristic Algorithms, pp. 81–96. Luniver Press, Bristol (2008)
2. Dong, G.Y.: Research on optimal configuration of distributed power supply based on firefly algorithm. Chin. J. Power Sources **41**(10), 1487–1489 (2017)
3. Duan, S.N., Dai, S.H.: Application of discrete firefly algorithm in high-speed train operation adjustment. Comput. Eng. Appl. **54**(15), 209–213 (2018)
4. Qi, X.M., Wang, H.T., Yang, J., Tang, Q.M., Chen, F.L., Ye, H.P.: Quantum glowworm swarm algorithm and its application to no-wait flowshop scheduling. Inf. Control **45**(02), 211–217 (2016)
5. Li, M.F., Zhang, Y.Y., Ma, J.H., Zhou, Y.X.: Research on path planning based on variable parameters firefly algorithm and maklink graph. Mech. Sci. Technol. Aerosp. Eng. **34**(11), 1728–1732 (2015)

6. Gong, Y.C., Zhang, Y.X., Ding, F., Hao, J., Wang, H., Zhang, D.S.: Projection pursuit model for assessment of groundwater quality based on firefly algorithm. J. China Univ. Mining Technol. **44**(03), 566–572 (2015)

7. Yu, S., Su, S., Lu, Q., et al.: A novel wise step strategy for firefly algorithm. Int. J. Comput. Math. **91**(12), 2507–2513 (2014)

8. Yu, S., Zhu, S., Ma, Y., et al.: A variable step size firefly algorithm for numerical optimization. Appl. Math. Comput. **263**, 214–220 (2015)

9. Wang, X.J., Peng, H., Deng, C.S., Huang, H.Y., Zhang, Y., Tan, X.J.: Firefly algorithm based on uniform local search and variable step size. J. Comput. Appl. **38**(3), 174–181 (2018)

10. Sarbazfard, S., Jafarian, A.: A hybrid algorithm based on firefly algorithm and differential evolution for global optimization. Int. J. Adv. Comput. Sci. Appl. **7**(6), 95–106 (2017)

11. Chen, S., Liu, Y., Wei, L., et al.: PS-FW: a hybrid algorithm based on particle swarm and fireworks for global optimization. Comput. Intell. Neurosci. (2018)

12. Mishra, A.K., Das, M., Panda, T.C.: A hybrid swarm intelligence optimization for benchmark models by blending PSO with ABC. Int. Rev. Model. Simul. **6**(1), 291–299 (2013)

13. Zhang, W., Ma, Y., Zhao, H.D., Zhang, L., Li, Y., Li, X.D.: Obstacle avoidance path planning of intelligent mobile based on improved fireworks-ant colony hybrid algorithm. Control Decis. 1–10 (2018). https://doi.org/10.13195/j.kzyjc.2017.0870

14. Lan, W.H., Zhen, Y.H., Li, L.X., Wang, X., Chen, H.T., Zhang, Y.: Regional fault diagnosis method for grounding grids based on glowworm-particle swarm hybrid optimiza. Insulators Surge Arresters (04), 92–99 (2015)

15. Li, M., Cao, D.X.: Hybrid optimization algorithm of cuckoo search and DE. Comput. Eng. Appl. (04), 92–99 (2015)

16. Zhang, J.L., Zhou, Y.Q.: A hybrid optimization algorithm based on artificial swarm and differential evolution. Inf. Control **40**(05), 608–613 (2011)

17. Tan, Y., Zhu, Y.: Fireworks algorithm for optimization. In: Tan, Y., Shi, Y., Tan, K.C. (eds.) ICSI 2010. LNCS, vol. 6145, pp. 355–364. Springer, Heidelberg (2010). https://doi.org/10.1007/978-3-642-13495-1_44

18. Yang, X.S.: Firefly algorithm, stochastic test functions and design optimisation. Int. J. Bio-Inspired Comput. **2**(2), 78–84 (2010)

19. Liang, J.J., et al.: Problem definitions and evaluation criteria for the CEC 2013 special session on real-parameter optimization. Computational Intelligence Laboratory, Zhengzhou University, Zhengzhou, China and Nanyang Technological University, Singapore, Technical Report 201212, pp. 3–18 (2013)

20. Rosner, B., Glynn, R.J., Ting Lee, M.L.: Incorporation of clustering effects for the Wilcoxon rank sum test: a large-sample approach. Biometrics **59**(4), 1089–1098 (2003)

21. Friedman, M.: The use of ranks to avoid the assumption of normality implicit in the analysis of variance. J. Am. Stat. Assoc. **32**(200), 675–701 (1937)

Enhanced Fireworks Algorithm
with an Improved Gaussian Sparks Operator

Jinglei Guo and Wei Liu[✉]

School of Computer Science, Central China Normal University,
No. 152 Luoyu Road, Wuhan 430074, Hubei, China
{guojinglei, liuwei}@mail.ccnu.edu.cn

Abstract. As a population-based intelligence algorithm, fireworks algorithm simulates the firework's explosion process to solve optimization problem. A comprehensive study on Gaussian spark operator in enhanced fireworks algorithm (EFWA) reveals that the search trajectory is limited by the difference vector and the diversity of swarm is not effectively increased by new sparks adding. An improved version of EFWA (IEFWA) is proposed to overcome these limitations. In IEFWA, a new Gaussian spark operator utilizes the location information of the best firework and randomly selected firework to calculate the center position and explosion amplitude, which enhance the search for potential region. Experiments on 20 well-known benchmark functions are conducted to illustrate the performance of IEFWA. The results turn out IEFWA outperforms EFWA and dynFWA on most testing functions.

Keywords: Fireworks algorithm · Gaussian distribution · Explosion

1 Introduction

In the last two decades, many swarm intelligence (SI) algorithms, which simulate the behavior of simple nature agents to produce the intelligent ability, have been proposed to solve engineering optimization problems. SI algorithms include such as ant colony algorithm (ACO) [1], particle swarm optimization (PSO) [2], firefly algorithm (FA) [3], cuckoo search [4], wolf colony algorithm (WCA) [5], whale optimization algorithm (WOA) [6], fireworks algorithm (FWA) [7] and so on. FWA is inspired by the explosion process of real fireworks in night sky and firstly proposed by Tan in 2010 [7]. The research work on FWA can be classified into two categories: (1) algorithm improvements: single objective FWA [8–11], multi-objective FWA [12], parallel FWA [13, 14], hybrid FWA with DE [15, 16]; (2) algorithm applications: FWA has been used in digital filter design [17], parameters optimization [18], harmonic elimination [19], multi-satellite control resource scheduling [20], and so on.

The remainder of this paper is organized as follows. Section 2 presents a detailed introduction of FWA. The review of well-known improvement FWA versions is presented in Sect. 3. In Sect. 4, the behavior of Gaussian sparks in EFWA is analyzed and a new Gaussian sparks operator is proposed to enlarge the search region. Experimental results are presented to validate the performance of IEFWA in Sect. 5. The conclusion is drawn in Sect. 6.

© Springer Nature Singapore Pte Ltd. 2019
H. Peng et al. (Eds.): ISICA 2018, CCIS 986, pp. 38–49, 2019.
https://doi.org/10.1007/978-981-13-6473-0_4

2 The Classical FWA

With generality, FWA [7] is for solving global minimal problem,

$$\min f(\vec{x}), \vec{x} = (x_1, \cdots, x_D) \in \Omega = \prod_{i=1}^{D} [a_i, b_i], \tag{1}$$

where $f: R^D \to R$ is a continuous problem, the dimension of $\vec{x}$ is D, a_i and b_i are the lower bound and upper bound of the ith component in feasible region Ω, and $-\infty < a_i < b_i < +\infty$.

FWA is a population-based heuristic algorithm which consists of three main operators: the explosion operator, the Gaussian sparks operator and the selection operator.

2.1 Explosion Operator

The explosion operator generates numerous sparks which explode with the center (firework x_i). For each firework x_i, its explosion sparks' number s_i is defined as follows,

$$s_i = M \frac{y_{max} - f(x_i) + \xi}{\sum_{i=1}^{n}(y_{max} - f(x_i)) + \xi} \tag{2}$$

where n is the number of fireworks, M is the total number of sparks generated by n fireworks, $y_{max} = \max(f(x_i))\,(i = 1, 2, \ldots, n)$ is the worst value of the objective function of the fireworks, and ξ is smallest constant to ensure the divisor is nonzero.

To avoid the overwhelming effects of the best fireworks, s_i is limited in a range, as follows:

$$s_i = \begin{cases} S_{min} & if\ s_i < S_{min} \\ S_{max} & if\ s_i < S_{max}, \\ S_i & otherwise \end{cases} \tag{3}$$

where S_{min} and S_{max} are the lower bound and upper bound for the spark number.

The firework's explosion amplitude is calculated as follows:

$$A_i = \hat{A} \frac{f(x_i) - y_{min} + \xi}{\sum_{i=1}^{n}(f(x_i) - y_{min}) + \xi}, \tag{4}$$

where $\hat{A}$ is the maximum explosion amplitude, $y_{min} = \min(f(x_i))\,(i = 1, 2, \ldots, n)$ is the best value of the objective function of the fireworks.

From the formula (2) and (4) above, it can be found out the better the firework's fitness is, the more sparks it generates and the smaller amplitude it produces. Thus, the firework's fitness determines the search behavior, that is, the firework with better fitness conducts exploitation and the firework with worse fitness conducts exploration.

Then using the formula (2) and (4), the explosion sparks are generated by Algorithm 1.

Algorithm 1. Generate an explosion spark of firework x_i

Initialize the location of the spark $\widetilde{p}_j = x_i$;

Randomly select z dimensions of $\widetilde{p}_j$;

Calculate the amplitude for $\widetilde{p}_j$ by formula (2), $h=A_i$*rand($-1,1$);

for each dimension $\widetilde{p_j^k} \in$ {pre-selected z dimensions of $\widetilde{p}_j$} do

$\quad \widetilde{p_j^k} = \widetilde{p_j^k} + h$

$\quad$ **if** $\widetilde{p_j^k} < b_k$ or $\widetilde{p_j^k} > a_k$ then

$\qquad \widetilde{p_j^k} = a_k + \left| \widetilde{p_j^k} \right| mod(b_k - a_k)$

$\quad$ **end if**

end for

2.2   Gaussian Sparks Operator

To keep the population diversity, Gaussian sparks operator is used to generate sparks in Gaussian distribution with the center which is the selected firework's location. The Gaussian sparks operator is computed by

$$\widetilde{p_j^k} = \widetilde{p_j^k} \cdot (1 + N(0,1)), \tag{5}$$

where $N(0,1)$ is the Gaussian distribution function with the mean value 0 and the standard deviation 1.

Then using the formula (5), the Gaussian sparks are generated by Algorithm 2.

Algorithm 2. Generate a Gaussian spark of firework x_i

Initialize the location of the spark $\widetilde{p}_j = x_i$;

Randomly select z dimensions of $\widetilde{p}_j$;

for each dimension $\widetilde{p_j^k} \in$ {pre-selected z dimensions of $\widetilde{p}_j$} do

$\quad$ Calculate the amplitude for $\widetilde{p}_j$ by formula (5), $\widetilde{p_j^k} = \widetilde{p_j^k} \cdot (1 + N(0,1))$;

$\quad$ **if** $\widetilde{p_j^k} < b_k$ or $\widetilde{p_j^k} > a_k$ then

$\qquad \widetilde{p_j^k} = a_k + \left| \widetilde{p_j^k} \right| mod(b_k - a_k)$

$\quad$ **end if**

end for

2.3   Selection of Locations

Like other EA algorithms, certain number sparks and fireworks should be survived for the next generation in FWA. Obviously, the best location (x^*) with the minimal objective function $f(x^*)$ is an optimal location in current generation and should be kept for the next generation. After that, for maintaining the diversity of the generation, the other locations are selected based on their distance to other locations. The total distance $R(x_i)$ between the spark x_i and other locations x_j is defined as follows:

$$R(x_i) = \sum_{j \in K} d(x_i, x_j), \tag{6}$$

where K is the number of fireworks and sparks.

The selection probability $P(x_i)$ of location x_i is calculated by formula (7).

$$P(x_i) = R(x_i) / \sum_{j \in K} R(x_j) \tag{7}$$

From (7), the selection probability is proportional to the distance. The larger total distance $R(x_i)$ is, the higher selection probability location x_i has. Thus, the locations which are far from other sparks and fireworks are prone to be selected. The selection scheme ensures the population diversity to some extent.

2.4 Framework of Basic FWA

The framework of basic FWA is described as follows.

Algorithm 3. Framework of the classical FWA

Randomly initialize n locations of fireworks
while stop condition is not satisfied **do**
    generate explosion sparks for fireworks by algorithm 1
    generate Gaussian sparks for fireworks by algorithm 2
    select the best location in the fireworks and sparks
    randomly select other n-1 locations according to the probability (7)
end while
---

3 Related Work

In enhanced Fireworks algorithm (EFWA) [8], for the problem that the explosion amplitude of the best fireworks is close to 0, the authors proposed a linear and non-linear decreasing method with the evolution process to set the lower bound A_{min} of explosion amplitude. Because the solutions out of feasible search space are mapped close to the origin by the mapping operator, FWA has worse results with increasing distance between function optimum and the origin of the search space. For this drawback, the mapping operator in EFWA is replaced by uniform random mapping operator in range $[a_i, b_i]$. In FWA, calculation of the distance between locations in selection strategy costs a high computational time. The Elitism-Random selection method whose computational complexity is linear with respect of the number of fireworks is applied in EFWA, therefore the runtime of EFWA is reduced significantly.

In [9], a new mutation operator with the covariance matrix (CM) is proposed. In FWACM, μ better sparks (v_i) are selected from the sparks in each generation and calculated the mean value $m = \frac{1}{\mu}\sum_{i=1}^{\mu} v_i$. Then the element $cov(v_i, v_j)$ in covariance matrix C is calculated. Finally, Gaussian sparks are produced according with Gaussian distribution $N(m,C)$ by mean value m and covariance matrix C. The covariance mutation operator produces Gaussian sparks nearly at the direction of the gradient of the function, which makes the new algorithm useful at finding the local optimum. From the experimental results on CEC 2015 competition problems, FWACM outperforms AFWA [10] on unimodal functions and hybrid functions.

The dynamic search fireworks algorithm (dynFWA) [11] is a state-of-the-art version of the fireworks algorithm. It outperforms FWA and EFWA on the 28 benchmark functions in CEC2013. There are two main improvements in dynFWA:

(1) Dynamic explosion amplitude for the elitist. In FWA and EFWA, the explosion amplitude solely depends on the fitness. But, in dynFWA, the explosion amplitude of the core firework (CF) which is the firework with the best fitness is dynamic in each generation. In the initial stage, CF is the best one among all randomly initialized fireworks. After that, if in generation g, the sparks of CF find a better location than the best in generation g-1, the amplitude will be enlarged by an amplification coefficient $C_a > 1$, otherwise it will be reduced by a coefficient $C_r < 1$. Thus, the explosion amplitude is dynamically adjusted according the search performance in the last generation,

$$A_{CF,g} = \begin{cases} A_{CF,g-1} * C_a & f(x_{CF,g}) < f(x_{CF,g-1}) \\ A_{CF,g-1} * C_r & f(x_{CF,g}) = f(x_{CF,g-1}) \end{cases}, \tag{8}$$

where $A_{CF,g}$ is the explosion amplitude of the CF in generation g.

(2) Elimination of the Gaussian sparks operator. Based on the analysis of the Gaussian sparks location, the Gaussian mutation operator is removed by dynFWA.

4   The IEFWA

4.1   Analysis of Gaussian Sparks Operator in EFWA

In EFWA, the Gaussian sparks are generated by the formula:

$$\widetilde{p}_j^k = \widetilde{p}_j^k + \left(x_{best}^k - \widetilde{p}_j^k\right) * e, \tag{9}$$

where x_{best} is the best firework that has been found so far and e is the Gaussian distribution $N(0,1)$.

From the formula (9), the new Gaussian sparks position will be located along the direction of difference vector $x_{best} - \widetilde{p}_j$. For 2D problem, it can be represented as Fig. 1. In Fig. 1, the black dot is the position of x_{best}, the white dot is the position of $\widetilde{p}_j$ and the grey dots are the possible locations that may be generated by Gaussian sparks.

According to the Gaussian sparks operator, the position of the sparks may be located at three situations: (1) close to the best firework x_{best}; (2) close to the selected firework $\widetilde{p}_j$; (3) some distance to both x_{best} and $\widetilde{p}_j$.

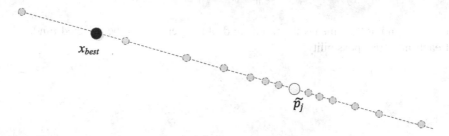

Fig. 1. Gaussian sparks' locations in EFWA.

Figure 2 is the bell-shaped curve of Gaussian distribution. From the mathematical statistic, the points have 95.45% possibility located in $[-2, 2]$. That means the first two situations have a high probability to occur. However, for the first two situations, it is similar to the effect of the explosion process made by the best firework x_{best} and the selected firework $\widetilde{p}_j$.

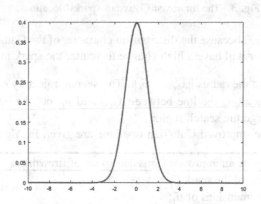

Fig. 2. Gaussian distribution N(0,1).

4.2 An Improved Gaussian Sparks Operator in EFWA

From the above discussion in Sect. 4.1, Gaussian sparks operator has been removed by dynFWA, because it has little effect in EFWA evolution process. In this section, a new Gaussian Sparks operator is proposed.

Similar to the Gaussian operator in EFWA, the best firework x_{best} found so far and the selected firework $\widetilde{p}_j$ are still selected in the improved Gaussian sparks operator. But in the new Gaussian sparks, the center of x_{best} and $\widetilde{p}_j$ is assigned a new vector, the

Euclidean distance $\|x_{best} - \widetilde{p}_j\|$ is the amplitude for the Gaussian distribution. The new Gaussian sparks formula is

$$\widetilde{p}_j^k = \frac{x_{best}^k + \widetilde{p}_j^k}{2} \pm \|x_{best} - \widetilde{p}_j\| * (1 + N(0, 1)), \tag{10}$$

where the symbol "$\pm$" means the minus and plus operator can be selected randomly, and each has 50% possibility.

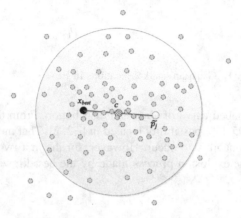

Fig. 3. The improved Gaussian sparks' locations.

As shown in Fig. 3, because the distribution character of the Gaussian function, the new mutation operator will have a high chance to scatter the spark in the area with the center $c = \frac{x_{best}^k + \widetilde{p}_j^k}{2}$ and the radius $\|x_{best} - \widetilde{p}_j\|$. The search trajectory of Gaussian sparks operator in EFWA is along the line between x_{best} and $\widetilde{p}_j$, but the improved Gaussian sparks operator enlarge the search region.

The details of the improved Gaussian operator are given in Algorithm 4.

Algorithm 4. Generate an improved Gaussian spark of firework x_i

Initialize the location of the spark $\widetilde{p}_j = x_i$;
Randomly select z dimensions of $\widetilde{p}_j$;
for each dimension $\widetilde{p}_j^k \in$ {pre-selected z dimensions of $\widetilde{p}_j$} **do**

Calculate the amplitude for $\widetilde{p}_j$ by formula (10), $\widetilde{p}_j^k = \frac{x_{best}^k + \widetilde{p}_j^k}{2} \pm \|x_{best} - \widetilde{p}_j\| *$
$(1 + N(0, 1))$
    if $\widetilde{p}_j^k < b_k$ or $\widetilde{p}_j^k > a_k$ **then**
    $\widetilde{p}_j^k = a_k + |\widetilde{p}_j^k| mod(b_k - a_k)$
    end if
end for

4.3   Framework of IEFWA

Algorithm 5 summarizes the framework of IEFWA. In each generation, the population goes through two types of explosions that generates explosion sparks and Gaussian sparks. After the evaluation process, the best one will be conserved to next generation. Suppose the algorithm is executed in T generations, the complexity of the IEFWA is O (T•(M + m)).

Algorithm 5. Framework of the IEFWA
Randomly initialize n locations of fireworks;

FEs=0;

While FEs<FEs_{max} **do**

$$A^k_{min}(t) = A_{init} - \frac{A_{init} - A_{final}}{evals_{max}} \cdot t;$$

    for i=1:n **do**

        Calculate the number s_i of sparks that the firework x_i produces according to (2);

        Calculate the amplitude A_i of sparks that the firework x_i produces according to (4);

        Limit the A_i above the low bound: If A_i<A_{min} A_i=A_{min};

        generate explosion sparks for fireworks by algorithm 1;

    end for

    for k=1:m **do**

    Randomly select a firework x_j;

    generate Gaussian sparks for fireworks by algorithm 4;

    end for

    $FEs = FEs + M + m;$

    select one best location among the fireworks and sparks;

    randomly select other n-1 locations;

end while

5   Experiments and Discussion

5.1   Benchmark Functions

To investigate the performance of the proposed IEFA, we conducted the experiments on 20 benchmark functions for 30 dimensions. The function name, the feasible bounds and the optimal fitness are listed in Table 1. The functions in Table 1 can be classified into three types, (1) unimodal functions; (2) multimodal functions; (3) shift functions.

Table 1. Benchmark functions

Type	Functions	Name	$f\left(\overrightarrow{X^*}\right)$	Search range
Unimodal functions	F_{01}	Sphere	0	[−100, 100]
	F_{02}	Schwefel 2.22	0	[−10, 10]
	F_{03}	Schwefel 1.2	0	[−100, 100]
	F_{04}	Schwefel 2.21	0	[−100, 100]
	F_{05}	Rosenbrock	0	[−100, 100]
	F_{06}	Step	0	[−100, 100]
	F_{07}	Quartic with Noise	0	[−1.28, 1.28]
Multimodal functions	F_{08}	Schwefel 2.26	−1259.5	[−500, 500]
	F_{09}	Rastrigin	0	[−5.12, 5.12]
	F_{10}	Ackley	0	[−32, 32]
	F_{11}	Griewank	0	[−600, 600]
	F_{12}	Penalized1	0	[−50, 50]
	F_{13}	Penalized2	0	[−50, 50]
Shift functions	F_{14}	Shift Sphere	2	[−100, 100]
	F_{15}	Shift Schwefel 1.2	2	[−100, 100]
	F_{16}	Shift Schwefel 1.2 with Noise	2	[−100, 100]
	F_{17}	Shift Griewank	2	[−600, 600]
	F_{18}	Shift Ackley	2	[−32, 32]
	F_{19}	Shift Penalized1	2	[−50, 50]
	F_{20}	Shift Penalized2	2	[−50, 50]

5.2   Comparison Experiments Among EFWA, dynFWA and IEFWA

In this section, we compare the performance of IEFWA with EFWA and dynFWA in terms of both convergence speed and optimization accuracy. The parameters are set as those used in the original literature.

(1) EFWA: $n = 5$, $M = 50$, $\hat{A} = 40$, $A_{init} = 0.02(b − a)$, $A_{final} = 0.001(b − a)$, $m = 5$;
(2) dynFWA: M_e(the maximum number of explosions sparks) $= 150$, $\hat{A} = 40$, $C_r = 0.9$, $C_a = 1.2$;
(3) IEFWA: $n = 5$, $M = 50$, $\hat{A} = 40$, $A_{init} = 0.02(b − a)$, $A_{final} = 0.001(b − a)$, $m = 5$;

Each algorithm is executed independently 50 times, the mean solution error and standard deviation are reported in Table 2 for D = 30. The wilcoxon's rank-sum test at the 0.05 significance level is employed to judge the significant difference between IEFWA and other algorithms, "+", "−" and "=" represent our proposed algorithm IEFWA is, respectively, better than, worse than and similar to the compared one in the Wilcoxon's rank-sum test.

Table 2. The results of EFWA, dynFWA and IEFWA

	EFWA Mean ± Std		dynFWA Mean ± Std		IEFWA Mean ± Std
F_1	1.53E−01 ± 2.43E−02	+	1.74E−15 ± 2.26E−15	+	**0.00E+00 ± 0.00E+00**
F_2	1.67E−01 ± 1.76E−02	+	8.91E−10 ± 6.77E−10	+	**0.00E+00 ± 0.00E+00**
F_3	1.09E+00 ± 3.22E−01	+	5.32E−04 ± 6.41E−04	+	**0.00E+00 ± 0.00E+00**
F_4	1.87E−01 ± 2.02E−02	+	2.72E−05 ± 2.84E−05	+	**0.00E+00 ± 0.00E+00**
F_5	9.91E+01 ± 1.22E+02	+	9.02E+01 ± 9.28E+01	+	**2.74E+01 ± 2.60E−01**
F_6	7.00E−01 ± 7.50E−01	+	4.63E+00 ± 1.96E+00	+	**0.00E+00 ± 0.00E+00**
F_7	1.98E−03 ± 9.36E−04	+	6.99E−03 ± 2.58E−03	+	**1.11E−04 ± 1.20E−04**
F_8	**−7.16E+03 ± 6.06E+02**	=	−7.38E+03 ± 7.77E+02	=	−7.19E+03 ± 7.74E+02
F_9	1.52E+02 ± 2.62E+01	+	2.36E+01 ± 9.39E+00	+	**0.00E+00 ± 0.00E+00**
F_{10}	4.69E+00 ± 8.22E+00	+	1.56E+00 ± 4.68E+00	+	**0.00E+00 ± 0.00E+00**
F_{11}	2.38E−01 ± 3.71E−02	+	3.21E−02 ± 2.60E−02	+	**0.00E+00 ± 0.00E+00**
F_{12}	6.78E+00 ± 2.14E+00	+	3.46E−03 ± 1.89E−02	+	**4.80E−06 ± 2.81E−06**
F_{13}	6.48E−03 ± 3.83E−03	+	**7.91E−12 ± 4.33E−11**	−	6.61E−05 ± 3.99E−05
F_{14}	1.56E−01 ± 2.75E−02	+	**9.80E−15 ± 2.79E−14**	−	1.47E−03 ± 6.41E−04
F_{15}	9.76E−01 ± 2.43E−01	+	**4.76E−04 ± 5.25E−04**	−	2.36E−01 ± 6.41E−02
F_{16}	2.08E+00 ± 9.36E−01	+	5.45E+02 ± 4.11E+02	−	**2.22E−01 ± 6.71E−02**
F_{17}	2.47E−01 ± 4.69E−02	+	**3.60E−02 ± 2.49E−02**	=	9.97E−02 ± 5.44E−02
F_{18}	9.27E+00 ± 9.61E+00	+	6.02E+00 ± 8.41E+00	+	**8.89E−03 ± 1.58E−03**
F_{19}	6.58E+00 ± 2.39E+00	+	2.37E−04 ± 1.30E−03	+	**5.61E−06 ± 3.45E−06**
F_{20}	5.68E−03 ± 1.12E−03	+	**2.28E−13 ± 1.23E−12**	−	7.19E−05 ± 4.20E−05

From Table 2, IEFWA obtains better results than EFWA and dynFWA on 14 out of 20 functions, respectively. For unimodal functions F_1–F_7, it is clear that IEFWA is the best one, it beats EFWA and dynFWA on each function. That may be the reason that IEFWA uses the globe best firework information in the Gaussian sparks operator and expand the search direction. For multimodal functions F_8–F_{13}, IEFWA outperforms EFWA on 5 out of 6 functions (except for function F_8 where they are even) and IEFWA performs better than dynFWA on 4 functions (except for function F_8 where they are even and function F_{13} where dynFWA is better). For shift functions F_{14}–F_{20}, IEFWA is better than EFWA, but worse than dynFWA on 4 functions. It might be because dynFWA's dynamic explosion amplitude method and removal of Gaussian explosion operator are suitable for shift type functions.

The convergence curves of EFWA, dynFWA and IEFWA on function F_7, F_{12}, F_{16}, F_{18} are shown in Fig. 4. The convergence curves show IEFWA has a fast convergence speed without loss of accuracy.

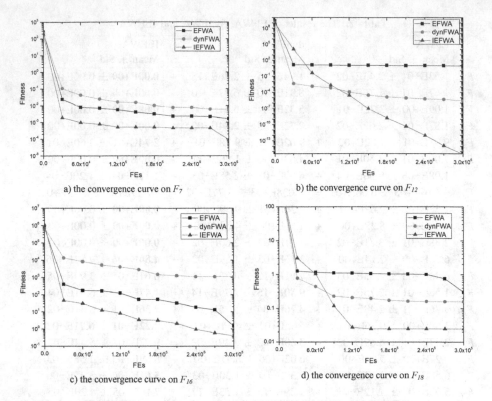

a) the convergence curve on F_7

b) the convergence curve on F_{12}

c) the convergence curve on F_{16}

d) the convergence curve on F_{18}

Fig. 4. The convergence curves of EFWA, dynFWA and IEFWA.

6   Conclusion

Based on the comprehensive study on EFWA, we propose an improved version of enhanced fireworks algorithm (IEFWA) in this paper. In IEFWA, to fix the problem of monotonous search trajectory in EFWA, a new Gaussian explosion operator which generates the sparks with Gaussian distribution character by the locations and the distance between the best firework and candidate firework is introduced.

Experimental results show that the IEFWA outperforms EFWA and dynFWA on most competition functions. However, some research work should be done on IEFWA to enhance the performance on shift functions.

Acknowledgment. This work is supported by the self-determined research funds of CCNU from the colleges basic research and operation of MOE (No. CCNU18QN018).

References

1. Dorigo, M., Gambardella, L.: Ant colony system: a cooperative learning approach to the traveling salesman problem. IEEE Trans. Evol. Comput. **1**(1), 53–66 (1997)
2. Kennedy, J.: Particle swarm optimization. In: IEEE International Conference on Neural Networks, Australia, pp. 1942–1948. IEEE (1995)
3. Yang, X.: Nature-Inspired Metaheuristic Algorithms. Luniver Press, London (2008)
4. Yang, X., Deb, S.: Cuckoo search via levy flights. In: IEEE World Congress on Nature & Biologically Inspired Computing, India, pp. 210–214. IEEE (2009)
5. Liu, C., Yan, X.: The wolf colony algorithm and its application. Chin. J. Electron. **20**(2), 212–216 (2011)
6. Mirjalili, S., Lewis, A.: The whale optimization algorithm. Adv. Eng. Softw. **95**, 51–67 (2016)
7. Tan, Y., Zhu, Y.: Fireworks algorithm for optimization. In: Tan, Y., Shi, Y., Tan, K.C. (eds.) ICSI 2010. LNCS, vol. 6145, pp. 355–364. Springer, Heidelberg (2010). https://doi.org/10.1007/978-3-642-13495-1_44
8. Zheng, S., Janecek, A., Tan, Y.: Enhanced fireworks algorithm. In: IEEE Congress on Evolutionary Computation, Mexico, pp. 2069–2077. IEEE (2013)
9. Yu, C., Tan, Y.: Fireworks algorithm with covariance mutation. In: IEEE Congress on Evolutionary Computation, Japan, pp. 1250–1256. IEEE (2015)
10. Li, J., Zheng, S., Tan, Y.: Adaptive fireworks algorithm. In: IEEE Congress on Evolutionary Computation, China, pp. 3214–3221. IEEE (2014)
11. Zheng, S., Janecek, A., Li, J., Tan, Y.: Dynamic search in fireworks algorithm. In: IEEE Congress on Evolutionary Computation, China, pp. 3222–3229. IEEE (2014)
12. Liu, L., Zheng, S., Tan, Y.: S-metric based multi-objective fireworks algorithm. In: IEEE Congress on Evolutionary Computation, Japan, pp. 1250–1256. IEEE (2015)
13. Ludwing, S., Dawar, D.: Parallelization of enhanced firework algorithm using MapReduce. Int. J. Swarm Intell. Res. **6**(2), 32–51 (2015)
14. Ding, K., Tan, Y.: Attract-repulse fireworks algorithm and its CUDA implementation using dynamic parallelism. Int. J. Swarm Intell. Res. **6**(2), 1–31 (2015)
15. Yu, C., Kelley, L., Zheng, S., et al.: Fireworks algorithm with differential mutation for solving the CEC 2014 competition problems, China, pp. 3238–3245. IEEE (2014)
16. Zheng, Y., Xu, X., Ling, H., et al.: A hybrid fireworks optimization method with differential evolution operators. Neurocomputing **148**, 75–82 (2015)
17. Gao, H., Diao, M.: Cultural firework algorithm and its application for digital filters design. Int. J. Model. Ident. Control **14**(4), 324–331 (2011)
18. Zheng, S., Tan, Y.: A unified distance measure scheme for orientation coding in identification. In: International Conference on Information Science and Technology, China, pp. 979–985. IEEE (2013)
19. Rajaram, R., Palanisamy, K., Ramasamy, S., et al.: Selective harmonic elimination in PWM inverter using fire fly and fireworks algorithm. Int. J. Innov. Res. Adv. Eng. **1**, 55–62 (2014)
20. Liu, Z., Feng, Z., Ke, L.: Fireworks algorithm for the multi-satellite control resource scheduling problem. In: IEEE Congress on Evolutionary Computation, Japan, pp. 1280–1286. IEEE (2015)

A Binary Particle Swarm Optimization for Solving the Bounded Knapsack Problem

Ya Li, Yichao He$^{(\boxtimes)}$, Huanzhe Li, Xiaohu Guo, and Zewen Li

College of Information and Engineering, Hebei GEO University,
Shijiazhuang 050031, China
921045813@qq.com, heyichao@hgu.edu.cn

Abstract. Bounded knapsack problem (BKP) is a classical knapsack problem. At present, methods for solving the BKP are mainly deterministic algorithms. The literature that using evolutionary algorithms solve this problem has not been reported. Therefore, this paper uses a binary particle swarm optimization (BPSO) to solve the BKP. On the basis of using the repair and optimization method to deal with the infeasible solutions, an effective method of using BPSO to solve the BKP is given. For three kinds of large-scale BKP instances, the feasibility and efficiency of BPSO are verified by comparing the results with whale optimization algorithm and genetic algorithm. The experimental results show that BPSO is not only more stable, but also can obtain the approximation ratio closer to 1.

Keywords: Bounded knapsack problem · Evolutionary algorithm ·
Binary particle swarm optimization · Repair and optimization method

1 Introduction

Knapsack problem (KP) [1–3] is a class of combination optimization problem, and it is also a kind of NP-hard problem. It has important theoretical significance and application value in the fields of industry, economy, and finance. The KP includes different expanded forms, such as the classic 0-1 knapsack problem (0-1KP) [4], the multidimensional knapsack problem (MDKP) [5], the multiple knapsack problem (MKP) [6], the bounded knapsack problem (BKP) [7], the unbounded knapsack problem (UKP) [8], the quadratic knapsack problem (QKP) [9], the randomized time-varying knapsack problem (RTVKP) [10] and the set-union knapsack problem (SUKP) [11] etc., and most of them have been successfully applied in various fields.

Because the time complexity of the deterministic algorithms for solving the KP is pseudo polynomial time, it is not suitable for solving the large-scale KP instances. Therefore, one often uses the evolutionary algorithms (EAs) to solve KP [12]. At present, many effective evolutionary algorithms have been proposed successively, such as genetic algorithm (GA) [13], particle swarm optimization (PSO) [14], differential evolution (DE) [15], ant colony optimization (ACO) [16], artificial bee colony (ABC) [17] and whale optimization algorithm (WOA) [18] etc. Among them PSO is a famous evolutionary algorithm proposed by Kennedy and Eberhart in 1995, and they proposed the binary particle swarm optimization (BPSO) in 1997 [19]. Since then,

© Springer Nature Singapore Pte Ltd. 2019
H. Peng et al. (Eds.): ISICA 2018, CCIS 986, pp. 50–60, 2019.
https://doi.org/10.1007/978-981-13-6473-0_5

several versions of discrete PSO have been proposed. For example, Clerc [20] proposed an improved discrete PSO for solving TSP problem. Van Den Bergh [21] introduced a new construction model of cooperative PSO and used it to solve IP problem. Liu et al. [22] presented a hybrid PSO for solving pipeline scheduling problem. Li et al. [23] proposed a binary particle swarm algorithm based on multiple mutation strategy to solve 0-1 KP. Bansal et al. [24] proposed an improved BPSO by limiting the update equation of position and used it to solve 0-1KP. He et al. [10, 11] solved RTVKP and SUKP respectively by BPSO, and obtained good results. Therefore, it is not difficult to see that BPSO is very suitable for solving combination optimization problems in discrete domain.

BKP is a classical KP problem, which has not been solved by evolutionary algorithms. Therefore, this paper uses BPSO to solve the BKP, and verifies the efficiency by comparing with other algorithms. The rest of this paper is organized as follows: Sect. 2 introduces the mathematical model of BKP. In Sect. 3, we firstly introduce the binary particle swarm optimization (BPSO), the repair optimization method is given to handle the infeasible solution, and the pseudo-code of BPSO to solve the BKP is given at the end. In Sect. 4, the feasibility and efficiency of this method are verified according to the calculation results of BPSO, improved whale optimization algorithm (IWOA) [25] and GA on three kinds of large-scale BKP instances. Finally, we summarize the whole paper and look forward to the future research directions.

2 Definition and Mathematical Model of BKP

BKP is defined as: Given a set of m items, each item i has a profit p_i, a weight w_i, and a bound b_i. The target is to select a number of each item i such that the sum of the profit is maximized, and the sum of weight is not exceed C.

BKP is an expanded form of the 0-1 KP, it can be converted to the 0-1KP. In the BKP, each item i has a bound b_i. Set the sum of the quantity of each item is $n = \sum b_i$, it can be regarded as a 0-1 KP with n items. Let the value set is $P = \{p_1, p_2, \ldots, p_n\}$, the weight set is $W = \{w_1, w_2, \ldots, w_n\}$, and the knapsack capacity is C. $p_i, w_i (1 \leq i \leq n)$, C are positive integers. According to the definition, a mathematical model of the 0-1KP form of BKP can be established. $X = [x_1, x_2, \ldots, x_n] \in \{0, 1\}^n$ stand for a feasible solution of the BKP. $x_i = 1$ means that item i is included in the knapsack, and $x_i = 0$ that it is not. The mathematical model of the 0-1KP form of BKP is as follows:

$$Max. \sum_{i=1}^{n} p_i x_i \tag{1}$$

$$s.t. \sum_{i=1}^{n} w_i x_i \leq C \, x_i \in \{0, 1\} \tag{2}$$

3 Solve BKP with BPSO

3.1 BPSO

In BPSO, each individual is treated as a particle in the n-dimensional space. $X_i = (x_{i1}, x_{i2}, \ldots, x_{in})$ and $V_i = (v_{i1}, v_{i2}, \ldots, v_{in})$ stand for the current position and velocity of the ith particle. $P_i = (p_{i1}, p_{i2}, \ldots, p_{in})$ is the local best position. Assuming that the problem to be solved is a minimum optimization problem, the P_i is determined by the formula (3):

$$P_i(t+1) = \begin{cases} P_i(t), & \text{if } f(X_i(t+1) \geq f(P_i(t)) \\ X_i(t+1), & \text{if } f(X_i(t+1) < f(P_i(t)) \end{cases} \tag{3}$$

The size of population is N. $P_g(t)$ is the global best position, and determined by the following formula:

$$P_g(t) \in \{P_0(t), P_1(t), \ldots, P_N(t)\} \,|\, f(P_g(t)) = min\{f(P_0(t)), f(P_1(t)), \ldots, f(P_N(t))\} \tag{4}$$

the evolution equation of BPSO can be described as:

$$v_{ij}(t+1) = v_{ij}(t) + c_1 r_{1j}(t)(p_{ij}(t) - x_{ij}(t)) + c_2 r_{2j}(t)(p_{gj}(t) - x_{ij}(t)), \tag{5}$$

$$x_{ij}(t+1) = \begin{cases} 0, & \text{sig}(v_{ij}(t+1)) \leq r_3(t) \\ 1, & \text{sig}(v_{ij}(t+1)) > r_3(t) \end{cases}. \tag{6}$$

where c_1 and c_2 are acceleration constants, and the values are usually between 0 and 2. $r_1 \sim U(0, 1)$, $r_2 \sim U(0, 1)$, $r_3 \sim U(0, 1)$ are three independent random functions. $sig(x) = 1/(1+e^{-x})$ is a fuzzy function, $1 \leq i \leq N, 1 \leq j \leq n$.

The initialization process of BPSO is as follows:

(1) Set the size of population is N.
(2) v_{ij} is subject to uniform distribution in $[-v_{max}, v_{max}]$.
(3) Randomly generate $x_{ij} = 0$ or $x_{ij} = 1$.

3.2 Repairing and Optimization Method

Because the BKP is a constrained optimization problem, the infeasible solution may be generated when solving it by BPSO. Therefore, the infeasible solution needs to be processed. There are three main methods to deal with this problem: penalty function method [26, 27], repair method [26] and repairing and optimization method [28, 29]. This paper refers to the idea of the literature [29, 30], and uses the repairing and optimization method to solve the BKP problems. Let p_i/w_i be the density of item i. In the repair phase, the items with less density corresponding to the infeasible solution are removed from the knapsack one by one to ensure that the sum of the weight is within C, that is, the infeasible solution is repaired as a feasible solution. In the optimization phase, the items that are not loaded with relatively large density are loaded into the knapsack as much as possible, and will not be overweight after loading.

According to the density, all items are sorted in descending order. The index of each item are stored in an array $H[1...n]$. The BKP-GROA is shown in Algorithm 1.

Algorithm 1. BKP-GROA

```
Input: A potential solution X=[x₁,...,xₙ]and array H[1...n]
Output: A feasible solution X=[x₁,...,xₙ] and f(X)
1.   fweight←∑ⁿⱼ₌₁wⱼxⱼ, j←n
2.   WHILE (fweight>C) DO
3.      IF (x_{H[j]}=1) THEN
4.         x_{H[j]}←0, fweight←fweight-w_{H[j]}
5.      END IF
6.      j←j-1
7.   END WHILE
8.   FOR j←1 to N do
9.      IF (x_{H[j]}=0) AND(fweight+w_{H[j]}≤C) THEN
10.        x_{H[j]}←1, fweight←fweight+w_{H[j]}
11.     END IF
12.  END FOR
13. RETURN (X, f(X))
```

3.3   Application of BPSO to BKP

The main steps to solve BKP by using BPSO are as follows: firstly, randomly initialize N particles, calculate the fitness of each particle, and determine P_g. Then, the following process is repeated until the termination condition is met: update the velocity and position according to formulas (5) and (6), and calculate the fitness of each particle; For each particle, if its fitness is better than the fitness of P_i, it will be the local best position at present. Then, the P_g can be determined. Finally, output the optimal solution and optimal value of BKP.

$H[1...n] \leftarrow QuickSort(\{p_j/w_j \,|\, p_j \in P, w_j \in W, 1 \leq j \leq n\})$, where $QuickSort$ is used for sorting all items to descending order according to the density, and all items' index are stored in an array $H[1...n]$. Then, the pseudo-code description of BPSO for the BKP is shown in Algorithm 2.

Algorithm 2. BPSO

```
Input: The population size N, the number of iterations
MaxIter, and c₁,c₂
```
Input: The population size N, the number of iterations $MaxIter$, and c_1, c_2
Output: Optimal position X^* and $f(X^*)$

1. $H[1...n] \leftarrow QuickSort(\{p_j/w_j \mid p_j \in P, w_j \in W, 1 \leq j \leq n\})$
2. Generate initial population X_i ($i=1...N$) randomly, calculate the fitness of each particle and set $P_i = X_i$;
3. $t \leftarrow 0$;
4. WHILE ($t \leq MaxIter$)
5.   FOR $i \leftarrow 1$ TO N
6.   Update position and velocity of the particles by formula (5)(6)
7. $(X_i, f(X_i)) \leftarrow$ BKP-GROA $(X_i, H[1...n])$;
8.   END FOR
9.   FOR $i \leftarrow 1$ TO N
10.   IF $f(X_i(t+1)) > f(P_i(t))$ then $P_i(t+1) \leftarrow X_i(t+1)$
11.   Else $P_i(t+1) \leftarrow P_i(t)$
12.   END IF
13. $P_g = \max\{P_i \mid 1 \leq i \leq N\}$
14.   END FOR
15. $t \leftarrow t+1$;
16. END WHILE

4 Experimental Results and Discussions

4.1 BKP Instance and Experimental Environment

In this section, we tested three different types of the BKP: Uncorrelated instances of BKP (UBKP), Weakly correlated instances of BKP (WBKP), and Strongly correlated BKP instances (SBKP), each of which contains 10 BKP instances of size 100, 200, ..., 1000, namely UBKP1 ~ UBKP10, WBKP1 ~ WBKP10 and SBKP1 ~ SBKP10. For specific data of all instances, please refer to the document from http://xxgc.hgu.edu.cn/uploads/heyichao/ThreekindsofBKPInstances.rar.

The HP 280 Pro G3 MT desktop computer is used for all the calculations in this paper. The hardware configuration is Intel (R) Core (TM) i5-7500 CPU@3.40 GHz with 4 GB. Programming with C language, the compiler environment is VC++ 6.0; The line charts are drawn with Python in JetBrains PyCharm.

4.2 Parameter Settings of Algorithms and Comparison of Calculation Results

In order to verify the effectiveness of BPSO, it is compared with IWOA and GA, the detailed parameters of each algorithm are set as follows: In IWOA, $N = 50$, $b = 0.5$. In GA, $N = 50$, the crossover probability $P_c = 0.8$, and the mutation probability $P_m = 0.001$. In BPSO, $N = 50$, $w = 1.0$, $c_1 = c_2 = 1.8$. The number of iterations of each algorithm is twice the size of the instance.

The calculation results of solving the BKP instances are shown in Tables 1, 2 and 3, where OPT is the optimal value of the instance calculated by the dynamic programming method (DP), and Best denote the best values by using all algorithms among 50 times. Mean and Std denote the average values and the standard deviations.

Table 1. Comparison of 3 algorithms for solving UBKP instances

Instance	Results	DP	IWOA	GA	BPSO
UBKP1	Best	201616	**201616**	**201616**	**201616**
	Mean		201609.16	**201616**	201615.18
	Std		23.4635	0	4.165
UBKP2	Best	414114	**414114**	**414114**	**414114**
	Mean		**414114**	413995.12	**414114**
	Std		0	69.4964	0
UBKP3	Best	594613	594586	**594610**	594603
	Mean		594580.98	**594610**	594602.12
	Std		6.562	0	3.5757
UBKP4	Best	831629	831612	831611	**831614**
	Mean		831601.72	831594.3	**831613.68**
	Std		11.2855	69.4067	0.7332
UBKP5	Best	1003643	1003628	1003602	**1003633**
	Mean		1003619.98	1003589.74	**1003633**
	Std		6.6588	71.1347	0
UBKP6	Best	1228085	1228083	1228073	**1228085**
	Mean		1228075.68	1227988.58	**1228085**
	Std		3.5465	254.3668	0
UBKP7	Best	1524770	**1524759**	1524739	**1524759**
	Mean		1524753.82	1524703.04	**1524757.88**
	Std		4.9018	121.1483	1.796
UBKP8	Best	1692853	1692835	1692835	**1692844**
	Mean		1692835	1692684.64	**1692841.78**
	Std		0	431.4943	2.8865
UBKP9	Best	1869142	1869131	1869095	**1869138**
	Mean		1869122.44	1868982.32	**1869135**
	Std		8.8253	360.0176	3.3941
UBKP10	Best	2066060	**2066060**	2066025	**2066060**
	Mean		2066043.78	2065995.86	**2066060**
	Std		10.6645	66.85	0

From Table 1, we can see that when using BPSO to solve the UBKP instances, the best values are better than IWOA and GA except for the instance UBKP3; Except for the instance UBKP1 and UBKP3, the average values of BPSO are better than IWOA and GA.

As can be seen from Table 2, when BPSO solves the WBKP instances, the best values and average values are better than IWOA and GA.

It can be seen from Table 3 that when BPSO solves the SBKP instances, all instances can reach the optimal value obtained by the deterministic algorithm. Except that the average values of the instance SBKP4 and SBKP5 are not as good as GA, the calculation results of other instances are better than IWOA and GA.

Table 2. Comparison of 3 algorithms for solving WBKP instances

Instance	Results	DP	IWOA	GA	BPSO
WBKP1	Best	119312	119309	119308	**119312**
	Mean		119306.68	119308	**119312**
	Std		3.1333	0	0
WBKP2	Best	297700	**297700**	**297700**	**297700**
	Mean		**297700**	**297700**	**297700**
	Std		0	0	0
WBKP3	Best	444156	444147	444147	**444156**
	Mean		444144.42	444145.36	**444155.82**
	Std		2.3246	7.375	1.26
WBKP4	Best	605678	605668	605653	**605676**
	Mean		605660.6	605652.68	**605675.76**
	Std		6.5635	1.0852	1.1926
WBKP5	Best	772191	772187	772168	**772188**
	Mean		772184.88	772168	**772188**
	Std		2.8889	0	0
WBKP6	Best	890314	890307	890303	**890313**
	Mean		890303.32	890300.6	**890313**
	Std		2.6566	6.3119	0
WSBKP7	Best	1045302	**1045297**	1045291	**1045297**
	Mean		1045294.38	1045272.3	**1045297**
	Std		2.125	56.1	0
WBKP8	Best	1210947	**1210944**	1210936	**1210944**
	Mean		1210941.14	1210936	**1210944**
	Std		2.9121	0	0
WBKP9	Best	1407365	**1407364**	**1407364**	**1407364**
	Mean		**1407364**	1407318.18	**1407364**
	Std		0	168.6493	0
WBKP10	Best	1574079	1574074	1574066	**1574075**
	Mean		1574071.92	1574000.56	**1574074.4**
	Std		2.2076	183.7961	0.4899

In order to compare the performance of IWOA, BPSO and GA more intuitively, the average approximation ratio and the best approximation ratio are used to verify the performance. The average approximation ratio is defined as OPT/Mean, and the best approximation ratio is defined as OPT/Best. Figures 1, 2 and 3 shows the comparison of the average approximation ratio and the best approximation ratio of IWOA, GA and BPSO for three types of BKP instances.

As can be seen from Fig. 1(a), the average approximation ratio of BPSO is better than GA except UBKP1 and UBKP3, and BPSO is better than IWOA in solving all UBKP instances. From Fig. 1(b), we can see that the best approximation ratio obtained by BPSO is better than IWOA and GA except UBKP3. As can be seen from Fig. 2, the

Table 3. Comparison of 3 algorithms for solving SBKP instances

Instance	Results	DP	IWOA	GA	BPSO
SBKP1	Best	144822	144821	**144822**	**144822**
	Mean		144815.12	**144822**	**144822**
	Std		7.8426	0	0
SBKP2	Best	259853	**259853**	259853	259853
	Mean		259844.92	**259853**	**259853**
	Std		5.5239	0	0
SBKP3	Best	433414	**433414**	**433414**	**433414**
	Mean		433406.42	**433414**	**433414**
	Std		6.2421	0	0
SBKP4	Best	493847	**493847**	**493847**	**493847**
	Mean		493841.46	**493847**	493846.94
	Std		4.8092	0	0.2375
SBKP5	Best	688246	**688246**	**688246**	**688246**
	Mean		688240.14	**688246**	688245.938
	Std		5.0991	0	0.1972
SBKP6	Best	849526	**849526**	**849526**	**849526**
	Mean		849523.98	849523.08	**849526**
	Std		3.3555	4.6897	0
SBKP7	Best	1060106	**1060106**	1060105	**1060106**
	Mean		1060104.38	1060100.82	**1060106**
	Std		1.7192	5.2486	0
SBKP8	Best	1171576	**1171576**	1171566	**1171576**
	Mean		1171570.18	1171554.18	**1171576**
	Std		5.2103	9.5408	0
SBKP9	Best	1263609	**1263609**	1263597	**1263609**
	Mean		1263606.02	1263591.72	**1263609**
	Std		3.1968	15.3467	0
SBKP10	Best	1412095	**1412095**	1412085	**1412095**
	Mean		1412089.16	1412074.88	**1412095**
	Std		3.7382	13.3396	0

average approximation ratio and the best approximation ratio of BPSO are better than IWOA and GA in solving WBKP instances, and the performance of BPSO is very stable for ten different scales of WBKP instances.

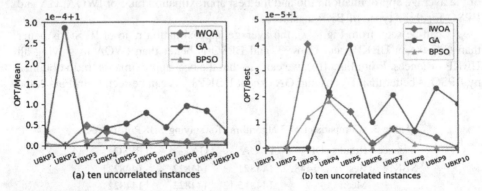

Fig. 1. The approximation ratio of 3 algorithms for solving UBKP instances

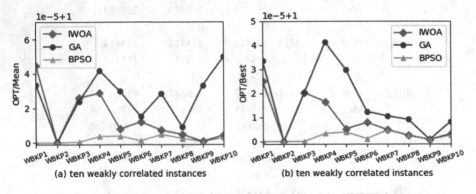

Fig. 2. The approximation ratio of 3 algorithms for solving WBKP instances

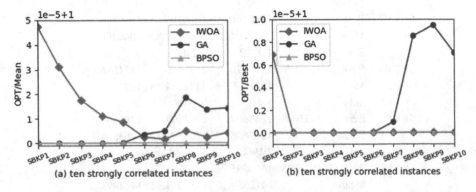

Fig. 3. The approximation ratio of 3 algorithms for solving SBKP instances

As can be seen from Fig. 3, the average approximation ratio and the best approximation ratio of BPSO are almost all 1 when solving SBKP instances, and the performance of BPSO is very stable for ten different scale SBKP instances; the performance of IWOA and GA is not as good as BPSO and the stability is inferior to BPSO when solving few instances.

5 Conclusion

In this paper, BPSO is used to solve the BKP problem, and the performance of BPSO is verified by three kinds of large-scale BKP instances. The comparison with the experimental results of IWOA and GA shows that the best values and average values obtained by BPSO are better when solving BKP instances. In addition, by comparing the average approximation ratio and the best approximation ratio, it is not difficult to see that BPSO not only has good stability, but also has the approximation ratio closer to 1, so the calculation effect is optimal. Although BKP is a classical combination optimization problem, the research of its solution by using evolutionary algorithms is relatively weak. Therefore, it is worthy of further research to explore the performance of BKP using other EAs.

Acknowledgments. This work was supported by the Scientific Research Project Program of Colleges and Universities in Hebei Province (ZD2016005), and the Natural Science Foundation of Hebei Province (F2016403055).

References

1. Karp, R.M.: Reducibility among combinatorial problems. In: Miller, R.E., Thatcher, J.W. (eds.) Proceedings of the Complexity of Computer Computations, pp. 110–137. Plenum Press, New York (1972)
2. Martello, S., Toth, P.: Knapsack Problems: Algorithms and Computer Implementations. Wiley, New York (1990)
3. Kellerer, H., Pferschy, U., Pisinger, D.: Knapsack Problems, pp. 55–75. Springer, Berlin (2004). https://doi.org/10.1007/978-3-540-24777-7
4. Mathews, G.B.: On the partition of numbers. Proc. Lond. Math. Soc. **28**, 486–490 (1897). https://doi.org/10.1112/plms/s1-28.1.486
5. Chu, P.C., Beasley, J.E.: A genetic algorithm for the multidimensional knapsack problem. J. Heuristics **4**(1), 63–86 (1998)
6. Khuri, S.L.: The zero/one multiple knapsack problem and genetic algorithms. In: Proceedings of the 1994 ACM Symposium of Applied Computing, pp. 188–193 (1994)
7. Pisinger, D.: A minimal algorithm for the bounded knapsack problem. In: Balas, E., Clausen, J. (eds.) IPCO 1995. LNCS, vol. 920, pp. 95–109. Springer, Heidelberg (1995). https://doi.org/10.1007/3-540-59408-6_44
8. Martello, S., Toth, P.: An exact algorithm for large unbounded knapsack problems. Oper. Res. Lett. **9**(1), 15–20 (1990)
9. Caprara, A., Pisinger, D., Toth, P.: Exact solution of the quadratic knapsack problem. Informs J. Comput. **11**(2), 125–137 (1999)

10. He, Y.C., Wang, X.Z., Li, W.B., Zhao, S.L.: Exact algorithms and evolutionary algorithms for randomized time-varying knapsack problem. Ruan Jian Xue Bao/J. Softw. (2016). (in Chinese with English abstract). http://www.jos.org.cn/1000-9825/4937.htm. https://doi.org/10.13328/j.cnki.jos.004937

11. He, Y., Xie, H., Wong, T.-L., Wang, X.: A novel binary artificial bee colony algorithm for the set-union knapsack problem. Future Gener. Comput. Syst. **87**(1), 77–86 (2018)

12. Wang, X.Z., He, Y.-C.: Evolutionary algorithms for knapsack problems. J. Softw. **28**, 1–16 (2017)

13. Goldberg, D.E.: Genetic Algorithm in Search, Optimization, and Machine Learning. Addison-Wesley, Reading (1989)

14. Kennedy, J., Eberhart, R.: Particle swarm optimization. In: 1995 Proceedings of the IEEE International Conference on Neural Networks, vol. 4, pp. 1942–1948 (1995)

15. Storn, R., Price, K.: Differential evolution – a simple and efficient heuristic for global optimization over continuous spaces. J. Global Optim. **11**(4), 341–359 (1997)

16. Dorigo, M., Birattari, M., Stutzle, T.: Ant colony optimization. IEEE Comput. Intell. Mag. **1**(4), 28–39 (2007)

17. Karaboga, D., Basturk, B.: A powerful and efficient algorithm for numerical function optimization: artificial bee colony (ABC) algorithm. J. Global Optim. **39**(3), 459–471 (2007)

18. Mirjalili, S., Lewis, A.: The whale optimization algorithm. Adv. Eng. Softw. **95**, 51–67 (2016)

19. Kennedy, J., Eberhart, R.C.: A discrete binary version of the particle swarm algorithm. In: Proceedings 1997 Conference on Systems, Man, and Cybernetics, pp. 4104–4109. IEEE Service Center, Piscataway (1997)

20. Clerc, M.: Discrete particle swarm optimization, illustrated by the traveling salesman problem. In: Clerc, M. (ed.) New Optimization Techniques in Engineering. STUDFUZZ, vol. 141, pp. 219–239. Springer, Heidelberg (2004). https://doi.org/10.1007/978-3-540-39930-8_8

21. Van Den Bergh, F.: An analysis of particle swarm optimizers. Ph.D. thesis (2007)

22. Liu, B., Wang, L., Jin, Y.H.: An effective PSO-based memetic algorithm for flow shop scheduling. IEEE Trans. Syst. Man Cybern. Part B Cybern. **37**(1), 18 (2007). A Publication of the IEEE Systems Man & Cybernetics Society

23. Li, Z., Li, N.: A novel multi-mutation binary particle swarm optimization for 0/1 knapsack problem. In: 2009 Chinese Control and Decision Conference, no. 2, pp. 3090–3095 (2009)

24. Bansal, J.C., Deep, K.: A modified binary particle swarm optimization for knapsack problems. Appl. Math. Comput. **218**(22), 11042–11061 (2012)

25. Hussien, A.G., Houssein, E.H., Hassanien, A.E.: A binary whale optimization algorithm with hyperbolic tangent fitness function for feature selection. In: Eighth International Conference on Intelligent Computing and Information Systems. IEEE (2018)

26. Michalewicz, Z.: Genetic Algorithm + Data Structure = Evolution Programs, pp. 13–103. Springer, Berlin (1996). https://doi.org/10.1007/978-3-662-03315-9

27. Zou, D.X., Gao, L.Q., Li, S., Wu, J.H.: Solving 0-1 knapsack problem by a novel global harmony search algorithm. Appl. Soft Comput. **11**, 1556–1564 (2011). https://doi.org/10.1016/j.asoc.2010.07.019

28. He, Y.C., Zhang, X.L., Li, X., Wu, W.L., Gao, S.G.: Algorithms for randomized time-varying knapsack problems. J. Comb. Optim. **31**(1), 95–117 (2016). https://doi.org/10.1007/s10878-014-9717-1

29. He, Y.C., Wang, X.Z., Li, W.B., Zhao, S.L.: Exact algorithms and evolutionary algorithms for randomized time-varying knapsack problem. Ruan Jian Xue Bao/J. Softw. (2016). (in Chinese with English abstract). http://www.jos.org.cn/1000-9825/4937.htm. https://doi.org/10.13328/j.cnki.jos.004937

30. He, Y.-C., Song, J.-M., Zhang, J.-M., et al.: Research on genetic algorithm for solving static and dynamic knapsack problems. Appl. Res. Comput. **32**(4), 1011–1015 (2015). (in Chinese)

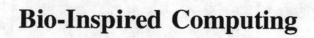

Bio-Inspired Computing

A New Multi-strategy Ensemble Artificial Bee Colony Algorithm for Water Demand Prediction

Hui Wang[1,2] and Wenjun Wang[3(✉)]

[1] Jiangxi Province Key Laboratory of Water Information Cooperative Sensing and Intelligent Processing, Nanchang Institute of Technology, Nanchang 330099, China
[2] School of Information Engineering, Nanchang Institute of Technology, Nanchang 330099, China
[3] School of Business Administration, Nanchang Institute of Technology, Nanchang 330099, China
wangwenjun881@126.com

Abstract. Artificial bee colony (ABC) is an efficient global optimizer, which has bee successfully used to solve various optimization problems. Recently, multi-strategy ensemble technique was embedded to ABC to make a good trade-off between exploration and exploitation. In this paper, a new multi-strategy ensemble ABC (NMEABC) is proposed. In our approach, each food source is assigned a probability to control the frequency of dimension perturbation. Experimental results show that NMEABC is superior to the original multi-strategy ensemble ABC (MEABC). Finally, NMEABC is applied to predict the water demand in Nanchang city. Simulation results demonstrate that NMEABC can achieve a good prediction accuracy.

Keywords: Artificial bee colony · Swarm intelligence · Multi-strategy · Ensemble · Water demand prediction

1 Introduction

Artificial bee colony (ABC) was proposed by Karaboga in 2005 [1]. It is inspired by the social behaviors of bees. Some research studies proved that ABC is better than or comparable to other swarm intelligence algorithms [2]. Therefore, ABC was widely applied to many optimization problems [3–12].

ABC has strong exploration ability, but it is not good at exploitation. Thus, the convergence of ABC is not fast. To deal with this problem, some improved methods were presented. In [13], the global best solution is used to lead the search and accelerate the convergence. Experiments demonstrated introducing the global best solution can help ABC find more accurate solutions under fixed iterations. In [14], the differential evolution (DE) mutation based on the global best solution was modified as the search equation in ABC. This modification also aims to accelerate the search. In [15], an external archive method was used to store some best solutions found at each iteration. New solutions are generated based on the external archive. The purpose of the external

© Springer Nature Singapore Pte Ltd. 2019
H. Peng et al. (Eds.): ISICA 2018, CCIS 986, pp. 63–70, 2019.
https://doi.org/10.1007/978-981-13-6473-0_6

archive is similar to the literature [14]. In [16], a multi-strategy ensemble ABC (called MEABC) algorithm was proposed. Different search models including the original ABC search model were used to improve the single search characteristic in ABC. Results show MEABC can help ABC find much better solutions on some test cases.

Water plays an important role in our life. It is the source of life and one of the most important and indispensable material resources for human survival and development. China is a populous country, but also a large water shortage country. Water resources in China are not abundant, and the problem of supply and demand is very prominent. The total water resources in China is about 2.81×10^8 m^3, which ranks the sixth place in the world after Brazil, the former Soviet Union, Canada, the United States and Indonesia. Although the absolute amount is abundant, the per capita water resources occupancy is much lower than the world average because of its large population. Therefore, how to improve the water use efficiency is very important. In order to achieve this goal, we must exactly predict the water demand at first. Water demand is related to many factors including location, economic, population, agricultural acreage, vegetation coverage, climate, water prices and some uncertain factors. So, how to exactly predict the water demand is difficult [17].

In this paper, a new MEABC called NMEABC is proposed by introducing probability parameters to control the frequency of dimension updating. Some classical benchmark functions are used to verify the performance of NMEABC. Finally, the new algorithm NMEABC is applied to predict the water demand of a city in central China.

The rest of this work is organized as follows. In Sect. 2, the original ABC is introduced. Our algorithm NMEABC is described in Sect. 3. In Sect. 4, we use NMEABC to solve some benchmark functions. In Sect. 5, NEMABC is used to predict the water demand. Finally, the conclusions of this work is given in Sect. 6.

2 Artificial Bee Colony

Like most swarm intelligence algorithms, ABC is based on population search. But ABC is different from them for individual representation and operations. In ABC, each member in the population is called food source, which is a potential solution in the search space. The purpose of ABC is finding the global optimal food source (solution) through iterations. In order to accomplish this task, ABC consists of three types of bees, where are namely employed bee, onlooker bee and scout bee, respectively [1].

For all food sources in the population, an employ bee flies to a food source with position X_i and tries to find a new food source V_i (solution) in its neighborhood by the following equation [1].

$$v_{ij}(t) = x_{ij}(t) + \phi_{ij}(x_{ij}(t) - x_{kj}(t)), \tag{1}$$

where $j \in [1, D]$ is a stochastic dimension index and D is the dimension size; $k \in [1, N]$ is an random individual index, N is the population size and $i \neq j$. $\phi_{ij} \in [-1, 1]$ is a random weight value.

According to the quality (fitness) of a food source (solution), ABC calculates its probability p_i as follows [1].

$$p_i = \frac{fitness_i}{\sum_{i=1}^{N} fitness_i},$$

(2)

where $fitness_i$ is the fitness value of the ith food source. The above equation also reflects the fitness proportion of each solution in the population. A better solution will has a larger probability p_i.

For each food source, an onlooker bee uses a probability test to judge whether it needs to search the neighborhood of the current food source. If the probability p_i is satisfied, the onlooker bee uses Eq. (1) to execute the search.

When the employed or onlooker bees carry out Eq. (1), new solutions V_i are created. ABC employs a simple greedy method to select which solution is entering the next iteration. If V_i is better than its parent X_i, then replace X_i with V_i.

The scout bee aims to help trapped solutions jump to new positions. When a solution cannot be improved *limit* iterations (*limit* is a parameter), the scout bee randomly creates a solution to replace it.

3   New Multi-strategy Ensemble ABC

Recently, a multi-strategy ensemble ABC (MEAB) algorithm was proposed [16]. In MEABC, three different search models, including the original ABC (S_1), global best guided ABC (S_2) [13] and a modified ABC/best (S_3), were utilized to construct the search pool. In the search process, each solution X_i is assigned a search model S_i, where $i = 1, 2, 3$. When searching the neighborhood of X_i, MEABC checks the search model tag S_i and selects the corresponding search model to complete the search. The search model for each solution is dynamically updated in terms of the quality of solution V_i. If V_i is better than X_i, MEABC remains use the current search model; otherwise it selects a different model to replace the current one. Many experiments showed MEABC is much better than the original ABC.

The original ABC modifies only one dimension of a solution to generate a new solution and the convergence speed is slowed down. The inventor of ABC pointed out that how many dimensions to be modified is very important to the performance of ABC [18]. Then, Akay and Karaboga [18] used a new parameter MR to control the frequency of the perturbation for the dimension updating. A larger MR means that more dimensions are modified and a smaller MR means fewer dimensions are updated.

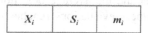

Fig. 1. The encoding of solutions in NMEABC.

Inspired by the idea of MR-ABC [18], we introduce a new parameter m_i for each solution X_i in MEABC. Then, the encoding of the new MEABC (called NMEABC) can be described in Fig. 1. From the figure, the ith solution has three components including position X_i, search model S_i, and probability of dimension updating m_i.

The probability m_i should not be too large. In our algorithm, we use a dynamic method to adjust the parameter m_i. Initially, the probability m_i is equal to $rand(0, 0.2)$, where $rand(0, 0.2)$ is a random value between 0 and 0.2. In the search process, the probability m_i is updated as follows.

$$m_i = \begin{cases} rand(m_i, \ 0.2), & \text{if } f(V_i) < f(X_i) \\ rand(0, \ m_i), & \text{otherwise} \end{cases} . \tag{3}$$

The changes of the probability m_i is determined by the quality of V_i. If the current search model S_i can find a better solution (it means that V_i is better than X_i), then increase the probability m_i. More dimensions are modified and it may accelerate the search. If the current search model S_i cannot find a better solution (it means that V_i is worse than X_i), then decrease the probability m_i. Fewer dimensions are modified and it may improve the exploration. It is noted that at least one dimension should be updated. To implement this, we use a simple method as described in Algorithm 1.

Algorithm 1: Dimension Updating Method
1: Input: $X_i=(x_{i1},x_{i2},...,x_{il},...,x_{iD})$
2: **for** $l=1$ to D **do**
3:   **if** $rand(0,1)<m_i \wedge l==j$ **then**
4:     Execute the corresponding search model;
5:   **end if**
6: **end for**
7: Output: $V_i=(v_{i1},v_{i2},...,v_{il},...,v_{iD})$

---

4   Experiments on Benchmark Functions

To verify the performance of NMEABC, ten well-known benchmark functions are used in this section. Table 1 briefly gives these benchmark functions.

In the experiments, we compare NMEABC with MEABC and ABC. The detailed parameter settings are listed as follows. The parameters N and limit are set to 50 and 100, respectively [16]. In NMEABC and MEABC, the constant C is equal to 1.5 [13]. Each algorithm is run 30 times and the average best fitness values are reported. For each run, when the number fitness evaluations reaches to 1.5e+05, the algorithm is terminated [16].

Table 2 presents the results of NMEABC, MEABC and ABC on the ten test functions. From the results, three ABCs can find the global optimum on f_6. For the rest of 9 functions, MEABC is better than ABC. However, NMEABC falls into local minima on this function. Compared to MEABC, NMEABC obtains more accurate solutions on 6 functions. They achieve the same solutions on 3 functions. The results demonstrate our probability strategy can improve the performance of MEABC.

Table 1. Benchmark functions

Functions	Search range	Global optimum
Sphere (f_1)	[−100, 100]	0
Schwefel 2.22 (f_2)	[−10, 10]	0
Schwefel 1.2 (f_3)	[−100, 100]	0
Schwefel 2.21 (f_4)	[−100, 100]	0
Rosenbrock (f_5)	[−30, 30]	0
Step (f_6)	[−100, 100]	0
Quartic with noise (f_7)	[−1.28, 1.28]	0
Schwefel 2.26 (f_8)	[−500, 500]	−12569.5
Rastrigin (f_9)	[−5.12, 5.12]	0
Ackley (f_{10})	[−32, 32]	0

Table 2. Comparison among NMEABC, ABC and MEABC.

Functions	ABC	MEABC	NMEABC
	Mean	Mean	Mean
f_1	1.14e−15	4.85e−40	**3.54e−58**
f_2	1.49e−10	1.25e−21	**1.09e−35**
f_3	1.05e+04	9.81e+03	**3.82e+03**
f_4	4.07e+01	4.89e+00	**2.04e+00**
f_5	1.28e+00	**2.86e−01**	2.31e+01
f_6	**0.00e+00**	**0.00e+00**	**0.00e+00**
f_7	1.54e−01	2.29e−02	**1.51e−02**
f_8	−12490.5	**−12569.5**	**−12569.5**
f_9	7.11e−15	**0.00e+00**	**0.00e+00**
f_{10}	1.60e−09	2.90e−14	**2.19e−14**

5   Application on Water Demand Prediction

As mentioned before, water demand is related to many factors including location, economic, population, agricultural acreage, vegetation coverage, climate, water prices and some uncertain factors. So, how to exactly predict the water demand is difficult. In this section, we try to use NMEABC to predict the water demand in Nanchang city of China. According to the Table 1 of [17], the water consumption of Nanchang city consists of four departments: industry, agriculture, resident and ecology. The first three departments account for 97%. So, we ignore the ecological water use when constructing the water demand prediction model.

By the suggestions of [17], three prediction models, namely linear, exponential and hybrid, are used in this paper.

Linear model (Y_l):

$$Y_l = x_1 \cdot W_1 + x_2 \cdot W_2 + x_3 \cdot W_3 + x_4, \tag{4}$$

Exponential model (Y_e):

$$Y_e = x_1 \cdot W_1^{x_2} + x_3 \cdot W_2^{x_4} + x_5 \cdot W_3^{x_6} + x_7, \tag{5}$$

Hybrid model (Y_h):

$$Y_h = x_0 \cdot Y_l + (1 - x_0) \cdot Y_e, \tag{6}$$

where x_i is weighting factor; W_1, W_2, and W_3 are the population, gross industrial production, and gross agricultural production, respectively. The historical data of W_1, W_2, and W_3 can be found in [17, 19].

To evaluate the quality of those models, we use sum of squared errors as the objective function. Therefore, to find the optimal prediction model, NMEABC aims to minimize the following objective.

$$\min \left[\sum_{i=1}^{M} (Y_{pre} - Y_{act})^2 \right], \tag{7}$$

where M is the number of training data, Y_{pre} is the predicted water demand, and Y_{act} is the actual water demand. Y_{pre} can be calculated by the corresponding prediction model.

Table 3. Prediction errors achieved by NMEABC under different models.

Models	Mean	Std dev	Best	Worst
Linear	4.97%	1.32e−02	3.52%	7.62%
Exponential	2.92%	7.71e−03	2.35%	4.72%
Hybrid	2.79%	5.29e−03	2.30%	4.06%

In the experiments, we use the data between 2003 and 2012 as the training sample $(M = 10)$. The rest of three years data (2013–2015) are used as testing sample. For other parameters of NMEABC, we use the same settings as described in Sect. 4.

Table 3 lists the prediction error achieved by NMEABC under different models. From the table, the linear model obtains the mean prediction error 4.97%, which is worse than exponential and hybrid models. The hybrid model achieves the high prediction accuracy 97.21%. For the worst linear model, the prediction accuracy is still up to 95.03%. So, NMEABC under three models can achieve good prediction accuracy.

6   Conclusions

Multi-strategy ensemble ABC (MEABC) is an efficient ABC variant. To further enhance the search ability of MEABC, a new MEABC (NMEABC) is proposed in this paper. The main contribution of NMEABC include two aspects: (1) introducing an independent dimension updating probability for each food source; and (2) a dynamic method to adjust the dimension updating probability. A simple experiment confirms that the proposed method can improve the search efficiency of MEABC. For water demand prediction, NMEABC also obtains good performance and the prediction accuracy is between 95.03% and 97.21%.

Acknowledgement. This work was supported by the Science and Technology Plan Project of Jiangxi Provincial Education Department (No. GJJ170994), the National Natural Science Foundation of China (No. 61663028), the Distinguished Young Talents Plan of Jiangxi Province (No. 20171BCB23075), the Natural Science Foundation of Jiangxi Province (No. 20171BAB202035), and the Open Research Fund of Jiangxi Province Key Laboratory of Water Information Cooperative Sensing and Intelligent Processing (No. 2016WICSIP015).

References

1. Karaboga, D.: An idea based on honey bee swarm for numerical optimization. Technical report-TR06, Erciyes University, engineering Faculty, Computer Engineering Department (2005)
2. Karaboga, D., Akay, B.: A comparative study of artificial bee colony algorithm. Appl. Math. Comput. **214**, 108–132 (2009)
3. Karaboga, D., Gorkemli, B., Ozturk, C., Karaboga, N.: A comprehensive survey: artificial bee colony (ABC) algorithm and applications. Artif. Intell. Rev. **42**(1), 21–57 (2014)
4. Zhao, J., et al.: Artificial bee colony based on special central and adapt number of dimensions learning. J. Inf. Hiding Multimed. Sig. Process. **7**(3), 645–652 (2016)
5. Panda, T.R., Swamy, A.K.: An improved artificial bee colony algorithm for pavement resurfacing problem. Int. J. Pavement Res. Technol. **11**(5), 509–516 (2018)
6. Sharma, N., Sharma, H., Sharma, A.: Beer froth artificial bee colony algorithm for job-shop scheduling problem. Appl. Soft Comput. **68**, 507–524 (2018)
7. He, Y., Xue, X.S., Zhang, S.M.: Using artificial bee colony algorithm for optimizing ontology alignment. J. Inf. Hiding Multimed. Sig. Process. **8**(4), 766–773 (2017)
8. Cui, L.Z., et al.: A smart artificial bee colony algorithm with distance-fitness-based neighbor search and its application. Future Gener. Comput. Syst. **89**, 478–493 (2018)
9. Cui, L.Z., et al.: A ranking-based adaptive artificial bee colony algorithm for global numerical optimization. Inf. Sci. **417**, 169–185 (2017)
10. Kumar, A., Kumar, D., Jarial, S.K.: A review on artificial bee colony algorithms and their applications to data clustering. Cybern. Inf. Technol. **17**(3), 3–28 (2017)

11. Wu, C.M., Fu, S.R., Li, T.T.: Research of the WSN routing based on artificial bee colony algorithm. J. Inf. Hiding Multimed. Sig. Process. **8**(1), 120–126 (2017)
12. Tang, L.L., Li, Z.H., Pan, J.S., Wang, Z.F., Ma, K.Q., Zhao, H.N.: Novel artificial bee colony algorithm based load balance method in cloud computing. J. Inf. Hiding Multimed. Sig. Process. **8**(2), 460–467 (2017)
13. Zhu, G., Kwong, S.: Gbest-guided artificial bee colony algorithm for numerical function optimization. Appl. Math. Comput. **217**, 3166–3173 (2010)
14. Gao, W., Liu, S.: A modified artificial bee colony algorithm. Comput. Oper. Res. **39**, 687–697 (2012)
15. Wang, H., Wu, Z.J., Zhou, X.Y., Rahnamayan, S.: Accelerating artificial bee colony algorithm by using an external archive. In: Proceedings of IEEE Congress on Evolutionary Computation, pp. 517–521 (2013)
16. Wang, H., Wu, Z.J., Rahnamayan, S., Sun, H., Liu, Y., Pan, J.S.: Multi-strategy ensemble artificial bee colony algorithm. Inf. Sci. **279**, 587–603 (2014)
17. Wang, H., Wang, W.J., Cui, Z.H., Zhou, X.Y., Zhao, J., Li, Y.: A new dynamic firefly algorithm for demand estimation of water resources. Inf. Sci. **438**, 95–106 (2018)
18. Akay, B., Karaboga, D.: A modified Artificial bee colony algorithm for real-parameter optimization. Inf. Sci. **192**, 120–142 (2012)
19. Wang, H., et al.: Firefly algorithm for demand estimation of water resources. In: Liu, D., Xie, S., Li, Y., Zhao, D., El-Alfy, E.S. (eds.) ICONIP 2017. LNCS, vol. 10637, pp. 11–20. Springer, Cham (2017). https://doi.org/10.1007/978-3-319-70093-9_2

Approximate Backbone Subsection Optimization Algorithm for the Traveling Salesman Problem

Feipeng Wang[1(✉)], Hu Peng[1], Changshou Deng[1(✉)], Xujie Tan[1], and Likun Zheng[2]

[1] School of Information Science and Technology, Jiujiang University, Jiujiang, Jiangxi, China
373779432@qq.com, csdeng@jju.edu.cn
[2] School of Computer and Information Engineering, Haerbin Commerce University, Haerbin, Heilongjiang, China

Abstract. Approximate backbone subsection optimization algorithm is proposed to solve the traveling salesman problem, for the precision accuracy of the basic ant colony algorithm for solving the larger traveling salesman problem is low. First, traveling salesman problem approximate backbone is obtained by the ant colony algorithm, and then the original traveling salesman problem is sectioned based on the approximate backbone. Then the ant colony optimization algorithm is applied to solve the subsections to improve the precision accuracy of the global optimal solution. The experimental results show that the algorithm is more precision accuracy than the basic ant colony algorithms in the solution of the typical traveling salesman problem.

Keywords: Traveling salesman problem · Approximate backbone · Subsection · Ant colony optimization

1 Introduction

Traveling Salesman Problem (TSP) is a classical NP-hard combinatorial optimization problem [1]. Its model is simple but difficult to solve. Ant Colony Optimization (ACO) is another heuristic search algorithm applied to combinatorial optimization problems after the meta-heuristic search algorithms such as simulated annealing algorithm, genetic algorithm, Tabu Search algorithm and artificial neural network algorithm.

Dorigo et al. applied ant colony algorithm to classical optimization problems such as TSP and the Quadratic Assignment Problem, and got good results. But using ant colony algorithm to solve the large scale TSP directly, the efficiency is low, and the quality of the solution is not high [2, 3].

Backbone refers to the intersection of all global optimal solutions of a problem instance [4]. He et al. [4] divides the backbone application in heuristic algorithm design into two types: probability type and deterministic type. Probabilistic backbone algorithm [5–7] mainly has three stages: first, the local optimal solution solving stage;

© Springer Nature Singapore Pte Ltd. 2019
H. Peng et al. (Eds.): ISICA 2018, CCIS 986, pp. 71–80, 2019.
https://doi.org/10.1007/978-981-13-6473-0_7

secondly, the approximate backbone probability computing stage; finally, the probability-oriented solution stage, mainly using the approximate backbone probability for the generation of initial solution, instance transformation or local search in the neighborhood determination [6]. The deterministic backbone algorithm can be further divided into space constrained and instance reduction [6]. Schneider [8, 9], Qi et al. [10], Fischer et al. [11], Dong et al. [12] improve the efficiency of solving TSP instances by conventions; Zou et al. [13] on the basis of conventions of TSP, through the analysis of the experimental results of the instances, concluded that about 80% of the local optimal solutions are the edges of the global optimal solution, and this generalization. The rate is not related to the scale of the problem. Based on this conclusion, an approximate backbone subsection of ACO (ABSACO) algorithm for TSP is proposed.

ABSACO algorithm is based on the set of local optimal solutions obtained by ant colony algorithm, through the statistics of the edges in the set of local optimal solutions, and according to a certain weight proportion from the statistical results, select a certain number of edges to form the approximate backbone of the optimal solution; then based on the approximate backbone, the current optimal solution obtained by ant colony algorithm is sectioned. Finally, the subsections are optimized by ant colony optimization algorithm. The strategy based on approximate backbone subsection effectively decomposes the original TSP, reduces the size of the solution, so that the basic ant colony algorithm can improve the efficiency of solving large-scale TSP and improve the quality of the solution.

2 Ant Colony Algorithm

Given a group of cities N, TSP can be described as finding a closed loop of the shortest length that passes through each city only once. Let d_{ij} be the length of the path from the city i to city j. In this paper, the Euclidean distance $(d_{ij} = [(x_i - x_j)^2 + (y_i - y_j)^2]^{1/2})$ is given. Then, a TSP is a known graph G(N, E), N represents a group of cities, E represents the edges between the groups of cities, and solves the problem of a shortest path through each city in the graph G. In this paper, we solve the symmetric TSP, that is, $d_{ij} = d_{ji}$.

2.1 Ant System

Ant colony algorithm is initially applied to solve TSP. A basic ant colony algorithm-ant system (AS) can be simply described as follows: initialization parameters, m ants randomly placed in one of the corresponding n cities, the construction of each ant's City taboo table and accessible table; then, each ant according to formula (1) in accordance with the probability of moving from city i to city j, all the ants complete a round trip after the N cycle; calculate the path length of each ant in a round trip, update the pheromone according to formula (2); record the shortest round trip length of m ants. Repeat this process until the maximum number of iterations is reached.

The formula (1) is the probability formula for ant k moving from city i to city j.

$$p_{ij}^k(t) = \frac{[\tau_{ij}(t)]^\alpha \cdot [\eta_{ij}]^\beta}{\sum_{l \in N_i^k} [\tau_{il}(t)]^\alpha \cdot [\eta_{il}]^\beta}, \quad if \ j \in N_i^k \tag{1}$$

Among, N_i^k is the collection of ant k to transfer cities. The $\tau_{ij}(t)$ indicates the pheromone concentration on the connection path between city i and city j at t time. The heuristic function $\eta_{ij} = 1/d_{ij}$ denotes the expected degree of the ant's transfer from the city i to the city j. The parameters alpha and beta are the parameters controlling the concentration of the pheromone and the expected degree of the transfer, respectively.

The formula (2) is the formula for updating pheromones.

$$\tau_{ij}(t+1) = (1 - \rho) \cdot \tau_{ij}(t) + \sum_{k=1}^m \Delta\tau_{ij}^k(t) \tag{2}$$

Among them, ρ is a parameter; $1 - \rho$ represents the evaporation of pheromone on the path between time t and time t + 1. The $\Delta\tau_{ij}^k(t)$ is the increment of pheromone released by the ant k on the edge e(i, j) from time t to time t + 1 per unit length. The $\Delta\tau_{ij}^k(t)$ is calculated by formula (3).

$$\Delta\tau_{ij}^k(t) = \begin{cases} \frac{Q}{L^k}(t) & \text{If the edge e(i, j) is used} \\ & \text{by the ant k at t time} \\ 0 & \text{Otherwise} \end{cases} \tag{3}$$

Q is a constant. L^k is the path length traveled by ant k.

2.2 Ant System with Elitist Strategy

The ant system with elitist strategy (AS$_{elite}$) mentioned in reference [14] is an improved pheromone concentration updating method based on the basic ant colony algorithm AS. The improved pheromone concentration updating formula is as follows:

$$\tau_{ij}(t+1) = \rho\tau_{ij}(t) + \sum_{k=1}^m \Delta\tau_{ij}^k(t) + \Delta\tau_{ij}^* \tag{4}$$

Among them, the $\Delta\tau_{ij}^*$ is the increment of pheromone on path ij caused by elite ants, which is calculated by formula (5).

$$\Delta\tau_{ij}^* = \begin{cases} \rho \cdot \frac{Q}{L^*} & \text{If the edge e(i, j) is part of the} \\ & \text{optimal solution found} \\ 0 & \text{Otherwise} \end{cases} \tag{5}$$

In formula (5), ρ is the number of elite ants, and L^* is the optimal solution path length.

3 Approximate Backbone Subsection of ACO

3.1 Approximate Backbone Subsection Strategy

There are a lot of random experiments on two typical examples in TSPLIB, in reference [13]. The experiments show that approximately 80% of the edges in the local optimal solution are the edges of the global optimal solution. Approximate Backbone Subsection (ABS) strategy is based on this discovery. The edges of the local optimal solution are counted and the approximate backbone of the optimal solution is obtained. From the approximate backbone, it is the starting edge of the subsection that we choose a part of the statistical results which appear more frequently. Then the current local optimal solution is sectioned. Sectioned subsections are then optimized separately. If there is a better result, then the atomic path subsection is better instead of. The final solution is the optimal solution. The main idea of approximate backbone subsection optimization strategy is shown in Fig. 1.

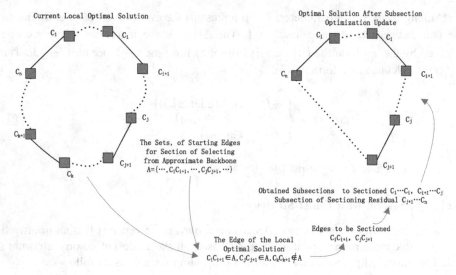

Fig. 1. Approximate backbone subsection optimization strategy main idea

For solving the traveling salesman problem in n cities, the current local optimal solution path is $C_1 \ldots C_i C_{i+1} \ldots C_j C_{j+1} \ldots C_k C_{k+1} \ldots C_n$. The Sets, of Starting Edges for Section of Selecting from Approximate Backbone, is $A = \{ \ldots, C_i C_{i+1}, \ldots, C_j C_{j+1}, \ldots \}$. Thus, the $C_i C_{i+1}$ is one of edges of current local optimal solution, it belongs to set A, and the $C_j C_{j+1}$ is too. The $C_k C_{k+1}$ is one of edges of current local optimal solution, but it does not belong to set A. Based on this, there are the subsection $C_1 \ldots C_i, C_{i+1} \ldots C_j$ and $C_{j+1} \ldots C_n$ from the current local optimal solution. Finally, the subsection $C_1 \ldots C_i, C_{i+1} \ldots C_j$ and $C_{j+1} \ldots C_n$ carries on the optimization separately, the solution path after the subsection optimization renewal is the optimal solution path, and the obtained solution is the optimal solution.

3.2   Approximate Backbone Subsection of ACO Algorithm

Approximate backbone subsection colony optimization algorithm flow chart is shown in Fig. 2.

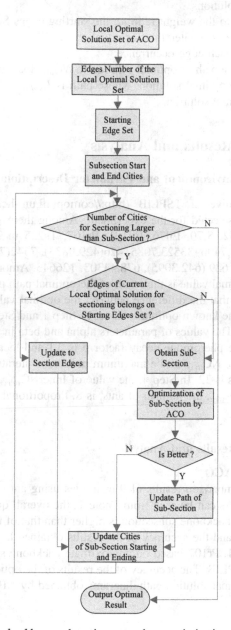

Fig. 2. Approximate backbone subsection ant colony optimization algorithm flow chart

The main steps of the algorithm are described below.

Step 1: ant colony algorithm iterates the maximum NC_{max} times to generate NC_{max} local optimal solutions.

Step 2: The number matrix *BorderNums* is obtained by counting the edges of NC_{max} local optimal solutions.

Step 3: According to the weight ratio ω, the starting edges Set SSSB is obtained, whose number of edge is greater than or equal to $\omega \cdot NC_{max}$, from the matrix BorderNums of times for each edge occurrence.

Step 4: The R_{ngb} is a path of optimal solution to NC_{max} local optimal solution. It is sectioned to obtain the optimal solution, whose path is R_{ugb}.

Step5: Output optimal solution.

4   Experimental Results and Analysis

4.1   Experimental Environment and Parameter Description

Nine examples of universal TSPLIB (http://comopt.ifi.uni-heidelberg.de/software/TSPLIB95/tsp/) were selected for the experiment. Among them, examples Oliver 30, Att48, Eil51, Berlin 52, St70, Eil76, Eil101, Pr107, Ts225 in TSPLIB provide the optimal values are 423.7406, 33523.7085, 426(429.9833), 7542(7544.3659), 675(678.5975), 538(558.7119), 629 (642.3095), 678.44303, 126643. Among them, the value in parentheses of the optimal value is the result of the optimal path provided by TSPLIB. Deviation is the result that the difference between the optimal value minus the known optimal value divide the known optimum value. In Step 1 and Step 4, ant system with elitist(AS_{elite}) is used. The values of parameters alpha and beta in ant colony algorithm are set to 1 and 5. The pheromone decay factor p is 0.1 and local pheromone adjustment factor Q is 1. The NC_{max} of the maximum number of iterations in Step 1 is 300 and the number of ants is 32. In Step 4, the value of $InnerNC_{max}$, maximum iterations number, is 200. The m_{inner}, the number of ants, is 8. Proportional weight Omega is set to 0.8.

4.2   Experimental Results and Analysis

1. Comparison with ACO

Table 1 shows the comparison results of 9 examples using ant colony algorithm and ABSACO algorithm. As can be seen from Table 1, the overall quality of the solution based on approximate backbone subsection is higher than that of the solution based on ant colony algorithm, and the accuracy of the results obtained by Att48, Eil51, Berlin 52, St70, Eil76, Eil101, Pr107 based on approximate backbone subsection is up to or higher than that of TSPLIB. The accuracy of the results of the optimal path is provided.

Figure 3 is the optimal solution path diagrams obtained by ABSACO algorithm for some instances.

Table 1. TSP instance test results of ACO and ABSACO

TSP instances	Optimal ACO/ABSACO	Average ACO/ABSACO	Deviation ACO/ABSACO
Oliver30	423.7406/423.7406	424.62568/423.7406	0.00000/0.00000
Att48	35221.8906/33523.7085	36061.26433/34122.03316	0.05066/0.00000
Eil51	449.2723/428.9816	460.58299/432.30439	0.05463/0.00700
Berlin52	7548.9927/7544.3659	7796.615208/7573.139225	0.00093/0.00031
St70	703.4685/677.1096	739.70106/701.960295	0.04218/0.00313
Eil76	572.4761/551.6946	588.080035/569.14083	0.06408/0.02545
Eil101	692.5415/641.0211	723.31598/680.26375	0.10102/0.01911
Pr107	46740.4675/44301.6837	47475.26795/44481.13528	0.05502/-0.00003
Ts225	131429.9493/128758.896	135826.9446/132692.7332	0.03780/0.01671

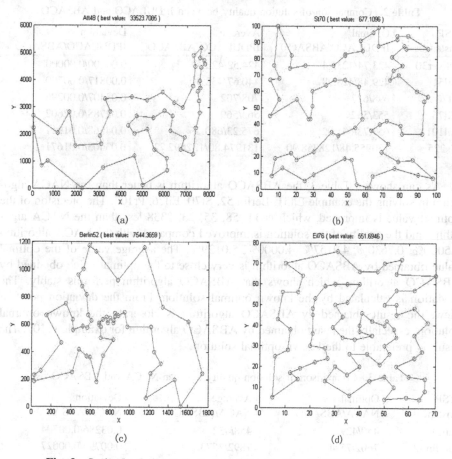

Fig. 3. Optimal solution path diagrams obtained by ABSACO algorithm

2. Comparison with IPDULACO and NACA

Compared with the existing IPDULACO [15] and NACA [16] algorithms, the quality of ABSACO algorithm is verified. As shown in Table 2, the accuracy of the solution obtained by ABSACO algorithm is higher than that obtained by IPDULACO algorithm for five instances, Eil51, St70, Eil76, Eil101, Ts225, etc. In these five instances, the quality of the solution obtained by ABSACO algorithm is improved by 0.5, 21, 1, 16.71 and 2196.58 respectively, and the relative improvement rate is 0.1164%, 3.0086%, 0.1808%, 2.5406%, 1.6773%. IPDULACO and ABSACO have the same precision for example Oliver 30, but the average value of ABSACO algorithm is 423.74. The algorithm only needs one time to get the global optimal solution; the two algorithms solve the example Oliver 30, Eil51, St70, and the average value of the optimal solution of ABSACO algorithm relative to IPDULACO algorithm is extracted respectively, to 0.78, 8.37 and 6 higher. The ABSACO algorithm is more stable.

Table 2. Comparison of solution quality between IPDULACO and ABSACO

TSP instances	Optimal IPDULACO/ABSACO	Average IPDULACO/ABSACO	Deviation IPDULACO/ABSACO
Oliver30	423.74/423.74	424.52/423.74	0.00000/0.00000
Eil51	429.48/428.98	440.67/432.30	0.00817/0.00700
St70	698/677	708/702	0.03407/0.00296
Eil76	553/552	563/569	0.02788/0.02602
Eil101	657.73/641.02	675.23/680.26	0.04568/0.01911
Ts225	130955.48/128758.90	131974.80/132692.73	0.03405/0.01671

As can show in Table 3, the ABSACO algorithm is better than the NACA algorithm in solving the example Eil51, Berlin 52, St70, Eil76, Pr107. The precision of the optimal value is improved, which is 11, 58, 35, 23, 2338 less than the NACA algorithm, and the quality of the solution is improved compared with the NACA algorithm 2.5000%, 0.7630%, 4.9157%, 4.0000%, 5.0129%. The average value of the optimal value obtained by ABSACO algorithm is very close to the optimal value obtained by ABSACO algorithm, which shows that ABSACO algorithm performs stably. The deviation is calculated by the known optimal solution. From the deviation point of view, the result obtained by ABSACO algorithm is closer to the known optimal solution, especially the result obtained by ABSACO algorithm for example Pr107. The result is preferable to the known optimal solution.

Table 3. Comparison of solution quality between NACA and ABSACO

TSP instances	Optimal NACA/ABSACO	Average NACA/ABSACO	Deviation NACA/ABSACO
Eil51	440/429	458/432	0.03286/0.00704
Berlin52	7602/7544	7892/7573	0.00796/0.00027
St70	712/677	768/702	0.05481/0.00296
Eil76	575/552	620/569	0.06877/0.02602
Pr107	46640/44302	48890/44481	0.05275/-0.00002

5　Summary

Aiming at the problem that the precision of basic ant colony algorithm for solving traveling salesman problem is not high, an optimization algorithm is proposed, which gets the approximate backbone by statistical local optimal solution edge and solves the traveling salesman problem piecewise on the basis of approximate backbone. The experiment shows that the algorithm based on approximate backbone subsection has high accuracy in solving large-scale traveling salesman problem, and can obtain the optimal solution in an acceptable time. On the basis of a certain amount of local optimal solution, the approximate backbone is obtained by statistics, and a certain proportion of the edges in the approximate backbone are taken as the sectioned edges. The original problem is sectioned to reduce the scale of the problem and improve the quality of the solution. The next step is to reduce the statistics and the number of subsections to improve the efficiency of solving the problem. The optimization strategy based on approximate backbone subsection is applied to other combinatorial optimization algorithms to solve other large-scale traveling salesman problems.

Acknowledgement. This work was supported by the National Natural Science Foundation of China (No. 61763019), the Natural Science Foundation of Heilongjiang Province (General Program:F2017019), the "Thirteenth Five-Year Plan" of Education Science in Jiangxi Province for 2017 (No.17YB211), and the Science and Technology Plan Projects of Jiangxi Provincial Education Department (No. GJJ161072, No. GJJ161076, No. GJJ170 953).

References

1. Garey, M.R., Johnson, D.S.: Computers and Intractability: A Guide to the Theory of NP-Completeness. W.H. Freeman, San Francisco (1979)
2. Colorni, A., Dorigo, M.: Heuristics from nature for hard combinatorial optimization problems. Int. Trans. Oper. Res. **3**(1), 1–21 (1996)
3. Dorigo, M., Gambardella, L.M.: Ant colony system: a cooperative learning approach to the traveling salesman problem. IEEE Trans. Evol. Comput. **1**(1), 53–66 (1997)
4. Jiang, H., Qiu, T., Hu, Y., Li, M.-C., Luo, Z.-X.: Backbone analysis and applications in heuristic algorithm design. Acta Autom. Sin. **37**(3), 257–269 (2011)
5. Helsgaun, K.: An effective implementation of the Lin-Kernighan traveling salesman heuristic. Eur. J. Oper. Res. **126**(1), 106–130 (2000)
6. Zhang, W.X., Looks, M.: A novel local search algorithm for the traveling salesman problem that exploits backbones. In: Proceedings of the 19th International Joint Conference on Artificial Intelligence, pp. 343–348. Morgan Kaufmann Publishers, San Francisco (2005)
7. Helsgaun, K.: General k-opt submoves for the Lin-Kernighan TSP heuristic. Math. Program. Comput. **1**(2–3), 119–163 (2009)
8. Schneider, J., Froschhammer, C., Morgenstern, I., Husslein, T., Singer, J.M.: Searching for backbones-an efficient parallel algorithm for the traveling salesman problem. Comput. Phys. Commun. **96**(2–3), 173–188 (1996)
9. Schneider, J.: Searching for backbones - a high-performance parallel algorithm for solving combinatorial optimization problems. Future Gener. Comput. Syst. **19**(1), 121–131 (2003)
10. Qi, Y.-T., Liu, F., Jiao, L.-C.: Immune algorithm with self-adaptive reduction for large-scale TSP. J. Softw. **19**(6), 1265–1273 (2008)

11. Fischer, T., Merz, P.: Reducing the size of traveling salesman problem instances by fixing edges. In: Cotta, C., van Hemert, J. (eds.) EvoCOP 2007. LNCS, vol. 4446, pp. 72–83. Springer, Heidelberg (2007). https://doi.org/10.1007/978-3-540-71615-0_7
12. Dong, C., Jäger, G., Richter, D., Molitor, P.: Effective tour searching for TSP by contraction of pseudo backbone edges. In: Goldberg, A.V., Zhou, Y. (eds.) AAIM 2009. LNCS, vol. 5564, pp. 175–187. Springer, Heidelberg (2009). https://doi.org/10.1007/978-3-642-02158-9_16
13. Zou, P., Zhou, Z., Chen, G.L., Gu, J.: A multilevel reduction algorithm to TSP. J. Softw. **14**(1), 35–42 (2003). http://www.jos.org.cn/1000-9825/14/35.pdf. (in Chinese with English abstract)
14. Dorigo, M., Maniezzo, V., Colorni, A.: The ant system: optimization by a colony of cooperating agents. IEEE Trans. Syst. Man Cybern.-Part B **26**(1), 29–41 (1996)
15. Xu, K., Lu, H., Cheng, B., Huang, Y.: Ant colony optimization algorithm based on improved pheromones double updating and local optimization for solving TSP. J. Comput. Appl. **37**(6), 1686–1691 (2017)
16. Zhang, C., Tu, L., Wang, J.: Application of self-adaptive ant colony optimization in TSP. J. Central South Univ. (Sci. Technol.) **46**(8), 2944–2949 (2015)

A Computing Model for Four-Valued Logic AND Gate Based on DNA Origami and DNA Displacement

Zhen Tang$^{(\boxtimes)}$, Zhixiang Yin, Xia Sun, Jing Yang, and Jianzhong Cui

Anhui University of Science and Technology, Huainan 232001, China
1179145666@qq.com

Abstract. A four-valued logic AND gate model is constructed by DNA origami and DNA strand displacement. Different input signals are designed into different input DNA strands, the results of the input signals are determined by observing whether the hairpin structures are unwound (the length of the long strand is changed) and the fluorescence colors are quenching. The biological expectation results show that the model can not only judge the false and true states of the four valued logic AND gate, other states in four-valued logic AND gate can also be well displayed by the long strand length changed and fluorescence quenching.

Keywords: DNA displacement · DNA origami · Four-valued logic AND gate

1 Introduction

Electronic computers have played a huge role in human society, but with the emergence of more complex nonlinear problems, such as NP complete problems, the shortcomings of electronic computers with small storage capacity, slow computing speed, and low intelligence are slowly emerging. Traditional electronic computers are difficult to solve these problems, and people are gradually turning their attention to the field of new computing. Due to the natural characteristics of DNA molecules: specificity, high parallelism and miniaturization, high-capacity preservation and parallel operation in the process of mass information storage and processing have significant advantages. DNA computing has become a hot research field with broad application prospects. Once a DNA computer is successfully researched, its calculation amount of ten hours is equivalent to the sum of all computer operations on the earth. In 1994, Adleman entered the field of DNA computing for the first time. He used DNA coding to solve the Hamiltonian path problem of directed graphs [1]. In 1995, Lipton solved the SAT problem on the basis of the Adleman test [2]. In 2000, Sakamoto skillfully used the hairpin structure of single-stranded DNA molecules to encode the constraints of logical operations in DNA molecules. Then he solved a 3-SAT problem by self-assembly of DNA molecules (forming hairpin structures) [3].

With the gradual development of molecular science and technology, Winfree proposes a high-precision computing model, molecular self-assembly model, from bottom to top, from disorder to order, and constantly self-correcting. DNA origami and

© Springer Nature Singapore Pte Ltd. 2019
H. Peng et al. (Eds.): ISICA 2018, CCIS 986, pp. 81–90, 2019.
https://doi.org/10.1007/978-981-13-6473-0_8

DNA strand displacement reactions are two new molecular biotechnologies developed on the basis of molecular self-assembly techniques. Due to the operability of the strand displacement reaction, the simple realization conditions, the predictability of the product and the high yield, the DNA strand displacement reaction has become an important application method and a popular research direction in the field of nanoscience. In 2000, Bernard and Andrew et al. used DNA molecules to design a molecular machine that was assembled from three single strands of DNA and controlled by "adding" and "closing" by adding two additional strands, When opening a "closed molecular machine, the biological manipulation technique used is the DNA strand displacement reaction [4]. In 2011, Qian and Winfree constructed a biochemical circuit that can solve the square root of a four-digit binary number based on the DNA strand displacement reaction [5]. In the same year, Qian and Winfree assembled into four interconnected artificial neurons using 112 different DNA strands based on the DNA strand displacement reaction. These four artificial neurons constitute a neural network with artificial intelligence [6]. DNA origami can successfully fold a target long strand (scaffold) into a variety of complex and controllable nanoscale patterns and shapes, which has the advantage that traditional DNA self-assembly does not have. The breakthrough in the field of DNA origami was in 2006, and DNA origami was first reported by Rothemund. In this technique, a long single-stranded DNA molecule (scaffold) extracted from M13mp18 phage is folded and assembled into squares, triangles, and pentagrams, and has short, single-stranded DNA oligonucleotides (staple) guidance. The invention of DNA origami quickly attracted the attention of many scholars and became one of the hot topics [7]. In the same year, Qian et al. established an asymmetric simulated Chinese map with a diameter of about 150 nm by DNA origami technology [8]. In 2008, Andersen designed the dolphin structure logo based on DNA origami, and can control the dolphin tail activity [9]. In 2012, the first autonomous nanodevice based on DNA origami was reported [10]. In 2013, bipedal DNA walkers took a critical step in the DNA origami orbit [11]. In 2014, DNA origami robots were used for routine calculations [12]. In 2017, Nature published four papers on DNA origami. Tikhomirov et al. used a square DNA origami tile with a pattern on the surface as a basic building block to construct a two-dimensional DNA origami lattice with a width of 0.5 μm [13]. Ong et al. designed a microscale self-assembly method for three-dimensional DNA structures [14]. Wagenbaue uses a multi-layer self-assembly method to achieve self-assembly of micron-sized three-dimensional DNA origami nanostructures [15]. Praetorius et al. used the virus to prepare single-stranded precursor DNA. Each DNA contains tens of thousands of sequences that can be cleaved and opened by DNase and assembled into a three-dimensional origami nanostructure [16].

In electronic computers, the theory and practice of binary logic have matured. However, many problems in life practice are not only "true or false", such as "true", "false", "no definition" in the subject of information processing and PLA. Three-state of "forward rotation", "stop" and "reverse rotation" of motor control. numerical boundaries can often be divided into "positive number", "zero", "negative number". Therefore, multi-valued logic is getting more and more attention from scholars at home and abroad. Multi-value logic refers to logic whose value of all logical values is greater than 2. For example, except for two logical values of "true" and "false", an intermediate value is allowed, which is three-valued logic. Four-valued logic means that the logical value has four values. In 2018, Yin and Zhao constructed a three-valued logic and gate calculation model based on DNA origami [17]. In 2001, Chen et al. designed a four-valued TTL non-gate and NAND using bipolar transistors. Both TTL non-gate and NAND gates are discrete logic circuits. These gates can be used to form quaternary combinational logic circuits and sequential logic circuits, and can also be used with DYL series circuits [18]. In 2017, George et al. introduced a logic inverter gate run by DNA strand displacement. This logic inverter gate has a modular feature that can be used anywhere in the circuit [19].

The amount of information that a four-valued logic can represent is twice as the amount of information represented by two-bit binary logic, the study of four-valued logic is more important. By applying four-valued logic in the programming language, four-branch and multi-way transitions can be established, avoiding the use of a large number of two-branch nesting, thus greatly simplifying the program and flow chart. The fault diagnosis of the digital system needs to consider the state of faulty and faultless, and only two logical values are not enough. On the other hand, if a four-valued logic circuit is used to form a binary digital system, the redundant logic values can be used to make the system a fault tolerant, self-checking, fail-safe or fail-safe digital system. In this paper, a four-valued logic and gate model is constructed by DNA origami and DNA strand displacement. The model has the advantages of simple operation, high precision and easy implementation.

2 DNA Strand Displacement and DNA Origami

2.1 DNA Strand Displacement

Early DNA self-assembly uses the DNA molecules as main assembly material. Based on the design of DNA coding and base-matching rules, the DNA molecule spontaneously form the primary structure of a certain rigidity. The structure as the basic unit further assembled into certain geometric shape of two-dimensional or three-dimensional structure. In recent years, the DNA strand displacement technology is based on the response of dynamic equilibrium, it has a simple principle, programmable reaction process and easy modularization. The DNA strand displacement can form a cascade circuit flexibly, which has attracted the attention of many scholars and has multidisciplinary characteristics. As a new molecular computing technique, DNA strand displacement has been widely used in many areas, such as scientific computing, nanomachines and biomedical.

The DNA strand displacement reaction is a spontaneous reaction between the DNA molecules, and the power of the reaction comes entirely from the intermolecular forces. The DNA strand displacement reaction refers to the process of producing a new double strand structure by replacing the single strand in the original structure and releasing the single strand in the original structure. The principle of DNA strand displacement reaction is: due to the different binding force between different DNA single strands, the free energy tends to be stable in the molecule hybrid system. With the input strand with strong binding force, the DNA strand with weak binding force on the part of the complementary structure is replaced. A simple understanding is that the longer DNA strand replaces the short DNA strand, and the replaced DNA strand is used as output signals to implement molecular logic operations. The basic process of DNA strand displacement reaction is shown in Fig. 1. Single-strand *ab*, which is an input signal, undergoes a DNA strand displacement reaction with a partial double-strand structure. First, the region *a* and region $\bar{a}$ form complementary double strands by certain binding force. Then, the single-stranded identification area *b* gradually replaces the single strand *b* of the original binding, until the single strand *b* is completely replaced and released. At the same time it releases the output signal, the structure reaches stability, and the DNA strand displacement reaction is completed.

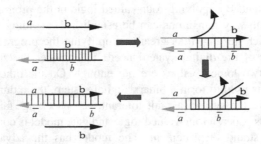

Fig. 1. Basic reaction process of DNA strand displacement.

2.2   DNA Origami

DNA origami is a technique that uses a special structure of DNA molecules and a complementary pairing of bases to fold a specific region of a long DNA single strand (scaffold) and fix it with short strands (staples) to construct an expectation. The structure in Fig. 2 is folded into a hairpin structure. Compared with the traditional self-assembly method, the obvious advantage of DNA origami is that it can not only accurately assemble and align the DNA strands at the nanometer scale, but also obtain more complicated and fine structures, and the experimental conditions are simple, easy to operate, and efficient in assembly. Using the structure obtained by DNA origami as a template to assemble functional nanomaterials or molecules, it is possible to obtain nanodevices or drug carriers with controllable properties such as optics and electromagnetism.

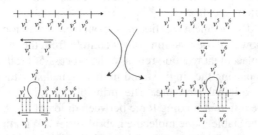

Fig. 2. Basic reaction process of DNA origami.

3 A Computing Model for Four-Valued Logic AND Gate Based on DNA Origami and DNA Displacement

3.1 The Design of Scaffold, Staples, Short Strands

The scaffold is designed to consist of two main parts, each representing an input signal x, y. Each part consists of five nucleotide fragments, respectively $x_1 \cdots x_5, y_1 \cdots y_5$. The constructed scaffold is shown in Fig. 3.

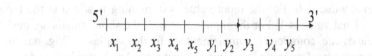

Fig. 3. Schematic diagram of the scaffold.

For the staples, it is designed for two main purposes: one is complementary to the part of the scaffold strand to form hairpin structures. the other is to replace the DNA strand displacement reaction, so that the hairpin structure can be opened. Therefore, the staples are designed in two parts (As shown in Fig. 4a). The area $\overline{x_1}, \overline{x_3}.\overline{y_1}, \overline{y_3}$ in Fig. 4a corresponds to the first portion of the staple strand, which are respectively complementary to the scaffold strand $x_1, x_3.y_1, y_3$. The area $\overline{t_x}, \overline{t_y}$ corresponds to the second part of the staple strand, which is used for DNA strand displacement reaction to open the hairpin structures.

For short strands, the purpose of designing it is to control the fluorescence to extinguish by the DNA strand displacement reaction (As shown in Fig. 4b). The $5'$ ends of the staples in Fig. 4b have blue, green fluorescent gene molecules, respectively. The area $\overline{x_4}, \overline{x_5}.\overline{y_4}, \overline{y_5}$ corresponds to the first part of the staple strand, which are respectively complementary to the scaffold strand $x_4, x_5.y_4, y_5$. The region $\overline{s_x}, \overline{s_y}$ corresponds to the second portion of the staple strand, which is used for DNA strand displacement reactions to control the brightness of the fluorescence.

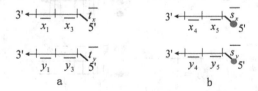

Fig. 4. (a) Schematic diagram of the staples, (b) Schematic diagram of the short strands. (Color figure online)

The scaffold strand, the staple strands and the short strands are mixed together, and a four-valued logical AND gate model based on DNA origami and DNA strand displacement is obtained (As shown in Fig. 5).

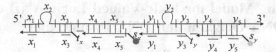

Fig. 5. Four-valued logical AND gate model based on DNA origami and DNA strand displacement.

3.2   The Design of Input Signals

The input signal value is 0: For the input value is 0, nothing is added at the input.

The input signal value is 1: For the input value is 1, the short strands are designed. The short strands are completely complementary to the staples of Fig. 4a, thereby achieving the purpose of opening the hairpin structures (As shown in Fig. 6).

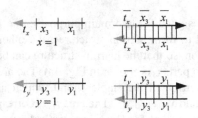

Fig. 6. Short strands diagram with input value of 1.

The input signal value is 2: For the input value is 2, the design of short strands are attached with a fluorescence quenching gene molecule at its $3'$ end to control the fluorescence extinction. These short strands are completely complementary to the short strands in Fig. 4b (As shown in Fig. 7).

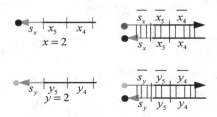

Fig. 7. Short strands diagram with input value of 2.

The input signal value is 3: For the input value is 3, design two short strands, that is, the two strands of the design with input values of 1, 2, can simultaneously open the hairpin structure and quench the fluorescent color (As shown in Fig. 8).

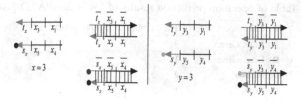

Fig. 8. Short strands diagram with input value of 3. (Color figure online)

3.3 Input Signals and Model Detection

A four-valued logical AND gate can be defined as a four-valued small operator,

$$G = \{0, 1, 2, 3\}, \quad \forall x, y \in G, F = x \wedge y = \min\{x, y\}$$

and its truth table is shown in Table 1.

Table 1. Four-valued small operator truth table

F	0	0	0	0	0	1	1	1	0	1	2	2	0	1	2	3
X	0	0	0	0	1	1	1	1	2	2	2	2	3	3	3	3
Y	0	1	2	3	0	1	2	3	0	1	2	3	0	1	2	3

The input signal value is 0, nothing is added, there are two hairpin structures, and the blue and green fluorescence are bright. At this time, the DNA long strand is also the longest of all input signal values, and can be detected by gel electrophoresis.

The input signal value is 1, as judged by the formation and unwinding of the hairpin structure, which can be displayed by gel electrophoresis.

The input signal value is 2, which is judged by the brightening of the fluorescent color, the detection result is accurate, and the realization condition is simple.

The input signal value is 3, which is judged by the formation and unwinding of the hairpin structure, and the fluorescence is extinguished at the same time. When the input signal is $x = 3, y = 3$, the two hairpin structures in the model are all unwrapped, and the blue and green fluorescence are completely quenched. The length of the DNA long strand at this time is also the shortest of all input signal values, and can be clearly separated by gel electrophoresis. Table 2 shows the expected results of the reaction after inputting different input signals.

The reaction diagrams of the input signals (1, 1), (2, 2), (3, 3) are given below (As shown in Fig. 9).

Table 2. Table of operation prediction results of four-valued AND gate model

X	Y	F	Fluorescent colors	The number of hairpin structures
0	0	0	Blue, Green	2
0	1	0	Blue, Green	1
0	2	0	Blue	2
0	3	0	Blue	1
1	0	0	Blue, Green	1
1	1	1	Blue, Green	0
1	2	1	Blue	1
1	3	1	Blue	0
2	0	0	Green	2
2	1	1	Green	1
2	2	2	nothing	2
2	3	2	nothing	1
3	0	0	Green	1
3	1	1	Green	0
3	2	2	nothing	1
3	3	3	nothing	0

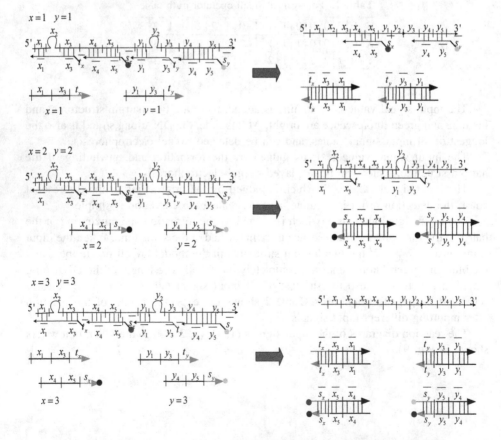

Fig. 9. The reaction diagram of the input signals are (1, 1), (2, 2), (3, 3).

4 Conclusion

In this paper, a four-valued logical AND gate model was constructed by using two methods of DNA origami and DNA strand displacement. The hairpin structures formed by DNA origami was unwrapped (the length of the long strand changed) and the fluorescent color. The detection of the result after the input signal is judged. This model has the following advantages:

(1) The model utilizes two main techniques of DNA molecular origami and DNA strand displacement in DNA molecule self-assembly, which are simple in implementation and accurate in response.
(2) After inputting the signal, the results are judged by gel electrophoresis and fluorescence detection, and the two detection methods are simple in operation and high in accuracy.
(3) Compared with some models, only the two states of the input signal (true, true) and others (other states other than "true, true" cannot be distinguished well). The model can clearly obtain the various conditions of the input signal according to the reaction result obtained after the input signal, instead of only judging (true, true). This greatly improves the possibility of using the model in practical problems. For example, in the use of machinery, "bad, repairable obstacles, non-repairable obstacles, good" is not only "good" is needed, "repairable obstacles" need to be detected.

Although the model design has many advantages, there are still many shortcomings. How to apply this model to practical problems, how to extend the model to a more general multi-valued logic gate will be our next step.

Acknowledgments. This work is supported by National Natural Science Foundation of China (NO. 61672001, 61702008) and National Natural Science Foundation of Anhui (NO. 1808085MF193).

References

1. Adleman, L.M.: Molecular computation of solutions to combinatorial problems. Science **266** (5187), 1021–1024 (1994)
2. Lipton, R.J.: Using DNA to solve NP-complete problems. Science **268**(5120), 542–545 (1995)
3. Sakamoto, K., Gouzu, H., Komiya, K., et al.: Molecular computation by DNA hairpin formation. Science **288**(5469), 1223–1226 (2000)
4. Yurke, B., Turberfield, A.J., Mills Jr., A.P., et al.: A DNA-fuelled molecular machine made of DNA. Nature **406**(6796), 605–608 (2000)
5. Qian, L.L., Winfree, E.: Scaling up digital circuit computation with DNA strand displacement cascades. Science **332**(6034), 1196–1201 (2011)
6. Qian, L.L., Winfree, E., Bruck, J.: Neural network computation with DNA strand displacement cascades. Nature **475**(7356), 368–372 (2011)
7. Rothemund, P.W.: Folding DNA to create nanoscale shapes and patterns. Nature **440**(7082), 297–302 (2006)

8. Qian, L., Wang, Y., Zhang, Z., et al.: Analogic China map constructed by DNA. Chin. Sci. Bull. **51**(24), 2973–2976 (2006)
9. Andersen, E.S., Dong, M., Nielsen, M.M., et al.: DNA origami design of dolphin-shaped structures with flexible tails. ACS Nano **2**(6), 1213–1218 (2008)
10. Douglas, S.M., Bachelet, I., Church, G.M.: A logic-gated nanorobot for targeted transport of molecular payloads. Science **335**(6), 831–834 (2011)
11. Tomov, T.E., Tsukanov, R., Liber, M., et al.: Rational design of DNA motors: fuel optimization through single-molecule fluorescence. J. Am. Chem. Soc. **135**(32), 11935–11941 (2013)
12. Amir, Y., Benishay, E., Levner, D., et al.: Universal computing by DNA origami robots in a living animal. Nat. Nanotechnol. **9**(5), 353–357 (2014)
13. Tikhomirov, G., Petersen, P., Qian, L., et al.: Fractal assembly of micrometre-scale DNA origami arrays with arbitrary patterns. Nature **552**(7683), 67–71 (2017)
14. Ong, L.L., Hanikel, N., Yaghi, O.K., et al.: Programmable self-assembly of three-dimensional nanostructures from 10,000 unique components. Nature **552**(7683), 72–77 (2017)
15. Wagenbauer, K.F., Sigl, C., Dietz, H.: Gigadalton-scale shape-programmable DNA assemblies. Nature **552**(7683), 78–83 (2017)
16. Praetorius, F., Kick, B., Behler, K.L., et al.: Biotechnological mass production of DNA origami. Nature **552**(7683), 84–87 (2017)
17. Yin, Z.X., Zhao, X.Y.: A computing model for three-valued logic AND gate based on DNA origami. J. Hefei Univ. Technol. (Nat. Sci.) **41**(2), 176–194 (2018)
18. Chen, S.K., Yan, B.C., Wu, J.H., et al.: The study on the discrete logic circuit of 4 values 'and not gate'. J. Electric Power Sci. Technol. **16**(4), 35–37 (2001)
19. George, A.K., Singh, H.: DNA strand displacement-based logic inverter gate design. Micro Nano Lett. **12**(9), 611–614 (2017)

0-1 Integer Programming Based on DNA Tetrahedral Probe

Jing Yang[1], Xinmu Yang[1], Zhixiang Yin[1(✉)], Zhang Qiang[1,2], and Jianzhong Cui[1]

[1] School of Mathematics and Big Data,
Anhui University of Science and Technology, Huainan, Anhui, China
jyangh82@163.com, zxyin66@163.com
[2] School of Computer, Dalian University of Technology,
Dalian, Liaoning, China

Abstract. It is difficult to find an effective algorithm for solving NP complete problems such as integer programming. The nanostructure constructed by DNA origami combines huge parallelism and massive storage capacity of DNA computing. In the calculation process, it can effectively avoid the number of experimental operations required by other DNA computing models. It greatly reduces the time consumption and the rate of misinterpretation, thus providing an effective way to efficiently solve integer programming. DNA tetrahedron is a nanostructure constructed by origami. It has stable structure, good toughness and compression resistance, simple production process, high yield, rich functional modification sites, good biocompatibility, but also resistance to a variety of specific or non-specific nuclease. Therefore it can reduce the misinterpretation rate of biochemical reactions using DNA tetrahedron and DNA single strand to construct probes, finding the true solution according to the constraint condition. And then it can improve the computational efficiency of the model.

Keywords: DNA tetrahedron · 0-1 integer programming · DNA origami · DNA computing

1 Introduction

DNA nanotechnology has been developing rapidly in the past 30 years [1, 2]. There are two main ways to construct self-assembled DNA nanostructures, including tile self-assembly developed by Seeman's team [3, 4] and DNA origami invented by Rothemund [5]. In 1980s, Seeman [6] put forward "structural DNA nanotechnology". Researchers then constructed different modules, such as DX (double-crossover) module [7–11], TX (triple-crossover) module [12], cross module [13] and symmetry module [14], and assembled various graphical structures (two-dimensional arrays, square meshes, polyhedrons, etc.) [15]. In 2006, Rothemund [5] proposed a new method of DNA self-assembly, DNA origami. By DNA origami, Rothemund obtained the intricate two-dimensional structures of triangles, squares, rectangles, pentagrams and smiling faces. Rothemund's research laid the foundation for the precise assembly of nanostructures, and then more complex and diverse nanostructures [16, 17] were

© Springer Nature Singapore Pte Ltd. 2019
H. Peng et al. (Eds.): ISICA 2018, CCIS 986, pp. 91–100, 2019.
https://doi.org/10.1007/978-981-13-6473-0_9

constantly designed and assembled, providing more sophisticated templates for the in-depth study of nanodevices. In 2007, Shih et al. [18] folded M13 as a scaffold stand to form 410 nm hexahelical nanotubes using DNA origami and site-specific design. This is the first time that researchers have used DNA origami to create a three-dimensional structure, which opens the prelude to the assembly of three-dimensional nano-DNA structures. Subsequently, the researchers designed and obtained many complex and exquisite three-dimensional DNA self-assembly structures.

Fig. 1. Smiles and stars folded in DNA origami

In 2008, Andersen et al. [19] successfully designed the school badge of dolphin structure of Aarhus University using DNA origami. By adjusting the number of Crossover at the tail to control the movement of the dolphin tail, the shapes of different shapes were obtained. This is the first asymmetric figure with holes. The next year, they designed a 3D box with M13mp18 as the scaffolding stand, and switched the lid of the box through the stand replacement reaction. Three months later, the lab's Dietz et al. devised a variety of twist patterns [20], with angles accurate to about 3 degrees. Soon after the separation, Ke et al. [21] designed a hollow tetrahedral structure. Subsequently, Han et al. [22] pushed the DNA origami to a climax in 2013. They used a nearly vertical DNA strand composed of a cross structure, and successfully obtained the structure of 21 bp, 42 bp, 63 bp network structure. Then by adjusting the scaffolding assembly mode, the node is slightly twisted to form a gridiron-like structure. The three-dimensional spherical structure and spiral structure of DNA were successfully designed to overcome the problem of charge mismatch of DNA molecules. Han et al. have greatly promoted the preparation of three-dimensional DNA nanostructures. The cavity of three-dimensional DNA nanostructures can be used to carry some drug molecules to achieve targeted therapy of diseases. In recent years, the research on DNA tetrahedron has attracted more and more scholars' attention. DNA tetrahedron structure is a three-dimensional DNA nanostructure with tetrahedron shape, which is composed by DNA origami, ingenious DNA sequence design, complementary pairing principle and automatic hybridization of each strand (Fig. 1).

The tetrahedron is closed by 4 triangular planes, and each side of the triangle is about 54 nm. It is hybridized by multiple staple stands and a scaffold of DNA, rather than each other, so the response requires relatively low accuracy in the measurement relationship. It can significantly improve the success rate and yield of the assembly.

DNA tetrahedron is a kind of nanostructure. It has stable structure, good toughness and compressive properties, simple manufacturing process, high yield, rich functional modification sites, good biocompatibility [23]. It can also resist a variety of specific or non-specific nucleases, and has good application potential in molecular diagnosis, bioimaging, molecular delivery and drug targeted therapy.

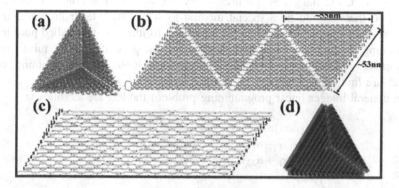

Fig. 2. The design of DNA tetrahedron by Ke et al. [21]

At present, there are many software packages for the design of DNA nanostructures [24], such as Uniquimer 3D [25] and NANEV [26]. The development and application of these software packages make it easier to design DNA nonmaterial including tetrahedral structures. DNA tetrahedrons suitable for integer programming will be constructed by DNA origami technology, and the computational complexity of integer programming will be reduced by combining the advantages of nanostructures in this paper (Fig. 2).

2 0-1 Integer Programming

Integer programming is an independent branch [27] formed by R.E. in 1958 after the cutting plane method was proposed. Generally, it is consistent with the combinatorial optimization problem, which is to find the best solution satisfying certain constraints among a limited number of alternatives. Such as backpack (or loading) problem, fixed cost problem, harmony exploration team problem (combinatorial pairing problem), effective exploration team problem (combinatorial coverage problem), traveling salesman problem, vehicle routing problem and so on. It can be transformed into integer programming problem to solve. Its method mainly includes branch and bound method, cutting plane method and exhaustive method. In addition, it also has wide applications in computer design, system reliability, coding and economic analysis.

Integer programming is an optimization problem with integer variables. That is, the optimization problem of maximizing or minimizing a multivariate function with all or part variables as integers under the constraints of a set of equations or inequalities. Integer programming is an important part of mathematical programming, and it has applications in many aspects of life. Nonlinear integer programming can be divided into linear part and integer part, so integer programming is often regarded as a special part of linear programming. In linear programming problems, some of the optimal solutions may be fractions or decimal. But for some specific problems, it is often required that the answer must be integers. In order to satisfy the integer requirement, it seems at first that only rounding off the non-integer solution already obtained is enough. In fact, the integer is not necessarily the feasible solution and the optimal solution, so there should be a special method to solve the integer programming. In integer programming, if all variables are restricted to integers, it is called pure integer programming. If only one variable is restricted to integers, it is called mixed integer programming. A special case of integer programming is the 0-1 programming, whose variables are limited to 0 or 1.

The general integer linear programming problem models are as follows:

$$\max(\min)z = c_1x_1 + c_2x_2 + \cdots + c_nx_n$$
$$\begin{cases} a_{11}x_1 + a_{12}x_2 + \cdots + a_{1n}x_n \leq (=, \geq)b_1 \\ a_{21}x_1 + a_{22}x_2 + \cdots + a_{2n}x_n \leq (=, \geq)b_2 \\ \quad\quad\quad\quad\quad \vdots \\ a_{m1}x_1 + a_{m2}x_2 + \cdots + a_{mn}x_n \leq (=, \geq)b_m \\ x_1, x_2, \cdots, x_n = 0, 1, a_{ij}, b_j \text{ is integer} \\ i = 1, 2, \cdots, m. j = 1, 2, \cdots, n \end{cases}$$

0-1 programming plays an important role in integer programming. On the one hand, many practical problems, such as assignment, location and delivery, can be attributed to such programming. On the other hand, any integer programming with bounded variables can be transformed into 0-1 programming [28]. Many nonlinear programming problems can also be expressed as integer programming problems by 0-1 programming method, so many scholars are devoted to this direction of research.

When the variable x_i takes only 0 and 1, and b_j takes the non negative integer, that is 0-1 integer programming, as follows:

$$\max(\min)z = c_1x_1 + c_2x_2 + \cdots + c_nx_n$$
$$\begin{cases} a_{11}x_1 + a_{12}x_2 + \cdots + a_{1n}x_n \leq (=, \geq)b_1 \\ a_{21}x_1 + a_{22}x_2 + \cdots + a_{2n}x_n \leq (=, \geq)b_2 \\ \quad\quad\quad\quad\quad \vdots \\ a_{m1}x_1 + a_{m2}x_2 + \cdots + a_{mn}x_n \leq (=, \geq)b_m \\ x_1, x_2, \cdots, x_n = 0, 1, b_j \text{ is } non\,negative\,integer \\ i = 1, 2, \cdots, m. j = 1, 2, \cdots, n \end{cases}$$

When the coefficient a_{ij} only takes 0 and 1, the variable x_i takes only 0 and 1, and b_j takes the non negative integer, that is 0-1 integer programming, as follows:

$$\max(\min)z = c_1x_1 + c_2x_2 + \cdots + c_nx_n$$

$$\begin{cases} a_{11}x_1 + a_{12}x_2 + \cdots + a_{1n}x_n \leq (=, \geq)b_1 \\ a_{21}x_1 + a_{22}x_2 + \cdots + a_{2n}x_n \leq (=, \geq)b_2 \\ \qquad\qquad \vdots \\ a_{m1}x_1 + a_{m2}x_2 + \cdots + a_{mn}x_n \leq (=, \geq)b_m \\ a_{ij}, x_j = 0, 1, b_j \text{ is nonnegative integer} \\ \qquad i = 1, 2, \cdots, m. j = 1, 2, \cdots, n \end{cases}$$

Since Adleman solved the problem of 7-vertex directed Hamilton path with DNA computing method in 1994 [29], DNA computing has become a hot topic for many scientists. Many scholars have tried to solve the integer programming problem with this method. The first breakthrough was the DNA computing model proposed by Yin in 2003 to solve the general 0-1 integer programming problem [30]. In the same year, Zhang Fengyue applied the surface DNA computing model to solve the 0-1 integer programming problem [31]. Yin et al. also applied DNA computing to 0-1 integer programming problem. He used DNA computing to solve a special 0-1 integer programming problem, that is, the generalization of assignment problem [32]. On the basis of reference [32], Wang gave an algorithm to solve the optimal solution of a special integer programming problem based on DNA computing [33]. Zhou et al. further extended the application of DNA computing model in 0-1 integer programming, and proposed 0-1 integer programming model with negative coefficients calculated by DNA [34]. Yang et al. gave the DNA calculation model [35] based on the three helix structure. Zhang et al. gave a self assembling DNA computing model [36] for the 0-1 integer programming problem and so on [37–39]. Integer programming theory and algorithm research is blending with other subjects of mathematical programming, but many algorithms cannot be applied to solve practical problems in society. DNA tetrahedron has the advantages of nanostructure and biochemical reaction. Therefore, it is meaningful to study the application of DNA tetrahedron structure in integer programming.

It is just beginning that using of DNA origami computing model is to solve integer programming problem. At present, the existing research results are basically around the establishment of 0-1 integer programming problem DNA computing model. Therefore, there are worthy of further study that how to construct the DNA origami computing model of 0-1 integer programming problem, how to realize the self-assembly computing model of 0-1 integer programming problem biologically, how to establish the self-assembly computing model of general integer programming problem and how to realize these problems.

3 0-1 Integer Programming Model Based on DNA Tetrahedron

3.1 Basic Algorithm

Step 1: Generate all possible combinations of variable 0 or 1 for given problem.
Step 2: Eliminate unfeasible solutions using every constraint inequality, and preserve feasible solutions.

Step 3: Generating residual solutions.

Step 4: Continue step 2,3 with the constraint inequality order, eliminate all unfeasible solutions and preserve residual solutions.

Step 5: Compare the value for object function corresponding with every feasible solution to obtain the optimum solutions.

3.2　Biological Algorithm

Step 1. We use DNA encoder to generate DNA single strand representing 0 and 1 values of n variables. There are 2n kinds of DNA short strands. Only n kinds of short strands are involved in reaction. The combination of 2n kinds of short strands should be $\underbrace{C_2^1 C_2^1 \cdots C_2^1}_{n} = 2^n$.

Step 2. In a certain constraint condition, if the variable is expressed as 1, it will not take 0 again. Similarly, if it is taken as 0, it will not take 1. Therefore, when constructing a data pool, only n kinds of DNA short strands are put into the test tube, and ligases are added to generate 2^n kinds of DNA long strands as the data pool.

Step 3. DNA tetrahedron is constructed by DNA origami. Three vertices of tetrahedron are modified and fixed on the chip. DNA single strands representing complementary strands with different constraints are constructed. DNA single strands are fixed on the remaining vertices of tetrahedron to construct DNA tetrahedron probes.

Step 4. The DNA tetrahedron probe is used to extract the DNA long stand satisfying the first constraint condition. The data pool at this time satisfies the first constraint.

Step 5. For other constraints, repeat steps (4) to exclude all solutions which do not satisfy the conditions. Finally, DNA strand satisfying all the conditions is obtained.

Step 6. Use PCR- amplification technology to read and interpret.

3.3　Case Analysis

To illustrate this algorithm, we use a simple 0-1 integer programming problem to demonstrate the biological algorithm. For a general 0-1 integer programming problem, $a_{ij}x = x_{j1} + x_{j2} + \cdots + x_{jk}, k = a_{ij}, i = 1, 2, \cdots, m, j = 1, 2, \cdots, n$, can be classified as a simple 0-1 programming [28].

$$minZ = 2x_1 - 3x_2 + 2x_3$$
$$\text{s.t.} \begin{cases} x_1 + x_2 - x_3 \geq 1 \\ x_1 + x_3 \leq 1 \\ x_2 + x_3 \leq 1 \\ x_1, x_2, x_3 = 0, 1 \end{cases}$$

In order to solve the 0-1 programming problem of the above formula, the 0-1 programming is reduced to a simple 0-1 programming. $x_1 + x_2 - x_3 \geq 1$ is represented as $x_1 + x_2 - (1 - \bar{x}_3) \geq 1$. $x_1 + x_2 + \bar{x}_3 \geq 2$ is reorganized. In this way, the above 0-1 integer programming becomes a simple 0-1 programming.

$$\min Z = 2x_1 - 3x_2 + 2x_3$$
$$\text{s.t.} \begin{cases} x_1 + x_2 + \bar{x}_3 \geq 2 \\ x_1 + x_3 \leq 1 \\ x_2 + x_3 \leq 1 \\ x_1, x_2, x_3, \bar{x}_1, \bar{x}_2, \bar{x}_3 = 0, 1 \end{cases}$$

Step 1: Construct 6 kinds of oligonucleotide fragments to express $x_1, x_2, x_3, \bar{x}_1, \bar{x}_2, \bar{x}_3$ If x_i takes 1, $\bar{x}_i$ takes 0, $i = 1, 2, 3$ For these 6 variables, there will be no $\bar{x}_i$ when x_i occurs in constraints. Therefore, ligases can be used to generate arbitrary combinations of $2^3 = 8$ kinds of DNA single strands without repetitive variables, and these eight single strands can be put into a test tube to form a data pool, $(x_1, x_2, x_3), (x_1, x_2, \bar{x}_3)$ $(x_1, \bar{x}_2, x_3), (\bar{x}_1, x_2, x_3), (\bar{x}_1, \bar{x}_2, x_3), (\bar{x}_1, x_2, \bar{x}_3), (x_1, \bar{x}_2, \bar{x}_3), (\bar{x}_1, \bar{x}_2, \bar{x}_3)$ (Fig. 3).

$$x_1 : AATCGTACGTCGTATAGCTA$$
$$x_2 : CAATTGGCGAGTGAATCGTG$$
$$x_3 : GCCTGTACGTCAGTCGTACG$$
$$\bar{x}_1 : TGGATCGTAGCTAGCTGAAC$$
$$\bar{x}_2 : GGTCATCGTACGATTCAGCT$$
$$\bar{x}_3 : CCTATGCTAGCTAGCTAGCT$$

Fig. 3. Encoding of variable $x_1, x_2, x_3, \bar{x}_1, \bar{x}_2, \bar{x}_3$

Step 2: DNA nanotetrahedron was constructed by origami, and the three vertices of the DNA tetrahedron were modified and fixed on the chip. The first constraint stand is encoded to construct DNA single stand. Then it is fixed on the vertex of the tetrahedron. Constitute DNA tetrahedral probe (as follow Fig. 4). The first constraint is $x_1 + x_2 + \bar{x}_3 \geq 2$. That is to say, at least two of $x_1, x_2, \bar{x}_3$ will take 1 to establish. So the combination $(x_1, x_2, \bar{x}_3)$ of constraint conditions is (1, 1, 0), (1, 0, 1), (0, 1, 1), (1, 1, 1). In order to extract the DNA strand satisfying the constraint condition 1, we need to construct these four probes. The combination (x_1, x_3) satisfying the second constraint condition is (0, 0), (0, 1), and (1, 0). The combination (x_2, x_3) satisfying the third constraint condition is (0, 0), (1, 0), (0, 1).

Step 3: DNA tetrahedron probes are placed in the data pool, and the strands satisfying the first constraint are hybridized with the probes to form double strands (as follow Fig. 5). The probe is taken out and cleaned to form a new data pool. The data pool thus formed satisfies the first constraint.

Step 4: repeat step 3, so we will find DNA stands that satisfy all constraints.

Step 5: the extracted DNA stand was purified and amplified by PCR. Finally, the feasible solution is read out. For all feasible solutions, we compare the value of the objective function. Finally, the optimal solution is obtained.

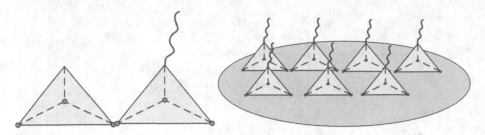

Fig. 4. DNA tetrahedral probe

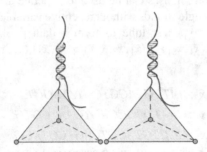

Fig. 5. Extraction of DNA stands satisfying constraints by using DNA tetrahedron probe

Each integer linear programming is equivalent to a 0-1 integer linear programming. The general integer linear programming can be transformed into a simple 0-1 integer programming [28] by mathematical methods. For satisfiability problem, it can also be transformed into a 0-1 integer programming problem.

3.4   Complexity Analysis

The complexity of the model generally includes time complexity and spatial complexity. The time complexity is usually related to its biochemical reaction time. And the spatial complexity is generally related to its computational depth. The short strand number used in this model is related to the representation of variables and the number of variables. The computational depth of the model is related to the constraints of the model, so the complexity of the model is linear with the number of variables n. The above analysis shows that the model greatly reduces the complexity of the integer programming problem, and is a more effective algorithm.

4   Conclusion

In this paper, DNA tetrahedron is constructed by origami, and DNA tetrahedron is used as a probe to solve 0-1 integer programming problem. The complexity of computation is linearly related to the number of variables. The model makes full use of the advantages of origami, such as convenient encoding, fast reaction, low cost and so on.

The tetrahedron has the advantages of stable structure, good toughness and compression resistance, simple fabrication process, high yield, abundant functional modification sites, and good biocompatibility. Therefore, the fabrication of probes with this structure can greatly reduce the generation of pseudo-solutions and improve the efficiency of the solution. With the improvement of experimental environment and the development of molecular biology technology, the biological operation of this DNA tetrahedron computing model will be better realized.

Acknowledgment. This project is supported by National Natural Science Foundation of China (No. 61702008, No. 61672001) and Anhui Natural Science Foundation (No. 1808085MF193).

References

1. Seeman, N.C.: Structural DNA nanotechnology: growing along with nano letters. Nano Lett. **10**(6), 1971–1978 (2010)
2. LaBean, T.H.: Nanotechnology: another dimension for DNA art. Nature **459**(7245), 331–332 (2009)
3. Yang, X., Wenzler, L.A., Qi, J., et al.: Ligation of DNA triangles containing double crossover molecules. J. Am. Chem. Soc. **120**(38), 9779–9786 (1998)
4. Winfree, E., Liu, F., Wenzler, L.A., et al.: Design and self-assembly of two-dimensional DNA crystals. Nature **394**(6693), 539–544 (1998)
5. Rothemund, P.W.K.: Folding DNA to create nanoscale shapes and patterns. Nature **440**(7082), 297–302 (2006)
6. Seeman, N.C.: Nucleic-acid Junctions and Lattices. J. Theor. Biol. **99**(11), 237–247 (1982)
7. Winfree, E., Liu, F.R., Sedman, N.C.: Design and self-assemble of two-dimensional DNA crystals. Nature **394**, 539–544 (1998)
8. Rothemund, P.W., Papadakis, N., Winfree, E.: Algorithmic self-assembly of DNA Sierpinski triangles. PLoS Biol. **2**, 2041–2053 (2004)
9. Sa-Ardyen, P., Vologodskii, A.V., Seeman, N.C.: The flexibility of DNA double crossover molecules. Biophys. J. **84**, 3829–38371 (2003)
10. Fu, T.J., Seeman, N.C.: DNA double-crossover molecules. Biochemistry **32**, 3211–3220 (1993)
11. Li, X.J., Yang, X.P., Qi, J., et al.: Antiparallel DNA double crossover molecules as components for nanoconstruction. J. Am. Chem. Soc. **118**, 6131–6140 (1996)
12. LaBean, T.H., Yan, H., Kopatsch, J., et al.: Construction, analysis, ligation, and self-assembly of DNA triple crossover complexes. J. Am. Chem. Soc. **122**, 1848–18601 (2000)
13. Yan, H., Park, S.H., Finkelstein, G., et al.: DNA-templated self-assembly of protein arrays and highly conductive nanowires. Science **301**, 1882–1884 (2003)
14. He, Y., Chen, Y., Liu, H.P., et al.: Self-assembly of hexagonal DNA two-dimensional (2D) arrays. J. Am. Chem. Soc. **127**, 12202–122031 (2005)
15. He, Y., Ye, T., Su, M., et al.: Hierarchical self-assembly of DNA into symmetric supramolecular polyhedral. Nature **452**, 198–201 (2008)
16. Zhang, F., Nangreave, J., Liu, Y., et al.: Reconfigurable DNA origami to generate quasifractal patterns. Nano Lett. **12**, 3290–3295 (2012)
17. Wei, B.R., Dai, M.J., Yin, P.: Complex shapes self-assembled from single-stranded DNA tiles. Nature **485**, 623–626 (2012)

18. Douglas, S.M., Chou, J.J., Shih, W.M.: DNA-nanotube-induced alignment of membrane proteins for NMR structure determination. Proc. Natl. Acad. Sci. USA **104**, 6644–6648 (2007)
19. Andersen, E.S., et al.: DNA origami design of dolphin-shaped structures with flexible tails. ACS Nano **2**(6), 1213–1218 (2008)
20. Dietz, H., Douglas, S.M., Shih, W.M.: Folding DNA into twisted and curved nanoscale shapes. Science **325**(5941), 725–730 (2009)
21. Ke, Y., Sharma, J., Liu, M., Jahn, K., Liu, Y., Yan, H.: Scaffolded DNA origami of a DNA tetrahedron molecular container. Nano Lett. **9**(6), 2445–2447 (2009)
22. Han, D., et al.: DNA gridiron nanostructures based on four-arm junctions. Science **339**(6126), 1412–1415 (2013)
23. Kim, K.R., Kim, D.R., Lee, T., Yhee, J.Y., Kim, B.S., Abn, D.R.: Drug delivery by a self-assembled DNA tetrahedron for overcoming drug resistance in breast cancer cells. Chem. Commun. **49**(20), 2010–2012 (2013)
24. Williams, S., Lund, K., Lin, C., Wonka, P., Lindsay, S., Yan, H.: Tiamat: a three-dimensional editing tool for complex DNA structures. In: Goel, A., Simmel, F.C., Sosík, P. (eds.) DNA 2008. LNCS, vol. 5347, pp. 90–101. Springer, Heidelberg (2009). https://doi.org/10.1007/978-3-642-03076-5_8
25. Zhu, J., Wei, B., Yuan, Y., et al.: UNIQUIMER 3D, a software system for structural DNA nanotechnology design, analysis and evaluation. Nucleic Acids Res. **37**(7), 2164 (2009)
26. Goodman, R.P.: NANEV: a program employing evolutionary methods for the design of nucleic acid nanostructures. Biotechniques **38**(4), 548–550 (2005)
27. Gomory, R.E.: Outline of an algorithm for integer solutions to linear programs. Bull. Am. Math. Soc. **64**, 275–278 (1958)
28. Wang, S.Y., Yang, A.M.: DNA solution of integer linear programming. Appl. Math. Comput. **170**, 626–632 (2005)
29. Adleman, L.M.: Molecular computation of solutions to combinatorial problems. Science **266**(11), 1021–1024 (1994)
30. Yin, Z.X., Zhang, F.Y., Xu, J.: The general form of 0-1 programming problem based on DNA computing. Biosystems **70**(1), 73–79 (2003)
31. Zhang, F.Y., Yin, Z.X., Xu, J.: Application of DNA chip on 0-1 planning problem. Biochem. Biophys. **30**(3), 412–415 (2003)
32. Yin, Z.X., Zhang, F.Y., Xu, J.: 0-1 DNA computing model for programming problem. J. Electron. Inf. **15**(1), 1–5 (2003)
33. Wang, L., Lin, Y.P., Li, Z.Y.: DNA computation for a category of special integer programming problem. J. Comput. Res. Dev. **42**(8), 1431–1437 (2005)
34. Zhou K., Tong X.J., Xu J.: The improvement on algorithm of DNA computing on 0-1 programming problem. In: Proceedings of the Fifth International Conference on Machine Learning and Cybernetics, Dalian, pp. 4282–4286 (2006)
35. Yang, J., Yin, Z.: 0-1 integer programming problem based on RecA- mediated triple-stranded DNA structure. Comput. Eng. Appl. **44**(2), 76–79 (2008)
36. Zhang, X.C., Niu, Y., Cui, G.Z., et al.: Application of DNA self-assembly on 0-1 integer programming problem. J. Comput. Theor. Nanosci. **7**(1), 165–172 (2010)
37. Li, F., Liu, J., Li, Z.: DNA computation model based on self-assembled nanoparticle probes for 0–1 integer programming problem. Math. Comput. Simul. **151**, 1–4 (2017)
38. Yin, Z., Cui, J., Yang, J.: Integer programming problem based on plasmid DNA computing model. Chin. J. Electron. **26**(6), 1284–1288 (2017)
39. Chen, Y.H., Sha, S.: Molecular beacon model of 0-1 integer programming based on microfluidic chip. J. Guangdong Polytech. Norm. Univ. **2**, 004 (2016)

A Novel Discrete Grey Wolf Optimizer
for Solving the Bounded Knapsack Problem

Zewen Li, Yichao He[✉], Huanzhe Li, Ya Li, and Xiaohu Guo

College of Information and Engineering, Hebei GEO University,
Shijiazhuang 050031, China
3521014180@qq.com, heyichao@hgu.edu.cn

Abstract. Grey Wolf Optimizer (GWO) is a recently proposed metaheuristic optimizer inspired by the leadership hierarchy and hunting mechanism of grey wolves. In order to solve the bounded knapsack problem by the GWO, a novel Discrete Grey Wolf Optimizer (DGWO) is proposed in this paper. On the basis of DGWO, the crossover strategy of the genetic algorithm is introduced to enhance its local search ability, and infeasible solutions are processed by a Repair and Optimization method based on the greedy strategy, which could not only ensure the effectiveness but also speed up the convergence. Experiment using three kinds of large-scale instances of the bounded knapsack problem is carried out to verify the validity and stability of the DGWO. By comparing and analyzing the results with other well-established algorithms, computational results show that the convergence speed of the DGWO is faster than that of other algorithms, solutions of these instances of the bounded knapsack problem are all well obtained with approximation ratio bound close to 1.

Keywords: Bounded knapsack problem · Grey Wolf Optimizer ·
Genetic algorithm · Repair and optimization method

1 Introduction

Grey Wolf Optimizer (GWO) [1] is a swarm intelligence optimization algorithm proposed by Mirjalili et al. in 2014, which simulates the leadership hierarchy and predatory behavior of grey wolves, it has shown a good result in the optimizing problems. For example, GWO has been used to solve the 0-1 knapsack problem (0-1 KP) [2], the numerical optimization [3], the multi-layer perceptron training [4], etc. Characteristic of less adjustment parameters make this optimizer easy to implement. Besides, GWO has been successfully applied to practical problems like optical buffer design, and engineering design problem such as compression spring, pressure vessel and welded beam design [5].

Knapsack problem (KP) is a well-known NP complete and combinatorial optimization problem [6] which has a wide range of applications in real life, for example, stock cutting [7], cargo loading [8], resource allocation [9], investment decision [10], etc. KP has many variations, such as the Bounded Knapsack Problem (BKP), the Unbounded Knapsack Problem (UKP), the Multidimensional Knapsack Problem (MKP), the Quadratic Knapsack Problem (QKP), and the Discounted {0-1} Knapsack

© Springer Nature Singapore Pte Ltd. 2019
H. Peng et al. (Eds.): ISICA 2018, CCIS 986, pp. 101–114, 2019.
https://doi.org/10.1007/978-981-13-6473-0_10

Problem (D{0-1}KP) [11], etc. The BKP is a typical extension of the 0-1KP, which removes the restriction that there is only one of each item but restricts the number of copies of each kind of item to a maximum non-negative integer value. At present, existing approaches for solving the BKP are mainly to transform it into an equivalent 0-1 KP and then use the relevant algorithms, but a disadvantage arise that duplication of massive items increases the complexity of 0-1 KP, which could result in low efficiency. Pisinger [12] proposed a minimal algorithm to solve BKP, which minimized the *core* (a subset of items with a high probability containing the optimal solution) and solved the expanding *core* problem. However, this algorithm is based on dynamic programming and has a pseudo-polynomial time complexity, therefore it is inapplicable for the large-scale BKP instances. To avoid this problem, the use of Evolutionary Algorithms (EAs) is a good choice. Comparing with the traditional optimization methods, EAs are a kind of efficient and fast randomized approximation algorithms [13], they are widely used global optimization methods with characteristics of self-organization, self-adaptive and self-learning, as they are not limited by feature of the problems, EAs could effectively deal with the complex problems which are difficult to solve by the traditional optimization algorithms.

Classical EAs including genetic algorithm (GA) [14], particle swarm optimization (PSO) [15], differential evolution (DE) [16], etc. are commonly used to generate high-quality solutions for optimization. Grey Wolf Optimizer (GWO) is a relatively new kind of EAs, which has been effectively applied in many optimization problems. Emary [17] et al. proposed a binary Grey Wolf Optimizer (BGWO) for feature selection in 2015, the results obtained have borne out that the proposed binary version outperforms other methods in the search capability. Kamboj et al. [18] used GWO to solve the power system economic load allocation (ELD) problem in 2016, computational results compared with PSO, GA, and DE indicated that GWO gives a better performance and shows faster convergence rate in this problem. In another study, Moradi et al. [19] tested the GWO for solving non-convex of the economic dispatch by the transmission loss, which was found that the GWO in economic dispatch appeared to be the most efficient solution in solving the big scale of the dispatch problem. Chandra et al. [20] proposed a modified GWO to select the optimum set of services from web services according to the quality of service, the results showed that the modified GWO is effective and powerful to extract the optimum services and even being compared with basic GWO and GA. In this paper, a Discrete Grey Wolf Optimizer (DGWO) based on natural number coding is proposed. By comparing with BGWO [17] and GA, this paper points out the superiority of DGWO for solving the BKP.

The remainder of the paper is organized as follows. Section 2 describes the definition and the mathematical model of BKP. In Sect. 3, the basic Grey Wolf Optimizer is described. In Sect. 4, the encoding transformation method for the discretization approach is provided, and a Repair and Optimization method is introduced to handle the infeasible solutions, pseudo-code and time complexity analysis of DGWO are given at the end. In Sect. 5, the experiment results are presented and DGWO is compared with BGWO, BGA and NGA. Section 6 is the summary and prospect.

2   Mathematical Model of the BKP

Definition of the BKP could generally be described as: Given a knapsack of capacity C and n item types, where the value of type j has a profit p_j, weight w_j, and a bound b_j on the availability. Consider selecting $x_j (0 \leq x_j \leq b_j)$ of each item type j such that the profit sum of the included items is maximized without having the weight sum exceed C. The BKP may thus define as the following mathematical model:

$$Maximize \quad f(X) = \sum_{j=1}^{n} p_j x_j \tag{1}$$

$$s.t. \quad \sum_{j=1}^{n} w_j x_j \leq C \tag{2}$$

$$x_j \in \{0, 1, \ldots, b_j\}, j = 1, 2, \ldots, n \tag{3}$$

where $p_j, w_j, b_j (1 \leq j \leq n)$ and C are all positive integers. $x_j = 0$ indicates that no item of type j is loaded in the knapsack, $x_j \neq 0$ indicates that x_j items of type j are loaded in the knapsack. Obviously, only an arbitrary integer vector $X = [x_1, x_2, \ldots, x_n]$ satisfies formula (2) is a feasible solution, otherwise it is a potential solution of the BKP.

3   Overview of Grey Wolf Optimizer

Grey Wolf Optimizer (GWO) [1] is a novel EAs proposed by Mirjalili et al. in 2014. The grey wolf society can be classified into four levels: alpha, beta, delta, omega. In the top of the hierarchy is the alpha wolf, considered as the leader of the pack, it is responsible for making decisions on hunting, resting and advancing. The beta wolf is the candidate to the alpha wolf and superior to delta wolf, both beta and delta wolves are subordinate to the alpha wolf, they help the alpha wolf in making decisions and reinforce alpha's decisions among other wolves in the lower level. The last level of the hierarchy is composed of omega wolves with no subordinates but subordinate to the wolves in the higher level and report to them, They are in the lowest level of this system and are allowed to eat the remaining food which is left after all the wolves in other levels are finished. In GWO, the population consists of several grey wolves. We consider the optimal solution to be alpha, the suboptimal solution and the third optimal solution to be beta and delta, and the other solutions to be omega. In the evolution, we use alpha, beta and delta to guide omega. GWO assigns the stages of tracking, encircling and attacking to different levels of grey wolves to complete the predatory behavior, thus realizing the process of global optimization. The three stages are summarized as follows:

3.1   Tracking

As the initial step, they track, chase and approach the prey. During the hunting process, the wolf's tracking behavior is described mathematically as follows:

$$\vec{X}(t+1) = \overrightarrow{X_p}(t) - \vec{A} \cdot \vec{D} \tag{4}$$

$$\vec{D} = \left| \vec{C} \cdot \overrightarrow{X_p}(t) - \vec{X}(t) \right| \tag{5}$$

where $\vec{X}$ represents the position of the grey wolf, t represents the current iteration, $\overrightarrow{X_p}$ represents the position of the prey, $\vec{D}$ represents the distance between the grey wolf and the prey calculated as formula (5). $\vec{A}$ and $\vec{C}$ are two coefficient vectors estimated as follows:

$$\vec{A} = 2\vec{a} \cdot \overrightarrow{r_1} - \vec{a} \tag{6}$$

$$\vec{C} = 2\overrightarrow{r_2} \tag{7}$$

where $\overrightarrow{r_1}$ and $\overrightarrow{r_2}$ are 2 random vectors with every dimension in range [0, 1]. Each element a in coefficient vector $\vec{a}$ decreases linearly from 2 to 0 with the increase of iterations, controlling the balance between exploitation (local search) and exploration (global search).

3.2   Encircling

Although the hunting process in nature is usually guided by alpha and coordinated by beta and delta, the position of the optimal solution is unknown in evolutionary computation. Therefore, a mathematical model can be established based on the characteristic that the position of the prey (the potential optimal solution) is more easily known by alpha (the optimal candidate solution), beta and delta. We save the three optimal solutions $\overrightarrow{X_\alpha}$, $\overrightarrow{X_\beta}$ and $\overrightarrow{X_\delta}$, then update the position of other grey wolves using the following equations:

$$\vec{X}(t+1) = \frac{\overrightarrow{X_1} + \overrightarrow{X_2} + \overrightarrow{X_3}}{3} \tag{8}$$

$$\overrightarrow{X_1} = \left| \overrightarrow{X_\alpha}(t) - \overrightarrow{A_1} \cdot \overrightarrow{D_\alpha} \right| \tag{9}$$

$$\overrightarrow{X_2} = \left| \overrightarrow{X_\beta}(t) - \overrightarrow{A_2} \cdot \overrightarrow{D_\beta} \right| \tag{10}$$

$$\overrightarrow{X_3} = \left| \overrightarrow{X_\delta}(t) - \overrightarrow{A_3} \cdot \overrightarrow{D_\delta} \right| \tag{11}$$

$$\overrightarrow{D_\alpha} = \left| \overrightarrow{C_1} \cdot \overrightarrow{X_a}(t) - \vec{X}(t) \right| \tag{12}$$

$$\overrightarrow{D_\beta} = \left| \overrightarrow{C_2} \cdot \overrightarrow{X_\beta}(t) - \vec{X}(t) \right| \tag{13}$$

$$\overrightarrow{D_\delta} = \left| \overrightarrow{C_3} \cdot \overrightarrow{X_\delta}(t) - \vec{X}(t) \right| \tag{14}$$

3.3 Attacking

Attacking is the last stage of hunting process, the wolves get the best solution by attacking and capturing their prey. This process is mainly realized by decreasing the value of a in Eq. (6). When the value of a decreases from 2 linearity to 0, the corresponding value of A also varies in the interval $[-a, a]$. In addition, when $|A|$ is less than 1, indicates that the next generation position of the wolves will be closer to the position of the prey. When $1 \le |A| \le 2$, the wolf pack would disperse towards the direction away from the prey, causing the GWO algorithm to lose the optimal position and thus fall into a local optimal. The update equation of a in GWO is as follows:

$$a = 2 - 2^* t / MaxIter \tag{15}$$

where t is the current iteration and *MaxIter* is the maximum number of iteration.

4 Discrete Grey Wolf Optimizer

4.1 Encoding Transformation

In dealing with the problem of numerical optimization, GWO uses the position of the grey wolf to find the optimal solution in continuous space, but the way that the position of a grey wolf updates is different in discrete space that it should be mapped to the discrete domain by a transfer function. In order to solve the problem of pure integer linear programming, $Y_i = [y_{i1}, y_{i2} \dots y_{in}]$ is introduced as the mapping vector of position $X_i = [x_{i1}, x_{i2} \dots x_{in}]$, corresponding to the solution of the problem. In DGWO, X_i participates in the evolution process, and use $f(Y_i)$ to evaluate the fitness of X_i.

Referring to the idea of literature [21], an encoding transformation function is proposed, which convert the real number vector, the position of an individual in continuous space into an integer vector by using the Eq. (16).

$$y_{ij} = \left\lfloor b_j * \frac{x_{ij} - lb}{ub - lb} + 0.5 \right\rfloor, j = 1, 2, \dots, n. \tag{16}$$

where x_{ij} is the position X_i in the jth dimension, y_{ij} is the value of the potential solution Y_i in the jth dimension of individual i. b_j is the total number of the item of type j. ub and lb are the upper and lower bounds of the search space respectively, which means that $x_{ij} \in [lb, ub]$.

4.2 Repair and Optimization

When EAs is used to solve constrained optimization problems, infeasible solutions would be generated. A key problem is to deal with these infeasible solutions reasonably. There are three main methods to deal with this problem: the penalty function method [22, 23], the repair method [22] and the repair and optimization method [24, 25]. In DGWO, repair and optimization methods are used to deal with the infeasible solutions, a Greedy Repair and Optimization Algorithm (GROA) is introduced in reference [25, 26], the pseudo-code shown in Algorithm 1 has a time complexity of $O(n)$. Array $H[1...n]$ stores $H[j]$,the sequence number of the density of each item (density of item j is p_j/w_j) by descending order.

Algorithm 1. GROA

```
Input: a potential solution Y=[y₁,y₂,…,yₙ], array H[1…n].
Output: a feasible solution Y=[y₁,y₂,…,yₙ] and f(Y).
```

1. $R \leftarrow \sum_{j=1}^{n} w_j x_j$; $j \leftarrow n$;

2. WHILE $(R>C)$ //repair phase

3.   IF $(y_{H[j]}>0)$

4. $y_{H[j]} \leftarrow y_{H[j]}-1$; $R \leftarrow R-w_{H[j]}$;

5.   ELSE

6. $j \leftarrow j-1$;

7.   END IF

8. END WHILE

9. $j \leftarrow 1$;

10. WHILE $(j \leq n)$ //optimize phase

11.   IF $(y_{H[j]}<b_j$ and $R+w_{H[j]} \leq C)$

12. $y_{H[j]} \leftarrow y_{H[j]}+1$; $R \leftarrow R+w_{H[j]}$;

13.   ELSE

14. $j \leftarrow j+1$;

15.   END IF

16. END WHILE

17. $f(Y) \leftarrow \sum_{j=1}^{n} p_j y_j$

18. RETURN $(Y, f(Y))$

4.3   Crossover

Crossover is an effective evolutionary method in the genetic algorithm, which could realize direct communication between the parent individuals and discover better solutions. In DGWO, there is no communication between the omega wolves so the crossover strategy introduced in the evolution of DGWO is an effective method to find the new solutions potentially. The crossover operator used in DGWO is single point crossover. Details of the crossover operators are introduced in literature [27].

The specific crossover operation in DGWO are as follows: In the $t+1(t \geq 0)$ iteration of the individual i, if $r<P_c$ (r is a random number in (0,1), P_c is the crossover probability), the single point crossover operator is used to act on the position X_i of individual i and X_j of another random selected individual j, they crossover to produce

two new vectors X_s and X_t, corresponding to their potential solution vector Y_s and Y_t. After processing GROA, their fitness values are compared with the fitness values of Y_i and Y_j, if the fitness value increase, that is, better solution has produced, then the individuals with higher fitness would be reserved to the next generation.

4.4 The Pseudo-code of DGWO

When DGWO is initialized, component of each dimensional of the individual X is randomly selected as the initial position coordinates in range $[lb, ub]$. For the BKP, X is converted to the corresponding potential solution Y by Eq. (16), and then Y would be evaluated after being repaired and optimized by GROA. The best three individuals with the largest fitness value are selected as alpha, beta and delta, which would guide the evolution for other individuals. In each subsequent generation, GROA is used to deal with abnormal encoding individuals.

$H[1...n] \leftarrow QuickSort(\{p_j/w_j | p_j \in P, w_j \in W, 1 \le j \le n\})$ means that sorting the n items by $p_j/w_j (1 \le j \le n)$ in descending order through the quick sort method, the subscript can be stored in an array $H[1...n]$. The pseudo-code of DGWO is shown as Algorithm 2 below.

Algorithm 2. DGWO

```
Input: N Number of grey wolves in the pack;
       MaxIter Number of iterations for optimization;
       Pc Probability of crossover.
Output: Optimal solution Y_α;
        Best fitness value f(Y_α).
1. H[1…n]← QuickSort({p_j/w_j | p_j∈P, w_j∈W, 1≤j≤n})
2. Generate initial population X_i (i=1…n) randomly and Y_i;
3. FOR i←1 TO N DO (X_i, f(Y_i))←GROA(Y_i, H[1…n]);
4. Find the α,β,δ positions based on fitness;
5. t←0;
6. WHILE (t ≤ MaxIter)
7.      a←2-2*t/MaxIter;
8.      FOR i←1 TO N
9.          Update position vector X_i by equation (8);
10.         Update solution vector Y_i by equation (16);
11.         (Y_i, f(Y_i))←GROA(Y_i, H[1…n]);
12.         Crossover operate by probability Pc;
13.     END FOR
14.     Update the α,β,δ positions based on fitness;
15.     t←t+1;
16.END WHILE
```

In DGWO, Step1 uses *QuickSort* implementation with time complexity $O(n log n)$. Time complexity of Step2 and Step3 are both $O(Nn)$. Step4 selects the alpha, beta, delta wolves which needs $3 N-3$ operations at most, the time complexity is $O(Nn)$.

Step9 needs $3(N-3)$ operations to calculate the distance between $X_\alpha, X_\beta, X_\delta$ and other individuals, and the complexity of the distance calculation is $O(n)$, thus the time complexity of Step9 is $4O(Nn)$. The time complexity of Step10 and Step11 are both $O(Nn)$. The time complexity of Step12 is $2O(Nn)$. Step14 has a time complexity of $O(N) + O(n)$. N and T are linear functions of n. Therefore, the time complexity of DGWO is $O(n\log n) + (8T + 3) \times O(Nn) = O(n^3)$.

5 Experimental Results and Discussion

5.1 BKP Instances and Experiment Settings

In this section, three classes of different BKP instances: UBKP, WBKP and SBKP are introduced to test the proposed algorithm. For each class of instances, ten instances with the sizes of $100 < n < 1000$ numbered as UBKP1–UBKP10, WBKP1–WBKP10 and SBKP1–UBKP10. For details of these data, please refer to the document from: http://xxgc.hgu.edu.cn/uploads/heyichao/ThreekindsofBKPInstances.rar

All the calculations are performed on a microcomputer configured for Intel Core i5-7500u @3.40 GHz CPU and 4 GB RAM 2.90 ghz, using the C Programming language compiled in Microsoft Visual C++ 6.0. Diagrams are drawn with Python in JetBrains PyCharm.

5.2 Performance Comparison and Analysis

To verify the performance of DGWO, this paper introduced three classes of standard BKP instances, and compares DGWO with BGWO [17], genetic algorithm based on natural number coding (NGA) and genetic algorithm based on binary coding (BGA). Parameters setting of each algorithm is shown in Table 1, where *popsize* represents the population size of the algorithms, *MaxIter* represents the maximum number of iterations and *dim* is the scale of the problem (for DGWO and NGA, $dim = n$. for BGWO and BGA, $dim = \sum_{j=1}^{n} b_j$), *lb* and *ub* are the upper bound and lower bound of the component value respectively, b_j is the total number of the item of class j.

Table 1. Parameter setting of DGWO, BGWO, BGA, NGA

Algorithm	Parameter					
	popsize	MaxIter	P_c	P_m	lb	ub
DGWO	30	2*dim	0.8	-	0	5
BGWO	30	2*dim	-	-	-5	5
BGA	30	2*dim	0.96	0.001	0	1
NGA	30	2*dim	0.9	0.001	0	b_j

Table 2. Experiment results of DGWO, BGWO, BGA, NGA for solving UBKP1–UBKP10

		UBKP1	UBKP2	UBKP3	UBKP4	UBKP5	UBKP6	UBKP7	UBKP8	UBKP9	UBKP10
DGWO	Best	**201616**	**414114**	594606	**831629**	1003628	**1228085**	1524759	**1692853**	1869132	**2066060**
	Mean	201570.12	414114	594574.6	831592.62	1003624	1228075	1524742.82	1692836	1869122	2066038.46
	Std	36.774	0	21.595	12.103	10.015	3.371	7.185	2.724	13.353	11.824
BGWO	Best	201590	**414114**	594497	831464	1003497	1227851	1524247	1692283	1868695	2065625
	Mean	201550.86	413870	594273.3	831134.46	1003074	1227290	1523385.26	1691357	1867768	2064526.34
	Std	42.856	175.047	169.657	178.451	259.079	289.801	615.851	571.506	509.324	464.602
BGA	Best	**201616**	**414114**	594610	831575	1003131	1226731	1521655	1685320	1785406	2052087
	Mean	201602.16	414037	594549.9	831166.1	1002490	1225629	1519055.1	1683225	1782782	2045624.12
	Std	20.305	51.265	85.882	168.418	336.98	522.681	1071.571	1231.258	1311.134	2270.995
NGA	Best	201590	**414114**	594601	831615	1003642	**1228085**	**1524770**	1692846	1869138	2066057
	Mean	201590	414114	594599.1	831608	1003630	1228075	1524759.8	1692841	1869129	2066052.36
	Std	0	0	0.392	5.161	5.752	4.258	7.141	3.905	10.494	2.278

Table 3. Experiment results of DGWO, BGWO, BGA, NGA for solving WBKP1–WBKP10

		WBKP1	WBKP2	WBKP3	WBKP4	WBKP5	WBKP6	WBKP7	WBKP8	WBKP9	WBKP10
DGWO	Best	**119312**	**297700**	444149	605675	772188	890312	1045298	1210944	1407364	1574075
	Mean	119308.7	297700	444144	605657.3	772178	890305.8	1045294.56	1210941	1407364	1574067.8
	Std	2.934	0	2.778	6.262	5.591	3.525	3.389	3.251	0	2.078
BGWO	Best	119309	**297700**	444109	605595	772051	890212	1045139	1210673	1407105	1573820
	Mean	119285.44	297640	444010.8	605436.88	771870.4	890009.5	1044923	1210484	1406839	1573450.16
	Std	10.553	36.541	65.258	135.069	113.435	119.435	118.786	136.368	153.729	195.362
BGA	Best	119308	**297700**	444092	605564	771955	889586	1044295	1209445	1404746	1570003
	Mean	119306.3	297692	444028.2	605462.58	771518.8	889113.4	1043695.14	1208964	1403749	1568901.32
	Std	2.369	9.218	44.35	65.428	172.242	222.157	239.854	287.577	403.996	535.316
NGA	Best	119295	**297700**	444153	605668	772188	890310	1045300	1210944	1407364	**1574079**
	Mean	119295	297700	444144.9	605660.86	772186.1	890309.5	1045297.94	1210944	1407364	1574074.34
	Std	0	0	4.825	5.363	1.489	0.877	1.605	1.68	0.196	1.861

Table 4. Experiment results of DGWO, BGWO, BGA, NGA for solving SBKP1–SBKP10

		SBKP1	SBKP2	SBKP3	SBKP4	SBKP5	SBKP6	SBKP7	SBKP8	SBKP9	SBKP10
DGWO	Best	**144822**	**259853**	**433414**	**493847**	**688246**	**849526**	**1060106**	**1171576**	**1263609**	**1412095**
	Mean	144816.54	259848	433412.8	493844.5	688243.7	849523.4	1060102.52	1171572	1263605	1412093.72
	Std	5.092	2.573	0.496	4.892	2.799	3.324	4.374	5.435	4.487	2.683
BGWO	Best	144811	259843	433404	493837	688236	849506	1060085	1171556	1263589	1412077
	Mean	144799.62	259833	433389.2	493820.14	688216.6	849490.3	1060064.48	1171537	1263571	1412058
	Std	7.707	6.46	9.851	11.085	8.975	11.058	11.28	17.689	10.042	10.292
BGA	Best	**144822**	**259853**	**433414**	**493847**	**688246**	849516	1060086	1171526	1263538	1411985
	Mean	144818.98	259853	433414	493847	688246	849506.5	1060065.34	1171509	1263514	1411960.7
	Std	2.47	0	0	0	0	3.812	7.29	9.379	12.301	12.713
NGA	Best	**144822**	**259853**	**433414**	**493847**	**688246**	**849526**	**1060106**	**1171576**	**1263609**	**1412095**
	Mean	144821.22	259852	433413.6	493845.74	688245.6	849526	1060106	1171576	1263609	1412095
	Std	1.316	0.458	0.494	1.11	0.494	0	0	0	0	0

Best, Mean, Std, ARB and *ARM* are used as evaluation indexes. *ARB* and *ARM* are respectively defined as $ARB = Opt/Best$ and $ARM = Opt/Mean$, where Opt is the best value of each instance calculated by the dynamic programming method.

As seen from Table 2, for ten UBKP instances, the *Best* value of DGWO for instances UBKP1,2,4,8,10 can reach *Opt*. BGWO can reach *Opt* for instance UBKP2. BGA can reach *Opt* for instance UBKP1,2, the *Mean* value of for instances UBKP1,3 is higher than that of the other three algorithms. The *Best* value of NGA for instance UBKP2,6,7 can reach *Opt*, and the *Mean* value of for instances UBKP4–UBKP10 is higher than that of the other three algorithms with the smallest standard deviation *Std*.

As seen from Table 3, for ten WBKP instances, the *Best* value of DGWO for instances WBKP1,2 can reach *Opt*, the *Mean* value of for instances WBKP1,9 is higher than that of the other three algorithms. The *Best* value of BGWO for instance WBKP2 can reach *Opt*, BGA can reach *Opt* for instance WBKP2. The *Best* value of NGA for instances WBKP2,10 can reach *Opt*, and the *Mean* value of instances WBKP3–8,10 is higher than that of the other three algorithms with the smallest standard deviation *Std*.

As seen from Table 4, DGWO and NGA showed good performance in solving instances of SBKP. Although the *Mean* and *Std* value of NGA are slightly better than DGWO, the *Best* of DGWO can reach *Opt*, which is superior to BGWO and BGA. For instances SBKP1–SBKP5 the *Mean* value of BGA is higher than that of DGWO, but for instances SBKP5–SBKP10 the *Mean* value of DGWO is higher than that of BGA.

Among 30 BKP instances, DGWO achieves *Opt* for 18 of them, BGA achieves *Opt* for 8 of them. NGA achieves *Opt* for 15 of them, BGWO cannot achieve *Opt* for any instance. Both DGWO and NGA show good optimization performance in experiments above. Data in Tables 2, 3 and 4 show that the standard deviation of NGA is the smallest and its *Mean* value is larger than that of the other algorithms, thus it has better stability. DGWO is slightly superior to NGA in the frequency of *Opt* achieved, its performance in solving UBKP and WBKP is obviously better than BGWO and BGA. The experimental results indicate that DGWO is very applicable for solving BKP, and GWO based on the natural number encoding is better than the binary encoding in solving these BKP instances.

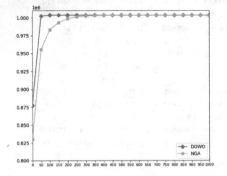

Fig. 1. Mean convergence curve for UBKP5

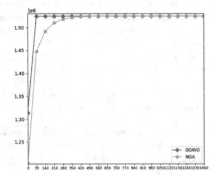

Fig. 2. Mean convergence curve for UBKP7

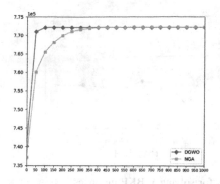

Fig. 3. Mean convergence curve for WBKP5

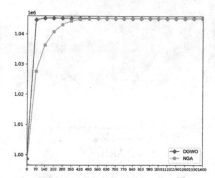

Fig. 4. Mean convergence curve for WBKP7

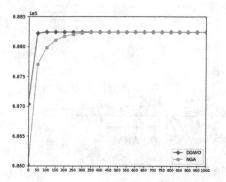

Fig. 5. Mean convergence curve for SBKP5

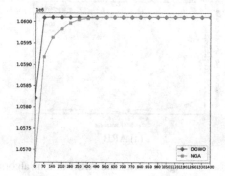

Fig. 6. Mean convergence curve for SBKP7

To compare the average performance of DGWO and NGA intuitively, the average convergence curves for instance UBKP5, UBKP7, WBKP5, WBKP7, SBKP5 and SBKP7 in 50 times run are given in Figs. 1, 2, 3, 4, 5 and 6. It can be seen that although the average results of DGWO and NGA are close but the convergence of DGWO is faster, optimal solution can be approximated within the iteration of $0.1 \times MaxIter$.

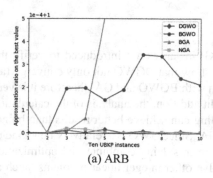

(a) ARB

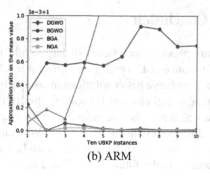

(b) ARM

Fig. 7. ARB and ARM of four algorithms for solving UBKP instances

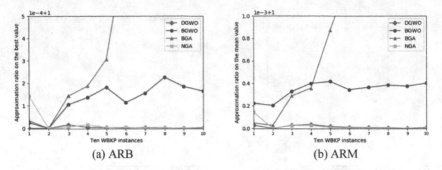

(a) ARB   (b) ARM

Fig. 8. ARB and ARM of four algorithms for solving WBKP instances

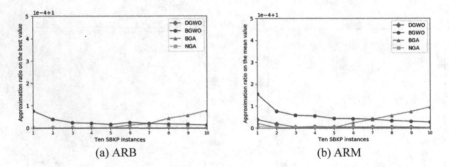

(a) ARB   (b) ARM

Fig. 9. ARB and ARM of four algorithms for solving SBKP instances

The ratio bound is one of the criteria for the accuracy measurement of approximation algorithm. The ARB and ARM diagrams in Figs. 7, 8 and 9 show that for the UBKP and WBKP types, as the dimension of the problem increases, the ARB and ARM curves of BGWO and BGA are on the rise. It is shown that DGWO and NGA are not affected by the increase of the scale of the problem, for three types of BKP instances, an approximate solution with ratio bound close to 1 can be achieved quickly, so they are more suitable for solving BKP problems.

6   Conclusion

In this paper, three classes of large-scale BKP instances are introduced to verify the performance of DGWO. Experimental results show that DGWO not only converge fast but also achieve better solutions in comparison with BGWO and GA, therefore it is very applicable and efficient for solving the BKP. In addition, the analysis of the calculation results also reveals that natural number encoding can achieve better results than binary encoding in solving the BKP with GWO and GA. Since GWO is a relatively new kind of EAs, it needs to be discussed and studied more in solving combinatorial optimization problems. In the future, we will attempt to solve other integer linear problems (such as facility location problem [28], discounted {0-1} knapsack problem [11]) with DGWO, and further investigate the effective method of discretization.

Acknowledgments. This work was supported by the Scientific Research Project Program of Colleges and Universities in Hebei Province (ZD2016005), and the Natural Science Foundation of Hebei Province (F2016403055).

References

1. Mirjalili, S., Mirjalili, S.M., Lewis, A.: Grey wolf optimizer. Adv. Eng. Softw. **69**, 46–61 (2014)
2. Masadeh, R., Yassien, E., Alzaqebah, A., et al.: Grey wolf optimization applied to the 0/1 knapsack problem. Int. J. Comput. Appl. **169**(5), 11–15 (2017)
3. Sharma, S., Salgotra, R., Singh, U.: An enhanced grey wolf optimizer for numerical optimization. In: International Conference on Innovations in Information, Embedded and Communication Systems, pp. 1–6 (2017)
4. Mirjalili, S.: How effective is the Grey Wolf optimizer in training multi-layer perceptrons. Appl. Intell. **43**(1), 150–161 (2015)
5. Hatta, N.M., Zain, A.M., Sallehuddin, R., et al.: Recent studies on optimisation method of Grey Wolf Optimiser (GWO): a review (2014–2017). Artif. Intell. Rev. May 2018. https://doi.org/10.1007/s10462-018-9634-2
6. Dantzig, G.B.: Discrete-variable extremum problems. Oper. Res. **5**(2), 266–288 (1957)
7. Gilmore, P.C., Gomory, R.E.: The theory and computation of knapsack functions. Oper. Res. **14**(6), 1045–1074 (1966)
8. Wei, S.: A branch and bound method for the multiconstraint zero-one knapsack problem. J. Oper. Res. Soc. **30**(4), 369–378 (1979)
9. Bitran, G.R., Hax, A.C.: Disaggregation and resource allocation using convex knapsack problems with bounded variables. Manag. Sci. **27**(4), 431–441 (1981)
10. Pendharkar, P.C., Rodger, J.A.: Information technology capital budgeting using a knapsack problem. Int. Trans. Oper. Res. **13**(4), 333–351 (2010)
11. He, Y.C., Wang, X.Z., Li, W.B., et al.: Research on genetic algorithms for the discounted 0–1 knapsack problem. Chin. J. Comput. **39**, 2614–2630 (2016)
12. Pisinger, D.: A minimal algorithm for the bounded knapsack problem. In: Balas, E., Clausen, J. (eds.) IPCO 1995. LNCS, vol. 920, pp. 95–109. Springer, Heidelberg (1995). https://doi.org/10.1007/3-540-59408-6_44
13. Wang, X.Z., He, Y.-C.: Evolutionary algorithms for knapsack problems. J. Softw. **28**, 1–16 (2017)
14. Goldberg, D.E.: Genetic Algorithms in Search, Optimization and Machine Learning. Addison-Wesley, Reading (1989)
15. Kennedy, J., Eberhart, R.: Particle swarm optimization. In: IEEE International Conference on Neural Networks, Proceedings, vol. 4, pp. 1942–1948 (1995)
16. Storn, R., Price, K.: Differential evolution – a simple and efficient heuristic for global optimization over continuous spaces. J. Glob. Optim. **11**(4), 341–359 (1997)
17. Emary, E., Zawbaa, H.M., Hassanien, A.E.: Binary Grey Wolf optimization approaches for feature selection. J. Neurocomputing **172**, 371–381 (2016)
18. Kamboj, V.K., Bath, S.K., Dhillon, J.S.: Solution of non-convex economic load dispatch problem using Grey Wolf optimizer. Neural Comput. Appl. **27**(5), 1301–1316 (2016)

19. Moradi, M., Badri, A., Ghandehari, R.: Non-convex constrained economic dispatch with valve point loading effect using a grey wolf optimizer algorithm. In: 2016 6th Conference on Thermal Power Plants (CTPP), pp 96–104. IEEE (2016)
20. Chandra, M., Agrawal, A., Kishor, A., Niyogi, R.: Web service selection with global constraints using modified Grey Wolf optimizer. In: 2016 International Conference on Advances in Computing, Communications and Informatics (ICACCI), pp 1989–1994. IEEE (2016)
21. He, Y.C., Wang, X.Z., Zhao, S.L., Zhang, X.L.: Design and applications of discrete evolutionary algorithm based on encoding transformation. Ruan Jian Xue Bao/J. Softw. **29** (9) (2018). (in Chinese). http://www.jos.org.cn/1000-9825/5400.htm
22. Michalewicz, Z.: Genetic Algorithm + Data Structure = Evolution Programs, pp. 13–103. Springer, Berlin (1996). https://doi.org/10.1007/978-3-662-03315-9
23. Zou, D.X., Gao, L.Q., Li, S., Wu, J.H.: Solving 0-1 knapsack problem by a novel global harmony search algorithm. Appl. Soft Comput. **11**, 1556–1564 (2011). https://doi.org/10.1016/j.asoc.2010.07.019
24. He, Y.C., Zhang, X.L., Li, X., Wu, W.L., Gao, S.G.: Algorithms for randomized time-varying knapsack problems. J. Comb. Optim. **31**(1), 95–117 (2016). https://doi.org/10.1007/s10878-014-9717-1
25. He, Y.C., Wang, X.Z., Li, W.B., Zhao, S.L.: Exact algorithms and evolutionary algorithms for randomized time-varying knapsack problem. Ruan Jian Xue Bao/J. Softw. (2016). (in Chinese with English abstract). http://www.jos.org.cn/1000-9825/4937.htm, https://doi.org/10.13328/j.cnki.jos.004937
26. He, Y.C., Song, J.M., Zhang, J.M., et al.: Research on genetic algorithm for solving static and dynamic knapsack problems. Appl. Res. Comput. **32**(4), 1011–1015 (2015). (in Chinese)
27. Mitchell, M.: An Introduction to Genetic Algorithms. MIT Press, Cambridge (1996)
28. Byrka, J., Li, S., Rybicki, B.: Improved approximation algorithm for k-level uncapacitated facility location problem (with penalties). Theory Comput. Syst. **58**, 19–44 (2016)

Novel Operators in Evolutionary Algorithms

Causes of the Imbalance Between Exploration and Exploitation in Evolutionary Computation

Zhe Chen[1,2]($\boxtimes$) (iD) and Chengjun Li[1,2] (iD)

¹ School of Computer Science, China University of Geosciences,
Wuhan 430074, Hubei, China
chenzhe@cug.edu.cn, cuglicj@126.com
² Hubei Key Laboratory of Intelligent Geo-Information Processing,
China University of Geosciences, Wuhan 430074, Hubei, China

Abstract. Evolutionary algorithms have been used in more and more research fields. However, it is very usual that an optimal of nontrivial problems cannot be found by an evolutionary algorithm. In fact, only if the balance between exploration and exploitation is achieved in runs, good solutions can be obtained. In this paper, we observe the changing trend of genotype diversity in runs, which cannot obtain the optimal, of different EAs. Then, we illustrate the main cause of the imbalance between exploration and exploitation in different situations.

Keywords: Evolutionary algorithm · Exploration and exploitation · Diversity · Causes

1 Introduction

Evolutionary algorithms (EAs) including genetic algorithm, genetic programming, evolutionary programming, evolution strategy and differential evolution are stochastic search methods and have been used in many field. An EA proceeds in an iterative manner by generating a new population, $P(t+1)$, from an old one, $P(t)(t \in [0, n])$. Every individual in a population is a tentative solution of the current problem encoded in a type of chromosome representation. For indicating suitability of an individual to problem, an evaluation function associates a fitness value to it. The initial population, $P(0)$, is produced randomly, Then, in each generation, crossover, mutation, etc are used to obtain new individuals based on the original ones. These new individuals are collected into a temporary population $P'(t)$. After that, $P(t+1)$ is produced through selection by picking up some individuals from $P(t)$ and some from $P'(t)$. The halting condition of EA is usually set as reaching a preprogrammed number of generations, or obtaining a satisfactory solution [1].

In theory, the task of EAs is to find the optimal of problem. However, for nontrivial problems, it very usual that EAs cannot find an optimal in runs. In

© Springer Nature Singapore Pte Ltd. 2019
H. Peng et al. (Eds.): ISICA 2018, CCIS 986, pp. 117–131, 2019.
https://doi.org/10.1007/978-981-13-6473-0_11

fact, exploration and exploitation require to be addressed for EAs. Exploration is the process of visiting entirely new regions in search space, while exploitation is the one of visiting the neighborhood of previously visited points [4]. They are two cornerstones in search [5]. Only if the balance between exploration and exploitation is achieved in runs, EAs can obtain good solutions.

In EAs, both exploration and exploitation are realized by operators. Moreover, population size and chromosome representation have important impacts on exploration and exploitation. Nevertheless, it is difficult to measure exploration or exploitation directly [4]. On many occasions, diversity, which can be measured at genotype level or phenotype level, is used to measure exploration and exploitation. In fact, existing methods for the balance between exploration and exploitation are classified according to their effect on diversity in [4]. Although there are methods to achieve the balance between exploration and exploitation, further studies need be done. Provided that causes of imbalance are better known, we can get more ideas for the balance. That is the motivation of this paper.

In this paper, experiments are carried out based on three EAs including a state-of-the-art EA. In our experiments, these EAs do not obtain the optimal in most cases. Thus, it can be inferred that the imbalance between exploration and exploitation occurs in runs of these EAs. Based on experimental results, the changing trend of genotype diversity in runs is shown in figures by us. By observing the trend, we illustrate causes of the imbalance between exploration and exploitation and propose a method to identify the main cause in certain runs.

The rest of this paper is organized as follows. Related works are introduced in Sect. 2. Then, experiments on different EAs are given in Sect. 3. In Sect. 4, we illustrate our finding based on experimental results. Finally, a conclusion and a prospect are dealt with in Sect. 5.

2   Related Works

As above mentioned, in the EA community, diversity is widely used to reflect exploration and exploitation. Diversity refers to differences among individuals. It can be measured at the genotype level or the phenotype one. Genotype diversity reveals differences among genomes within a population, while phenotype one just shows differences among fitness values. Compared with phenotype diversity, genotype diversity is more costly to calculate. So far, for both genotype diversity and phenotype diversity, many different measures have been proposed. Nonetheless, diversity measures are problem-specific [2,6,9]. Consequently, calculation steps of the same measure may be still distinct in EAs if these EAs are based on different chromosome representation. According to [4], most of existing approaches applied in EAs for the exploration and exploitation balance can be explained through their effect on diversity.

Although causes of the imbalance between exploration and exploitation are remained to be studied, phenomena arisen from the imbalance are widely known.

In practice, the imbalance between exploration and exploitation can be judged when no better individual can be obtained any more in a run in spite of an optimal not found. Based on diversity $d \in [0, 1]$, which refers to the differences among individuals, two phenomena can be distinguished from the situation that no better individual can be obtained any more in spite of an optimal not found. One is premature convergence, which features low diversity. The other is stagnation, which features much higher diversity. When premature convergence occurs, there is almost no difference between any two individuals in population. In other words, diversity tends to be zero. When stagnation comes, there are still differences among individuals. That is, diversity value is still high [4].

Here are examples to make these phenomena be understood well. After enough generations, individuals are fairly good in fitness. In this case, the probability of mutated individuals winning in selection may become less and less since their competitors have fairly good fitness. Provided that current diversity level has been low, it is difficult for crossover to generate offspring which are different from their parents since parents are very similar or even identical. Consequently, premature convergence comes soon. If well maintained diversity still can support crossover generating offspring different with their parents, the probability of they selected may become less and less for their competitors is good in fitness. As a result, stagnation happens soon.

3   Experiments to Show the Changing Trend of Genotype Diversity in Different EAs

In this section, three EAs based on different chromosome representations are involved in our experiments to cover the three main types of chromosome representations. In detail, they are a Genetic Algorithm (GA) for the Travelling Salesman Problem (TSP), a GA for the one-max problem and the Differential Evolution (DE) based on the covariance matrix learning and the bimodal distribution parameter setting (CoBiDE) for continuous function optimization. In the three EAs, the CoBiDE is a state-of-the-art one. For different tasks, each EA runs thirty times, respectively. We set enough generations for all algorithms. In each runs, genotype diversity is computed at every interval. Based on these data of genotype diversity, we draw figures showing the changing trend of genotype diversity during runs for each task.

3.1   Experiment on the EA for TSP

The EA for the TSP proposed by [14] and discussed in recent papers, such as [7,8,10], is employed by us. Details of the algorithm can be found in [14]. This EA are based on integer chromosome representation. It uses only one parameter, p, to control both crossover and mutation. In its crossover, a parent plays a major role and can be called the primary one. In crossover, two parents produce only one offspring. Then, in its selection, every offspring competes only with its primary parent. Thus, this algorithm is good at maintaining diversity. Datasets of TSP from TSPLIB [11], which are difficult for this EA, are used in the experiment. Settings this TSP EA are shown in Table 1.

Table 1. Settings of the EA for the TSP

Population size	100
p	0.02
Length of interval	4000 generations
Terminal criterion	400000 generations done

The method for genotype diversity computation in this EA comes from [3]. Let x_i and x_j be two individuals. Matrix M in Formula 1 is connection matrix of TSP tour. In the matrix, k is the number of cities and $a_{lm} \in \{0,1\}, (0 \le l \le k-1, 0 \le m \le k-1)$. $a_{lm} = 1$ represents that there is a connection from city $(l+1)$ to city $(m+1)$ in tour, while $a_{lm} = 0$ denotes that such a connection does not exist. Then, a $k \times k$ connection matrix can be built for x_i and x_j, respectively. Let k' be the number of rows which are same in the two matrixes. Then, the distance between x_i and x_j, $D(x_i, x_j)$, can be defined as Formula 2. Further, diversity, PD, can be defined as Formula 3, where NP is population size and C means combination.

$$\mathbf{M} = \begin{bmatrix} a_{00} & a_{01} & \cdots & a_{0(k-1)} \\ a_{10} & a_{11} & \cdots & a_{1(k-1)} \\ \cdots & \cdots & \cdots & \cdots \\ a_{(k-1)0} & \cdots & \cdots & a_{(k-1)(k-1)} \end{bmatrix} \tag{1}$$

$$D(x_i, x_j) = 1 - \frac{k'}{k} \tag{2}$$

$$PD = \frac{\sum_{i=1}^{NP} \sum_{j=1}^{NP} D(x_i, x_j)}{C_{NP}^2} \tag{3}$$

For lin318, linhp318, rd400, fl417, pr439, pcb442 and d493, the TSP EA runs thirty times, respectively. Diversity value is recorded at each interval in runs. Then, for every dataset, the thirty time average of diversity at every interval is plotted in Fig. 1 to show the changing trend of diversity in runs. It can be seen that, for each dataset, the trend in runs is very similar. In detail, after the sharp and short decrease at the initial stage, diversity stays at a low level in the remaining part of run. Such a type of trend shows runs go to stagnation soon after the initial stage.

3.2   Experiment on the EA for the One-Max Problem

We design a EA with binary chromosome representation for this problem which employ the uniform crossover [13], the bit string mutation and rank-based selecting model. Settings of this EA are listed as below.

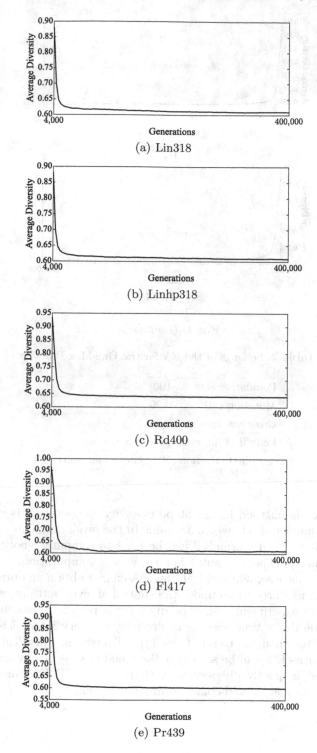

Fig. 1. The average diversity during runs of the EA for the TSP

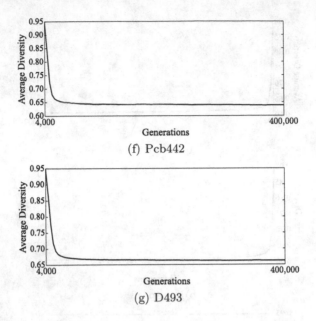

(f) Pcb442

(g) D493

Fig. 1. (*continued*)

Table 2. Settings of the EA for the One-Max Problem

Population size	100
Mutation rate	0.20
Crossover rate	0.80
Length of interval	Five generations
Terminal criterion	500 generations done

In this EA, the method for genotype diversity computation is very simple. Let k' be the number of bits which are same in the two individuals and k be the that of total bits. Then, Formula 2 can be used to compute genotype distance between x_i and x_j. Then, Formula 3 is for diversity computation.

When the scale is set 300 and 500, this EA cannot obtain an optimal. In this case, the EA runs thirty times under the control of given settings, respectively. As the previous experiment, genotype diversity is recorded at each interval in runs. Then, the thirty time average of diversity at every interval is plotted in Fig. 2 to show the changing trend of genotype diversity in runs (Table 2).

For each dataset, it can be seen that the trend in runs is very similar. However, the trend is quietly different with that of the TSP EA runs. In detail, diversity declines sharply and comes to minimum soon.

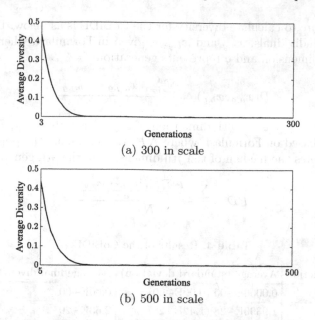

(a) 300 in scale

(b) 500 in scale

Fig. 2. The average diversity during runs of the EA for the One-Max Problem

3.3 Experiment on CoBiDE

Wang et al. [15] proposed the CoBiDE. The covariance matrix learning based coordinate system is established in the algorithm. Besides, the bimodal distributing parameter setting is employed to control parameters. This algorithm has been tested on benchmark test functions provided by [12], which can be classified into four categories, unimodal functions, basic multimodal ones, expanded multimodal ones and hybrid composition ones. Experimental results in [15] show it has overall better performance compared with some earlier DE variants and other state-of-the-art EAs. The detailed procedure of covariance matrix learning based coordinate system and that of setting two groups of parameter, $F_{i,g}$ and $CR_{i,g}$, can be found in [15]. Settings for the CoBiDE are given in Table 3.

Table 3. Settings of the CoBiDE

Function dimension	30
Population size	60
pb	0.40
ps	0.50
Length of interval	500 generations
Terminal criterion	50000 generations done

The measure to calculate diversity for the CoBiDE is as below. Distance, D, between two individuals, $x_{a,g}$ and $x_{b,g}$, is given in Formula 4, where d denotes the function dimension and g represents generations.

$$D(x_{a,g}, x_{b,g}) = \frac{\sum_{j=1}^{d} |x_{a,j,g} - x_{b,j,g}|}{d} \tag{4}$$

In the formula, $x_{i,j,g}$ is the jth dimension of $x_{i,g}$. Then, diversity, PD, is given in Formula 5 based on Formula 4, where NP still represents the population size and $m_{j,g}$ denotes the median of the jth dimension in the gth generations.

$$PD = \frac{\sum_{i=1}^{NP} \frac{\sum_{j=1}^{d} |x_{i,j,g} - m_{j,g}|}{d}}{NP} \tag{5}$$

Table 4. Results of the CoBiDE

Function	Average (standard deviation)	Average final diversity
F1	0.0000E+00 (0.00E+00)	0.00E+00
F2	1.9390E−28 (1.42E−28)	2.63E−20
F3	1.1434E+02 (1.60E+02)	4.92E−05
F4	2.0600E−28 (1.27E−28)	2.65E−20
F5	7.0031E−12 (9.30E−13)	5.30E−17
F6	1.3829E−26 (3.11E−26)	0.00E+00
F7	2.5449E−03 (5.39E−03)	1.38E−11
F8	2.0001E+01 (2.88E−03)	2.39E−11
F9	0.0000E+00 (0.00E+00)	6.67E−11
F10	4.4942E+01 (1.51E+01)	6.64E−11
F11	6.1589E+00 (3.08E+00)	2.92E−17
F12	3.7778E+03 (4.28E+03)	4.44E−10
F13	1.6766E+00 (4.12E−01)	1.27E−10
F14	1.2356E+01 (4.32E−01)	4.81E−06
F15	4.0667E+02 (5.83E+01)	1.49E−10
F16	9.2541E+01 (6.78E+01)	5.01E−12
F17	7.9355E+01 (2.75E+01)	2.00E−04
F18	9.0423E+02 (8.80E−01)	8.38E−19
F19	9.0429E+02 (1.10E+00)	4.45E−19
F20	9.0411E+02 (5.82E−01)	4.62E−19
F21	5.0000E+02 (0.00E+00)	2.49E−10
F22	8.3259E+02 (2.20E+01)	1.28E−18
F23	5.3416E+02 (1.83E−04)	9.50E−03
F24	2.0000E+02 (0.00E+00)	1.52E−09
F25	2.0962E+02 (5.22E−01)	1.35E−01

We run the CoBiDE 30 times for each of the 25 functions. Results are given in Table 4. According to Table 4, the CoBiDE can obtain an optimal at 100% for F1 and F9. In fact, when we observe the detailed results, we find that the CoBiDE obtains an optimal in a part of runs for F2, F4, F6 and F7. In other words, the CoBiDE cannot obtain an optimal of F3, F5, F8 and F10-F25 in the 25 benchmark test functions under the above settings. Therefore, genotype diversity is recorded at each interval in runs for these functions. Then, the average of diversity at every interval is plotted to show the changing trend of diversity in runs for them. In Figs. 3, 4, 5 and 6, we show the changing trend of genotype diversity of the selected 19 functions.

It can be seen that the trend in runs shows difference in different functions. During the whole course, genotype diversity of runs for F3 shows constantly decrease, while that for F23 shows high fluctuates. For remaining functions, the trend in runs consists of one or several declining periods and flat ones. However, details are different. That of F5, F10-F13, F15-F17, F21 and F24-F25 begins with a declining period and then has a flat one. Meanwhile, a declining period and a flat one alternately appear in the trend in runs of F8, F14, F18-F20 and F22. Besides, the trend of these functions except F8 always ends in a flat period. For all functions, diversity never comes to zero.

4   Discussion

In the experiment on the EA for the TSP, runs for all datasets are similar in the changing trend of diversity. In detail, diversity declines only at the beginning and then remains at a level. The value of genotype diversity stable in the later stage shows that runs come to the steady state. On one hand, these runs never find an optimal. On the other hand, diversity value is still high after the steady state coming. It can be inferred that runs of this EA are always trapped into premature stagnation.

The experiment on the EA for the one-max problem shows that genotype diversity in runs declines to the minimum soon. However, no optimal is obtained in runs. The above phenomena illustrate that runs of this EA fall into premature convergence.

In the experiment on the CoBiDE, the changing trend of genotype diversity is very complicated and needs be further analyzed. Since the trend of runs for F3, F8 and F23 does not finish with a flat period, it can be inferred that they still do not fall into premature stagnation or premature convergence after 50000 generations. Meanwhile, the trend of runs for other functions always ends in a flat period with a value larger than zero. Besides, an optimal is never obtained in these runs. Therefore, these runs fall into premature stagnation. Further, the fact that the trend in runs of F14, F18-F20 and F22 shows more than one flat period can be attributed to the effect of particular procedures applied in the CoBiDE, such as the covariance matrix learning. In detail, though the sign of premature stagnation, a flat period with diversity value higher than zero, appears in runs, the particular procedures may make runs jump out of premature stagnation for one or more times.

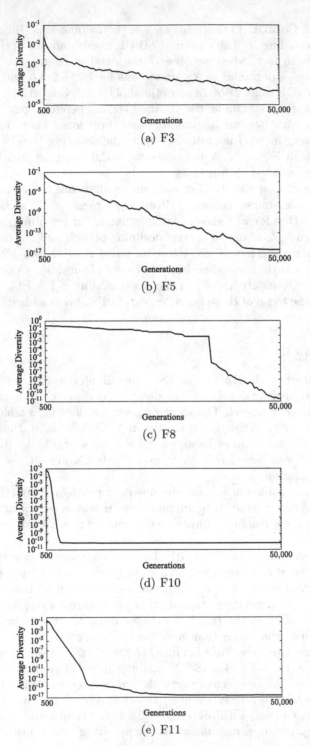

(a) F3

(b) F5

(c) F8

(d) F10

(e) F11

Fig. 3. The average diversity during runs of the CoBiDE (part 1)

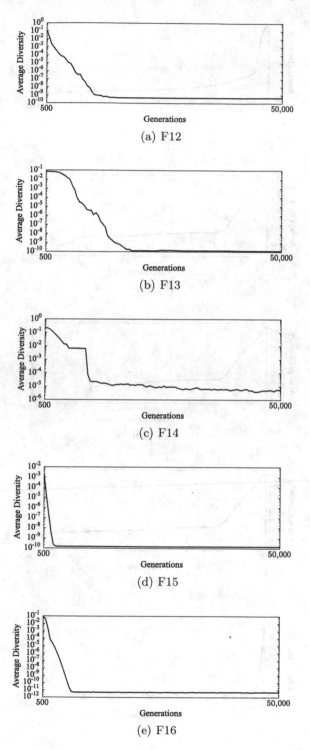

Fig. 4. The average diversity during runs of the CoBiDE (part 2)

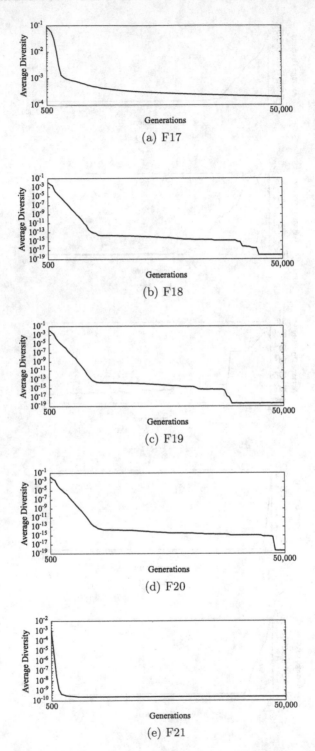

Fig. 5. The average diversity during runs of the CoBiDE (part 3)

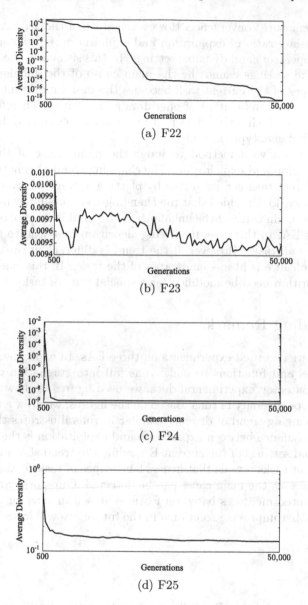

Fig. 6. The average diversity during runs of the CoBiDE (part 4)

Based on our experimental results, we can explain causes of the imbalance between exploration and exploitation as follow. In general, the combination of operators and settings of an EA is the main cause of the imbalance. When it is the main cause, runs of an EA for different tasks show the similar changing trend of diversity. For example, runs of the GA for the TSP for the seven datasets show premature stagnation, while those of the GA for the one-max problem for the two scales show premature convergence. However, a state-of-the-art EA can provide a more appropriate ratio of exploration and exploitation by its combination of well-designed operators and dynamic settings. In this situation, the combination of operators and settings cannot be the main cause of the imbalance. Instead, fitness landscapes of the current task becomes the more important cause of the imbalance than the combination of operators and settings. Therefore, runs for different functions which are distinct in fitness landscapes show difference in the changing trend of genotype diversity.

Hence, we can give a method to judge the main cause of the imbalance between exploration and exploitation. The changing trend of genotype diversity in runs for different task can be gotten by plotting average of diversity at every interval just as we do. Provided that the changing trend is similar in runs for different tasks, the main cause of the imbalance is the combination of operators and settings of this EA. In this case, modifying algorithm may lead to improvement on solutions for all tasks. However, if the trend is different in runs for different tasks, the main cause is fitness landscapes of the tasks. In this case, to improve solutions, algorithm need be modified for a special type of tasks.

5   Concluding Remark

In this paper, we executed experiments on three EAs. In experiments, we select datasets, scales and functions to make runs fall into stagnation or premature convergence. Based on experimental data, we used figures to show the changing trend of genotype diversity in runs. Based on the figures, we drew a conclusion as follow. The changing trend of diversity similar in runs illustrates that the main cause of the imbalance between exploration and exploitation is the combination of operators and settings of the current EA, while the trend showing different in runs for different tasks reveals that fitness landscapes of tasks is the main cause, instead. In this way, the main cause can be detected. Our work can help to find some more pointed measures based on features shown in runs for achieving the balance for further improving solutions. In the future, we will focus on proposing such measures.

References

1. Alba, E., Tomassini, M.: Parallelism and evolutionary algorithms. IEEE Trans. Evol. Comput. **6**(5), 443–462 (2002)
2. Burke, E.K., Gustafson, S., Kendall, G.: Diversity in genetic programming: an analysis of measures and correlation with fitness. IEEE Trans. Evol. Comput. **8**(1), 47–62 (2004)
3. Chang, P.C., Huang, W.H., Ting, C.J.: Dynamic diversity control in genetic algorithm for mining unsearched solution space in TSP problems. Expert Syst. Appl. **37**(3), 1863–1878 (2010)
4. Črepinšek, M., Liu, S.H., Mernik, M.: Exploration and exploitation in evolutionary algorithms: a survey. ACM Comput. Surv. (CSUR) **45**(3), 35 (2013)

5. Eiben, A.E., Schippers, C.A.: On evolutionary exploration and exploitation. Fundamenta Informaticae **35**(1–4), 35–50 (1998)
6. Galván-López, E., McDermott, J., O'Neill, M., Brabazon, A.: Towards an understanding of locality in genetic programming. In: Proceedings of the 12th Annual Conference on Genetic and Evolutionary Computation, pp. 901–908. ACM (2010)
7. Izzo, D., Getzner, I., Hennes, D., Simões, L.F.: Evolving solutions to TSP variants for active space debris removal. In: Proceedings of the 2015 Annual Conference on Genetic and Evolutionary Computation, pp. 1207–1214. ACM (2015)
8. Mavrovouniotis, M., Müller, F.M., Yang, S.: Ant colony optimization with local search for dynamic traveling salesman problems (2016)
9. Paenke, I., Jin, Y., Branke, J.: Balancing population-and individual-level adaptation in changing environments. Adapt. Behav. **17**(2), 153–174 (2009)
10. Pan, G., Li, K., Ouyang, A., Li, K.: Hybrid immune algorithm based on greedy algorithm and delete-cross operator for solving TSP. Soft Comput. **20**(2), 555–566 (2016)
11. Reinelt, G.: TSPLIB—A traveling salesman problem library. ORSA J. Comput. **3**(4), 376–384 (1991)
12. Suganthan, P.N., et al.: Problem definitions and evaluation criteria for the CEC 2005 special session on real-parameter optimization. KanGAL Rep. **2005005**, 2005 (2005)
13. Syswerda, G.: Uniform crossover in genetic algorithms (1989)
14. Tao, G., Michalewicz, Z.: Inver-over operator for the TSP. In: Eiben, A.E., Bäck, T., Schoenauer, M., Schwefel, H.-P. (eds.) PPSN 1998. LNCS, vol. 1498, pp. 803–812. Springer, Heidelberg (1998). https://doi.org/10.1007/BFb0056922
15. Wang, Y., Li, H.X., Huang, T., Li, L.: Differential evolution based on covariance matrix learning and bimodal distribution parameter setting. Appl. Soft Comput. **18**, 232–247 (2014)

Analysis of Optimization Capability of Selection Operator for DE Algorithm

Huichao Liu[⊠] and Fengying Yang

College of Information Engineering, Huanghuai University,
Zhumadian 463000, China
huichao_liu@qq.com, happyay2008@126.coom

Abstract. Differential Evolution Algorithm (DE) is an intelligent algorithm widely used in recent years. Many scholars have studied DE algorithm from many aspects, such as theory and application. Selection operator using greedy strategy is an important part of DE algorithm. Traditionally thought, the DE selection operator is only a means to maintain effective population evolution of DE. In fact, the DE selection operator also has some capability to optimize. For this reason, this paper constructs some DE variants, and compares the optimization results of them with the standard DE algorithm. Simulation results show that the new algorithm which only using greedy selection can achieve certain optimization results, meanwhile, DE algorithm which removing its greedy selection operator only has poor performance. This proves that DE selection operator has certain optimization capability.

Keywords: Algorithm analysis · Differential evolution algorithm ·
Selection operator

1 Introduction

Differential Evolution Algorithm (DE) [1] is an intelligent algorithm widely used at present, which has the advantages of simplicity, high efficiency and fast convergence speed. The DE algorithm includes four main operators: population initialization, mutation, crossover and selection. It is generally believed that the optimization performance of DE is mainly provided by its mutation and crossover operators, different mutation and crossover strategies and corresponding parameters have important influence on the performance of DE algorithm. There are many related researches for this topic. For example, Brest et al. [2] proposed an adaptive DE variant (jDE), in which parameters F and Cr are encoded into each individual and evolve with them. Through parameter control, F and Cr can be randomly selected in interval [0.1, 1.0] and [0.0, 1.0] respectively. Qin et al. [3] proposed a strategy-adaptive DE algorithm (SaDE), and four DE evolutionary strategies were used to form a strategy pool, and the success rate of each strategy used in the past LP generation evolution was calculated as the basis for selecting the evolutionary strategy. Mallipeddi and Sugaranthan [4] applied a strategy of combining mutation and controlling parameters to DE and proposed EPSDE algorithm. Three DE mutation strategies are used to form a mutation strategy pool, and nine Cr values in the interval [0.1, 0.9] and six F values in the

© Springer Nature Singapore Pte Ltd. 2019
H. Peng et al. (Eds.): ISICA 2018, CCIS 986, pp. 132–141, 2019.
https://doi.org/10.1007/978-981-13-6473-0_12

interval [0.4, 0.9] are used to form a parameter pool. Each strategy or parameter in the pool competes with each other to produce offspring. Wang et al. [5] proposed a new algorithm CoDE which combining a new mutation strategy and control parameters. Based on other researches, CoDE algorithm selects three mutation strategies to form a mutation strategy pool, and selects three combinations of F and Cr values as a parameter pool. There are many similar studies, which can be referred to some reviews [6, 7].

Selection operator is an important part of DE algorithm, initially only designed as a greedy and elite reservation mechanism. This mechanism makes the individual in population have a greater selection pressure, and promotes the rapid convergence of the algorithm. At the same time, it also increases the risk of the algorithm falling into local optimum. Some literatures have studied the advantages and disadvantages of DE selection operator and made some improvements. For example, Literature [8] proposed that individual survival time can be considered when performing selection operations. Zhou [9] proposed discrete differential evolution algorithm with average fitness selection. Hu et al. [10] proposed a hybrid algorithm which combines artificial immune system and differential evolution. In the differential evolution process, clonal selection operation and receptor editing mechanism were introduced to enhance the local search ability and population diversity of the algorithm. In order to solve the problems of "premature convergence" and "slow search" in the process of function optimization, Literature [11] proposed a new clonal selection differential evolution algorithm which introducing clonal selection operation into differential evolution algorithm.

Generally speaking, the research on the selection operator of DE algorithm is relatively few. Moreover, researchers generally use selection operators as a means to maintain the evolution process of DE. Some improvement of DE selection operator is also focused on improving the selection pressure of the algorithm. In fact, the DE selection operator also has some capability to optimize. For this reason, this paper proposes some evolutionary variants based on DE algorithm, and compares their optimization results with the standard DE algorithm. The results show that the DE selection operator truly has certain optimization capability.

This article contains five sections. The first section introduces the background of the study. The second section introduces the basic structure of DE algorithm briefly. The third section proposes some DE variants for next experiments. The fourth section, some simulation experiments were carried out, and the experimental results are also analyzed theoretically. The fifth section summarizes the whole paper.

2 Differential Evolution Algorithm

The DE algorithm first initializes the population and then begins the population evolution process. Each generation evolves through three operators: mutation, crossover and selection. Classical DE algorithms have a variety of alternative strategies besides selection operators. These different strategies are combined to form different DE evolutionary schemes. Each evolutionary scheme is usually represented as *DE/a/b/c*, *DE* is represented as DE algorithm, *a* denotes the characteristic of disturbed base vectors, *b* denotes the number of difference vectors used to disturb base vectors, and *c* denotes the type of crossover operator. After several generations of evolution, DE will trigger the stop condition of the algorithm (such as the algorithm has found the optimal solution, reached the predetermined search time or algorithm stagnation) and then stop running and output the optimization results. A basic DE algorithm evolution framework is shown in Fig. 1.

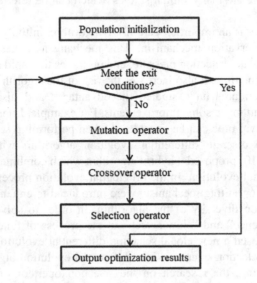

Fig. 1. Basic framework of DE algorithm

2.1   Population Initialization

DE similar with many other intelligent algorithms (such as GA, PSO, etc.), are in the way of group collaboration to find the optimal solution of the problem. Population initialization is the starting point of DE algorithm for optimization, and the results of initialization have an important impact on the subsequent evolution process. Generally, DE initializes the population by random method, that is, the algorithm randomly generates an initial population $P(G = 0) = \{X_i^G\}$, $X_i^G = \{x_{i1}^G, x_{i2}^G, \ldots, x_{in}^G\}$, $i = 1, 2, \ldots, NP$, in the definition space of the problem to be solved. G represents the current evolution generation, NP is the population size, and n is the dimension of the problem.

2.2   Mutation Operator

The main function of mutation operator is to generate the corresponding variant vectors (or donor vectors) $V_i^G = \{v_{i1}^G, v_{i2}^G, \ldots, v_{in}^G\}$, $i = 1, 2, \ldots, NP$ of the current individuals X_i^G, $i = 1, 2, \ldots, NP$. Mutation operator includes many strategies, which is the most abundant content in DE algorithm. There are five common mutation strategies, in which an element $v_{i,j}^G$, $j = 1, 2, \ldots, n$ of each variation vector are defined as:

- DE/rand/1:

$$v_{i,j}^G = x_{r1,j}^G + F \cdot \left(x_{r2,j}^G - x_{r3,j}^G \right)$$

- DE/best/1:

$$v_{i,j}^G = x_{best,j}^G + F \cdot \left(x_{r1,j}^G - x_{r2,j}^G \right)$$

- DE/target-to-best/1:

$$v_{i,j}^G = x_{i,j}^G + F \cdot \left(x_{best,j}^G - x_{i,j}^G \right) + F \cdot \left(x_{r1,j}^G - x_{r2,j}^G \right) \tag{1}$$

- DE/best/2:

$$v_{i,j}^G = x_{best,j}^G + F \cdot \left(x_{r1,j}^G - x_{r2,j}^G \right) + F \cdot \left(x_{r3,j}^G - x_{r4,j}^G \right)$$

- DE/rand/2:

$$v_{i,j}^G = x_{r1,j}^G + F \cdot \left(x_{r2,j}^G - x_{r3,j}^G \right) + F \cdot \left(x_{r4,j}^G - x_{r5,j}^G \right)$$

The **best** represents the subscript position of the optimal individual vector in the population, $r_k \in [1, NP]$, $k = 1, 2, \ldots, 5$ is the subscript of different individuals randomly selected, and the **best**, i, r_k need to be completely different from each other. F is the scaling factor.

In addition, some scholars also put forward some special mutation operators. Such as trigonometric variation [12], arithmetic reorganization [13] and *DE/current-to-pbest/* 1 mutation strategy [14] etc.

2.3 Crossover Operator

The crossover operator used to generate new trial vectors U_i^G by exchanging some elements of the target vector X_i^G and mutation vector V_i^G. DE algorithm mainly has two kinds of crossover strategies, namely binomial crossover (**bin**) and exponential crossover (**exp**). Different crossover strategies have different crossover modes and evolution effects. But the two crossover strategies should be implemented under the control of cross rate parameter (*Cr*). For binomial crossover (**bin**) strategy, whether each element in the mutation vector can enter the trial vector or not is independently selected under the control of parameter *Cr*. When the random number is less than the parameter *Cr*, the element in the mutation vector enters the trial vector; otherwise, the element in the target vector acts as the element of the trial vector. Each element in the trial vector is generated as follows:

$$u_{i,j}^G = \begin{cases} v_{i,j}^G, (rand(0,1) < Cr) \ or \ (j_{rand} == j) \\ x_{i,j}^G, otherwise \end{cases} \tag{2}$$

In which, $(j_{rand} == j)$ means that there is at least one element in the mutation vector need to enter the trial vector.

For the exponential crossover (exp) strategy, the algorithm first randomly generates two integers $s \in [1, n]$ and $c \in (1, n)$ under the control of the crossover factor (Cr), s specifies the starting position of element for exchanging, and c specifies the number of exchanged elements. Each element is generated as follows:

$$u_{i,j}^G = \begin{cases} v_{i,j}^G, if \ j = s_n, s + 1_n, \ldots, s + c - 1_n \\ x_{i,j}^G, otherwise \end{cases} \tag{3}$$

In which, $\langle x \rangle_n$ represents the modular operation.

2.4   Selection Operator

The selection operator of DE algorithm is relatively simple. Almost all DE literatures adopt the method of survival of the fittest to decide whether the trial vector U_i^G can enter the next generation population $P \ (G + 1)$ to continue evolution. For the minimization problem $f(x)$, the selection mechanism is as follows:

$$X_i^{G+1} = \begin{cases} U_i^G, if \ f(U_i^G) \le f(X_i^G) \\ X_i^G, otherwise \end{cases} \tag{4}$$

3   Constructing Variants of DE for Comparison

In order to further verify the optimization capability of the selection operator of DE algorithm, it is necessary to construct some DE variants by removing or just reserving the selection operator of DE algorithm. For simplicity, all variants are based on the DE/rand/1/bin strategy.

3.1   DE Variant Without Greedy Selection

This variant aims to remove the influence of greedy selection of DE algorithm, and to find the optimization capability of DE. For this reason, the new variant keeps the basic framework of DE algorithm unchanged, but the selection operator is reformed as the random selection operation shown in the formula (5). In each generation, the generated candidate vectors and target vector is randomly selected to join the new population, regardless its fitness is better or not. For convenience, the new algorithm is named DE_RS (means DE with Random Selection).

$$X_i^{G+1} = \begin{cases} U_i^G, & \text{if } rand() < 0.5 \\ X_i^G, & \text{otherwise} \end{cases} \tag{5}$$

3.2 DE Variant Without Mutation and Crossover

The purpose of this variant is to reserve the selection operator and remove the mutation and crossover operator, and to investigate the optimization capability of greedy selection in DE algorithm. For this purpose, the new variant keeps the basic frame of DE algorithm unchanged, and the mutation and crossover operators are replaced by the random search shown in formula (6). So that, the candidate vectors are randomly generated in the search space $[a, b]^n$ of the problem, and then the greedy selection operator is performed to produce a new population. For convenience, the new variant is named DE_RE (means DE with Random Evolution).

$$u_{i,j} = a + rand \cdot (b - a) \tag{6}$$

3.3 DE Variant Only Randomly Search

The new variant arms to construct an algorithm with random search behavior, but still uses DE algorithm framework. So after population initialization, variant adopts evolutionary operators and selection operators according to formula (6) and formula (5) respectively to generate the next generation population. Therefore, the evolution process is essentially random search. For convenience, the new algorithm is still named DE_RES (means DE with Random Evolution and Selection).

4 Experimental Results and Analysis

4.1 Experimental Setup

In the following experiments, 13 global optimization functions, which are widely used, are chosen as the experimental bed [1, 15]. In these functions, the first five are uni-modal functions, and F_6 is a step function which has a minimum and is discontinuous. F_7 is a noisy quartic function. F_8–F_{13} are multi-modal functions with many local minima. In the following experiments, two groups of experimental results were compared. The first group set the problem dimension D to 10 and the second set the problem dimension D to 30.

In order to compare and analyze the optimization capability of selection operator, four algorithms, include the standard DE algorithm (DE) with *DE/rand/1/bin* scheme and other three DE variants (DE_RE, DE_RS and DE_RES) introduced in Sect. 3, are used to obtain different results. The scaling factor (F) is set to 0.9, and the crossover factor (Cr) is set to 0.1. All algorithms are run 25 times, and the average value of 25 runs was taken as the final result.

4.2 Performance Comparison When D Is 10

In order to show the optimization capability of selection operator in DE algorithm, the first group experiment is carried out when $D = 10$. The experimental results are shown in Table 1. From Table 1, it can be seen that the standard DE algorithm achieves the optimal results, DE_RES get the worst results, Although DE_RS and DE_RE are not the worst, they are significantly worse than DE. This shows that mutation, crossover and selection operator play different but important roles respectively in DE algorithm. Moreover, the results of DE and DE_RS are far from almost all functions, which show that the optimization capability of DE algorithm is greatly reduced without the greedy selection operators. The comparison between DE_RE and DE_RES shows that DE_RE is superior to DE_RES in almost all functions, which shows that DE algorithm still has certain optimization capability when it adopts random evolution but retains the greedy selection operator. The results of DE_RES algorithm are the worst among the four algorithms, which shows that the random search method is difficult to achieve ideal results for complex problems. In general, the greedy selection operator in DE does have some optimization capability.

Table 1. The performance comparison results of the 4 algorithms when D = 10

Function	DE (ave. ± std.)	DE_RS (ave. ± std.)	DE_RE (ave. ± std.)	DE_RES (ave. ± std.)
F_1	2.24E−70 ± 5.73E−70	2.32E+03 ± 6.40E+02	3.08E+03 ± 9.45E+02	3.89E+03 ± 7.66E+02
F_2	1.15E−37 ± 1.63E−37	1.18E+01 ± 1.48E+00	1.50E+01 ± 1.70E+00	1.64E+01 ± 2.28E+00
F_3	1.26E−14 ± 6.29E−14	2.39E+03 ± 6.50E+02	3.29E+03 ± 7.11E+02	4.48E+03 ± 8.87E+02
F_4	1.83E−02 ± 9.14E−02	2.69E+01 ± 3.68E+00	3.24E+01 ± 3.68E+00	3.56E+01 ± 5.32E+00
F_5	4.88E+00 ± 1.88E+00	6.16E+05 ± 2.81E+05	1.42E+06 ± 6.43E+05	1.50E+06 ± 8.26E+05
F_6	0.00E+00 ± 0.00E+00	2.41E+03 ± 5.42E+02	3.35E+03 ± 7.67E+02	3.95E+03 ± 1.06E+03
F_7	1.46E−03 ± 6.96E−04	3.56E−01 ± 1.22E−01	6.70E−01 ± 1.83E−01	7.35E−01 ± 2.30E−01
F_8	4.74E+00 ± 2.37E+01	2.02E+03 ± 1.10E+02	1.65E+03 ± 1.69E+02	1.80E+03 ± 1.32E+02
F_9	0.00E+00 ± 0.00E+00	5.46E+01 ± 6.50E+00	6.01E+01 ± 5.78E+00	6.59E+01 ± 6.78E+00
F_{10}	3.27E−15 ± 9.84E−16	1.35E+01 ± 1.16E+00	1.55E+01 ± 1.04E+00	1.62E+01 ± 6.74E−01
F_{11}	1.97E−03 ± 4.97E−03	2.20E+01 ± 5.03E+00	3.61E+01 ± 4.51E+00	3.39E+01 ± 1.01E+01
F_{12}	4.71E−32 ± 1.12E−47	5.18E+04 ± 7.36E+04	3.31E+05 ± 2.65E+05	5.31E+05 ± 4.83E+05
F_{13}	1.35E−32 ± 5.59E−48	8.84E+05 ± 6.56E+05	3.86E+06 ± 1.93E+06	6.27E+06 ± 2.99E+06

Table 2. Friedman rank sum test results between the four algorithms when $D = 10$

Algorithm	DE	DE_RS	DE_RE	DE_RES
Ranking	1.00	2.15	3.00	3.85

Table 3. The performance comparison results of the 4 algorithms when $D = 30$

Function	DE (ave. ± std.)	DE_RS (ave. ± std.)	DE_RE (ave. ± std.)	DE_RES (ave. ± std.)
F_1	7.02E−71 ± 6.34E−71	2.09E+04 ± 2.57E+03	3.67E+04 ± 1.54E+03	3.85E+04 ± 2.96E+03
F_2	3.47E−39 ± 2.03E−39	1.05E+02 ± 8.47E+01	1.20E+04 ± 2.38E+04	9.24E+04 ± 1.21E+05
F_3	2.56E−14 ± 3.39E−14	2.92E+04 ± 4.04E+03	4.02E+04 ± 3.57E+03	4.33E+04 ± 3.06E+03
F_4	1.94E−04 ± 7.28E−04	5.33E+01 ± 3.89E+00	6.54E+01 ± 2.95E+00	6.67E+01 ± 3.36E+00
F_5	2.33E+01 ± 1.44E+00	2.76E+07 ± 6.79E+06	7.54E+E+07 ± 1.23E+07	8.66E+07 ± 1.10E+07
F_6	0.00E+00 ± 0.00E+00	2.04E+04 ± 2.28E+03	3.63E+04 ± 2.90E+03	3.81E+04 ± 3.17E+03
F_7	5.01E−03 ± 1.45E−03	1.35E+01 ± 2.82E+00	3.43E+01 ± 5.78E+00	3.81E+01 ± 6.75E+00
F_8	1.42E+01 ± 3.93E+01	8.31E+03 ± 3.67E+02	7.86E+03 ± 2.06E+02	7.94E+03 ± 3.84E+02
F_9	0.00E+00 ± 0.00E+00	2.78E+02 ± 1.13E+01	3.15E+02 ± 1.33E+01	3.21E+02 ± 1.91E+01
F_{10}	3.69E−15 ± 7.11E−16	1.80E+01 ± 3.63E−01	1.95E+01 ± 2.00E−01	1.96E+01 ± 1.93E−01
F_{11}	2.96E−04 ± 1.48E−03	1.89E+02 ± 1.84E+01	3.22E+02 ± 2.68E+01	3.43E+02 ± 2.85E+01
F_{12}	1.57E−32 ± 5.59E−48	2.28E+07 ± 7.51E+06	1.22E+08 ± 2.00E+07	1.36E+08 ± 2.05E+07
F_{13}	1.35E−32 ± 5.59E−48	8.71E+07 ± 2.00E+07	2.88E+08 ± 5.85E+07	3.09E+08 ± 5.44E+07

Table 2 lists the nonparametric test results of the Friedman rank sum test between the four algorithms (the significance is less than 0.05). It can be seen that DE algorithm has the best performance, and DE_RS, DE_RE and DE_RES are arranged in sequence. This further validates our analysis above, and illustrate the optimization capability of greedy selection operator is remarkable.

4.3 Performance Comparison When D Is 10

In order to further verify the catholicity of optimization capability of DE selection operator, the second group of experiments were carried out under the condition of

$D = 30$. The results of experiment are shown in Table 3. It is found that the results in Table 3 are similar in Table 1. That is DE still obtains the best solution, and DE_RES also is the worst. Moreover, DE_RS variant with random selection operator is quite different from DE, and DE_RE variant has significant advantage in almost all functions when compared with DE_RES variant. All these show that DE selection operator still has certain optimization capability when the dimension is increased. That is to say, the capability of DE's selection operator is independent of the dimension of the problem. The Friedman rank sum test results between the four algorithms are also shown in Table 4. The contents of Table 4 are very similar to Table 2, which further validates our analysis above.

Table 4. Friedman rank sum test results between the four algorithms when $D = 30$

Algorithm	DE	DE_RS	DE_RE	DE_RES
Ranking	1.00	2.15	2.92	3.92

5   Conclusions

Traditionally, the selection operator of DE algorithm is regarded as a mechanism only to maintain the population evolution process. But in fact, the selection operator of DE algorithm also has certain optimization capability. In this paper, we construct some DE variants with different strategies, and further verify the optimization capability of greedy selection operator by two groups of experiments. Moreover, this optimization capability is independent with the problem dimension.

It can also be found from the experiments that although the separate mutation, crossover or selection operator has its optimization capability, but the optimization effect of each independent operator are obviously worse than their combination. Moreover, the optimization capability of each operator is different. What role each operator will play in DE algorithm will be a topic for future research.

Acknowledgements. This work was supported in part by Henan Science and Technology Project (No.182102210411) and Henan University Key Research Project (No.18A520040).

References

1. Storn, R., Price, K.: Differential evolution – a simple and efficient heuristic for global optimization over continuous spaces. J. Global Optim. **11**(4), 341–359 (1997)
2. Brest, J., Greiner, S., Boskovic, B., Mernik, M., Zumer, V.: Self-adapting control parameters in differential evolution: a comparative study on numerical benchmark problems. IEEE Trans. Evol. Comput. **10**(6), 646–657 (2006)
3. Qin, A.K., Huang, V.L., Suganthan, P.N.: Differential evolution algorithm with strategy adaptation for global numerical optimization. IEEE Trans. Evol. Comput. **13**(2), 398–417 (2009)
4. Mallipeddi, R., Suganthan, P.N., Pan, Q.K., Tasgetiren, M.F.: Differential evolution algorithm with ensemble of parameters and mutation strategies. Appl. Soft Comput. **11**(2), 1679–1696 (2011)

5. Wang, Y., Cai, Z., Zhang, Q.: Differential evolution with composite trial vector generation strategies and control parameters. IEEE Trans. Evol. Comput. **15**(1), 55–66 (2011)
6. Das, S., Suganthan, P.N.: Differential evolution: a survey of the state-of-the-art. IEEE Trans. Evol. Comput. **15**(1), 4–31 (2011)
7. Das, S., Mullick, S.S., Suganthan, P.N.: Recent advances in differential evolution – an updated survey. Swarm Evol. Comput. **27**, 1–30 (2016)
8. Storn, R.: System design by constraint adaptation and differential evolution. IEEE Trans. Evol. Comput. **3**(1), 22–34 (1999)
9. Zhou, Y.L., Zhu, Y.H.: Discrete differential evolution with fitness uniform selection scheme. J. Chin. Comput. Syst. **33**(1), 151–154 (2012)
10. HU, C.-J., Zhang, J.: Immune differential evolution algorithm using clone selection. Appl. Res. Comput. **30**(6), 1635–1640 (2013)
11. Yang, G., Jin, H.: Optimization algorithm based on differential evolution and clonal selection mechanism. Comput. Eng. Appl. **49**(10), 49–50 (2013)
12. Fan, H.Y., Lampinen, J.: A trigonometric mutation operation to differential evolution. J. Global Optim. **27**(1), 105–129 (2003)
13. Corne, D., Dorigo, M., Glover, F., Dasgupta, D., Moscato, P., Poli, R., et al.: New Ideas in Optimization, pp. 11–32. UK, McGraw-Hill Ltd (1999)
14. Zhang, J., Sanderson, A.C.: JADE: adaptive differential evolution with optional external archive. IEEE Trans. Evol. Comput. **13**(5), 945–958 (2009)
15. Wang, H., Rahnamayan, S., Sun, H., Omran, M.G.: Gaussian bare-bones differential evolution. IEEE Trans. Cybern. **43**(2), 634–647 (2013)

A New Quantum Evolutionary Algorithm in 0-1 Knapsack Problem

Jialin Li[1] and Wei Li[2(✉)]

[1] School of Science and Technology, Gannan Normal University, Ganzhou,
Jiangxi Province, China
lijialin8@hotmail.com
[2] School of Information Engineering, Jiangxi University of Science
and Technology, Ganzhou, Jiangxi Province, China
nhwslw@gmail.com

Abstract. As a common optimization problem in the field of operations research. Knapsack problem (KP) is often used in many areas, such as business, combinatorial mathematics, computational complexity theory, cryptography and applied mathematics. Based on the characteristics of 0-1 knapsack problem, this essay proposes an improved quantum evolutionary algorithm (IQEA) based on dynamic rotation angle catastrophe technology and designs a quantum rotating gate operator which adaptively adjusts the values of rotation angle according to the fitness value and evolution generations. In the process of evolution, the early quantum rotation angle is used to carry out the catastrophic operation of some individuals. The individual and the individual after the catastrophe are evolved in parallel, and the multipath optimization is carried out to improve the parallelism of the algorithm. This can effectively make the population jump out of the current optimal solution, increase the diversity of the population, carry out multi direction search, and maintain the stability of the population, and ensure that the excellent information in the subpopulation will not be lost. The experimental results of the typical knapsack problem show that the performance of the algorithm is better than the traditional evolutionary algorithm and the traditional quantum evolutionary algorithm in solving the knapsack problem.

Keywords: Knapsack problem · Quantum evolutionary algorithm ·
Dynamic quantum angle · Catastrophic technology

1 Introduction

As a common optimization problem in the field of operations research. Knapsack problem (KP) is often used in many areas, such as business, combinatorial mathematics, computational complexity theory, cryptography and applied mathematics. The problem of blanking in the factory, resource allocation in management, capital budgeting, investment decision and loading problem can be modeled as knapsack problem. It is very important to study the solution to this problem in theory and practice. The study of the knapsack problem can be traced back to 1897 [1]. Because it is difficult to find the global optimal solution in a limited time, the solution of the knapsack problem is mainly based on some heuristic algorithms, such as tabu search algorithm, simulated

© Springer Nature Singapore Pte Ltd. 2019
H. Peng et al. (Eds.): ISICA 2018, CCIS 986, pp. 142–151, 2019.
https://doi.org/10.1007/978-981-13-6473-0_13

annealing algorithm and so on. There are also some papers using evolutionary algorithms to solve this problem, but when the scale of the problem is large, the traditional evolutionary algorithms are not very effective [2].

Narayanan and Moore first proposed the quantum genetic algorithm (QGA) In 1996, and successfully solved the TSP problem [3], and created the research direction of the fusion of quantum evolutionary algorithms and evolutionary computation. The fusion point of quantum computation and evolutionary algorithm mainly lies in the construction of population encoding and evolution strategies. Simply speak, the population adopts quantum bit based coding, and the population evolution adopts quantum bit phase rotation of quantum gates, using quantum Not gate or catastrophic operation to maintain the diversity of the population. It is based on some concepts and theories of quantum computing, such as quantum bit, quantum state superposition, etc., using quantum bit coding to express chromosomes, and use quantum gate updating to complete evolutionary search. The quantum genetic algorithm (QGA) proposed by Han (2000–2006) successfully solves the knapsack problem. The algorithm uses a quantum rotating gate to make a chromosome change to generate a new individual, moreover, the strategy of gene transformation can make the realization of quantum computer possible in the future [4–6]. Quantum genetic algorithm is superior to traditional genetic algorithm in population diversity and computational parallelism, which can effectively improve the convergence speed and reduce premature convergence. Scholars at home and abroad have made many attempts to improve the research of quantum evolutionary algorithms, including the structure of the algorithm, the way of evolution and the coding method. For example, Yang of University of Science and Technology of China proposed a multi universe parallel quantum genetic algorithm [7]. Zhang of Southwest Jiao Tong University adopts the quantum bit phase comparison method to update quantum gates and adjust the strategy of adaptive search grid [8]; Chen of Southwest Jiao Tong University, and so on, proposes a quantum genetic algorithm for chaos updating the rotation angle of rotating gate [9]; and Tsinghua University's Ling gives a hybrid quantum genetic algorithm based on two input coding and based on it. A real coded hybrid quantum genetic algorithm [10]. Li and others proposed a double-chain quantum genetic algorithm based on real coding and gradient information of objective function to solve continuous optimization problems [11]; other studies in optimization problems [12]. Based on the characteristics of 0-1 knapsack problem, this essay proposes an improved quantum evolutionary algorithm (IQEA) based on dynamic rotation angle catastrophe technology and designs a quantum rotating gate operator which adaptively adjusts the values of rotation angle according to the fitness value and evolution generations. In the process of evolution, the early quantum rotation angle is used to carry out the catastrophic operation of some individuals. The individual and the individual after the catastrophe are evolved in parallel, and the multipath optimization is carried out to improve the parallelism of the algorithm. This can effectively make the population jump out of the current optimal solution, increase the diversity of the population, carry out multi direction search, and maintain the stability of the population, and ensure that the excellent information in the subpopulation will not be lost. The experimental results of the typical knapsack problem show that the proposed algorithm outperforms traditional evolutionary algorithms and traditional quantum evolution algorithms in solving the knapsack problem.

2 Knapsack Problem

The 0-1 knapsack problem is the most basic KP problem. This is also an NP puzzle. It can be described as: Given a set of projects, each project has its own weight and value. In a limited total weight, study how to maximize the total value of the project. We assume that the weight and value of all items are non-negative, and that the maximum weight that a backpack can bear is W, limiting each item to 0 or 1. The mathematical model is expressed as follows:

$$\max \sum_{i=1}^{n} c_i x_i \tag{1}$$

$$s.t. \quad \sum_{i=1}^{n} w_i x_i \leq W \quad x_i \in \{0, 1\}, i = 1, 2, \cdots, n \tag{2}$$

In which formula 1 is the target, that is, the value of the items loaded into the knapsack is the maximum value; formula 2 is a constraint condition that represents the volume limit of the knapsack, n represents the total number of items, "i" is the identifier of items, W_i represents the weight of the item "i", C_i is the value of the item "i", W is the capacity of the backpack, and the total number of items in the backpack is m (m <= n). X_i represents a binary variable, which is used to measure whether the item I is loaded into the backpack variable. The value is 0 or 1. When 1 is taken, it indicates that the item I is selected, for example: N = 10, X = 1100010110 means putting items 1, 2, 6, 8 and 9 in a backpack (m = 5).

3 Quantum Evolution Algorithm

Quantum evolution algorithm (QEA), based on the concepts of quantum bit and quantum state superposition in quantum computing, uses the probability amplitude of qubits to represent the coding of chromosomes, so a qubit chromosome can represent the superposition of multiple states. Compared with traditional evolutionary algorithms, the algorithm has better population diversity and higher computational parallelism. The random observation of simulated quantum collapse makes the population more abundant. It can improve the convergence speed of the algorithm, and can make the balance between the exploration and development of the algorithm, and improve the optimization efficiency of the algorithm [13].

3.1 Qutbit

In QEA, a qubit-based encoding method is used, and (qutbit) is a two-state quantum system that acts as a physical medium for an information storage unit, which is a unit vector defined in Hilbert space. A pair of real number vectors $\begin{pmatrix} \alpha_i \\ \beta_i \end{pmatrix}$ can be used to define a quantum bit. The probability that a quantum is in a spin-down state is $|\alpha_i|^2$, and the probability that a quantum is in a spin-up state is $|\beta_i|^2$. And meet $|\alpha_i|^2 + |\beta_i|^2 = 1$.

3.2 Quantum Coding

In quantum evolutionary algorithms, a quantum bit is defined by a pair of real number vectors $\begin{pmatrix} \alpha_i \\ \beta_i \end{pmatrix}$ using a quantum bit-based encoding scheme, so the Ith quantum chromosome with k bits can be expressed as:

$$\begin{bmatrix} \alpha_{i1} & \alpha_{i2} & \cdots & \alpha_{ik} \\ \beta_{i1} & \beta_{i2} & \cdots & \beta_{ik} \end{bmatrix} \tag{3}$$

Among them, 0 states and 1 states are obtained with a certain probability $|\alpha_i|^2$ and $|\beta_i|^2$ respectively, and satisfy $|\alpha|^2 + |\beta|^2 = 1$.

Therefore, each multivariate variable (N dimension) can be composed of N quantum genes. Obviously, if the dimension of the problem is n and the chromosome population of the T generation is q^t, each quantum individual is composed of N quantum genes, so each quantum individual can be encoded in the following form of quantum coding:

$$q_j^t = \begin{bmatrix} \alpha'_{11} & \alpha'_{12} & \cdots & \alpha'_{1k} & \alpha'_{21} & \alpha'_{22} & \cdots & \alpha'_{2k} & \cdots & \alpha'_{n1} & \alpha'_{n2} & \cdots & \alpha'_{nk} \\ \beta'_{11} & \beta'_{12} & \cdots & \beta'_{1k} & \beta'_{21} & \beta'_{22} & \cdots & \beta'_{2k} & \cdots & \beta'_{n1} & \beta'_{n2} & \cdots & \beta'_{nk} \end{bmatrix} \tag{4}$$

Among them, q_j^t is the jth member of the t generation, and k is the qubit number used for the components of each independent variable.

Take a 3 bit quantum chromosome as an example to illustrate quantum individuals:

$$Q = \begin{bmatrix} 1 & \frac{1}{3} & 0 \\ 0 & \frac{\sqrt{8}}{3} & 1 \end{bmatrix} \tag{5}$$

This individual contains states: $|000, |001, |010, |011, |100, |101, |110,$ and $|111$. The probability is 0, 1/9, 0, 8/9, 0, 0, 0, 00 (The proportion of the state $|001\rangle$ is $(1)^2 \times (1/3)^2 \times 1^2 = 1/9$). From this example, We can see that $2^3 = 8$ states only need 3 quantum chromosomes to represent, so the quantum chromosome has the characteristics of diversity. As the quantum chromosomes $|\alpha_i|^2$ and $|\beta_i|^2$ gradually approach 1 or 0, the quantum chromosomes gradually converge to a single state, the diversity of the population disappears, and the algorithm converges.

4 Application of Improved Quantum Evolutionary Algorithm in 0-1 Knapsack Problem

Based on the characteristics of 0-1 knapsack problem, this essay proposes an improved quantum evolutionary algorithm (IQEA) based on dynamic rotation angle catastrophe technology and designs a quantum rotating gate operator which adaptively adjusts the values of rotation angle according to the fitness value and evolution generations. In the process of evolution, the early quantum rotation angle is used to carry out the catastrophic operation of some individuals. The individual and the individual after the catastrophe are evolved in parallel, and the multipath optimization is carried out to improve the parallelism of the algorithm. This can effectively make the population jump out of the current optimal solution, increase the diversity of the population, carry out multi direction search, and maintain the stability of the population, and ensure that the excellent information in the subpopulation will not be lost.

4.1 Quantum Coding of the 0-1 Knapsack Problem

In this essay, the 0-1 knapsack problem is quantum coded, and the matrix representation is used to characterize the 0-1 knapsack problem. Each qubit satisfies $|\alpha_i|^2 + |\beta_i|^2 = 1$ and can be represented by $\begin{pmatrix} \alpha_i \\ \beta_i \end{pmatrix}$. After observation, the population is a binary coded 0-1 backpack matrix. Hypothesis that the quantum population size is SizePop and the number of 0-1 knapsack nodes is n, the length of each quantum chromosome is L = 2n. Then, the coding form of the ith individual in the group $Q(t) = \{q_1^t, q_2^t, \ldots, q_{sizepop}^t\}$ is:

$$q_i^t = \begin{pmatrix} \alpha_1 & \alpha_2 & \cdots & \alpha_j & \cdots & \alpha_n \\ \beta_1 & \beta_2 & \cdots & \beta_j & \cdots & \beta_n \end{pmatrix} \tag{6}$$

In this essay, $\frac{1}{\sqrt{2}}$ is used as the initial of α_i and β_i in the population, which effectively guarantees that all states appear with the same probability.

4.2 IQEA Algorithm Flow

Step1: Make t = 0, generate the initial population Q(t) by using the probability quantum chromosome;
Step2: The initial population is measured and the classical chromosomal state P(t) that solves the 0-1 knapsack problem is obtained;
Step3: Calculate each state fitness value;
Step4: Record the fitness of the best individual;
Step 5: while (Maximum number of iterations or no update generation)
{
t++;
Improved quantum revolving door for updating individual populations;
{
When the evolution of the population tends to stagnate;
A group of catastrophic technology is initiated by using a certain probability as trigger;
}
The quantum measurement and decoding of the population Q(t) is carried out. The state P(t) is obtained;
The fitness of each state is calculated;
Record the fitness of the best individual.
}

4.3   A New Quantum Rotation Gate Operation

In this IQEA, make the quantum rotation gate $U_R(\theta) = \begin{pmatrix} \cos\theta & -\sin\theta \\ \sin\theta & \cos\theta \end{pmatrix}$ act on the quantum chromosome to update its gene bit. The quantum rotating gate is a 2×2 matrix to represent a bit, and the quantum bit is updated by changing the direction and size of the quantum rotation angle. The corresponding operation is [14]:

$$\begin{pmatrix} \alpha_i' \\ \beta_i' \end{pmatrix} = U_R(\theta) \cdot \begin{pmatrix} \alpha_i \\ \beta_i \end{pmatrix} = \begin{pmatrix} \cos\theta & -\sin\theta \\ \sin\theta & \cos\theta \end{pmatrix} \cdot \begin{pmatrix} \alpha_i \\ \beta_i \end{pmatrix} \tag{7}$$

In which θ is rotation angle, the quantum chromosome $\begin{pmatrix} \alpha_i \\ \beta_i \end{pmatrix}$ is transformed into $\begin{pmatrix} \alpha_i' \\ \beta_i' \end{pmatrix}$ after quantum rotation gate operation. The rotation angle θ and the rotation direction are selected from the Table 1 quantum rotation angle direction and size selection table.

Table 1. Quantum rotation angle direction and size selection table

x_i	b_i	$f(x_i) > f(b_i)$	$\Delta\theta$	$S(\alpha_i, \beta_i)$			
				$\alpha_i \beta_i > 0$	$\alpha_i \beta_i < 0$	$\alpha_i = 0$	$\alpha_i = 0$
0	0	F	0	0	0	0	0
0	0	T	0	0	0	0	0
0	1	F	0	0	0	0	0
0	1	T	δ	-1	1	± 1	0
1	0	F	δ	-1	1	± 1	0
1	0	T	δ	1	-1	0	± 1
1	1	F	δ	1	-1	0	± 1
1	1	T	δ	1	-1	0	± 1

The $\Delta\theta$ value of the quantum rotation angle in the upper table is generally a fixed value, which is fixed by selecting the rotation angle to update the gene location of the quantum chromosome through the look-up table, which can easily lead to the loss of the diversity of the population, thus making the search easy to fall into the local optimal. In this essay, a quantum rotating gate operator is designed for the 0-1 knapsack problem, which adaptively adjusts the value of the rotation angle according to the fitness value and the evolutionary generations. The concrete realization is as follows: It is assumed that the values of ith bit in the individual x and the best individual b after the use of quantum measurements in a population are represented by xi and b_i respectively. The fitness functions F(xi) and F(bi) are used to represent individual fitness values, respectively. Combined with Table 1 of this paper, the value of the dynamic quantum rotation angle can be defined by the following formula:

$$\theta = S\Delta\theta(e^{\frac{abs(F(x_i)-F(b_i))}{t}} - 1) \tag{8}$$

In which $\Delta\theta$ is an initial rotation angle, the rotation direction of the quantum rotation angle S can be shown in combination with Table 1, and 't' is the current evolutionary generations carried out by the algorithm. The values of the functions $F(x_i)$ and $F(b_i)$ change as the evolutionary generation increases. In the course of evolution, the quantum rotation angle is dynamically changed according to the rate of convergence. When the algorithm is in the initial stage of evolution and continuously searches for better solutions, the quantum rotation angle is larger, so that the algorithm can search in a larger range of space. As the evolutionary generations of the algorithm is increasing, the value difference of the optimal solution of the contemporary solution is slowly changing hours, and the quantum rotation angle is becoming smaller and smaller, with the convergence of the algorithm gradually approaching zero.

4.4 Group Catastrophe Technology

In the evolution of quantum evolutionary algorithm, the quantum chromosome collapses to a certain direction under the action of the quantum rotation gate adjustment strategy. If the algorithm does not join the mutation operation during the evolution process, when the equivalent sub bit appears in the convergence state, the measured value will be fixed to 0 or 1. It is difficult to jump out again, and the algorithm is easy to have a prematurity problem. When the algorithm does not change for several generations in the optimal solution, it shows that the algorithm falls into the local optimal value. At this point, catastrophic operation can be carried out on the population, and a greater disturbance will be imposed on the population in the process of evolution, so that it will be separated from the local optimum. When the continuous N generations are not renewed, the quantum gates are triggered by mutation probability to perform quantum dyeing catastrophic operation.

Because quantum individuals are uncertain in the measurement of decoding, the decoding process may be out of the local optimum, so the catastrophic operation uses the rotation angle in the early stage of evolution to greatly disturb some individuals. Realize the parallel evolution of contemporary superior individuals and post-catastrophe individuals, perform multi-path optimization, and improve the parallelism of the algorithm. This can effectively make the population jump out of the current optimal solution, increase the diversity of the population, conduct multi-directional search, and also maintain the stability of the population, ensuring that the excellent information in the offspring population will not be lost.

4.5 Quantum Measurement

The process of quantum measurement is mainly the process of transforming a quantum chromosome into a classical body, making them corresponding to the classical chromosomes, and establishing the corresponding relationship with the solution of the problem. Specific description is: when measuring (or selecting state), it is based on qubit probability amplitude $|\alpha_{ij}|^2$ (or $|\beta_{ij}|^2$) to select 0 or 1 of the corresponding gene position. The specific method of this paper is: use the random function rand(0,1) to generate a random number r, how its value is greater than and if it is greater than the value of $|\alpha_{ij}|^2$ (or $|\beta_{ij}|^2$), then generate 0 or 1, the measurement result is 1; otherwise, it takes 0 (or vice versa).

5   Results Analysis

In this essay selects the 0-1 knapsack optimization problem with 100 items to carry out experiment. For simplicity, it is recorded as KP100. Each item is encoded in a quantum bit, so the quantum chromosome length is the number of items. In this paper, MATLAB is used to implement the algorithm. The population sizes are set to 10 and 20 respectively. The maximum evolution generations is 500. The algorithm is solved by traditional EA, QEA and IQEA respectively. Each case runs continuously for 10 times. Then the data of 10 highest fitness values searched 10 times are analyzed statistically. When optimizing the knapsack problem, m denotes the population size, f(x) denotes the maximum fitness value that is searched for every 10 times. "Best", "Worst" and "Average" represent the maximum fitness values, the minimum fitness values and the average fitness values for the 10 best results found in 10 consecutive experiments respectively. In this essay, all termination conditions for knapsack optimization are the largest evolution generations is 500. In this essay, the most important index to judge the effect of optimization is "mean", that is, the average fitness of 10 searches.

According to the data in Table 2, the quantum evolution algorithm based on the dynamic rotation angle catastrophe technique has obvious advantages in obtaining the accuracy of the optimal solution. For different initial population sizes, the search ability is different. When the population size is small, the three algorithms do not find the optimal solution in 500 generations. When the population size reaches a certain number, the result of the algorithm is better. Enhanced, IQEA can better find the optimal solution, and the average result is also close to the optimal result, but continue to increase the population size, and does not greatly improve the accuracy of the results.

Table 2. KP100's experimental data table

m	f(x)	EA	QEA	IQEA
10	Best	3264	3938	3943
	Worst	3099	3776	3907
	Mean	3192	3878	3930
20	Best	3342	3960	3979
	Worst	3176	3936	3961
	Mean	3245	3953	3968

Figure 1 is a graph of three algorithms for KP100 with a population of 20. From the convergence graph of Fig. 1, it can be seen that the improved quantum evolution algorithm is more difficult to fall into local optimum and the convergence speed is faster.

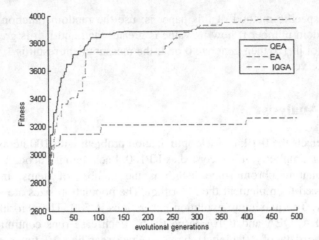

Fig. 1. Comparison of KP100 experiments

6 Conclusion

Based on the characteristics of 0-1 knapsack problem, this essay proposes an improved quantum evolutionary algorithm (IQEA) based on dynamic rotation angle catastrophe technology and designs a quantum rotating gate operator which adaptively adjusts the values of rotation angle according to the fitness value and evolution generations. In the process of evolution, the early quantum rotation angle is used to carry out the catastrophic operation of some individuals. The individual and the individual after the catastrophe are evolved in parallel, and the multipath optimization is carried out to improve the parallelism of the algorithm. This can effectively make the population jump out of the current optimal solution, increase the diversity of the population, carry out multi direction search, and maintain the stability of the population, and ensure that the excellent information in the subpopulation will not be lost. The experimental results show that the improved quantum evolution algorithm is better than the evolutionary algorithm and the traditional quantum evolution algorithm in solving the 0-1 knapsack problem.

References

1. Mathews, G.B.: On the partition of numbers. Lond. Math. Soc. **28**, 486–490 (1897)
2. Wang, X.Z., He, Y.C.: Evolutionary algorithms for knapsack problems. Ruan Jian Xue Bao/J. Softw. **28**(1), 1–16 (2017). (in Chinese)
3. Narayanan, A., Moore, M.: Quantum inspired genetic algorithm. In: IEEE International Conference on Evolutionary Computation, Iscataway, pp. 61–66 (1996)
4. Han, K.-H., Kim, J.-H.: Genetic quantum algorithm and its application to optimization problem. In: Proceedings of the 2000 IEEE Congress on Evolutionary. IEEE Press, USA, pp. 1354–1360 (2000)

5. Han, K.-H., Park, K.-H., Lee, C.-H.: Parallel quantum inspired genetic combinatorial optimization problem. In: Proceedings of the 2001 IEEE Congress on Combinatorial Computation algorithm for Evolutionary Computation. IEEE Press, USA, pp. 1422–1429 (2001)
6. Han, K.-H., Kim, J.-H.: On the analysis of the quantum-inspired evolutionary algorithm with a single individual. In: Proceedings of the 2006 IEEE Congress on Evolutionary Computation. IEEE Press, USA, pp. 2622–2629 (2006)
7. Yang, J.A., et al.: Multi-cosmic parallel quantum genetic algorithm. Chin. J. Electron. 32(6), 923–928 (2004)
8. Zhang, G.X., et al.: A novel quantum genetic algorithm and its application. ACTA Electr. Sin. 32(3), 476–479 (2004)
9. Chen, H., et al.: Chaos updating rotated gates quantum-inspired genetic algorithm. In: Proceedings of the International Conference on Communications, Circuits and systems, vol. 2, pp. 1108–1112 (2004)
10. Ling, W., et al.: Hybrid numerical optimization genetic algorithm based on quantum computing for and parameter estimation. Appl. Math. Comput. 171, 1141–1156 (2005)
11. Li, S., et al.: Quantum genetic algorithm based on real coding and gradient of objective function. J. Harbin Univ. Technol. 38(8), 1216–1218, 1223 (2006)
12. Liang, X.: Research on the application of evolutionary algorithms and quantum computing in optimization problems. China University of Science and Technology (2012). https://doi.org/10.7666/d.y2125828
13. Bhatia, A.K., Basu, S.K.: Tackling 0/1 knapsack problem with gene induction. Soft. Comput. 8(1), 1–9 (2003)
14. Li, J.L., et al.: A new quantum rotation angle of quantum-inspired evolutionary algorithm for TSP. Int. J. High Perform. Syst. Arch. 7(4), 223–230 (2017)

A General Selection Method for Mutation Strategy in Differential Evolution

Dahai Xia[1,3](✉), Song Lin[2], Meng Yan[1], Caiquan Xiong[1], and Yuanxiang Li[3]

[1] Computer School, Hubei University of Technology, Wuhan, China
xdh628@163.com, x_cquan@163.com, ym620@126.com
[2] Strategic Teaching and Research Section, Naval Command College, Nanjing, China
2100162ls@163.com
[3] College of Computer Science, Wuhan University, Wuhan, China
yxli@whu.edu.cn

Abstract. How to balance exploration and exploitation is a key issue for evolution algorithm including differential algorithm (DE). Many researchers propose various improved mutation strategies to solve this issue for DE. Most of them can be classified as deterministic rules. That is to say, they select individuals according to predetermined methods and so the balance is static. However, different evolution stages require different balance between exploration and exploitation. In order to solve this problem, a general selection method named adaptive stochastic ranking based mutation strategies in DE(ASR-DE). In ASR-DE, it uses stochastic ranking method to rank all individuals according to their contribution in exploration and exploitation. The parameter P_f in stochastic ranking is adaptive controlled by a transform version of success rate. The individuals with the smaller ranking are more likely to be selected. 28 functions of CEC2013 is used here to verify the validity of testing method. The test results show that ASR-DE improves the standard DE and improved DE comparing with other methods.

Keywords: Different evolution · Exploration and exploitation · Mutation operator · Adaptive stochastic ranking

1 Introduction

Exploration and exploitation are the two cornerstones for evolution algorithms [1] including differential evolution (DE) [2]. Mutation strategy is very important in DE, and many researchers propose various improved mutation strategies to balance exploration and exploitation. Zhang [3] proposes a new mutation strategy named DE/current to pbest/1 operator. In order to release the selection pressure, DE/current to pbest/1 will choose the pbest vector to promote the exploration. Chiang [4] proposed a new mutation strategy named DE/2-Opt/1 operator. The base vector will be selected as the better member that forming the first difference vector in the operator to make faster convergence speed. Zhou

© Springer Nature Singapore Pte Ltd. 2019
H. Peng et al. (Eds.): ISICA 2018, CCIS 986, pp. 152–161, 2019.
https://doi.org/10.1007/978-981-13-6473-0_14

[5] proposed two intersect mutation strategies. The two operators select individuals from the better part and the worse part according to their fitness, and so promote exploration and exploitation respectively.

Recently, two selection frameworks for mutation strategies named rank based mutation in DE(rank-DE) [6] and multiobjective sorting-based mutation strategies in DE(MS-DE) [7] are proposed. In rank-DE, some individuals in the mutation strategies are selected according to their fitness rankings in the population. The individuals which get higher rankings will has greater chance to be selected. MS-DE can be regarded as a improved version of rank-DE. In MS-DE, the fitness is used to measure exploitation and the diversity contribution is used to measure exploration, a multiobjective technical named nondominated sorting method is used to sort the population. And also the individuals which get higher rankings will more likely to be selected. The ranking standard in rank-DE and MS-DE are unchanged in whole evolution stages, which means the balance between exploration and exploitation is static. However, different evolution stages require different balance between exploration and exploitation. So in this paper, a general selection method named adaptive stochastic ranking based mutation strategies in DE(ASR-DE) is proposed. In ASR-DE, all individuals in current generation are adaptive stochastic ranked according to different evolution stages. Then the individuals with smaller rankings will more likely to be selected in mutation operators.

The overall arrangement is as follows. Section 2 present standard DE. Section 3 introduces the specifics of ASR-DE. In Sect. 4, some experiments are used to test the validity of the method. Finally, Sect. 5 gives the conclusions.

2   Standard DE

DE will generate a population at first. The most common method is randomly generate each individual of population in definition domain. And the individual will be expressed as $x_{i,G} = [x_{i,1,G}, x_{i,2,G}, \ldots, x_{i,D,G}]$, where $i = 1, 2, \ldots, NP$. G denotes the iteration of evolution and NP denotes population size. D is the dimension of the individual. The definition domain is defined by the lower and upper bounds, i.e. $L = [L_1, L_2, \ldots, L_D]$ and $U = [U_1, U_2, \ldots, U_D]$. The procedure of generating the initial individual is:

$$x_{i,j,0} = L_j + rnd_j(0,1) \cdot (U_j - L_j) \tag{1}$$

rnd(0,1) means generated randomly number in the domain of [0,1].

A mutated vector $v_{i,G}$ is generated by mutate strategies for $x_{i,G}$. And $x_{i,G}$ is called target vector. The frequently used mutation strategies are:

(1) DE/rand/1

$$v_{i,G} = x_{i_1,G} + F \cdot (x_{i_2,G} - x_{i_3,G}) \tag{2}$$

(2) DE/rand/2

$$v_{i,G} = x_{i_1,G} + F \cdot (x_{i_2,G} - x_{i_3,G}) + F \cdot (x_{i_4,G} - x_{i_5,G}) \tag{3}$$

(3) DE/best/1

$$v_{i,G} = x_{best,G} + F \cdot (x_{i_1,G} - x_{i_2,G})) \tag{4}$$

(4) DE/best/2

$$v_{i,G} = x_{best,G} + F \cdot (x_{i_1,G} - x_{i_2,G})) + F \cdot (x_{i_3,G} - x_{i_4,G}) \tag{5}$$

(5) DE/rand to best/1

$$v_{i,G} = x_{i_1,G} + F \cdot (x_{best,G} - x_{i_1,G}) + F \cdot (x_{i_2,G} - x_{i_3,G}) \tag{6}$$

(6) DE/current to best/1

$$v_{i,G} = x_{i,G} + F \cdot (x_{best,G} - x_{i,G}) + F \cdot (x_{i_1,G} - x_{i_2,G}) \tag{7}$$

The $x_{best,G}$ denotes the best individual of current generation, and the numbers i_1, i_2, i_3, i_4, i_5 are selected from the set$[1, 2, \ldots, NP]\backslash i$. $F > 0$ is a real positive parameter that controls the scaling of the vectors.

Following mutation, the crossover strategy is applied to exchanges some components of the mutant vector $v_{i,G}$ with the target vector $x_{i,G}$ to generate trial vector $u_{i,G}$. The binomial strategy is express as:

$$u_{i,j,G} = \begin{cases} v_{i,j,G}, & if \ rand_j(0,1) \leqslant CR \ or \ j = j_{rand} \\ x_{i,j,G}, & otherwise \end{cases} \tag{8}$$

$CR \in (0,1)$ is a crossover parameter, $j_{rand} \in (1,D)$ is an integer randomly chosen form 1 to D.

Lastly, a one-to-one selection scheme is used between target vector $x_{i,G}$ and trial vector $u_{i,G}$. The better vector will be chosen to update the population:

$$x_{G+1} = \begin{cases} u_{i,G}, & if \ f(u_{i,G}) \leqslant f(x_{i,G}) \\ x_{i,G}, & otherwise \end{cases} \tag{9}$$

3   Details of ASR-DE

The detailed content of ASR-DE is present at first. Then the whole method of ASR-DE is given.

3.1   Measurement of Diversity Contribution

Here we used different metric to measure individuals' contribution to the exploration and exploitation. The fitness is used to express exploitation. And a method that based on individuals' distance is used to express the exploitation which is the same as MS-DE. Lower fitness indicate the individual is more useful for exploitation. The distance-based method which is used to measure exploration is defined as:

$$f_{diversity}(x_i) = \sum_{i=1}^{NP} ||x_i - x_j|| \tag{10}$$

where

$$||x_i - x_j|| = \sqrt{\sum_{k=1}^{D}(x_{i,k} - x_{j,k})^2}, \tag{11}$$

and D is the dimension of individual. $f_{diversity}(x_i)$ equals to the sum of the distances of i'th individual from other members in the population. Greater $f_{diversity}(x_i)$ value denotes the individual is more useful for exploration.

3.2 Stochastic Ranking

Stochastic ranking is a constraint manage method [8]. The method ranks the whole individuals according to their constraint violation and objective function value. A parameter P_f is used to control the swap standard and so the balance between constraint violation and objective function value is achieved. Here we use stochastic ranking method to rank whole individuals according to their fitness values and diversity metrics. The details are as follows.

Algorithm 1.   Stochastic Ranking

Input:Indexs of whole individuals $\{1, 2, \cdots, NP\}$;fitness $\{f(x_1), f(x_2), \cdots, f(x_{NP}\}$; diversity metrics $\{f_{diversity}(x_1), f_{diversity}(x_2), \cdots, f_{diversity}(x_{NP}\}$, $P_f \in [0,1]$.

Output:rankings of whole individuals $\{R_1, R_2, \cdots, R_{NP}\}$

(1). for i=1 to NP do
(2).   for j=1 to NP-1 do
(3).   u=rand[0,1]
(4).   if u< P_f
(5).   if $f_{diversity}(x_j) < f_{diversity}(x_{j+1})$
(6).   swap the position of x_j and x_{j+1};
(7).   end if
(8).   else
(9).   if f(x$_j$)>f(x$_{j+1}$)
(10).   swap the position of x_j and x_{j+1};
(11).   end if
(12).   end if
(13).   end for
(14).   if no swap
(15).   break;
(16).   end if
(17). end for

When the current population is ranked according to Algorithm 1, every individual will get a ranking value. And better individuals will get smaller ranking values.

3.3 Setting Method of P_f

The parameter $P_f \in [0,1]$ controls the swap standard in Algorithm 1. Larger P_f value will encourage the individuals with higher $f_{diversity}(x_i)$ values to get smaller ranking values, thus promoting exploration. Smaller P_f value will encourage the individuals with lower fitness values to get smaller ranking values, thus promoting exploitation. In [9], the author use success rate to distinguishing evolution stages. When the success rate is greater than a threshold, the population is in the early evolution stage and will be more explored. Otherwise, the population is in the later evolution stage and will be more exploited. Inspired by this, an adaptive technique is used here to adjust P_f. The core conception is using success rate as feedback to adjust P_f. Furthermore, the P_f is higher when success rate is higher, otherwise P_f is smaller.

Success rate (SR) is defined as follows:

$$SR_G = \frac{NS}{NP} \tag{12}$$

NS denotes the number of trial vectors that successfully entering the next generation in G'th generation.

Specific equation for P_f is defined as follows:

$$P_{f,G} = \begin{cases} 0.95, & \text{if } G = 0 \text{ and } SR_0 \neq 0 \\ 0.05, & \text{else if } SR_0 = 0 \\ 0.05 + \dfrac{SR_{G-1}}{SR_{max}} * 0.9, & \text{else} \end{cases} \tag{13}$$

SR_0 denotes initial value of SR in the first generation. SR_{max} denotes the maximum value of SR in evolutionary history.

It can be seen from the Eq. (13) that $P_{f,G}$ is dependent on SR_{G-1}. The initial value of $P_{f,G}$ is set as 0.95 if SR_0 is not equal to zero, so the population can be relatively mostly explored in the initial generation. If SR_0 is equal to zero, it means the function is too hard for algorithm. So $P_{f,G}$ is set as 0.05 in the whole generations to strengthen exploitation. It should be noted that the upper and lower bounds of $P_{f,G}$ is set to 0.95 and 0.05. Because when the upper and lower bounds of $P_{f,G}$ is set to 1 and 0, then the whole population will be ranked only according to $f_{diversity}(x_i)$ values or fitness values if $P_{f,G}$ equal to 1 or 0. And the stochastic ranking will turn to static ranking. So here we set the upper and lower bounds of $P_{f,G}$ as a slightly smaller number than 1(0.95) and a slightly larger number than 0(0.05).

3.4 Selection Procedure

After stochastic ranking, the ranking values R_i is transformed as:

$$R_i = NP + 1 - R_i, \ i = 1, 2, \cdots, NP \tag{14}$$

The chosen probability will be computed as:

$$P_i = \frac{R_i}{NP}, i = 1, 2, \cdots, NP \tag{15}$$

From Eqs. (14)(15), we can see that better individuals with the smaller ranking values will get larger selection probability. At last, the chosen probability will be normalized. Then roulette wheel selection is used to choose individuals for mutation strategies.

3.5 Execution Process of ASR-DE

ASR-DE is an general method. And the execution of ASR-DE for DE/rand/1 will be renamed as ASR-DE/rand/1. The detailed execution process is express in Algorithm 2.

Algorithm 2. ASR-DE/rand/1
---
(1). Calculate the fitness and diversity metric for each individual according to (10)(11);
(2). Calculate $P_{f,G}$ according to (12)(13);
(3). Ranking the population according to Algorithm 1;
(4). Calculate chosen probability for all individuals on the basis of (14)(15);
(5). The roulette wheel method is used to choose individuals;
(6). The DE/rand/1 strategy is used to generate the corresponding mutant vector.

The best individual that used in the mutation strategies(such as "DE/best/1", "DE/best/2", etc) will regenerated for each individual. At first, the population will be re-ranked according to line(2–13) in Algorithm 1 for every individual. Then the best individual is set as the first individual in the ranked population. Then more better individuals may be set as best individual and release the selection pressure.

4 Experiment Results

In this section, 28 benchmark functions from CEC2013 [10] is implemented to check validity of ASR-DE. Firstly, standard DE with six different mutation strategies(DE/rand/1/bin, DE/rand/2/bin, DE/best/1/bin, DE/rand to best/1/bin) based on ASR-DE versions are compared with the original versions, MS-DE versions and rank-DE versions. Secondly, four advanced DEs (SaDE [11], CoDE [12], jDE [13], OBDE [14]) based on ASR-DE versions are comparing with the original versions, MS-DE versions and rank-DE versions. The transboundary processing method has great influence on the performance of DE. Therefore, we use the reinitialization method for all mentioned DEs to make a fair competition, i.e., the decision variable will be regenerated randomly if it is beyond its boundary constraint.

4.1   Experiment Setup

For standard DE, the parameter NP is set as 100, and F and CR are set as 0.5 and 0.9 respectively.

For four advanced DE, the parameters are not change. The experimental parameters are set as follow:

(1). Dimension of fucntions: $D = 30$;
(2). Maximun number of function evaluations (MaxFEs): 300000;
(3). Independent number of runs: 51

4.2   Validity in Standard DE

Standard DE with six mutation operators based on ASR-DE versions are comparing with their standard versions, rank-DE versions and MS-DE versions. Table 1 gives the experimental results. Here wilcoxon signed-rank test is used as the comparing standard.

Table 1. Experimental results in standard DEs.

Algorithm	vs Algorithm	w/t/l	R+	R−	p-value	$\alpha = 0.05$	$\alpha = 0.1$
ASR-DE/rand/1/bin	DE/rand/1/bin	14/10/4	289	82	1.73E-02	Yes	Yes
	rank-DE/rand/1/bin	7/13/8	146	199	7.84E−01	No	No
	MS-DE/rand/1/bin	13/10/5	289	92	1.88E-02	Yes	Yes
ASR-DE/rand/2/bin	DE/rand/2/bin	22/6/0	380	26	0.00E+00	Yes	Yes
	rank-DE/rand/2/bin	17/11/0	369	43	0.00E+00	Yes	Yes
	MS-DE/rand/2/bin	22/6/0	375	31	0.00E+00	Yes	Yes
ASR-DE/best/1/bin	DE/best/1/bin	22/3/3	340	65	3.00E−03	Yes	Yes
	rank-DE/best/1/bin	21/5/2	338	71	4.00E−03	Yes	Yes
	MS-DE/best/1/bin	11/12/5	194	212	6.34E−01	No	No
ASR-DE/best/2/bin	DE/best/2/bin	17/10/1	325	79	4.00E−03	Yes	Yes
	rank-DE/best/2/bin	18/8/2	315	88	1.61E−02	Yes	Yes
	MS-DE/best/2/bin	19/8/1	380	26	0.00E+00	Yes	Yes
ASR-DE/r2b/1/bin	DE/r2b/1/bin	20/5/3	385	16	0.00E+00	Yes	Yes
	rank-DE/r2b/1/bin	15/10/3	365	42	1.00E−02	Yes	Yes
	MS-DE/r2b/1/bin	14/6/8	265	139	8.03E−02	No	Yes
ASR-DE/c2b/1/bin	DE/c2b/1/bin	24/3/1	345	62	3.00E−03	Yes	Yes
	rank-DE/c2b/1/bin	22/3/3	386	20	5.00E−02	Yes	Yes
	MS-DE/c2b/1/bin	17/3/9	321	86	1.42E−02	Yes	Yes

In the unimodel functions (F1–F5), ASR-DE/rand2/bin and ASR-DE/best2/bin achieve prominent better results than other three versions (original DE, rank-DE, and MS-DE) in all functions. ASR-DE/rand1/bin, ASR-DE/best1/bin, ASR-DE/rand-to-best1/bin and ASR-DE/current-to-best1/bin achieve better results in one or functions. Thus, the advantages of ASR-DE are not obvious in unimodel functions.

In the multimodal functions (F6–F20). ASR-DE versions obviously better results comparing with standard versions and MS-DE versions in most cases. In the hybrid compositon functions (F21–F28), ASR-DE/rand/2/bin, ASR-DE/rand-to-best1/bin and ASR-DE/current-to-best1/bin are significantly better than other three versions in most functions. Overall, ASR-DE versions obtain obvious advantages in most multimodal functions comparing with other versions.

4.3   Validity in Advanced DE

In this section, four advanced DEs (CoDE, jDE, SaDE, OBDE) with ASR-DE versions are comparing with their original versions, rank-DE versions and MS-DE versions. The four advanced DE algorithms have different features. CoDE uses three couples of different mutation operators and parameters to generate three offsprings for each target vector. jDE and SaDE use adaptive method to select mutation operators or set parameters CR and F. Opposition learning strategy is introduced in OBDE for population initialization and generation jumping.

Table 2. Experimental results in advanced DE.

Algorithm	vs Algorithm	w/t/l	R+	R−	p-value	$\alpha = 0.05$	$\alpha = 0.1$
ASR-CoDE	CoDE	15/13/0	383	23	0.00E+00	Yes	Yes
	rank-CoDE	9/19/0	247	155	4.45E−01	No	No
	MS-CoDE	16/12/0	362	38	0.00E+00	Yes	Yes
ASR-jDE	jDE	12/10/6	238	65	6.97E−02	No	Yes
	rank-jDE	7/16/5	196	153	6.89E−01	No	No
	MS-jDE	11/10/7	273	72	3.00E−03	Yes	Yes
ASR-SaDE	SaDE	19/5/4	343	35	0.00E+00	Yes	Yes
	rank-SaDE	7/14/7	194	181	7.13E−01	No	No
	MS-SaDE	14/10/4	261	114	1.82E−01	No	No
ASR-OBDE	OBDE	17/7/4	315	91	1.10E−02	Yes	Yes
	rank-OBDE	11/12/5	223	151	5.57E−01	No	No
	MS-OBDE	13/8/7	273	133	1.96E−01	No	No

Table 2 shows the detailed results.

In the unimodel functions (F1–F5), ASR-CoDE, ASR-jDE and ASR-SaDE achieve significantly better results in most functions. ASR-OBDE is significantly better than other versions in one function. Overall, ASR-DE versions takes obvious advantages in most test functions.

In the multimodal functions (F6–F20), ASR-CoDE, ASR-jDE and ASR-OBDE achieve significantly better results in most fucntions. ASR-SaDE achieves significantly better results only in four functions. In the hybrid compositon functions (F21–F28), ASR-CoDE, ASR-jDE and ASR-OBDE achieve significantly better results in five fucntions. ASR-SaDE achieve significantly better results in three functions. Overall, ASR-DE versions are better than the original versions, ran-DE versions and MS-DE versions in most multimodal functions.

Through the above analysis, it can be seen that ASR-DE versions are significantly better than other versions both in most unimodel functions and multimodal functions.

5   Conclusion

In this paper, a new selection framework named ASR-DE is proposed to balance exploration and exploitation for DE. ASR-DE uses stochastic ranking method to rank all individuals in each generation. Success rate is regarded as a standard to adaptive control the parameter P_f in stochastic ranking method. Specifically, P_f is directly proportional to value of success rate between the interval [0.05, 0.95]. After stochastic ranking, selection probabilities are calculated for each individual. Better individuals will get greater selection probabilities. Then roulette wheel method is used to choose individuals. Comprehensive experimental results show that ASR-DE versions take obvious advantage comparing with original versions, rank-DE versions and MS-DE versions in original DE with six different mutation operators and four advanced DEs.

Acknowledgement. Supported by National Key Research and Development Program of China under grant number 2017YFC1405403, and National Natural Science Foundation of China under grant number 6107505961300127, and Green Industry Technology Leding Project (product development category) of Hubei University of Technology under grant number CPYF2017008, and Doctor's program of Hubei University of Technology under grant number BSQD2017047, BSQD2017045.

References

1. Liu, S.H., Mernik, M.: Exploration and exploitation in evolutionary algorithms: a survey. ACM Comput. Surv. **45**(3), 1–33 (2013)
2. Storn, R., Price, K.: Differential Evolution - A Simple and Efficient Heuristic for Global Optimization over Continuous Spaces, 1st edn. Kluwer Academic Publishers, Holland (1997)
3. Zhang, J., Sanderson, A.C.: JADE: adaptive differential evolution with optional external archive. IEEE Trans. Evol. Comput. **13**(5), 945–958 (2009)
4. Chiang, C.W., Lee, W.P., Heh, J.S.: JA 2-Opt based differential evolution for global optimization. Appl. Soft Comput. **10**(4), 1200–1207 (2010)
5. Zhou, Y., Li, X.P., Gao, L.: A differential evolution algorithm with intersect mutation operator. Appl. Soft Comput. **13**(1), 390–401 (2013)
6. Gong, W., Cai, Z.: Differential evolution with ranking-based mutation operators. IEEE Trans. Cybern. **6**(43), 2066–2081 (2013)

7. Wang, J., Liao, J., Zhou, Y., et al.: Differential evolution enhanced with multiobjective sorting-based mutation operators. IEEE Trans. Cybern. **12**(44), 2792–2805 (2014)
8. Runarsson, T.P., Yao, X.: Stochastic ranking for constrained evolutionary optimization. IEEE Trans. Evol. Comput. **3**(4), 284–294 (2000)
9. Tang, L., Dong, Y., Liu, J.: Differential evolution with an individual-dependent mechanism. IEEE Trans. Evol. Comput. **4**(19), 560–574 (2015)
10. Liang, J.J., Qu, B.Y., Suganthan, P.N., Hernández-Díaz, A.G.: Problem definitions and evaluation criteria for the CEC 2013 special session on real-parameter optimization. In: IEEE Congress on Evolution Computation 2013, pp. 1–20. IEEE Press, Singapore (2013)
11. Qin, A.K., Huang, V.L., Suganthan, P.N.: Differential evolution algorithm with strategy adaptation for global numerical optimization. IEEE Trans. Evol. Comput. **2**(13), 398–417 (2009)
12. Wang, Y., Cai, Z., Zhang, Q.: Differential evolution with composite trial vector generation strategies and control parameters. IEEE Trans. Evol. Comput. **1**(15), 55–66 (2011)
13. Brest, J., Greiner, S., Boskovic, B., et al.: Self-adapting control parameters in differential evolution: a comparative study on numerical benchmark problems. IEEE Trans. Evol. Comput. **6**(10), 646–657 (2007)
14. Rahnamayan, S., Tizhoosh, H.R., Salama, M.M.A.: Opposition-based differential evolution. IEEE Trans. Evol. Comput. **1**(12), 64–79 (2008)

Automatic Object Segmentation and Detection, and Image Colorization

An Enhanced Region-Based Model for Segmentation Images with Intensity Inhomogeneity

Haiping Yu[1,2(✉)] and Xiaoli Lin[3]

[1] Wuhan College of Foreign Languages and Foreign Affairs, Wuhan, China
seapingyu@163.com
[2] City College of Wuhan University of Science and Technology, Wuhan, China
[3] Wuhan University of Science and Technology, Wuhan, China

Abstract. Segmentation of images with intensity inhomogeneity is always challenging due to low resolution, blurred boundaries and poor illumination. Although existing image segmentation methods were widely used, there exists some shortcomings in segmenting intensity inhomogeneous images, such as not considering the spatial interrelation within the central pixel and its neighborhood. Therefore, this paper proposes an enhanced region-based active contour model for segmenting images with intensity inhomogeneity. In this model, a range-based adaptive bilateral filter is utilized to preserve edge structures and resist the noise of the image. Then an effective energy functional is constructed into the level set framework. With the permission of keeping the original shape of the image, a regularization term is utilized to refrain from the process of re-initialization and speed up the curve evolution. In the end, some experiments on synthetic and real images and contrast with the classic segmentation models are executed. The proposed model is more accuracy than other classic models.

Keywords: Image segmentation · Region-based model · Level set

1 Introduction

Image segmentation plays a vital role in image processing and computer vision such as pattern recognition, image analysis and medical diagnosis. However, due to the complete noise, intensity inhomogeneity and lower gray contrast, these features cause it is extremely challenging in many fields. Particularly, the characteristics of intensity inhomogeneity is a huge problem in the segmentation fields. The idea of image segmentation is to split an image into some sub-regions that do not overlap each other. In particular, for each pixel x in the image domain Ω. We assume that the domain of the image contains N non-overlapping Sub-regions, which means that: $\Omega = \cup \Omega_i (i = 1, 2, 3, \ldots \ldots N)$, $\Omega_i \cap \Omega_j = \Phi$, $\forall i \neq j$. Many of segmentation methods have been proposed, such as fuzzy clustering methods [1–3], deep learning based methods [4–6], and super pixel based methods [7, 8] and active contour methods (ACM) [9–15]. Fuzzy clustering methods work well on noise free images, however, these methods cannot accurately segment images corrupted by severe noise, low contrast and intensity inhomogeneity. Recently, deep learning based methods are currently in a stage of rapid

© Springer Nature Singapore Pte Ltd. 2019
H. Peng et al. (Eds.): ISICA 2018, CCIS 986, pp. 165–176, 2019.
https://doi.org/10.1007/978-981-13-6473-0_15

development and have been approved in segmentation fields. However, this type of method requires a large number of training sample sets, which is not suitable for a small number of intensity inhomogeneous images, especially medical images. Super pixel segmentation methods generally require preprocessing and are prone to over-segmentation. ACM has been widely used to segmenting images, it is several desirable advantages for segmentation images with intensity inhomogeneity over the above mentioned segmentation methods.

In ACMs, they are divided into two major categories: one is edge-based model and the other is region-based model. Edge-based model uses the gradient of the image to get the segmentation result, which is effective to images with sharp contours. Recent years, region-based ACM and its variant models have been well addressed for image segmentation, which utilizes spatial statistical information to guide the curve evolution. The superiority is that it utilizes the local statistical information and the intensity of image itself in the local region-based models [16]. The Chan-Vese (CV) model, addressed by Chan and Vese in the Ref. [9], is one of the famous region-based model. Later, many region-based segmentation models are addressed to segment intensity inhomogeneous images. In related works, we will introduce some related models.

The rest of this paper is composed as follows: we review three typical region-based methods for image segmentation in Sect. 2. In Sect. 3, we detailed elaborate the proposed model with three subsections. Section 4 analyzes the comparison results with the representative segmentation models on artificial and real images. Finally, in Sect. 5, we end with conclusion and our future work.

2   Related Works

2.1   The CV Model

The CV model, a well-known region-based model, has been proposed by Chan and Vese in 2002. It is on the assumption that there is the same intensity value in two partitions, which refer the target to be segmented and background. Specifically, we use $I(x)$ as the test image and ϕ as its domain, the contour C is the curve, the energy functional is defined as follows:

$$
\begin{aligned}
E^{CV}(\phi) = \mu \int_{\Omega} \delta(\phi)|\nabla\phi|dxdy + v \int_{\Omega} H(\phi)dxdy \\
+ \lambda_1 \int_{in(C)} |I(x,y) - c_1|^2 dxdy + \lambda_2 \int_{out(C)} |I(x,y) - c_2|^2 dxdy
\end{aligned}
\tag{1}
$$

Here, $\mu, v, \lambda_1, \lambda_2$ are non-negative constant weight parameters. $I(x, y)$ represents the observed image, $H(\phi)$ is a Heaviside function shown in Eq. (2), and $\delta(\phi)$ (see Eq. (3)) is the derivative of $H(\phi)$. $in(C)$ and $out(C)$ are the region inside and outside of the contour C, respectively.

$$H(x) = \frac{1}{2}\left[1 + \frac{2}{\pi}\arctan\left(\frac{x}{\varepsilon}\right)\right] \tag{2}$$

$$\delta(x) = \frac{\partial H(x)}{\partial x} = \frac{\varepsilon}{\pi \cdot (\varepsilon^2 + x^2)} \tag{3}$$

2.2 The Local Image Fitting Model

To accurately segment intensity inhomogeneous images, Zhang et al. constructed a model based on local information, which utilized a truncated Gaussian function as local constraint information. It improved the computational efficiency and reduced the chance of the curve evolution function falling into local optimum. The LIF energy functional is defined as follows:

$$E^{LIF}(\phi) = \frac{1}{2}\int_\phi \left|I(x) - I^{LFI}(x)\right|^2 dx, x \in \Omega \tag{4}$$

Where $I^{LFI}(x)$, named a local fitted image formulation, the mathematical formulation is defined as follows:

$$I^{LFI} = m_1 H_\varepsilon(\phi) + m_2(1 - H_\varepsilon(\phi)) \tag{5}$$

Here, m_1 and m_2 are respectively the average intensity of inside and outside the region. The definition see the Ref. [17].

2.3 The Local Statistical Active Contour Model (LSACM)

Though the LIF model was more computationally effective in segmenting intensity inhomogeneous images. When the image is disrupted by noise, lower resolution and more overlapping. This model will not perform well. Therefore, Zhang et.al have addressed a new model, named a locally statistical active contour model (LSACM) [18]. In this model, a clever mapping was created, which was mainly used to minimize overlapping. The energy function was defined:

$$E_{\theta,B}^L = \sum_{i=1}^n \int_\Omega \int_{\Omega_i} K_\rho(x,y)\left(\log(\sigma_i) + \frac{(I(y) - B(x)c_i)^2}{2\sigma_i^2}\right) dy dx \tag{6}$$

In Eq. (6), $\Omega = \sum_{i=1}^n \Omega_i$, with $\Omega_i \cap \Omega_j = \emptyset$, for all $i \neq j$, $K_\rho(x,y)$ is the indicator function of local region O_x. ρ controls the size of the local region. $\theta_i = \{c_i, \sigma_i\}, \theta = \{\theta_i, i = 1, \ldots, n\}$.

Compared with CV model and LIF model, this LSACM segment well in intensity inhomogeneous images, especially medical images. However, the model has limitations which is the noise of the image are assumed to be Gaussian distribution. In addition, the model cannot consider the influence of spatial constraint information.

3 The Proposed Model

Base on the above analysis, we address a novel enhanced region-based model, in which edge properties can be well preserved and segmentation results have more accurate. The main idea is to construct a data-driven energy model, which is based on the enhanced range-based bilateral filter. Different from other models, the filter can preserve edge sharpness and reduce noise.

3.1 The Enhanced Region-Based Bilateral Filter

The basic bilateral filter has some merit over other filter technology. It is based on two aspects [19–21]: one is for considering the relationship among the pixels of the image; the other is for considering the image spatial information, which is vital to accurate segmentation.

In our model, we construct an efficient enhanced bilateral filter. For an image $f(x)$, the mathematical expression description is defined as:

$$h(x) = k_r^{-1} \int_\Omega f(\xi)c(\xi,x)s(\xi,x,\zeta)d\xi \tag{7}$$

With the normalization

$$k(x) = \int_\Omega c(\xi,x)s(\xi,x,\zeta)d\xi \tag{8}$$

And the function of c is used to measure the geometric closeness in the local area; s is used for gauging the spatial information. The definitions are followed as:

$$c(\xi,x) = exp\left(\frac{||\xi - x||^2}{2\sigma_1^2}\right) \tag{9}$$

$$s(\xi,x,\zeta) = exp\left(\frac{||f(\xi) - f(x) - \zeta(x)||^2}{2\sigma_2^2}\right) \tag{10}$$

To boost the robustness of noise, we set a local region as an enhanced filter region. In Eq. (10), the function $\zeta(x)$ controls the scale of the local region. The definition is followed as:

$$\zeta(x) = \begin{cases} |f(x) - M(\Omega_y)|, & |x - y| \le \rho \\ = 0, & otherwise \end{cases} \tag{11}$$

Where Ω_y means the neighborhood centered the image of pixel x; $M(\bullet)$ represents the mean intensity value within the neighborhood centered on the pixel x.

3.2   The Energy Model Based on Enhanced Region-Based Bilateral Filter

In this subsection, we propose and analyze the level set energy model in detail. In the proposed model, all notations is followed as:

(1) $I : \Omega \to \mathcal{R}^d$ represents the observed image I, Ω means the domain of the image, d means the dimension of the image;
(2) C is the closed contour in the domain Ω of I;
(3) $h(x)$ comes from the Eq. (7).
(4) λ_i, $(i = 1, 2)$ are non-negative constants.
(5) f_i, $(i = 1, 2)$ are the average intensity value inside and outside of the closed C, respectively

Therefore, we construct the proposed energy function as follows:

$$\varepsilon = \sum_{i=1}^{2} \lambda_i \int_{\Omega_i} K(x - y)|h(y)I(y) - f_i(x)|^2 dy \tag{12}$$

Where $K(\bullet)$ is an indicator function, the value is 1 in the neighborhood of the pixel, otherwise is zero.

In the domain Ω, we get the energy function:

$$E(C, f_1, f_2) = \int_{\Omega} \varepsilon(f_1, f_2) + v|C| \tag{13}$$

Using the LSF ϕ to replace the contour C, we redefine the equation as:

$$E(\phi, f_1(x), f_2(x)) = \sum_{i=1}^{2} \lambda_i \int \int K_\rho |h(y)I(y) - f_i|^2 M_i(\phi) dy dx \tag{14}$$

Here, $M_1(\phi) = H(\phi), M_2(\phi) = 1 - H(\phi)$. In order to keep the LSF's stability during the curve evolution. In our model, we add a regularization term. Therefore, the final energy function can be rewritten as:

$$\mathcal{F}(\phi, f_1, f_2) = \sum_{i=1}^{2} \lambda_i \int \int K_\rho |h(y)I(y) - f_i|^2 M_i(\phi) dy dx \\ + v \int \delta |\nabla \phi| dx + \frac{1}{2} \mu \int |\nabla \phi - 1|^2 dx \tag{15}$$

Here μ and v are nonnegative constants. Next, we minimize the Eq. (15) by using gradient flow method [22–24] described in Subsect. 3.3.

3.3   Energy Minimization

In Eq. (15), we first fix the implicit function ϕ, and minimize the energy functional about $f_1(x)$ and $f_2(x)$. Therefore, we get the following Euler-lagrange equations:

$$\int K(x-y)M_i(\phi)(h(y)I(y)-f_i(x))^2 dy = 0, i = 1,2 \tag{16}$$

Accordingly, we get the expression about f_i ($i = 1, 2$):

$$f_i(x) = \frac{K_\rho(x)*[M_i(\phi)h(x)I(x)]}{K_\rho(x)*M_i(\phi)} \tag{17}$$

In fact, the values of $f_i(x)$ ($i = 1, 2$) are mean value of the intensities within the neighborhood of the pixel x. And the size is related to the parameter ρ.

Finally, we get the energy functional about ϕ, by solving the following the equation:

$$\frac{\partial\phi}{\partial t} = -\delta(\phi)(\lambda_1 e_1 - \lambda_2 e_2) + \upsilon\delta(\phi)div\left(\frac{\nabla\phi}{|\nabla\phi|}\right) + \mu\left(\nabla^2\phi - div\left(\frac{\nabla\phi}{|\nabla\phi|}\right)\right) \tag{18}$$

And, e_1 and e_2 are followed as:

$$e_i(x) = \int K_\rho(y-x)|h(x)I(x)-f_i(y)|^2 dy, i = 1,2 \tag{19}$$

4 Experimental Results

4.1 Experimental on Artificial Images

In the first experiment, we verify the proposed model effectiveness. Figure 1 shows the segmentation results for artificial images and their level set function. The first image has no noise, the latter three images are corrupted by noise. It is obvious that our model can successfully extracts the object boundaries. Their level set functions can keep good stability.

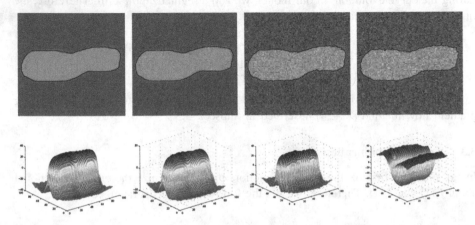

Fig. 1. Segmentation results of our model for artificial image, its noisy image and its level set function.

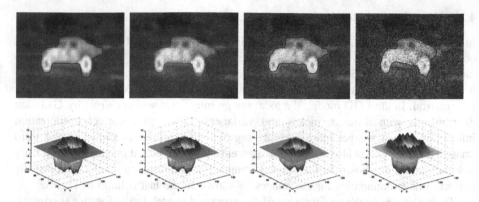

Fig. 2. Segmentation results of our model for synthetic image, its noisy image and its level set function.

In the second experiment, we also evaluated the effectiveness of the proposed model on an edge-blurred image and its noisy image. As shown in Fig. 2, the image boundaries are quite weak. It is clearly shown that our model accurately segments the object shapes.

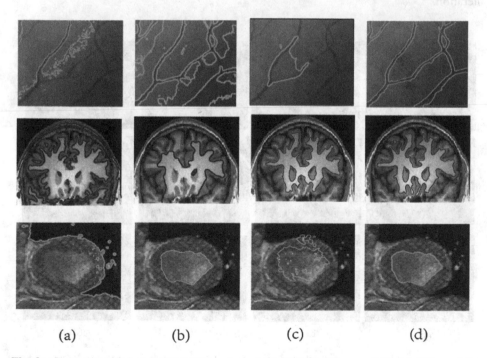

     (a)   (b)   (c)   (d)

Fig. 3. Comparisons of our model with other classic segmentation models: (a) CV model, (b) LGD model, (c) LSACM, (d) our model.

4.2 Experimental Results

In the third experiment, comparison results in segmenting the real images are executed between the proposed model and other classic models: the CV model [9], the LGD model [25] and the LSACM [18]. As shown in Fig. 3, the CV model has poor performance in segmenting the images. The reason lies in it is based on the global intensity information. In the LGD model, the local image intensities was construct by Gaussian distributions with different means and variances. If we give correct initialization information, then we get more accurate segmentation results as shown in the third image. The LSACM is also suitable for segmenting MRI medical images with intensity inhomogeneity as shown in the second image. By contrast, our model successfully extracts image boundaries for the images as shown in the last column of Fig. 3.

To further verify the performance of the proposed model, in the fourth experiment, we test the proposed model for three images with severe intensity inhomogeneity, the results in Fig. 4 show that the RSF model can accurately segment two images. And our model successfully extracts all the boundaries of the images. For the LVC model [26], it cannot segments the first image, because the image has the feature of poor illumination. The main reason lies that the enhanced range-based bilateral filter can preserve edge sharpness and reduce noise.

We implemented the proposed model in MatlabR2013b. In the proposed model, the main computational time is closely related to the scale of the image. The complexity of the four models' competitive algorithms is $O(N)$, here N represents the number of iteration.

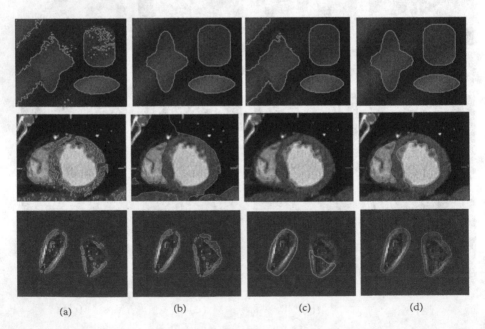

(a)   (b)   (c)   (d)

Fig. 4. Comparisons of our model with other classic segmentation models: (a) the CV model, (b) the RSF model, (c) the LVC model, (d) our model.

5   Quantity Analysis

In this section, we evaluate the efficiency of the proposed model using similarity measurement. In segmentation fields, Jaccard similarity (*JI*) coefficient is a well statistic used for measuring similarity between the ground truth and the real segmentation result. The JI can be computed by

$$JI(S_1, S_2) = \frac{|S_1 \cap S_2|}{|S_1 \cup S_2|} \qquad (20)$$

In segmentation fields, S_1 and S_2 are the segmented object region and the ground truth, respectively.

Next, we use a synthetic image with different Gaussian noise to evaluate the efficiency of our proposed model as shown in Fig. 5, and the *JI* values are listed in Table 1. When the noise is small, the JI values are relatively similar. As image noise increases, the boundaries of the image become increasingly blurred. The improved bilateral filter can resist the noise and preserve the detail of the image, the CV model cannot resist the noise of the image. For the LCV and the RSF models, when the influence of noise is small, the method can effectively segment the image. However, when the noise is gradually increased, the method cannot resist the influence of noise, and thus cannot be correctly segmented. Obviously, comparison results shows that the proposed model is more efficient than other models shown in Fig. 5.

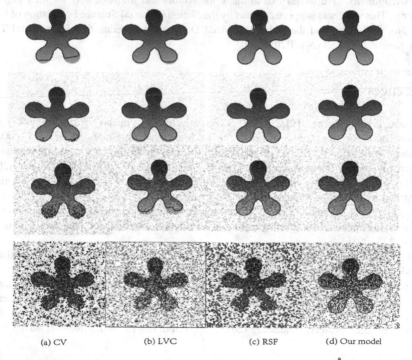

(a) CV   (b) LVC   (c) RSF   (d) Our model

Fig. 5. Comparisons among the CV, the LVC, the RSF model and our model with different noise: (a) the CV model, (b) the LVC model, (c) the RSF model, (d) our model.

Table 1. Comparisons of Jaccard Index with different Gaussian noise.

Line number	CV	LVC	RSF	Our model
Line 1	0.9872	0.9921	0.9799	0.9965
Line 2	0.9821	0.9899	0.9831	0.9913
Line 3	0.8919	0.9822	0.9841	0.9901
Line 4	0.7692	0.7312	0.6954	0.9853

6 Conclusions and Future Works

In this paper, we have proposed an enhanced region-based model for image segmentation. The proposed model efficiently utilizes a range-based adaptive bilateral filter to preserve the sharp edges and reduce the noise of the image. In addition, the model use a regularization term to ensure the regularity of the level set function and to avoid the process of the expensive re-initialization. Comparisons with the well-known models in the literature [9, 10, 18, 25] and [26], the proposed model is more efficient.

In future work, we mainly focus on three directions but not limited: (1) we will utilize intelligent algorithms and hardware resources to enhance the efficiency of the proposed model [27–29]. (2) We will absorb other related fields methods to improve the efficiency of the proposed model, such as image retrieval [30–32] and image super-resolution [33–35].

Acknowledgments. We would like to thank the editors and the reviewers for their pertinent comments. This work was supported in part by the National Natural Science Foundation of China (Grant No. 61502356) and the Hubei Provincial Department of Education Science and Technology Research Project (No. B2016590).

References

1. Chuang, K.S., Tzeng, H.L., Chen, S., et al.: Fuzzy c-means clustering with spatial information for image segmentation. Comput. Med. Imaging Graph. **30**(1), 9–15 (2006)
2. Gong, M., Liang, Y., Shi, J., et al.: Fuzzy c-means clustering with local information and kernel metric for image segmentation. IEEE Trans. Image Process. **22**(2), 573–584 (2013)
3. Han, Y., Shi, P.: An improved ant colony algorithm for fuzzy clustering in image segmentation. Neurocomputing **70**(4–6), 665–671 (2007)
4. Xu, J., Luo, X., Wang, G., et al.: A deep convolutional neural network for segmenting and classifying epithelial and stromal regions in histopathological images. Neurocomputing **191**, 214–223 (2016)
5. Qi, C.R., Su, H., Mo, K., et al.: PointNet: deep learning on point sets for 3D classification and segmentation. Proc. Comput. Vis. Pattern Recognit. (CVPR) **1**(2), 4 (2017)
6. Prasoon, A., Petersen, K., Igel, C., Lauze, F., Dam, E., Nielsen, M.: Deep feature learning for knee cartilage segmentation using a triplanar convolutional neural network. In: Mori, K., Sakuma, I., Sato, Y., Barillot, C., Navab, N. (eds.) MICCAI 2013. LNCS, vol. 8150, pp. 246–253. Springer, Heidelberg (2013). https://doi.org/10.1007/978-3-642-40763-5_31

7. Achanta, R., Shaji, A., Smith, K., Lucchi, A., Fua, P., Süsstrunk, S.: SLIC superpixels compared to state-of-the-art superpixel methods. IEEE Trans. Pattern Anal. Mach. Intell. **34** (11), 2274–2282 (2012)

8. Cheng, J., et al.: Superpixel classification based optic disc and optic cup segmentation for glaucoma screening. IEEE Trans. Med. Imaging **32**(6), 1019–1032 (2013)

9. Chan, T.F., Vese, L.A.: Active contours without edges. IEEE Trans. Image Process. **10**(2), 266–277 (2001)

10. Li, C., Kao, C.Y., Gore, J.C., et al.: Minimization of region-scalable fitting energy for image segmentation. In: IEEE Transactions on Image Processing: A Publication of the IEEE Signal Processing Society, vol. 17, no. 10, p. 1940 (2008)

11. Zhao, Y., Rada, L., Chen, K., et al.: Automated vessel segmentation using infinite perimeter active contour model with hybrid region information with application to retinal images. IEEE Trans. Med. Imaging **34**(9), 1797–1807 (2015)

12. Zhou, S., Wang, J., Zhang, S., Liang, Y., Gong, Y.: Active contour model based on local and global intensity information for medical image segmentation. Neurocomputing **186**, 107–118 (2016)

13. Niu, S., Chen, Q., de Sisternes, L., et al.: Robust noise region-based active contour model via local similarity factor for image segmentation. Pattern Recognit. **61**, 104–119 (2017)

14. Yu, H., He, F., Pan, Y.: A novel region-based active contour model via local patch similarity measure for image segmentation. Multimed. Tools Appl. **77**, 1–23 (2018)

15. Sun, W., Dong, E., Qiao, H.: A fuzzy energy-based active contour model with adaptive contrast constraint for local segmentation. Signal Image Video Process. **12**(1), 91–98 (2018)

16. Haiping, Yu., Huali, Z.: Regularized level set method by incorporating local statistical information and global similarity compatibility for image segmentation. In: Huang, D.-S., Bevilacqua, V., Prashan, P. (eds.) ICIC 2015. LNCS, vol. 9225, pp. 388–399. Springer, Cham (2015). https://doi.org/10.1007/978-3-319-22180-9_38

17. Zhang, K., Song, H., Zhang, L.: Active contours driven by local image fitting energy. Pattern Recognit. **43**(4), 1199–1206 (2010)

18. Zhang, K., Zhang, L., Lam, K.M., et al.: A level set approach to image segmentation with intensity inhomogeneity. IEEE Trans. Cybern. **46**(2), 546–557 (2016)

19. Zhang, B., Allebach, J.P.: Adaptive bilateral filter for sharpness enhancement and noise removal. IEEE Trans. Image Process. **17**(5), 664–678 (2008)

20. Farbman, Z., Fattal, R., Lischinski, D., et al.: Edge-preserving decompositions for multi-scale tone and detail manipulation. ACM Trans. Graph. (TOG) **27**(3), 67 (2008)

21. Kang, X., Li, S., Benediktsson, J.A.: Spectral–spatial hyperspectral image classification with edge-preserving filtering. IEEE Trans. Geosci. Remote Sens. **52**(5), 2666–2677 (2014)

22. Michailovich, O., Rathi, Y., Tannenbaum, A.: Image segmentation using active contours driven by the Bhattacharyya gradient flow. IEEE Trans. Image Process. **16**(11), 2787–2801 (2007)

23. Adams, S., Dirr, N., Peletier, M.A., et al.: From a large-deviations principle to the Wasserstein gradient flow: a new micro-macro passage. Commun. Math. Phys. **307**(3), 791 (2011)

24. Fritzsch, P., Ramos, A.: The gradient flow coupling in the Schrödinger functional. J. High Energy Phys. **2013**(10), 8 (2013)

25. Wang, L., He, L., Mishra, A., et al.: Active contours driven by local Gaussian distribution fitting energy. Signal Process. **89**(12), 2435–2447 (2009)

26. Zhang, K., Zhang, L., Song, H., et al.: Active contours with selective local or global segmentation: a new formulation and level set method. Image Vis. Comput. **28**(4), 668–676 (2010)

27. Zhou, Y., He, F., Qiu, Y.: Dynamic strategy based parallel ant colony optimization on GPUs for TSPs. Sci. China Inf. Sci. **60**(6), 068102 (2017)

28. Zhou, Y., He, F., Qiu, Y.: Optimization of parallel iterated local search algorithms on graphics processing unit. J. Supercomput. **72**(6), 2394–2416 (2016)

29. Alsmirat, M.A., Jararweh, Y., Al-Ayyoub, M., et al.: Accelerating compute intensive medical imaging segmentation algorithms using hybrid CPU-GPU implementations. Multimed. Tools Appl. **76**(3), 3537–3555 (2017)

30. Xia, Z., Wang, X., Zhang, L., et al.: A privacy-preserving and copy-deterrence content-based image retrieval scheme in cloud computing. IEEE Trans. Inf. Forensics Secur. **11**(11), 2594–2608 (2016)

31. Gonde, A.B., Murala, S., Vipparthi, S.K., Maheshwari, R., Balasubramanian, R.: 3D local transform patterns: a new feature descriptor for image retrieval. In: Raman, B., Kumar, S., Roy, P.P., Sen, D. (eds.) Proceedings of International Conference on Computer Vision and Image Processing. AISC, vol. 460, pp. 495–507. Springer, Singapore (2017). https://doi.org/10.1007/978-981-10-2107-7_45

32. Lu, X., Zheng, X., Li, X.: Latent semantic minimal hashing for image retrieval. IEEE Trans. Image Process. **26**(1), 355–368 (2017)

33. Liu, Y., Lu, Y., Yang, X., et al.: Amplified stimulated emission in up conversion nanoparticles for super-resolution nanoscopy. Nature **543**(7644), 229 (2017)

34. Shi, X., Garcia III, G., Van De Weghe, J.C., et al.: Super-resolution microscopy reveals that disruption of ciliary transition-zone architecture causes Joubert syndrome. Nat. Cell Biol. **19**(10), 1178 (2017)

35. Mo, G.C.H., Ross, B., Hertel, F., et al.: Genetically encoded biosensors for visualizing live-cell biochemical activity at super-resolution. Nat. Methods **14**(4), 427 (2017)

Algorithm Research on Distributed Pattern Recognition

Zelin Wang[✉], Zhengqi Zhou, and Muyan Zhou

College of Computer Science and Technology, NanTong University,
Nantong, JiangSu, China
whwzl@whu.edu.cn

Abstract. The methodology of tradition pattern recognition is a that of from macroscopic to microcosmos, the source of a pattern is refused or mistake recognition lie in impropriety abstraction and choiceing the character. A framework of distributed pattern recognition be presented in this paper, it is a methodology of from microcosmos to macroscopic. The main innovation are: (1) avoid the difficulty of abstraction and choiceing the character, provide a new technology for complex object recognition, (2) spread pattern recognition of static sate and concentration into dynamic state and distributed.

Keywords: Pattern recognition · Distributed · Agent

1 Introduction

Pattern recognition is a basic human intelligence, in daily life, people often conduct "pattern recognition". With the advent of 1940s and 50s the rise of computer artificial intelligence, pattern recognition, in early 1960s the rapid development and become a new subject. In just 50 years, emerge in an endless stream pattern recognition methods: Classification based identification of statistical patterns [1] and Syntax pattern recognition [2]; Bionic pattern recognition based on cognition [3] Cooperative pattern recognition based on self-organization [4]; synergetic pattern recognition based on self-organization; based on subspace pattern recognition [5] algebra and so on. They have been in the weather forecast, satellite aerial photograph interpretation, many aspects of industrial product testing, character recognition, voice recognition, fingerprint recognition biological feature recognition, medical image analysis has been applied to [6]'s success but all these methods are the problems and The nature is inseparable, and there is a big gap with the human pattern recognition process.

Patterns reflect the essence of the system (macro level), features reflect the appearance of the system (micro level), and the task of pattern recognition is to establish the connection between the essence and appearance of the system, a complex system. In order to complete the identification activities, countless neurons need to collaborate in a highly regular and highly orderly manner, due to collaboration. New properties emerge at the macro level, reflecting an integrative effect, and these new attributes are not present in the micro level [7].

© Springer Nature Singapore Pte Ltd. 2019
H. Peng et al. (Eds.): ISICA 2018, CCIS 986, pp. 177–189, 2019.
https://doi.org/10.1007/978-981-13-6473-0_16

Pattern recognition is similar to decision-making, requiring thought and concurrency and collaboration between the elements that make up the system [8]. The literature shows that the various components of the brain (neurons), which work at milliseconds, can process a very high amount of information in a few seconds at a point, despite the slowness of their components. In contrast, computer components are very fast, but the recognition images are so slow that they are impotent [9].

With the rapid development of distributed computing, Internet of things, and large data processing technologies, artificial intelligence research has begun to shift its emphasis to Agent computing. Through Agent's research, researchers are trying to find a crowdsourcing mechanism to overcome the limitations of a single system [10]. With the rapid development of distributed computing, Internet of things, and large data processing technologies, artificial intelligence research has begun to shift its focus to Agent computing, and researchers are trying to overcome the limitations of a single system by finding a crowdsourcing mechanism through Agent's research. Research and applications of Agent and MAS (Multi-Agent System) have made great progress [11].

Inspired by MAS, according to the pattern recognition of the goals and tasks of the individual can be completed independently, we propose a distributed pattern recognition framework, the main work: the pattern recognition process is divided into two stages: the emergence of pattern modeling and modeling mode. To solve the "memory", "classification" problem solving pattern emerge.

2   Limitations of Traditional Pattern Recognition Method

The human pattern recognition process is divided into two types. The first case: if the input mode has never seen, the need for feature extraction, establish the model of input pattern, then the pattern recognition process is actually a model, is a bottom-up process (micro and macro); second cases: if the pattern had seen, often using reasoning method the essence of the pattern recognition is a pattern emerged, is a process of top-down (macro and micro) computer. The traditional pattern recognition methods confuse pattern modeling and pattern emerge the two distinct processes, basically is a "micro macro", which is caused by pattern recognition are difficult to be used one of the basic reasons to solve practical problems.

Pattern recognition is bringing hope to people. At the same time, we should also see that due to the diversity and complexity of the problem, the existing theories and methods are far away from the actual requirements. Some fundamental problems need further study.

Feature extraction problem. The starting point of traditional pattern recognition theory is that the recognition object can be described by a set of features. Therefore, the quality of feature selection plays a decisive role in the recognition result. The problem of feature extraction is [12]:

In theory, there is a lack of a unified feature extraction method that is suitable for various problems. In many cases, the image feature extraction method is more dependent on experts. Therefore, we must explore a new research way to solve this problem;

Nowadays, there are many criteria for feature extraction, but there is a lack of a unified metric to evaluate the advantages and disadvantages of feature extraction methods under various criteria, so the design of classifiers is somewhat blindness;

The research on the relationship between feature space dimension, sample size and classifier recognition rate is mostly limited to experimental data, and has not been completely solved in theory;

So far, many important identification problems, such as word, voice, face, some biological signal and image recognition, are still the main difficulties in feature extraction.

The structure identification problem. In structural pattern recognition method, that the model is composed of some basic structural features (called primitives) according to a certain correlation between the composition, the composition can be a string, a tree or a graph to represent the syntactic parsing methods studied, a very good application and in the waveform analysis, chromosome recognition. Some scholars have put forward the statistical method and structure method combined with the idea. But most stay in division combination, there is not a kind of their organic fusion method together, no element of effective cooperation mechanism. So how to play the role of structural recognition has not been solved [13].

Statistical decision theory often assumes that the density of the sample is known, or that the sample volume is large, but in many pattern recognition problems we do not know the distribution of the sample. Making decisions based on a small sample is a pending issue [14].

Feature space has nothing to do with application. As far as image recognition is concerned, medical image, remote sensing image, fingerprint image and face image are all the same.

No distinction is made between simple, quantitative and qualitative features (see Definition 5-3). The qualitative features of the pattern, also known as invariant features, refer to features that cannot be reflected from pixel grayscale, such as human invariant features: shape, limbs, head, torso, hair … The quantitative feature of the model, also known as variable feature, is mainly based on some amount calculated from image gray scale.

Pattern memory is the foundation and premise of pattern emergence. Memory is the key to pattern recognition. Memory is not stored, but it is encoded to realize semantic interpretation of pattern. Model emergence includes feature matching, association and reasoning. There are many problems with association and reasoning [15].

This problem is related to [6], because there is no pattern coding, so that the storage contains a large amount of information, in some cases information is a good thing, but in many cases, too much detail will make pattern recognition more difficult. For example, the printing of Chinese characters on the small stains or gaps will make computer Chinese characters recognize errors. However, people don't even notice these stains or gaps at all. This is because human recognition involves conscious attention, which is not discussed in the current pattern recognition approach, but is important for improving the recognition [16].

Patterns include tangible patterns, such as graphics, images, videos, text, sounds, magnetic fields, optical signals, and intangible patterns.

At present, pattern recognition only works on algorithms, and there has been no substantial progress in the study of human cognitive mechanisms. Humans see pattern recognition as a perceptual process, a process of perception that accepts sensory input and converts it into more abstract code [5]. Past knowledge experience and real stimuli are prerequisites for perception, so pattern recognition involves two interrelated processes: bottom-up processing and top-down processing. Bottom-up processing refers to the process that begins with an external stimulus, usually by analyzing the smaller perception units before turning to the larger perception units to achieve the interpretation of sensory stimuli through a series of successive stages; Top down processing refers to perceptual processing guided by general knowledge, the higher level of processing restricts the lower level of processing. The former is called data driven processing, while the latter is called concept driven processing. The bottom up processing and the top down processing are two different processes. In turn, bottom processing alone cannot cope with the pun nature or uncertainty of some stimuli.

Categorization is absolute. The question is: What features are extracted? How many features are extracted? How to extract features? Both are pre-determined, that is, describe the network is fixed. Human classification is relative, the view of the problem different impact classification results.

3   Distributed Pattern Recognition Framework Description

Studies have shown that each neuron in the brain's nervous system has no intelligence or consciousness of its own, but through the dynamic interaction of groups of neurons, the entire brain's neural network exhibits intelligent behavior and the emergence of consciousness [10]. One of the goals of distributed pattern recognition is to simulate human group behavior in pattern recognition.

Complex systems consist of a large number of complex interacting parts (Agent). The basic strategy for analyzing complex systems is to break them down into increasingly basic subsystems until they are fully mastered. Therefore, solving the semantic gap between micro level and macro level is another goal of the distributed pattern recognition framework.

The traditional method of feature extraction is difficult, the workload is enormous, no one can guarantee the completeness of the collection, so we have to establish a model evolution simulation mechanism. When we understand the molecular motion as a whole, we only feel some temperature. The third goal of the distributed pattern recognition framework is to extract and select features by using the self-organization evolution process.

In order to achieve this goal, the approach, inspired by the theory of approximation, is to find a set of bases (I.E. Agent) that allow the input pattern to approach the pattern to be identified. This representation highlights the importance of a particular side. For example, wavelet coefficients can clearly provide the type and location of signal singularity. There are two approaches to approximation:

Linear Approximation

Linear approximation is a set of indexes projected from mode F to the previously selected M vector from the specification Zhengjiaoji B = {GM} mN.

$$fM = \sum_{m=0}^{M-1} <f, gm> gm \tag{1}$$

Fourier Ji is an excellent linear approximation tool for uniform smooth functions. It projects the signal onto M low frequency sine waves, when M increases, the error $\varepsilon[M] = |F - fM|$ is related to the integral regularity of F. In wavelet bases, the projection of a signal under the M-scale wavelet atom is equivalent to the approximation of the signal with a fixed resolution.

Nonlinear Approximation

Nonlinear approximation is based on the property of F, the amplitude of the previous M product $|<F, gM>|$ the largest vector as an indicator set, recorded as IM, the nonlinear approximation of f is:

$$fM = \sum_{m \in I_M} <f, gm> gm \tag{2}$$

In wavelet base, the integral amplitude is related to the local singularity of the signal, and the nonlinear approximation keeps the maximum wavelet product, which is equivalent to the adaptive approximation network [17].

The distributed pattern recognition framework is based on nonlinear approximation, which is based on input mode. The model we want is:

$$\vec{q}(t+1) \sum_{k=1}^{n} Ag_k(\vec{q}(t))\vec{v}_k + \vec{w}(t) \tag{3}$$

Is a set of Ji (the standard pattern set), is the time of system evolution, is the system evolution uncertainty (is a smooth random process), we call the coefficient = Agent. $\vec{v}_k$ is a set of Ji (standard pattern sets), t is the time of systematic evolution, $\vec{w}(t)$ is an uncertain term of the evolution of the system (a stationary random process). We call the coefficient $\xi_k = Ag_k(\vec{q}(t))$ is Agent. We will prove it later $Ag_k(\vec{q}(t))$ reflects the overall characteristics of $\vec{q}(0)$. In the evolution equation:

$$\dot{\xi}_k = -\frac{\partial V}{\partial \xi_k}, \qquad V = -\frac{1}{2}\sum_{k} \lambda_k \xi_k^2 + B \sum_{k,k'} \xi_k^2 \xi_{k'}^2 \tag{4}$$

Under the constraint, complete: $\vec{q}(0) \rightarrow \vec{q}(t) \rightarrow \vec{v}_{k0}$.

For the distributed pattern recognition framework, the key issue is the mutual communication and coordination between Agent, to complete any single Agent were unable to independently complete the recognition task. Usually the communication and coordination based on semantic communication and knowledge inference. Therefore, language and knowledge of the letter agreement the same logic to form a distributed pattern recognition research frame research of the core content. For example, if we want to complete the face recognition, due to limited knowledge (visual scope, feature selection, noise, etc.) every single camera (Agent) were not aware of the full face information, but Agent exchange with other Agent reconstruction of the face of complete information, trying to reach a consensus, when distributed system to achieve a stable condition, between the identity of the agreement, will complete face recognition. Then we will find that it really realizes each member alone are unable to complete the task, and through the system to complete the group since the emergence.

The derivation of a model

Define 1: Set $\{\vec{v}_k\}$ is a vector set, if there is a vector set $\{\vec{v}_k^+\}$, inner product $<\vec{v}_j^+, \vec{v}_i> = \delta_{ji}$, then $\vec{v}_k^+$ referred to as generalized inverse vector of $\vec{v}_k$.

Theorem 1: Set $\vec{v}_k^+$ referred to as generalized inverse vector of $\vec{v}_k, Ag_k(\vec{q}(t)) = <\vec{v}_k^+, \vec{q}(t)>$.

Proof: For (1) at both ends with $\vec{v}_k^+$ left inner product:

$$<\vec{v}_k^+, \vec{q}(t)> = \sum_{k=1}^{n} Ag_k(\vec{q}(t)) <\vec{v}_k^+, \vec{v}_k> + <\vec{v}_k^+, \vec{w}(t)>$$
$$= Ag_k(\vec{q}(t)) + <\vec{v}_k^+, \vec{w}(t)> \tag{8}$$

Because $\vec{w}(t)$ is a stationary random process, get $<\vec{v}_k^+, \vec{w}(t)> = 0$, so:

$$Ag_k(\vec{q}(t)) = <\vec{v}_k^+, \vec{q}(t)> \tag{9}$$

By the nature of the inner product: $<\vec{v}_k^+, \vec{q}(t)> = <\vec{q}(t), \vec{v}_k^+>$

Define 2: Set $\vec{q}(t)$ is a dynamic system, ξ_u and ξ_s is the system of unstable and stable mode respectively, ξ_u referred to as the order parameter of the system [18].

Theorem 2: Set $\vec{q}(t)$ is a dynamic system, ξ_s is the system of stable mode, ξ_u is the system of unstable mode. The evolution of ξ_u satisfies equation:

$$\frac{d\xi_u}{dt} = \lambda_s \xi_u - \beta \xi_u^3 + \vec{F}$$

Where, λ_s is matrix characteristic root for studying, $\xi_u = Ag_u(\vec{q}(t))$.

Proof: By the principle of dynamics, $\vec{q}$ satisfies Eqs. (10) and (11):

$$\vec{q} = \vec{q}_0 + \vec{q}_1$$

Derivation to:

$$\frac{\partial \vec{q}}{\partial t} = \frac{\partial \vec{q}_0}{\partial t} + \frac{\partial \vec{q}_1}{\partial t} = \frac{\partial \vec{q}_1}{\partial t} \tag{10}$$

$$\frac{\partial \vec{q}}{\partial t} = N(\vec{q}_0) + L\vec{q} + \hat{N}(\vec{q}) + \vec{w}(t) \tag{11}$$

$\vec{q}_0$ Indicates that the system initial state (rest), $\vec{q}_1$ Said system motion state, L is learning matrix. First only related with the system initial state, the second for linear system, the third for the system of high order, due to $|\vec{q}|$ very small, so it can omit. The first three systems determine the force. (5) is generally not solution, when ignore the item 3 and 4 (5) and using (4): $N(\vec{q}_0) = 0$, (5) can be written:

$\frac{d\vec{q}}{dt} = L\vec{q}$, Can solve: $\vec{q} = e^{Lt}\vec{q}_0$

Set λ_j is eigenvalue of L, $\vec{v}_j$ corresponds to feature vector of λ_j, i.e. $L\vec{v}_j = \lambda_j \vec{v}_j$. By the matrix function spectrum decomposition theorem get:

$$\vec{q} = e^{\vec{\lambda} t}\vec{v} = \sum_j \xi_j(t)\vec{v}_j \tag{12}$$

$$\text{or } \vec{q}(\vec{x}, t) = \vec{q}(0) + \sum_u \xi_j(t)\vec{v}_j(\vec{x}) \tag{13}$$

To the left (6) both ends with $\vec{v}_j^+$ inner product:

$$\xi_j = <\vec{v}_j^+, \vec{q}(t)>$$

Get by Theorem 1: $Ag_k(\vec{q}(t)) = \xi_k$ According to the Define 2, ξ_k is Agent. To (6) on both ends of the derivation:

$$\frac{d\vec{q}}{dt} = \sum_j \frac{d\xi_j(t)}{dt}\vec{v}_j \tag{14}$$

Plug in (14) into (7):

$$\sum_j \frac{d\xi_j(t)}{dt}\vec{v}_j = \sum_j \xi_j(t)L\vec{v}_j + \hat{N}[\sum_j \xi_j(t)\vec{v}_j] \tag{15}$$

Using generalized inverse of $\vec{v}_k$ (8) on both sides of the left inner product:

$$\frac{d\xi_u}{dt} = \lambda_u \xi_u + \tilde{N}_u(\xi_{u'}, \xi_{s'}) \approx \lambda_u \xi_u + \xi_u \xi_s \tag{16}$$

$$\frac{d\xi_s}{dt} = \lambda_s \xi_s + \tilde{N}_s(\xi_{u'}, \xi_{s'}) \tag{17}$$

ξ_u dominant ξ_s, ξ_s At the critical point with large damping, fast attenuation and the parameters of system evolution process doesn't work, ξ_u, on the other hand. Because ξ_u without damping, so they got the majority of the response of the subsystem, and often is growing exponentially, have an effect in the process of evolution from beginning to end, and plays A leading role subsystem behavior. In the specific processing parameter, the two differentiate from their critical damping coefficient, relies on the fluctuation, its coefficient is often A difference of several orders of magnitude. Because:

$$\frac{d\xi_s}{dt} = \lambda_s \xi_s + \xi_u^2 + \ldots \approx 0 \tag{18}$$

This is λ_u very small very little (ξ_u is very small), ξ_u Only slowly changes over time. We acquired:

$$\xi_s \approx -\frac{\xi_u^2}{\lambda_s}$$

Plug into (19): $\frac{d\xi_u}{dt} = \lambda_u \xi_u - \beta \xi_u^3$, where, $\beta = -\frac{1}{\lambda_s}$ ∎

By the relationship between force and potential and Theorem 2:

$$\frac{\partial \xi_k}{\partial t} = -\frac{\partial V}{\partial \xi_k} \quad \text{where,}$$

$$\begin{aligned} V &= -\frac{1}{2}\sum_k \lambda_k \xi_k^2 + B\sum_{k,k'} \xi_k^2 \xi_{k'}^2 \\ &= -\frac{1}{2}\sum_k \lambda_k \xi_k^2 + D\sum_{k \neq k'} \xi_k^2 \xi_{k'}^2 + C\left(\sum_k \xi_k^2\right)^2 \end{aligned} \tag{19}$$

Formula (19) for the potential function and potential function right end the meaning of each item: λ_u. To pay attention to the parameters, only when $\lambda_u > 0$, patterns can be identified, otherwise can't identify. Due to the first item is negative, so when $\vec{q}$ increase, V fall, when $\vec{q}$ increases to A certain extent, the third dominant, and ultimately faster than the first change, so the interaction between the first and the third show valleys. The second can cause the formation of the ridge; it is based on this, to achieve the distinction between different modes.

4   Design and Implementation of the Algorithm

In the 4th section we get the expression of potential function:

$$V = -\frac{1}{2}\sum_k \lambda_k \xi_k^2 + D\sum_{k \neq k'} \xi_k^2 \xi_{k'}^2 + C\left(\sum_k \xi_k^2\right)^2 \tag{20}$$

Because, $\vec{q}(t) = \vec{q}(0) + \sum_u \xi_u(t)\vec{v}_u$, and

So, $\dfrac{\partial \vec{q}}{\partial t} = \sum_u \dfrac{d\xi_u}{dt}\vec{v}_u = \sum_k \lambda_k \vec{v}_k \xi_k - D\sum_{k \neq k'} \xi_k^2 \xi_{k'} \vec{v}_k - C<\vec{q}^+,\vec{q}>\vec{q}$ or $\vec{q}(t+1)$

$$= \vec{q}(t) + \sum_k \lambda_k \vec{v}_k \xi_k - D\sum_{k \neq k'} \xi_k^2 \xi_{k'} \vec{v}_k - C<\vec{q}^+,\vec{q}>\vec{q} \qquad (21)$$

The following Theorem 3 and formula (1) is the foundation of the wet distributed identification algorithm design.

Theorem 3. Set matrix $A_{n \times m} = (\vec{a}_1, \vec{a}_2, \ldots, \vec{a}_m)$ for prototype model row vector of n line matrix and normalized handle, *i.e.* $\|\vec{a}_i\| = 1$, $i = 1, \ldots, n$, $B_{m \times n} = \left(\vec{b}_1, \vec{b}_2, \ldots, \vec{b}_m\right)^T$ for A generalized inverse and normalized handle, then: $<\vec{a}_i, \vec{b}_j> + <\vec{a}_j, \vec{b}_i> = \delta_{ij}$

Proof: If B is A generalized inverse, and $(AB)^T = AB$, i.e. AB is real symmetric matrices $<\vec{a}_i, \vec{b}_j>$ is the ith row, the jth column elements of AB, and $\|\vec{a}_i\| = \left\|\vec{b}_j\right\| = 1$, when $i \neq j$, defined by the generalized inverse: $<\vec{a}_i, b_i> = 0$, when i = j, divided into two kinds of circumstances, $\vec{a}_i$ and $\vec{b}_i$ Overlap, or in separate the sum of the projection direction is 1, namely: $<\vec{a}_i, \vec{b}_j> + <\vec{a}_i\vec{a}_i, \vec{b}_i> = \delta_{ij}$.

According to the Theorem 1 we get algorithm as follows:

Algorithm based on the theorem 1

Step 1: Stretch the input mode and standard mode to "grey value + prior knowledge" of the vector;

Step 2: Tow times wavelet transform, applied to the secondary low frequency information as a prototype vector, complete dimension reduction of more than 80%;

Step 3: For dimension reduction after the vector normalization into to A standard pattern of matrix A column vector; The normalized input mode to $\vec{q}(0)$;

Step 4: Calculation of the generalized inverse matrix of A,we get:B=$(\vec{v}_1^+, \vec{v}_2^+$,..., $\vec{v}_n^+)$, and $\vec{q}_k^+$;

Step 5: Execution Agent form module;

Step 6: the distribution of task decomposition module;

Step 7: initialization parameters: the evolution of time t, pay attention to the parameters

Step 8: according to the evolution of (11) $\vec{q}(0)$;

Step 9 : If the agent reach a consensus in a moment or evolutionary timeout, then go Step 10, otherwise Step 8;

Step 10 : END

According to the above algorithm, Matlab simulation of face recognition experiment ORL face image database. After entering the system shows that the main interface as shown in Fig. 1.

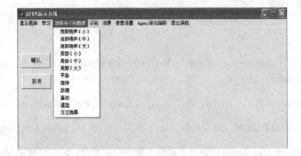

Fig. 1. Distributed pattern recognition simulation main interface

System is mainly composed of study, identification, the input mode selection, parameter setting, and Agent evolution curve of such modules. Learning module to complete the standard model selection, normalization, orthogonalization, dimension reduction, the choice of prior knowledge, etc. Recognition module can complete single pattern recognition, pattern recognition, the recognition rate calculation, etc. Input mode selection module determine the way and the way of interaction, Fig. 1 is the recognition result of the Gaussian noise, evolutionary step 2 to complete identification. Figure 2 is the recognition result of overlapping noise, evolutionary step 6 complete recognition. Figure 3 is the recognition result of zooming noise, evolutionary step 17 complete recognition. Figures 2 and 3 using PCA method to identify a failure.

Fig. 2. Results of overlapping noise identification

Fig. 3. Recognition results of select 7 numbers from 48 face

Table 1. Comparison of five pattern recognition methods

	Traditional method	Synergetic method	Bionic method	Subspace method	Distributed pattern recognition framework
Evolution mode	Static state	Dynamic	Dynamic	Static state	Dynamic
Control mode	Focus	Focus	Focus	Focus	Distribution
Primitives	Features	Pixel	Features	Vector	Semantics
Schema representation	Feature vector	Grayscale vector	Feature vector	Subspace	Nonlinear combination of agent
Method	Bottom-up	Top-down	Top-down	Bottom-up	Bottom-up and top-down
Principle	Model modeling	Pattern emergency	Pattern recognition	Pattern recognition	Model modeling + pattern emergency

5 Concluding Remarks

This paper analyzes the characteristics of top-down pattern recognition method and the bottom-up pattern recognition methods and the advantages and disadvantages, multi agent theory and technology based on the distributed pattern recognition framework of two kinds of methods of integration. First use the bottom-up approach to modeling, which is conducive to classification; classification method and top-down model of purpose. Is that the computer pattern recognition is more consistent with the human cognitive process.

The research of traditional pattern recognition method is based on feature, while the attention of distributed pattern recognition framework focuses on the activity of the whole feature network. Therefore, the distributed pattern recognition framework examines the whole of the schema. In Table 1, the comparison of centralized pattern recognition methods is presented.

In traditional pattern recognition, based on algorithm, it means that the whole system works in a deterministic way. The distributed pattern recognition framework is based on the self-organizing + algorithm, and the system state is determined by deterministic events and contingencies.

Statistical pattern recognition, pattern recognition, collaborative problem of subspace pattern recognition and biomimetic pattern recognition is not supported by distributed computing, and pattern recognition often requires distributed environment. This paper simply explains the basic idea of distributed pattern recognition framework, in the following article; we will discuss the design and implementation of the key technology of distributed mode the identification of the framework.

Acknowledgement. The National Natural Science Foundation of China (61771265, 61340037), the Natural Science Foundation of Jiangsu (BK20151272), the "333" Talents of Jiangsu (BRA2017475), the Nantong Science Plan Project (BK2014064).

References

1. Luo, J.: Multi class statistical pattern recognition model and its application. Master's degree thesis of Chongqing University, Chongqing (2009)
2. Hao, B.: Research and implementation of Chinese relationship extraction based on syntactic pattern recognition. Master's degree thesis of the University of Electronic Science and Technology, Chengdu (2017)
3. Chen, Y., Qin, H., Li, W.: Research and application progress of bionic pattern recognition technology. J. Intell. Syst. **11**(1), 1–14 (2016)
4. Liu, B., Wang, W., Fang, X.: Synergetic pattern recognition method. Syst. Eng. Electron. Technol. **25**(6), 758–763 (2003)
5. Mo, J., Zhu, G., Lv, Y.: I-VLDNS: an improved linear discriminant algorithm Besshi spatial pattern recognition. Comput. Appl. Softw. **7**, 172–177 (2016)
6. Xu, L.: Theoretical research and application of pattern recognition kernel method. Doctoral dissertations of Anhui University, Hefei (2017)
7. Haken, H.: Principle of Brain Functioning: A Synergetic Approach to Brain Activity, Behavior and Cognition. Shanghai Scientific & Technological Education Publishing House, Shanghai (2000). (Guo, Z., et al. translated)
8. Bai, L., Hancock, E.R.: Depth-based complexity traces of graphs. Pattern Recogn. **47**(3), 1172–1186 (2014)
9. Da San Martino, G., Navarin, N., Sperduti, A.: Exploiting the ODD framework to define a novel effective graph kernel. In: Proceedings. Presses universitaires de Louvain, pp. 219–224 (2015)
10. Zhou, C.: Calculation of heart, pp. 16–17. Tsinghua University Press, Beijing (2003)
11. Su, D.: Research on multi agent pursuit based on cooperative mechanism. Doctorate in Harbin Institute of Technology, Harbin (2017)
12. Xie, Y.: Research on some problems of face feature extraction and classifier design. Doctoral dissertations of Nanjing University of Science and Technology, Nanjing (2006)
13. Li, R., Zhang, L.: Design of syntactic parsing unit for structural pattern recognition system based on relational algebra. J. Dalian Jiaotong Univ. **33**(3), 59–63 (2012)
14. Chen, F., Shui, A., Li, L.: Small sample pattern recognition method for pipeline plugging in storage and transportation process. Comput. Appl. Res. **31**(7), 2031–2034 (2014)

15. Du, P.: Research on brain activity of paired association learning in visual haptic cross pattern. Doctoral dissertations of East China Normal University, Shanghai (2015)
16. Cheng, X.: Research on pattern recognition framework APRF based on multi agent. Doctoral dissertations of Nanjing University of Science and Technology, Nanjing (2006)
17. Di, J., Yin, J.: Application of wavelet analysis. Science Press, Beijing (2017)
18. Haken, H.: Work with computer and cognitive - top-down method of neural network. Tsinghua University Press, Beijing (1994). (Yang, J. translated)

Anime Sketch Coloring with Swish-Gated Residual U-Net

Gang Liu(✉), Xin Chen, and Yanzhong Hu

School of Computer Science, Hubei University of Technology, Wuhan 430072, China
lg0061408@126.com, ghj9527@163.com, 15738443@qq.com

Abstract. Anime sketch coloring is to fill the color into the anime sketches to obtain the colorful anime images and it is a new research direction in deep learning technology. Currently, generative adversarial networks (GANs) have been used for anime sketch coloring and achieved some results. However, the colorful images generated by the anime sketch coloring methods based on GANs generally have poor coloring effects. In this paper, an efficient anime sketch coloring method based on swish-gated residual U-net (SGRU) is proposed to solve the above problems. In SGRU, the proposed swish layer and swish-gated residual blocks (SGRBs) effectively filter the information transmitted by each level and speed up the convergence of the network. The perceptual loss and the per-pixel loss are used to constitute the final loss of SGRU. The final loss function reflects the coloring results more realistically and can control the effect of coloring more effectively. SGRU can automatically color the sketch without providing any coloring hints in advance and can be trained end-to-end with the sketch and the corresponding color image. Experimental results show that our method performs better than other state-of-the-art coloring methods, and can achieve the colorful images with higher visual quality.

Keywords: Anime sketch coloring · U-net · Swish layer · Swish-gated residual blocks

1 Introduction

Anime sketch coloring is the process of converting the black-and-white anime sketches into the colorful anime images. It needs to fill the appropriate colors into the black-and-white anime sketch, and also adjust the illumination and shadows to create the desired anime images. Due to the complexity of the coloring process, anime sketch coloring mainly relies on the professional anime artists to complete. For the anime artists, anime sketch coloring requires a lot of time and effort, and it has high requirements for the professional ability. Hence, it is very necessary to design an appropriate automatic coloring method for the black-and-white anime sketches. The automatic coloring methods can avoid the complicated work procedures generated by manual coloring, and also enable ordinary people to easily create more vivid anime images.

© Springer Nature Singapore Pte Ltd. 2019
H. Peng et al. (Eds.): ISICA 2018, CCIS 986, pp. 190–204, 2019.
https://doi.org/10.1007/978-981-13-6473-0_17

With the development of deep learning [14], anime sketch coloring methods based on deep learning have been used to automatically color the black-and-white anime sketches, such as Style2paints [19], Paintschainer [18], Auto-painter [11] and so on. These methods automatically convert the black-and-white anime sketches into the colorful anime images by using deep neural networks. And the coloring speed of these methods is faster than that of manual operations. The network structures of these automatic coloring models are primarily based on generative adversarial networks (GANs) [16]. GANs usually have the problems such as the difficulties of network training, unstable generating effects and non-convergence of the network. Therefore, the automatic coloring models based on GANs tend to generate the low-quality color anime images. The color images generated by these automatic coloring models usually have some serious problems, such as unreasonable color mixing, unnatural color gradient, coloring beyond the filled areas and so on. Altogether, the color rendering effects of the current anime sketch coloring models based on GANs are far less effective than that of manual coloring.

The U-net [13] is a U-shaped convolutional neural network that is originally used in the field of medical image segmentation [4]. It has two symmetrical branches and is considered to be an encoder-decoder network structure. Therefore, the U-net is also commonly used in the field of image synthesis. In order to improve the quality of the synthesized images, it is necessary to improve the U-net to generate higher quality images.

In order to solve the above problems, we propose the swish-gated residual U-net (SGRU) for coloring the black-and-white anime sketches into the vivid color anime images. SGRU is an improvement to the U-net. The black-and-white anime sketches are input into the SGRU, and then the color anime images are output. A novel type of residual blocks, called the swish-gated blocks (SGBs) which are inspired by the swish activation function [12], are proposed and embedded in SGRU. SGBs can further accelerate the convergence of the network and filter the feature information transmitted in the residual blocks by the proposed swish layers. Furthermore, the proposed swish layers are used to filter the information transmitted between the same levels in the left and right branches. SGRU combines the perceptual loss [8] and the per-pixel loss to constitute the final loss. The perceptual loss can effectively improve the quality of the color images generated by SGRU and solve the coloring problems caused by the automatic coloring models based on GANs. Compared with the U-net, SGBs and the swish layers effectively improve the learning ability of the U-net and accelerates the convergence of the network. Experimental verifications are conducted on the Danbooru2017 dataset [1]. Experimental results show that SGRU is significantly better than other state-of-the-art methods and the quality of the color images generated by SGRU is close to or reaches the level of manual coloring.

The remainder of this paper is organized as follows. The architecture of the U-net and the related work are described in Sect. 2. The architecture of SGRU is presented in Sect. 3. The baseline methods are introduced in Sect. 4.

Experimental datasets and results are reported in Sect. 5. Finally, some conclusions are given in Sect. 6.

2   The U-Net and Related Work

The U-net is usually used in the field of image segmentation, especially in the field of medical image segmentation [10,21]. The architecture of the U-net is illustrated in Fig. 1. The architecture of the U-net consists of two symmetric branches. The left branch of U-net is used to encode the input and reduce the resolution of the feature maps. The right branch is used to decode the output and increase the resolution of the feature maps. The left branch (contracting path) in the U-net can be considered as an encoder, The right branch (expanding path) in the U-net can be considered as a decoder.

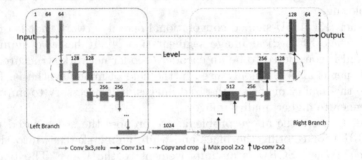

Fig. 1. The architecture of the U-net. Each blue box represents a multi-channel feature map. The number of channels is denoted on top of the box. Black boxes represent copied feature maps. The arrows denote the different operations. The resolution of the feature maps output by the convolutional layers in the same level is the same. In the left branch, the resolution of the feature maps output by the convolutional layers is gradually decreased and the resolution of the feature maps output by the convolutional layers in the right branch is gradually increased. (Color figure inline)

The left branch follows the typical architecture of the convolutional network. The right branch includes the upsampling operations and the convolution layers to build the image from the bottom to up. In the U-net, the resolution of the feature maps output by the convolutional layers in the same level is the same. The feature maps output by the convolutional layers in the first level have the highest resolution, and the resolution of the feature maps output by the final level is the smallest. As the serial number of the level increases, the resolution of the feature maps output by the convolutional layers gradually decreases. And the feature maps output by each level of the left branch will be spliced to the input feature maps of the corresponding level of the right branch. That is, copying low level features to the corresponding high levels actually creates a path for information propagation allowing signals propagate between low and high levels in a much easier way, which not only facilitating backward propagation during training, but also compensating low level finer details to high level semantic features.

Recently, the combination of the U-net and GANs has been used for automatic coloring [7,11,18,19] and achieved some results. In these studies, the generator in GANs uses the architecture based on the U-net. The literature [19] integrated residual U-net to apply the style to the gray-scale sketch with auxiliary classifier generative adversarial network (AC-GAN). In fact, Style2paints can be considered as the coloring model. But it needs to provide the color reference images in advance when converting the animation sketches into the color images. The literature [11] investigated the sketch-to-image synthesis problem by using conditional generative adversarial networks (cGAN). Auto-painter which can automatically generate painted cartoon images from a sketch is proposed and Wasserstein distance is used in training cGAN to overcome model collapse and enable the model converged much better. The new model is not only capable of painting hand-draw sketch with compatible colors, but also allowing users to indicate preferred colors. Isola [7] investigates conditional adversarial networks as a general-purpose solution to image-to-image translation problems. These networks not only learn the mapping from input image to output image, but also learn a loss function to train this mapping. This makes it possible to apply the same generic approach to problems that traditionally would require very different loss formulations. This approach is effective at synthesizing photos from label maps, reconstructing objects from edge maps, and colorizing images, among other tasks.

3   Our Method

3.1   Swish Layer and Swish-Gated Residual Blocks

This paper proposes a novel type of residual blocks, which is an improvement on the residual blocks in Resnet [6]. The novel residual blocks are called the swish-gated blocks (SGBs). SGBs are composed of the proposed swish layers and the residuals. The proposed swish layer contains the convolutional layer and the swish activation function [12]. The structure of the residual block, the swish layer and SGB are shown in Fig. 2. In Fig. 2, x represents the input data and $F(x)$ represents the residual. $F(x) + x$ is the output of the residual block. The $H(x)$ represents the output of the convolution layer in the swish layer. The "$\cdot$" denotes the element-wise multiplication and "$+$" means the element-wise addition. The $R(x)$ represents the output of the convolution layers using the nonlinearity function LReLU [5] in SGB. The $S(x)$ represents the output of the swish layer. The "$\oplus$" indicates the concatenation operation of the feature maps. The $R(x) \oplus S(x)$ represents the output of SGB.

As shown in Fig. 2, x are added directly to the residuals in the residual block without any processing. In order to process x, the swish layer is proposed to control the propagation of x. In fact, the swish layer can be considered as the swish-inspired adaptive gating mechanism. Compared to the residual block, SGB

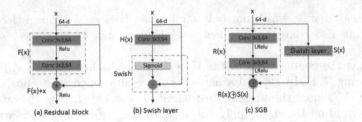

Fig. 2. The structures of the residual block, swish layer and SGB. Each blue box represents the corresponding data operation in the network. The arrows indicate data flow. (Color figure online)

uses the swish layer to filter x. The purpose of SGB is to control the data sent to the higher layers through the shortcut connection [6]. Formally, the swish layer can be defined as:

$$S(x) = x \cdot \sigma(H(x)) \tag{1}$$

where x and $S(x)$ are the input and output of the swish layer. The $H(x)$ represents the output of the convolution layer in the swish layer. The "σ" denotes the sigmoid function. The "$\cdot$" denotes the element-wise multiplication.

SGBs combine the residual blocks and the swish layers. In SGBs, the swish layers are used as the learnable gating mechanism which can filter the transmitted information. The x is filtered by the swish layer and the filtered information is concatenated to $R(x)$ to obtain the output of SGBs. SGB can be expressed as:

$$y = R(x) \oplus S(x) \tag{2}$$

where $R(x)$ can be considered as the residuals of SGB and $S(x)$ is the output of the swish layer in SGB. The "$\oplus$" denotes $R(x)$ and $S(x)$ are concatenated together.

3.2 Architecture

The proposed swish-gated residual U-net (SGRU) is the U-net with the swish-gated residual blocks. SGRU is an end-to-end automatic coloring model. The structure of SGRU is shown in Fig. 3. The network has 6 different resolution levels. With the increase of the serial number of the level, the resolutions of the feature maps decrease gradually.

In the vertical direction of SGRU, the swish layers are embedded between two adjacent levels. The swish layers and the stacked convolutional layers in the left (right) branches constitute SGBs. The structures inside the dashed boxes in Fig. 3 are SGBs. There are 10 SGBs in SGRU. In the horizontal direction of SGRU, the swish layers are embedded in each skip connection between the left and right branches to filter the information passed from the encoding path to the decoding path. The swish layers in the skip connections can accelerate the convergence of the network and improve the performance of the network.

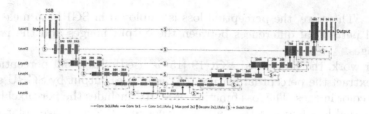

Fig. 3. The architecture of SGRU. Each blue box represents a multi-channel feature map. Each brown box represents a multi-channel feature map output by the swish layer. Each black box represents the copies of the feature maps of the left branch. The number on the box indicates the number of channels. The arrows denote the different operations. The S indicates the swish layer. Each structure inside the dashed box is SGB. From the 1st level to the 6th level, the resolution of the feature maps is halved in turn. (Color figure online)

Except for the last convolutional layer used in the output of SGRU, all other convolutional layers use layer normalization [2] and nonlinearity LReLU. In SGRU, the input of SGBs in the ith level is the output of the 1×1 convolutions in the $(i-1)th$ level and the output of SGBs in the ith level is concatenated to the input of the 1×1 convolutions in the $(i+1)th$ level. From the 1st level to the 6th level, the number of convolution kernels in each convolutional layer of SGB in ith level is the same as the number of the 1×1 convolutional kernels in the $(i-1)th$ level. Like the U-net, the upsampling still uses the deconvolution method.

The last convolutional layer of the right branch will output the final color images. It has 27 1×1 convolution kernels and does not use the normalization operations and the activation functions. SGRU contains 6 levels, in each convolutional layer from level 1 to level 6, the number of the convolution kernels is 96, 192, 288, 384, 480, 512, respectively.

3.3 Training

SGRU is trained end-to-end and uses the training pair $D = \{S, C\}$ as the input training dataset. A black-and-white anime sketch S is the input data and the corresponding reference color image C is considered as the label. For the tasks of coloring, simply comparing the pixel colors of the generated image and the reference color image can severely penalize the quality of the output image because the transformation from the anime sketch to the color image is not a one-to-one transformation. In fact, anime sketch coloring is a one-to-many transformation. For example, the hair color in the reference color image is red, but the hair color in the output color image may be black or silver. These hair colors are reasonable for anime. However, the difference between color of two kinds of hairs is huge when using the per-pixel loss and the per-pixel losses do not capture perceptual differences between the output images and the reference color images. In this situation, the perceptual features of the color of two kinds of hairs may be similar. Therefore, the perceptual loss is employed in SGRU to measure the high-level perceptual differences between the output images and the reference color images.

In our work, the pretrained VGG19 [15] is used as a visual perception network to extract the perceptual features of the images output by SGRU and the reference color images. The loss function of SGRU includes the per-pixel loss and the perceptual loss between the output images and the reference color images. Let φ be the pretrained VGG19. The φ_l represents a collection of layers in the network φ. The total loss function of SGRU can be represented as:

$$L_f = \sum_l \lambda_l ||\varphi_l(T) - \varphi_l(C)||_1 \tag{3}$$

where T represents the output color image. $\varphi_l(T)$ and $\varphi_l(C)$ represent the feature maps output from the lth layer in VGG19 when T and C are respectively input to VGG19. $l \in \{0, 1, 2, 3, 4, 5\}$ and φ_1 to φ_5 represent the convolutional layers (conv1_2, conv2_2, conv3_2, conv4_2 and conv5_2) that are selected to calculate the perceptual loss in VGG19. When $l = 0$, $\varphi_0(T)$ and $\varphi_0(C)$ represent the original input T and C. The hyperparameters λ_l is used to balance the contribution of the lth layer to the total loss L_f and $\lambda_l = \{0.88, 0.79, 0.63, 0.51, 0.39, 1.07\}$. Adam optimizer [9] is applied to minimize the total loss.

The Eq. 3 is used to color a single image for a given input S. Because the given black-and-white anime sketch can correspond to many images, it also makes sense to generate a diverse set of images as output. We use the method of diversity loss in CRNs [3] and output a collection of images in one shot. It can be represented as:

$$L_{df} = \min_u \sum_{l=0}^{5} \lambda_l \sum_j ||S^l \otimes (\varphi_l^j(T^u) - \varphi_l^j(C))||_1 \tag{4}$$

where T^u is the uth image in the output collection. φ_l^j is the jth feature map in φ_l, S^l is the mask downsampled to match the resolution of φ_l, and "$\otimes$" is the Hadamard product. This loss constructs a color image by adaptively taking the best generated content from the whole collection, and scoring the collection based on this assembled image.

4 Baselines

In this section, four alternative approaches are used as baselines. These methods are the U-net, the deep residual U-net (ResUnet) [20], SGRU with SGBs in the vertical direction (SGRU_V) and SGRU with the swish layers in the horizontal direction (SGRU_H). For the coloring tasks, SGRU will be compared to these baseline methods. Although the network structures of these methods are different, their loss functions are the same. The dataset and the training process are also the same for all of the convolutional networks.

The U-Net and ResUnet. The U-net has 6 levels. In our experiments, the upsampling method in the U-net uses the deconvolution method. ResUnet embeds the residual blocks between the adjacent levels in the U-net. The architecture of ResUnet is shown in Fig. 4. In ResUnet, the input of the residual blocks in the ith level is the output of the 1×1 convolutions in the $(i-1)th$ level and the output of the residual blocks in the ith level is concatenated to the input of the 1×1 convolutions in the $(i+1)th$ level. ResUnet has five more 1×1 convolutions than the U-net.

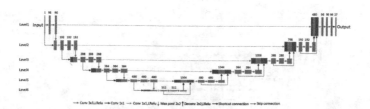

Fig. 4. The architecture of ResUnet.

SGRU_V and SGRU_H. Both SGRU_V and SGRU_H are the branches of SGRU. The structures of SGRU_V and SGRU_H are shown in Fig. 5. For SGRU_V, the swish layers are embedded between two adjacent levels in the vertical direction of the network to form SGBs. The skip connections in the horizontal direction are the same as the U-net. Like SGRU, SGRU_V also has 10 SGBs. The difference between them is that SGRU_V has no swish layer in the horizontal direction. For SGRU_H, the swish layers are embedded into the skip connections in the horizontal direction to form the swish connections. In the vertical direction, SGRU_H uses the same shortcut connections as ResUnet. Unlike SGRU, there are no SGBs in SGRU_H. There are 5 swish connections in SGRU_H.

5 Experiments

5.1 Datasets and Evaluation Metrics

In order to verify the performance of the proposed approach, a comprehensive set of experiments has been conducted on the large-scale public dataset Danbooru2017 [1]. The Danbooru2017 dataset is a large-scale crowdsourced and tagged anime illustration dataset. We selected $18,560$ color anime images and their corresponding the black-and-white sketches for training. In our experiments, the resolution of all training images is adjusted to 256×256.

For the Danbooru2017 dataset, when using the same black-and-white anime sketch as the input, the different networks may color different colors at the same location. Therefore, the standard quantitative measures such as the peak signal-to-noise ratio (PSNR) and structural similarity (SSIM) [17] fail to capture and accurately assess image quality. A reliable methodology to evaluate the quality of the colored images is the perceptual experiments with human observers.

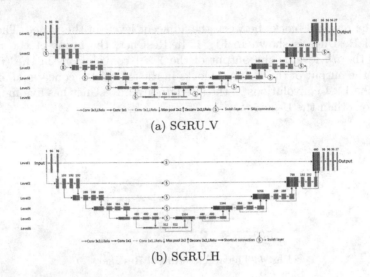

(a) SGRU_V

(b) SGRU_H

Fig. 5. The architectures of SGRU_V and SGRU_H.

5.2   Results

The qualitative results of several coloring models on the Danbooru2017 dataset are shown in Fig. 6. Compared with the color images colored by the baselines, the images colored by SGRU are more vivid and saturated. In addition, the color gradient process and the colour brightness and shadow of the images colored by SGRU are smoother and more natural.

Figure 7 shows the performance of the different networks. It shows that with the increase of epoch, the loss of SGRU can obtain the better result and our network converges faster. The loss of all methods on the dataset is presented in Table 1. The best results are shown in **boldface**. From Table 1, SGRU achieves the best result among other methods. When the epoch is 50, the loss of our network is 32560.918. Compared with other networks, our network can reach a lower loss. The above results show that the performance of our networks is significantly better than that of other networks. The results also show that SGBs and the swish layers effectively improve the performance of the network and accelerate the convergence of the network.

In order to investigate the effect of the perceptual loss, SGRU and SGRU without the perceptual loss are compared. The results of the comparison of the two methods are shown in Fig. 8. It can be clearly seen that compared with SGRU, the color images generated by SGRU without the perceptual loss are not rich enough and have fewer changes in color gradation. In addition, the color saturation is lower and the color processing on the texture details is rougher in SGRU without the perceptual loss.

The comparison results of SGRU, Style2paints [19] and Paintschainer [18] are shown in Fig. 9. As shown in Fig. 9, the color images output by SGRU have higher visual quality than other state-of-the-art coloring models. SGRU can effectively

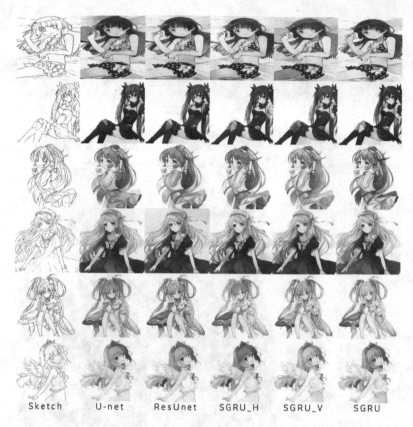

Sketch   U-net   ResUnet   SGRU_H   SGRU_V   SGRU

Fig. 6. Qualitative comparison of the colored images on the Danbooru2017 dataset. (Color figure online)

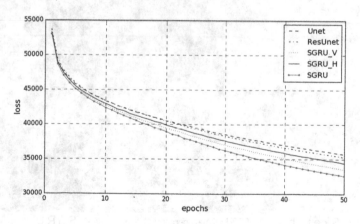

Fig. 7. The loss curve of all networks on the dataset.

Sketch   SGRU without perceptual loss   SGRU

Fig. 8. Qualitative comparison of SGRU and SGRU without the perceptual loss. (Color figure online)

Fig. 9. Qualitative comparison of the state-of-the-art coloring models. (Color figure online)

Table 1. Comparison of the loss of the different networks on the Danbooru2017 dataset

	The $1st$ epoch	The $25th$ epoch	The $50th$ epoch
U-net	53115.192	39470.028	35695.601
ResUnet	53732.840	39366.829	35262.385
SGRU_H	53256.047	38686.936	34394.662
SGRU_V	53525.884	38206.232	33492.846
SGRU	**52992.809**	**37535.647**	**32560.918**

Fig. 10. Effect of coloring diversity. A diverse collection of 9 images with different hues is output for a given black-and-white anime sketch. (Color figure online)

avoid the coloring problems existing in the latest Style2paints and Paintschainer, such as unreasonable color mixing, poor color gradient effect, coloring beyond the filled areas and so on. Therefore, the coloring effect of SGRU is not only superior to the state-of-the-art coloring methods, but also is closer to the coloring ability of the anime artists.

The effect of the diversity loss is shown in Fig. 10. The model outputs a collection of 9 colored images at a time. As seen from Fig. 10, for the same sketch, SGRU can produce different coloring effects. The diversity loss function effectively improves the coloring diversity of SGRU.

6   Conclusions

This paper presents a swish-gated residual U-net (SGRU) for coloring the black-and-white anime sketches into the vivid color anime images. The swish layers and the swish-gated blocks (SGBs) are proposed and embedded in SGRU to improve the performance of the network. SGRU also uses the swish-gated blocks (SGBs) to accelerate network convergence. SGRU can be easily trained end-to-end with the perceptual loss and the per-pixel loss. On the Danbooru2017 dataset, the experimental results show that the proposed method has obvious advantages over other state-of-the-art methods in the complicated sketch coloring tasks. Compared with other state-of-the-art methods, the output images colored by SGRU have the higher visual quality and SGRU converges faster. The coloring effect of SGRU is close to the level of the anime painters. SGRU also has the good coloring diversity. Future work includes using GANs to optimize our coloring model.

Acknowledgment. The work described in this paper was support by National Natural Science Foundation of China Foundation No. 61300127. Any conclusions or recommendations stated here are those of the authors and do not necessarily reflect official positions of NSFC.

References

1. Anonymous, The Danbooru Community, Branwen, G., Gokaslan, A.: Danbooru2017: a large-scale crowdsourced and tagged anime illustration dataset. https://www.gwern.net/Danbooru2017
2. Ba, J.L., Kiros, J.R., Hinton, G.E.: Layer normalization. CoRR abs/1607.06450 (2016). https://arxiv.org/abs/1607.06450v1
3. Chen, Q., Koltun, V.: Photographic image synthesis with cascaded refinement networks. In: Proceedings of International Conference on Computer Vision 2017 (ICCV 2017), Venice, Italy, pp. 1511–1520, October 2017
4. Dong, H., Yang, G., Liu, F., Mo, Y., Guo, Y.: Automatic brain tumor detection and segmentation using U-Net based fully convolutional networks. In: Valdés Hernández, M., González-Castro, V. (eds.) MIUA 2017. CCIS, vol. 723, pp. 506–517. Springer, Cham (2017). https://doi.org/10.1007/978-3-319-60964-5_44
5. He, K., Zhang, X., Ren, S., Sun, J.: Delving deep into rectifiers: surpassing human-level performance on imagenet classification. In: Proceedings of 2015 IEEE International Conference on Computer Vision (ICCV 2015), Santiago, Chile, pp. 1026–1034 (2015)
6. He, K., Zhang, X., Ren, S., Sun, J.: Deep residual learning for image recognition. In: Proceedings of 29th IEEE Conference on Computer Vision and Pattern Recognition, CVPR 2016, Las Vegas, NV, United states, pp. 770–778 (2016)
7. Isola, P., Zhu, J.Y., Zhou, T., Efros, A.A.: Image-to-image translation with conditional adversarial networks. In: Proceedings of 30th IEEE Conference on Computer Vision and Pattern Recognition (CVPR 2017), Honolulu, HI, United States, pp. 5967–5976, July 2017

8. Johnson, J., Alahi, A., Fei-Fei, L.: Perceptual losses for real-time style transfer and super-resolution. In: Leibe, B., Matas, J., Sebe, N., Welling, M. (eds.) ECCV 2016. LNCS, vol. 9906, pp. 694–711. Springer, Cham (2016). https://doi.org/10.1007/978-3-319-46475-6_43

9. Kingma, D.P., Ba, J.: Adam: a method for stochastic optimization. In: Proceedings of the 3rd International Conference for Learning Representations (ICLR 2015), San Diego, CA, United States, pp. 1–15, May 2015

10. Lin, B.S., Michael, K., Kalra, S., Tizhoosh, H.R.: Skin lesion segmentation: U-nets versus clustering. In: Proceedings of 2017 IEEE Symposium Series on Computational Intelligence (SSCI 2017), Honolulu, HI, United States, pp. 1–7, November 2017

11. Liu, Y., Qin, Z., Wan, T., Luo, Z.: Auto-painter: cartoon image generation from sketch by using conditional Wasserstein generative adversarial networks. Neurocomputing **311**, 78–87 (2018)

12. Ramachandran, P., Zoph, B., Le, Q.V.: Searching for activation functions. CoRR abs/1710.05941 (2017). http://arxiv.org/abs/1710.05941

13. Ronneberger, O., Fischer, P., Brox, T.: U-Net: convolutional networks for biomedical image segmentation. In: Navab, N., Hornegger, J., Wells, W.M., Frangi, A.F. (eds.) MICCAI 2015. LNCS, vol. 9351, pp. 234–241. Springer, Cham (2015). https://doi.org/10.1007/978-3-319-24574-4_28

14. Schmidhuber, J.: Deep learning in neural networks: an overview. Neural Netw. **61**, 85–117 (2015)

15. Simonyan, K., Zisserman, A.: Very deep convolutional networks for large-scale image recognition. CoRR abs/1409.1556 (2014). http://arxiv.org/abs/1409.1556

16. Wang, K., Gou, C., Duan, Y., Lin, Y., Zheng, X., Wang, F.Y.: Generative adversarial networks: introduction and outlook. IEEE/CAA J. Autom. Sinica **4**(4), 588–598 (2017)

17. Wang, Z., Bovik, A.C., Sheikh, H.R., Simoncelli, E.P.: Image quality assessment: from error visibility to structural similarity. IEEE Trans. Image Process. **13**(4), 600–612 (2004)

18. Yonetsuji, T.: Paintschainer. https://paintschainer.preferred.tech/index_en.html

19. Zhang, L., Ji, Y., Lin, X.: Style transfer for anime sketches with enhanced residual U-net and auxiliary classifier GAN. In: Proceedings of Asian Conference on Pattern Recognition (ACPR 2017), Nanjing, China, November 2017

20. Zhang, Z., Liu, Q., Wang, Y.: Road extraction by deep residual U-net. IEEE Geosci. Remote Sens. Lett. **15**(5), 749–753 (2018)

21. Zhao, H., Sun, N.: Improved U-net model for nerve segmentation. In: Zhao, Y., Kong, X., Taubman, D. (eds.) ICIG 2017. LNCS, vol. 10667, pp. 496–504. Springer, Cham (2017). https://doi.org/10.1007/978-3-319-71589-6_43

A Novel Moving Object Detection Algorithm of the Monitor Video in the Foggy Weather

Chunyu Xu[1], Yufeng Wang[2,3](✉), and Wenyong Dong[2]

[1] College of Computer and Information Engineering,
Nanyang Institute of Technology, Nanyang 473000, Henan, China
[2] Computer School, Wuhan University, Wuhan 430072, Hubei, China
wangyufeng@whu.edu.cn
[3] Software School, Nanyang Institute of Technology, Nanyang 473000, Henan, China

Abstract. In severe weather, the traditional three-frame difference method is prone to "hole" phenomenon in the moving object detection of the monitor video. In order to solve this problem, a novel moving object detection algorithm (MOD-DT) is proposed, which is combining dark color prior and oriented filtering. MOD-DT first detects the foggy image of the Monitor video, then de-haze the foggy image by dark primary color, and finally detects the moving object in the Monitor video image by the three-frame difference algorithm. Thus, MOD-DT can reduce the impact of the severe weather on the moving object detection. The experimental results show that this algorithm is superior to the traditional moving object detection algorithm in terms of integrity and accuracy, and can realize fast moving object extraction in the complex background environment.

Keywords: Moving object detection · Three-frame difference · De-haze

1 Introduction

At present, moving object detection has been widely used in military reconnaissance, intelligent traffic, video monitoring, video retrieval and other fields [1]. However, on the severe weather conditions, the detection of the moving target still have some difficult problem, especially in the case of haze.

Firstly, the flow of fog will form irregular dynamic background noise in the field of view, which will cause certain interference from the detection of moving objects. Second, in the case of fog, the moving target is often not clear, and the movement is slow. Third, in the case of foggy weather, the haze may block the object, which is similar to the background color and difficult to distinguish, resulting in the existence of voids in the detected objects and the difficulty in detecting the complete moving target. Therefore, it is of great significance

© Springer Nature Singapore Pte Ltd. 2019
H. Peng et al. (Eds.): ISICA 2018, CCIS 986, pp. 205–215, 2019.
https://doi.org/10.1007/978-981-13-6473-0_18

to analyze the disturbance factors of moving target detection in foggy days, study the static and dynamic characteristics of moving foreground target and background in foggy days, and design a detection method applicable to moving target detection in foggy days [2].

At present, the existing detection methods for moving targets mainly include background difference method [3], optical flow method [1] and frame difference method [4]. The background difference method is to make the frame difference between the current frame and the background frame image. The background difference method is simple in principle and easy to implement. However, this method requires a high degree of environmental background and is very sensitive to background changes. According to the velocity vector characteristics of each pixel of each frame in video sequence, the optical flow method is used to analyze the image dynamically. When the target moves, the light flow vector formed by the moving target changes, thus detecting the moving target. However, the optical flow method is not suitable for practical application because of its time-consuming calculation, poor real-time performance and high noise impact.

The frame difference method is to make difference between two adjacent frames in the sequence of video, so as to get the feature information of the moving target. The frame difference method has simple algorithm, good adaptability to environment and good stability. However, for objects with slow moving speed or under severe weather conditions (such as foggy weather), the frame difference method can not completely extract the information of moving objects, and even for some objects with slow moving, light and shadow have a great influence on the detection effect. Therefore, aiming at the problem of the frame difference method, this paper proposes a three frame difference method combining the background frame defogging and adaptive threshold to realize the detection of moving object.

2   Three Frame Difference Algorithm

The frame-to-frame difference method is a method to obtain the moving target wheel profile by differential operation calculation of two adjacent frames of the image sequence of video [5], which can be well applied to the case where there are multiple moving targets and camera movement. When abnormal object motion occurs in the monitoring scene, there will be obvious differences between frames. Two frames are subtracted to obtain the absolute value of the brightness difference between the two frames [6], and it is judged whether it is greater than the threshold value to analyze the motion characteristics of video or image sequence, so as to determine whether there is object motion in the image sequence. However, the motion object it extracts is usually larger than the actual object, and "ghost" phenomenon usually occurs. In addition, because the detected object is the part that changes relative to the previous two frames, the reduplication part cannot be detected, resulting in the "hole" phenomenon of the detected target. The three-frame difference method is improved on the basis of two-frame difference.

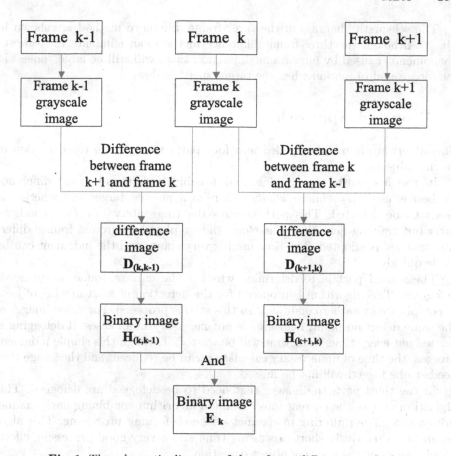

Fig. 1. The schematic diagram of three frame difference method

The principle of three-frame difference method is as follows. It select the continuous three-frame image of the image sequence $J_{k-1}(x,y)$, $J_k(x,y)$, $J_{k+1}(x,y)$, and calculate the difference between two adjacent frames:

$$\begin{cases} D_{(k,k-1)}(x,y) = |J_k(x,y) - J_{k-1}(x,y)| \\ D_{(k+1,k)}(x,y) = |J_{k+1}(x,y) - J_k(x,y)| \end{cases} \quad (1)$$

The obtained difference image was binarized by the appropriate threshold Q:

$$\begin{cases} H_{(k,k-1)}(x,y) = \begin{cases} 1 & D_{(k,k-1)}(x,y) \geq Q \\ 0 & D_{(k,k-1)}(x,y) < Q \end{cases} \\ H_{(k+1,k)}(x,y) = \begin{cases} 1 & D_{(k+1,k)}(x,y) \geq Q \\ 0 & D_{(k+1,k)}(x,y) < Q \end{cases} \end{cases} \quad (2)$$

The logical "and" operation is performed on the obtained image classification:

$$E_k(x,y) = \begin{cases} 1 & H_{(k-1,k)}(x,y) \bigcap H_{(k+1,k)}(x,y) = 1 \\ 0 & H_{(k-1,k)}(x,y) \bigcap H_{(k+1,k)}(x,y) = 0 \end{cases} \quad (3)$$

The schematic diagram of the three-frame difference method are shown in Fig. 1. Although the three-frame difference method can eliminate the "ghost" phenomenon caused by inter-frame difference, there will still be large "holes" in the foreground of motion when the target speed is slow.

3   Proposed Approach

This algorithm is mainly divided into four parts to complete the detection of moving objects.

In the first part, the simplest and feasible background frame difference method is used to estimate whether there is a moving target and whether it needs to be detected. This part requires the time interval of Ts seconds to carry out training detection. Therefore, the simplest background frames difference method is adopted. The time used is very short, and the judgment can be made quickly.

The second part is to determine whether the current frame image needs defogging. This algorithm is proposed for the detection of most moving objects of complicated weather conditions, so this step is proposed. For video images of the same detection point, defogging is not necessary in all cases. If defogging is carried out every time, more time will be wasted. Through this simple judgment process, the time of unnecessary calculation can be reduced, and the image that needs to be fogged will not be missed.

In the third part, the images that need to be defogged are defogged. This algorithm adopts the current most common algorithm combining dark channel priory and guided filtering to conduct image de-fogging processing. This algorithm has a relatively short processing time and a very good processing effect, which can meet the needs of object detection.

In the fourth part, three frame difference methods is used to detect the moving object. The main flow chart is shown in Fig. 2.

3.1   Background Difference

Background difference method is the most commonly used algorithm for moving object detection. Its basic idea is to establish the background model firstly, and then subtract the current frame image pre-background model. If the pixel threshold is greater than a certain threshold, the pixel region of these positions in the current image is determined to be the foreground motion region and vice versa.

$$D_{(k)}(x,y) = |J_k(x,y) - J_a(x,y)| \qquad (4)$$

$$R_{(k)}(x,y) = \begin{cases} 1 & D_{(k)}(x,y) \geq Q_a \\ 0 & D_{(k)}(x,y) < Q_a \end{cases} \qquad (5)$$

Where $J_k(x,y)$ is Current frame image, $J_a(x,y)$ is the background image, $D_{(k)}(x,y)$ is the difference image, Q_a is the threshold value, 1 is stands for sports region, 0 is stands for background region. According to the formulas (4) and (5), When $R_k(x, y) = 1$, the moving target detection is required, and when $R_k(x, y) = 0$, the polling detection is continued. Whether to carry out the object detection flowed chart is shown in Fig. 3.

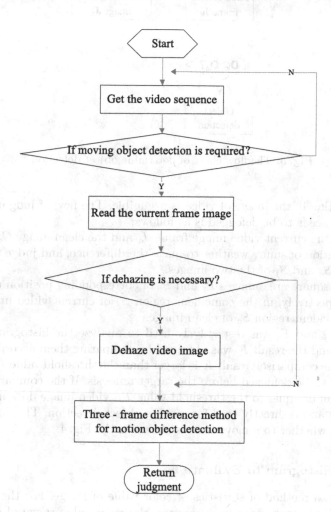

Fig. 2. Main function flow chart.

3.2   Haze Image Preprocess

In this algorithm, the first step of video image processing is to make the judgment on whether to remove fog. Video images are divided into two categories. The first category is foggy video images. Before the target detection, the used video image frames should be defogged. The other type is the fog-free video image. The fog-free image is not completely fog-free, but the effect of fog of the accuracy of

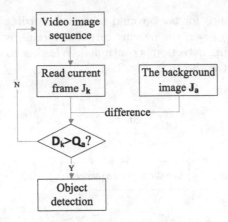

Fig. 3. The flow chart of determine object detection

target detection in the image of video is negligible. The flow of judging whether video image needs to be defogged is as follows:

1. Select the current video image frame J_a and the clean image C_a prepared for the condition of sunny weather to make the difference, and judge the coincident region S_c and S_j of the two images.

2. Select square area images F_j and F_c of corresponding position and size of $W \times H$, respectively, in the coincident region S_j of current video image frame and the coincident region S_c of clean image.

3. The F_j and F_c was respectively used to analyze the histogram of RGB three-path, and the result K was obtained by comparing them according to Eq. (6). When the comparison result K is larger than the threshold value T_a, monitor images need tȯ be defogged before the target analysis. If the comparison result K is less than or equal to the threshold value T_a, video image does not need to be degassed, and is directly used for moving object detection. The flowchart for determining whether to remove haze is shown in the Fig. 4.

3.3   Use Histogram to Evaluate K

Histogram is a method of statistics of color value of image. For the bitmap of 8-bit depth commonly used by computer, the color value range of each channel is 0 to 255. When the color value range is represented by abscissa and the ordinate is the statistical number of the same color value, such two-dimensional rectangular coordinate chart is the color histogram of the image [7]. The value range of the histogram ordinate is related to the size of the image and the distribution of its color value. Then there is the property that when the color grade is determined, it corresponds to a unique histogram; But the histogram is the same, not necessarily the same bitmap. Suppose you divide the color value of N grades, each level is represented by v_i $(i = 1, 2, 3, N)$, g_i $(i = 1, 2, 3, N)$ represents

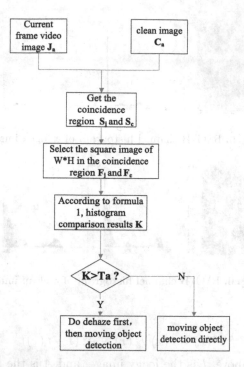

Fig. 4. Determining whether to remove haze flowchart.

the number of statistics when the color grade is v_i. Then, the statistical value of this group of pixel grades g_1, g_2, g_3, g_N is the histogram of this image.

$$K = \sum_{i=1}^{N} \left[(g_{aRi} - g_{bRi}) + (g_{aGi} - g_{bGi}) + (g_{aRi} - g_{bRi}) \right] \tag{6}$$

g_{ai} is used to represent the statistical number of the color grade v_i of fogged images, and g_{bi} is used to represent the statistical number of the color grade v_i of clean images in the same monitoring point. Obviously, g_{aRi} represents the red channel statistical number, and g_{aBi} represents blue, g_{aGi} represents green. The value of T_a can be obtained through multiple experiments. If the value is larger than 50, the image is considered to be foggy and needs to be de-fogged.

Figure 5 is a foggy image from road monitoring video, and Fig. 6 is a clean image from the same monitoring point. Then, RGB three-channel color values is extracted from them, and histogram analysis is carried out for each channel.

3.4 Defogging Algorithm Based on Improved Dark Channel Prior

In the field of computer vision and computer graphics, the imaging equation of atmospheric scattering model is used to describe the haze and fog environment [8]:

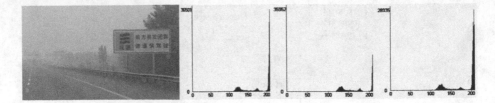

Fig. 5. R\G\B channel histogram of a foggy image

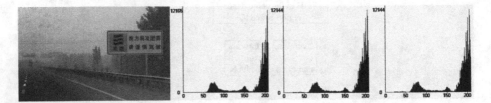

Fig. 6. R\G\B channel histogram of a clean image

$$I^c(x) = t(x) J^c(x) + A^c (1 - t(x)) \tag{7}$$

As mentioned above, I is the foggy image, and A is the global atmospheric light. In general, it is assumed to be a global constant, which is independent of local position x, J is a clean image or scene radiance, t is a medium transmission or transmittance, which is exponentially attenuated with image depth value. $t(x).J^c(x)$ is direct attenuation. $A^c(1 - t(x))$ is airlight.

He et al. [9], based on the statistical observation of a large number of clean images, found that for some pixels in the local area of the non-sky part of the natural image, at least one color channel has a low brightness value and tends to 0. Based on this, He proposed the dark channel prior model, that is, for any natural clear image J, Its dark channel satisfy Eq. (9)

$$\min_{y \in \Omega(x)} \left(\min_{c \in \{r,g,b\}} \frac{I^c(y)}{A^c} \right) = \tilde{t}(x) \min_{y \in \Omega(x)} \left(\min_{c \in \{r,g,b\}} \frac{J^c(y)}{A^c} \right) + 1 - \tilde{t}(x) \tag{8}$$

According to the aforementioned dark channel precedence theory:

$$J_{dark}(x) = \min_{y \in \Omega(x)} \left(\min_{c \in \{r,g,b\}} J_c(y) \right) = 0 \tag{9}$$

The Eq. (9) is brought into the Eq. (8), which can be obtained:

$$\tilde{t}(x) = 1 - \min_{y \in \Omega(x)} \left(\min_{c \in \{r,g,b\}} \frac{J^c(y)}{A^c} \right) \tag{10}$$

Obviously, $\min_{y \in \Omega(x)} \left(\min_{c \in \{r,g,b\}} \frac{J^c(y)}{A^c} \right)$ is the dark color image of foggy image, when the atmospheric light value A is normalized. So, the transmittance t can be calculated roughly. Considering the authenticity of the picture, the parameter α is introduced, and the range of values is $[0, 1]$. With a purposeful retention of the foggy, we make $\alpha = 0.95$, and can obtain that:

$$t\left(x\right) = 1 - \alpha \min_{y \in \Omega(x)} \left(\min_{c \in \{r,g,b\}} \frac{J^c(y)}{A^c} \right) \tag{11}$$

4 Compare with Other Moving Object Detection Algorithms

In our experiments, the simulation is done on an Intel(R) Core(TM) i5 3.30 GHz computer with 8 GB RAM, our codes are implemented in Matlab.

In order to analyze the simulation results quantitatively, the simulation results were compared with the Precision (Pre) and Re-call (Re). The precision rate is the ratio to the correct number of tests and the total number of tests. The re-call rate is the ratio of the correct number detected to the total number manually marked. The higher values of the two indexes at the same time indicate that the foreground detection is more effective. The recall and precision rates of the three methods of different video sets are shown in the Table 1.

Table 1. Comparison of precision ratio and recall ratio

	Evaluation index	Walking	Fight	Haze	Average
Three-frame difference	Re (%)	10	31	7	16
	Pre (%)	5	56	4	22
Background difference	Re (%)	21	37	16	25
	Pre (%)	7	79	5	30
MOD-DT	Re (%)	31	43	40	38
	Pre (%)	15	81	20	28

As can be seen from Table 1, the recall rate of this algorithm is 57% higher than that of the three-frame difference method, and the accuracy rate is 42% higher. Especially in foggy weather, the recall rate and accuracy rate are 82% and 80% higher than the three-frame difference method respectively. Therefore, the accuracy and integrity of the proposed algorithm is superior to the other two moving target detection algorithms in foggy environment with complicated weather conditions.

In order to analyze the speediness of the algorithm in this paper, the three detection algorithms of moving objects are compared on video with three groups by taking time complexity as the evaluation index. The comparison results are shown in Table 2.

Table 2. Comparison of times

	Walking	Fight	Haze	Average
Three-frame difference	1.02 s	1.41 s	1.22 s	1.22 s
Background difference	1.48 s	1.26 s	1.56 s	1.43 s
MOD-DT	1.23 s	1.56 s	2.43 s	1.74 s

5 Conclusion and Future Work

In this paper, we proposed a novel moving object detection algorithm based on the dark color prior and oriented filtering (MOD-DT). MOD-DT employs dark color prior and oriented filtering to de-haze the monitor video image, and then employs the three-frame difference method to detect the moving object. Therefore, it can improve the accuracy of moving object detection in severe weather conditions. The "hole" problem existed on the detection process of the traditional three-frame difference method can be eliminated, and the moving object can be accurately and completely extracted.

Acknowledgements. This research was supported by the National Natural Science Foundation of China (Nos. 61672024, 61170305 and 60873114), and National Key R&D Program of China (No. 2018YFB0904200), and the Key Research Program in Higher Education of Henan (No. 17A520046), and the Research on Application Foundation and Advanced Technology Program of Nanyang (No. JCQY2018012), and the Research on Education and Teaching Reform Program of NYIST (Nos. NIT2017JY-001 and NIT2017JY-032).

References

1. Kim, J., Ye, G., Kim, D.: Moving object detection under free-moving camera. In: IEEE International Conference on Image Processing, pp. 4669–4672 (2010)
2. Akinlar, C., Topal, C.: EDPF: a real-time parameter-free edge segment detector with a false detection control. Int. J. Pattern Recognit. Artif. Intell. **26**(01), 898–915 (2012)
3. Barnich, O., Droogenbroeck, M.V.: ViBe: a universal background subtraction algorithm for video sequences. IEEE Trans. Image Process. **20**(6), 1709–1719 (2011)
4. Archetti, F., Manfredotti, C.E., Messina, V., Sorrenti, D.G.: Foreground-to-ghost discrimination in single-difference pre-processing. In: Blanc-Talon, J., Philips, W., Popescu, D., Scheunders, P. (eds.) ACIVS 2006. LNCS, vol. 4179, pp. 263–274. Springer, Heidelberg (2006). https://doi.org/10.1007/11864349_24
5. Sengar, S.S., Mukhopadhyay, S.: A novel method for moving object detection based on block based frame differencing. In: International Conference on Recent Advances in Information Technology, pp. 10–23 (2016)
6. Yang, W., Tan, R.T., Feng, J., Liu, J., Guo, Z., Yan, S.: Deep joint rain detection and removal from a single image. In: The IEEE Conference on Computer Vision and Pattern Recognition (CVPR), pp. 1357–1366 (2017)

7. He, K., Sun, J., Tang, X.: Guided image filtering. IEEE Trans. Pattern Anal. Mach. Intell. **35**(6), 1397–1409 (2013)
8. Narasimhan, S.G., Nayar, S.K.: Contrast restoration of weather degraded images. IEEE Trans. Pattern Anal. Mach. Intell. **25**(6), 713–724 (2003)
9. He, K., Sun, J., Tang, X.: Single image haze removal using dark channel prior. IEEE Trans. Pattern Anal. Mach. Intell. **33**(12), 2341–2353 (2010)

Multilingual Automatic Document Classification and Translation

Language-Ontology-Based Russian-Chinese Basic Sentence Bank Construction

Aigang Yao[1] and Wuying Liu[1,2]([✉])

[1] Laboratory of Language Engineering and Computing,
Guangdong University of Foreign Studies, Guangzhou 510420,
Guangdong, China
wyliu@gdufs.edu.cn
[2] School of Information Science and Technology,
Jiujiang University, Jiujiang 332005, Jiangxi, China

Abstract. Language ontology is one of the research hotspots in artificial intelligence, knowledge engineering and natural language processing. This paper discusses what kind of language ontology is needed for natural language processing and how to construct such language ontology, and tries to establish a Russian-Chinese bank of basic sentences for natural language processing based on language ontology. The final implementation of the language resource engineering shows the effectiveness of our novel construction approach.

Keywords: Language ontology · Knowledge engineering ·
Basic sentence bank construction · Russian · Chinese

1 Introduction

Ontology has always been one of the basic subjects in philosophy research. From the end of the 20th century to the beginning of the 21st century, language ontology has become a hot research topic in the fields of artificial intelligence, knowledge engineering, natural language processing and so on [1]. At the same time, building domain ontology has gradually become one of the main ways of knowledge representation, knowledge management, knowledge sharing and knowledge reuse in many fields.

This paper holds that WordNet, FrameNet, HowNet, semantic dictionary established by Tuzov V. A., and concept dictionary compiled by Rubashkin V. Sh. and Lahuti D. G. belong to language ontology. This paper intends to explore what kind of language ontology is needed for natural language processing and how to construct such language ontology, and try to establish a Russian – Chinese bank of basic sentences based on language ontology.

2 Ontological Research in Computer Science

In recent years, there are more and more literatures on ontology in computer science in China. However, many researchers simply point out that the term comes from philosophy, emphasize the new features of the term after the introduction into computer

© Springer Nature Singapore Pte Ltd. 2019
H. Peng et al. (Eds.): ISICA 2018, CCIS 986, pp. 219–226, 2019.
https://doi.org/10.1007/978-981-13-6473-0_19

science and information science, and even some people think that it has a new meaning completely. This understanding is not comprehensive. After the term ontology was introduced into computer science, it really has new characteristics. However, in computer science the term ontology has no other unnecessary additional meaning, for those who understand its philosophical connotation and evolution history, it just contains the connotation which is consistent with its new definition, that is, a logical - systematic description and logical formalization of the real world. The essential difference between the new definition of this term and the previous philosophical definition is that it is not only a logical systematization and formal analysis of "being", but also a logical analysis of a specific conceptual system. In this way, the traditional connotation of the term has been extended, not only focus on abstract concepts, but also related to specific concepts, at the same time, it must also be expressed as a formal model, become a reusable computing resources. According to Rubashkin and Lahuti [2], in computer science ontology is more suitable to be called engineering ontology or computational ontology.

This paper holds that although the upsurge of ontological construction has arisen in computer science since the end of last century, there are still many problems in the research of ontology. First of all, the ontological construction method is far from perfect, there is no a unified and universally recognized ontological representation language. Secondly, most of the common research of ontology in computer science is construction of domain ontologies. Because of the lack of uniform standards for ontological construction, many domain ontologies use different ontological representation languages and ontological development tools. Building domain ontology can make full use of the limitations of the domain, more easily formalized, ensure its completeness in the selected domain, and avoid contradictions. However, the compatibility between various ontologies is very poor; the knowledge representation of each domain is incompatible with each other. Therefore, instead of developing and improving various tools to determine the corresponding relationship between independently constructed ontologies, it is better to build a general ontology, and building a general ontology should be the main direction of building ontology. Finally, In addition to the technical issues such as ontological description language and development tools, the research of ontological engineering should also pay attention to the long-term concerns of philosophy such as knowledge extraction and knowledge classification. Whether general ontology or domain ontology, in essence, is the model of the world or the fragment of reality, what kind of model can be closest to the objective world to be described? This is the essential problem in ontological construction. In addition, the reuse and mapping between different domain ontologies is not only related to the unity of description language, the key is the philosophical basis of knowing, describing the world is consistent. In ontological engineering, it is necessary to establish a unified primitive ontology (or top-level general ontology), and then build specific domain ontologies based on it, which should be the direction of future research.

3 What Kind of Language Ontology Is Needed for Natural Language Processing?

3.1 Classification of Knowledge

The term ontology was first introduced into computer science because of the need of knowledge representation. The development of computer science put forward urgent requirements for formal description of knowledge. In order to formalize knowledge for computer processing, we must first solve the problem of how to represent all kinds of knowledge. It is generally believed that conceptual knowledge, pure language knowledge and world knowledge should not be mixed together, so, how should they be represented separately, and can be linked to each other?

Nirenburg and Raskin [3] advocated the construction of static knowledge sources with ontology as the core, describing various kinds of knowledge that people use when processing language information. Static knowledge sources include ontology, lexicon and fact databank. Ontology is a constructed world model, which can be used as the main resource to extract and characterize the meaning of natural language texts and to use the knowledge in texts for reasoning. It can be used as a tool for the transformation between formal textual meaning representation and natural language text, in other words, using ontology can transform natural language text into formal textual meaning representation, in turn, can also generate natural language text according to formal textual meaning representation. Ontology provides a set of metalanguage to describe the meaning of a lexical unit and to explain formal textual meaning representation. The fact databank (world knowledge) contains instances of ontology concepts. For example, the ontology has a concept of "city", the fact databank includes London, Paris or Rome. Such ontology is language ontology. Language ontology is language - independent, and only in this way can they be shared among languages. Information related to specific natural languages is recorded in the lexicon, and there is a mapping relationship between lexicon and ontology.

Ontological semantics emphasizes that the strategy of classifying and representing knowledge can be adopted at the macro level, but different knowledge is not clearly defined, and the breadth and depth of knowledge description can be determined according to the needs of different tasks. For example, world knowledge is useful for disambiguating lexical and referential ambiguities, and the more knowledge about events and objects in a fact databank, the more likely the analyzer is to find the information needed for disambiguation.

3.2 Formal Knowledge Representation Language

Choosing the right knowledge representation language is critical to building ontologies. For the language ontology, because of the complexity of the knowledge contained in it, the requirement of knowledge representation language is higher. Some researchers point out that ontological builders are always too dependent on their native language. The natural language is the symbolic of the concept, the concept must be expressed in a specific language, and the expression of the concept in his own language is the most convenient way for the ontological builder. Because of the ambiguity and fuzziness of natural language, it is not competent for the role of knowledge representation language. Therefore, while building ontologies must rely on a natural language (usually the builder's mother tongue), it is necessary to formalize it, or to convert the concept of natural language into formalized notation and to establish a mapping relationship between the two.

The semantic metalanguage designed by Russian scholar Tuzov V.A. is a combination of physical symbol and Russian vocabulary. The semantic language of Tuzov [4] has the following characteristics: First, it is an abstract language which is equivalent to natural language and is completely formal in semantics, and only the computer can communicate in this language, it has no direct connection with any natural language; second, it is a formalized computer language, textual meaning can be represented as a form which the computer can understand.

Rubashkin and Lahuti [2, 5] set up a concept dictionary which has its own set of formal representation language. They chose the logical language, and believe that only using logical language can fully, orderly and formally descript the meaning relation between the words. Their view is too absolute. Logical language is not the only formal language suitable for semantic expressions, and some elements of natural language text can't exist in logical expressions, or they do not have equivalent units, but these elements are necessary for correctly establishing the semantic expressions of sentences.

Martynov [6] has been devoted to the study of computer-oriented Universal Semantic Code (универсальный семантический код, УСК) since 1970s, and proposed УСК-6 in 2001. УСК-6 uses X, Y, Z, W as Primitive/conceptual primitive, X is the subject, Y is the tool, Z - object, W - result. Give a simple example: ((XY)Z) ((ZW)Y) indicates that X works by Y to Z, creating W, which means X creating W. It should be noted that ((XY) Z) ((ZW) Y) is actually abbreviated ((X → Y) → Z) → ((Z → W) → Y).

3.3   How to Construct Language Ontology

Many researchers have summed up the method of constructing language ontology according to their practice experience. Rubashkin and Lahuti [5] pointed out that to construct the concept dictionary, it is necessary to solve the following basic theoretical and methodological issues: The classification of the natural language vocabulary should be reasonable and easy to model; determination of the composition of the dictionary description; delimitation of the boundary between the semantic primitives and the derivational concepts, the derivational concepts need to be formalized; determination of the description mode of the semantic pattern.

Nirenburg and Raskin [3] summarized the following steps to build the ontology: developing the specifications of the most general concepts at top levels of the ontological hierarchy; acquiring a rather detailed set of properties, the primitives in the representation system (for example, case roles, properties of physical objects, of events, etc.), because these will be used in the specifications of all the other ontological concepts; acquiring representative examples of ontological concepts that provide models (templates) for specification of additional concepts; acquiring examples of ontological concepts that demonstrate how to use all the expressive means in ontology specification.

Ontological semantics adopts the method of separating ontology from lexicon, so the acquisition of ontological concepts and the acquisition of vocabulary in lexicon are two separate and closely related tasks. Nirenburg and Raskin [3] list the steps to acquire ontological concepts: determining whether a meaning is worth introducing a new concept; finding a place for the concept in the ontology, that is determining which of the existing concepts in the ontology would best serve as the parent or sibling of the newly acquired concept; specifying properties for the new concept, making sure that it is different from its parents, children and siblings. When describing an ontological concept, the compiler minimizes the modification of the existing concepts and generates new concepts. Thus, the definition of a new concept often requires only a slight modification of properties and property values as compared to the definition of a parents or siblings. There are two ways to extend the list of candidate concepts: one is deductive or domain-driven, when a concept is added to the concept hierarchy, next step is to collect its sibling concepts, and the other is inductive or corpus-driven, when new concepts are needed to describe new words or phrases, they can be validated in a corpus.

Acquisition of ontology is a complex knowledge engineering task. Knowledge engineering or knowledge-based systems often have the problem of high cost of development. Therefore, how to implement automation as much as possible in the process of knowledge acquisition, editing, and how to minimize human expenditure is a problem that can't be neglected in acquisition of ontology. The language ontology oriented to natural language processing involves not only the knowledge of a restricted domain, so the acquisition of language ontology is more complex than the domain ontology. In addition to theoretical basis, acquisition of language ontology requires a variety of development tools, including editing interfaces, corpus, statistical tools, machine-readable dictionaries, databank management systems and knowledge acquisition guides. Because it is a large-scale knowledge engineering task, it must be completed by a team, so it also includes the personnel training, the unified arrangement of task, quality control and so on.

4 Ontology-Based Russian-Chinese Bank of Basic Sentences

Relying on "Russian Verb Sentences: an Experimental Syntax Dictionary" (here in after referred to as "syntax dictionary"), edited by Russian scholar Babenko L. A., We intend to construct a basic sentence class system based on language ontology, and build a Russian - Chinese bank of basic sentences.

Babenko [7] regards cognitive linguistics as the theoretical basis for dividing the semantic field of verbs. She holds that one of the main tasks of cognitive linguistics is to reveal the general concept system, which constitutes the concept space and serves as the backbone in dividing the concept space. Natural language is the main form of recording our knowledge about the world, or the main means by which we encode it. The compilation purpose of the "syntax dictionary" is not oriented to natural language processing, but its structure and consistency are good, so it can be transformed for natural language processing.

We regard the semantic field of verbs as an important core part of language ontology, and build a sentence class system based on it. This sentence class system is based on language ontology and has cross-language commonality. Each language has its own characteristics. When classifying specific subclasses, it may be more beneficial to find commonalities if multiple languages are used as references. From the perspective of Russian and Chinese languages, we try to establish and describe the sentence class system. We establish the sentence class system and its corresponding concepts and verbs. At the same time, we use Chinese as the reference language to verify whether the concept and sentence class system have cross-language commonality, and investigate the characteristics of various sentence classes through examples of Russian and Chinese languages.

The basis of the sentence classification in the "syntax dictionary" is the semantic field of verbs, which can be regarded as the sentence class system based on language ontology in nature. The sentence class system of "syntax dictionary" completely bases on the šentence class of the verbs in Russian, and the sentence class system contains only the verb sentences. First, it divides the verb sentences into three categories: behavioral, state and relational. Each class has the subclasses. Most sentences with nouns, adjectives and adverbs as predicates describe the state or characteristics, and they can also be classified into existing categories (most of them can be classified into subclass of state sentences). In this way, we initially set up the Russian-Chinese bank of basic sentences which consists of three major sentence classes: A–behavior sentence, taken from English "art", S – state sentence, from English "state", R – relation sentence, from English "relation". Basic sentence classes are: A1 – emphasis on position change of the subject, A2 – emphasis on position change of the object, A3 – placing something, A4 – physical effect sentences, A5 – create activity sentences, A6 – mental activity sentences, A7 – speech activity sentences, A8 – social activity sentences, A9 – physiological function sentences, S1 – sentences of existential state, S2 – sentences of character, R1 – mutual relation sentences, R2 – possession relation sentences, R3 – interpersonal relationship sentences, R4 – social relation sentences. Basic sentence classes divide into subclasses.

In the following, we take the physical effect sentence as an example to illustrate the specific division and description of sentence subclasses in Russian – Chinese bank of basic sentences. We divide the physical effects of subject on object into: strike, press, touch, reformat, remove, process, damage, negatively effect, liberate, get rid of, full up, connect, join, separate, and disassemble. Correspondingly, the physical effect sentence (a subclass of the behavior sentence) is subdivided according to the above physical effects.

The basic contents of the sentence class description are as follows:

The ontological concept corresponding to the sentence class: named after a Russian and Chinese word or phrase.

Sentence class expression: The semantic structure of a sentence, composed of semantic roles, converts the semantic structure of a sentence into a representation of letters and numbers, which is convenient for computer identification and use.

Sentence class Knowledge: The concept priority of each semantic component in a sentence class (the choice limit of each semantic role). According to the distinction of each component of sentence semantic structure (i.e. the subject, the predicate verb, the object, the tool), the sentence class divides into subclasses. The special sentence patterns in Russian and Chinese and the rules of translation.

Here we try to cite one example:

A44. The sentence that expresses change of place

Sentence class expression: subject—verb—object A44 = S + V + O

Datum predicates: изменять, 改变 (change).

Table 1. Seven subclasses

No.	Description of subclasses	Examples (Russian, Chinese, English)
1	Human being, animals, inanimate objects change the shape of the object	*По грязи шёл парнишка, босой, с засученными выше колен штанами.* 小伙子裤腿卷到膝盖以上，光着脚在泥里走。 *The lad rolled his pant above his knees and walked barefoot in the mud.*
2	Human being, animal, inanimate objects change the space state of the object	*Ветер слегка кренил лодку.* 风把船吹得有点倾斜。 *The wind heeled the boat a little.*
3	Human being, animals, inanimate objects change their own space state	*Дерево клонится к земле.* 树弯向地面。 *The tree bends to the ground.*
4	Human being, animals change the state of the body or part of the body	*Солдат вытянулся перед командиром.* 战士直挺挺地站在指挥官面前。 *The soldier stood stiffly in front of the commander.*
5	The plant changes the space state	*Эта пшеница не полегает.* 这种小麦不倒伏。 *This kind of wheat does not lodging.*
6	A certain part of the body change physical state due to the physiological reasons	*Ноги у меня подкосились от страха и слабости.* 我的腿由于害怕和虚弱弯曲发软。 *My legs bent due to fear and weakness.*
7	Human being changes the state of the body (the head) due to the emotional factors	*Девушка потупилась от смущения.* 姑娘羞得低下头去。 *The girl bowed her head in embarrassment.*

This example predicate at least includes seven subclasses. The detailed description of subclasses and corresponding example sentences are shown in Table 1. These examples indicate the hierarchical sentence semantic structure and sentence class knowledge.

5   Conclusion

Russian-Chinese bank of basic sentences still needs to be perfected. In the future, we will focus on solving the following issues:

(1) Combining the method of deduction and induction to perfect the sentence class system. On the one hand, we will sum up the characteristics of sentences in Russian and Chinese on the basis of language examples; on the other hand, we will draw lessons from the previous classification system, pay attention to extract the principles and mechanisms of building sentence class system from the relevant research in philosophy and computer science, and try to make the sentence class system suitable for natural language processing.

(2) Making full use of the existing research results in China and abroad, using a set of symbols (numbers, letters, keyboard symbols, etc.), which the computer can identify and use, to describe the language ontology, generate sentence class expression, represent sentence knowledge, and unify the specification of sentence bank.

Acknowledgements. The research is supported by the Key Project of State Language Commission of China (No. ZDI135-26), the Natural Science Foundation of Guangdong Province (No. 2018A030313672), the Featured Innovation Project of Guangdong Province (No. 2015KTSCX035), the Bidding Project of Guangdong Provincial Key Laboratory of Philosophy and Social Sciences (No. LEC2017WTKT002), and the Key Project of Guangzhou Key Research Base of Humanities and Social Sciences: Guangzhou Center for Innovative Communication in International Cities (No. 2017-IC-02).

References

1. Yao, A., Wu, B., Yi, M.: Automatic Analysis of Russian Semantics Based on Semantic Dictionary. Natural language understanding and large-scale content computation. Tsinghua University Press, pp. 645–647 (2005)
2. Rubashkin, V.Sh., Lahuti, D.G.: Ontology: from Natural Philosophy to Scientific Vision and Knowledge Engineering. Issues of Philosophy, no. 1 (2005). (Рубашкин В.Ш., Лахути Д.Г. Онтология: от натурфилософии к научному мирозрению и инженерии знаний. Вопросы философии № 1 (2005))
3. Nirenburg, S., Raskin, V.: Ontological Semantics. MIT Press, Cambridge (2004)
4. Tuzov, V.A.: Russian Computational Semantics. Publishing House of St. Petersburg State University, St. Petersburg (2004). (Тузов В.А. Компьютерная семантика русского языка. СПб.: Изд-во СПбГУ (2004))
5. Rubashkin, V.Sh., Lahuti, D.G.: Semantic (Conceptual) Dictionary for Information Technology (1). STI, Ser. 2, (1, 5, 7) (1998). (Рубашкин В.Ш., Лахути Д.Г. Семантический (концептуальный) словарь для информационных технологий (1). НТИ, Сер. 2, (1, 5, 7) (1998))
6. Martynov, V.V.: Fundamentals of Semantic Coding. Experience in the Representation and Transformation of Knowledge. EHU, Minsk (2001). (Мартынов В.В. Основы семантического кодирования. Опыт представления и преобразования знаний. Мн.: ЕГУ (2001))
7. Babenko, L.A.: Russian Verb Sentences: an Experimental Syntax Dictionary, M., Flint (2002). (Бабенко Л.А. и др. Русские глагольные предложения: экспериментальный синтаксический словарь. М., Флинта (2002))

Chinese Text Classification Based on Character-Level CNN and SVM

Huaiguang Wu[1], Daiyi Li[1(✉)], and Ming Cheng[2]

[1] School of Computer and Communication Engineering,
Zhengzhou University of Light Industry, Zhengzhou 450000, China
lidaiyiyy@163.com
[2] The First Affiliated Hospital of Zhengzhou University,
Zhengzhou 450000, China

Abstract. With the rapid development of the Internet, the high dimensional text data has increased rapidly. How to build an efficient and extensible text classification algorithm has become a hot topic in the field of data mining. Aiming at the problems of high feature dimension, sparse data and long computation time in traditional SVM classification algorithm based on TF-IDF (Term Frequency-Inverse Document Frequency), we propose a novel hybrid system for Chinese text classification: CSVM, which is independent of the hand-designed features and domain knowledge. Firstly, the encoding words are done by constructing a text vocabulary of size m for the input language, and then quantize each word using 1-of-m encoding. Secondly, we exploit the CNN (Convolutional Neural Network) to extract the morphological features of character vectors from each word, and then through large scale text material training the semantic feature of each word vectors are be obtained the semantic feature of each word vectors. Finally, the text classification is carried out with the SVM multiple classifier. Testing on a text dataset with 10 categories, the experimental results show that the CSVM algorithm is more effective than other traditional Chinese text classification algorithm.

Keywords: TF-IDF · SVM · Character-level CNN · Text vectorization · Text classification

1 Introduction

With the rapid development of the Internet, various kinds of information data have grown rapidly. However, the current social information foundation is weak, and the information resources are large and scattered. Therefore, the development of information data collection, storage, analysis and processing faces enormous challenges. In addition, massive text data makes information difficult to be digested and identified, meanwhile the information security is also difficult to guarantee. Therefore, how to obtain useful information from massive and high-dimensional text data has become a hot topic in current information retrieval research [1]. Text classification technology is an important branch of information retrieval. By constructing the organizational structure of the text sets, the problem of information confusion is effectively solved, thereby greatly improving the efficiency of text processing.

© Springer Nature Singapore Pte Ltd. 2019
H. Peng et al. (Eds.): ISICA 2018, CCIS 986, pp. 227–238, 2019.
https://doi.org/10.1007/978-981-13-6473-0_20

In recent years, great progress has been made in machine learning research. The machine learning techniques have been shown to be very successful in many recognition tasks. For example, SVM have some attractive characteristics such as a convex loss function and a maximum margin criterion, which provides good generalization capabilities [2]. However, the total number of words in Chinese is more than 200,000. The high-dimensional feature space makes the classification algorithms to increase computation complexity. In order to solve these problems, Manning et al. [3] improved the Bayesian model to extract features such as word frequency and morphological of the keywords in the sentence; Silva et al. [4] combined of lexical, syntactic and semantic features, and weighted according to the importance of combination features. Then they used the linear kernel function of SVM to classify the text; Ji et al. [5] extracted text features from the semantic knowledge base in the CNKI (China National knowledge Infrastructure), and then they used the maximum entropy model to classify the text; Negri et al. [6] extracted text features by using "bag model" and syntactic dependency tree techniques, and improved the model by calculating the value of kernel function. Although these methods could address the high dimensionality and data sparsity of text features, the artificially formulated features and various combinations of features may have a certain degree of subjectivity, which limited the generalization ability of feature extraction.

In this paper, we investigate and proposed the CSVM text classification model which used the Character-level CNN [7] to extract high-level features from the texts. This algorithm does not need to consider the grammatical and semantic structure of Chinese text, and it could facilitate rapid classification of multiple languages. In summary, the major contributions of our paper include three aspects. (a) Investigating a novel hybrid system for Chinese text classification: CSVM, which integrating CNN and SVM into a Chinese classifier, thus improving the prediction performance of classification models. (b) This article only applies CNN on characters. When trained on largescale Chinese text datasets, CNN is independent of the text syntax structure and background vocabulary knowledge. Thus it can work for different languages, since characters always constitute a necessary construct regardless of whether segmentation into words is possible. (c) The design of SVM multi-classifier and the parallel implementation of CNN under GPU, to solve the nonlinear problem while avoiding the dimensional disaster and greatly shorten the training time of classification model.

2   Research and Design of CSVM Model

2.1   Text Vectorization

Due to high complexity of Chinese text, the problem of high dimension of feature vectors and sparse data occurs when traditional vector space model is used to represent text information. As a result, computational complexity is increased, which leads to sharp increase in computing time. In this paper, a vocabulary is constructed by text characters, and text is vectorization according to frequency and location of words in text. The experimental data is from THUCNews [8], which contains 10 candidate classification categories: sports, furnishing, entertainment, education, games, fashion, finance, technology, real estate and current politics. The process of data preprocessing is as follows:

1. Training set, validation set and test set needed to build the classification model: 8,000 data were extracted from 10 candidate classifications to constitute the training set, validation set and test set. The training set contained 60,000 text data were, and the validation set and test set contained 10,000 text data, respectively.
2. Build and store vocabulary: The size of vocabulary is set to 6000, which is sorted according to the number of occurrences of characters in the training set text, and the first 5999 characters are selected to construct vocabulary. The characters in vocabulary are represented by $c_i(i = 1, 2, ..., 5999)$, and the last character is 0, which is used to represent characters that are not in vocabulary. Then, character is represented according to its location in vocabulary. Assuming that the length of the text sequence is n, as shown the following:

$$T = \{'c_1' : 0, 'c_2' : 1, ..., 'c_n' : n\} \tag{1}$$

3. Candidate classification vectorization: In this paper, 10 categories of news texts are selected for experiment. Assuming that M represents classification directory, labels and corresponding serial numbers of 10 category texts are represented in a dictionary format as shown the following:

$$M = \{'sports' : 0, 'finance' : 1, 'real estate' : 2, 'furnishing' : 3, ..., 'games'$$
$$: 8, 'entertainment' : 9\} \tag{2}$$

According to the stored vocabulary, text data and category labels for train, validation and test are vectorization. The pad_sequences function provided by keras module in Python is used to set the sequence length of each data to 600 uniformly. The format of the vectorization data is shown in Table 1:

Table 1. Text data vectorization.

Data	Shape	Date	Shape
X_train	[60000, 600]	Y_train	[60000, 10]
X_val	[10000, 600]	Y_val	[10000, 10]
X_test	[10000, 600]	Y_test	[10000, 10]

2.2 Construction of CSVM Model

CSVM classification model is mainly divided into two parts, feature extraction of CNN and text classification of SVM. Firstly, CNN is used to extract deep features of text represented by character vectors based on multi-GPU parallelization. Then text is classified by SVM multi-classifier.

1. Design of CNN

Feature extraction of CNN is inseparable from parameters in network model [9]. For example, sharing weights can reduce complexity of network model. Multidimensional images can be directly used as input of network to avoid complex feature extraction and data reconstruction process. CNN training algorithm mainly includes the following four steps:

Step 1: Select a sample (X, Y) from sample set and enter X into network;
Step 2: After operation of network model, output actual result O;
Step 3: Calculate the difference between actual output O and ideal output Y;
Step 4: Backward propagation according to minimization error, adjust corresponding weight matrix.

Step 1 and 2 are forward transmission phases, while Step 3 and 4 are reverse transmission phases (feedback phase).

Convolution layer is an important part of CNN. It has local connection and weight sharing characteristics [10]. Suppose window height of convolution kernel is h, the dimension of word vector of each word is d, and the length of a sentence composed of words $w_1, w_2, \ldots, w_n$ is n. Then input text data is $n \times d$ 2-D matrix, and the size of the convolution kernel is $h \times d$. Finally, the eigenvectors after convolution operation are shown as follows:

$$c_i = f(\sum W \cdot X_{i:i+h-1} + b) \tag{3}$$

Where, c_i is activation output; $X_{i:i+h-1}$ is words vector matrix in first i to $i + h - 1$ windows; W is convolution kernel (weight matrix); b is the offset; f is activate function for ReLU [11].

After text features are obtained by convolution, the main features are extracted by pooling in order to simplify computational complexity of network. Generally, there are two kinds of pooling operations: average pooling and maximum pooling. In this paper, maximum value of each feature is selected by maximum pooling, and pooling operation is as follows:

$$\hat{c} = \max\{c_i(i = 1, 2, \ldots, n - h + 1)\} \tag{4}$$

Where, $\hat{c}$ represents calculation result of maximum pooling; $c_i(i = 1, 2, \ldots, n - h + 1)$ is result after convolution calculation. Finally, text feature vector which needs to be input to classifier is obtained through full connection layer [12].

2. Design of SVM Multi-classifier

Multiple classifiers were built using SVM. In this paper, the method of one-to-many [13] is used to transform multi-classification into several two classifications. It is assumed that three text categories (a, b and c) are classified by SVM. The steps are as follows:

Step 1: "a" is treated as positive classes, while "b" and "c" together are treated as negative classes, and the decision function $f_1 = \text{sgn}(g_1(x))$ constructed by SVM is used to separate "a" text.

Step 2: Similarly, "b" and "c" are used as positive classes to construct decision tree $f_2 = \text{sgn}(g_2(x))$ and $f_3 = \text{sgn}(g_3(x))$, then "b" and "c" text is separated.
Step 3: Ideally, constructed SVM decision function can correctly reflect actual situation, so for any input x, there is only one positive value in decision function f_1, f_2 and f_3. If constructed decision function has error, category of input text x is determined according to maximum of $g_1(x)$, $g_2(x)$ and $g_3(x)$.

Suppose that the number of categories is m, one-to-many method is to construct m subclass two classifications with SVM. For the n-th subclass two classifications, samples belonging to the n class are marked as positive and the others as negative. The diagram of one-to-many classification is as follows (Fig. 1):

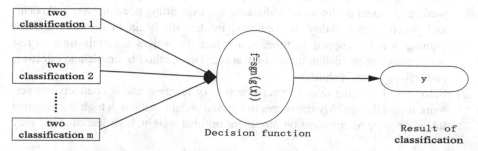

Fig. 1. One-to-many classification structure. f is classification function, y is the result of classification.

3. Parameter Optimization in CSVM Model

CSVM classification model has been trained on different parameter settings, so as to obtain feature extraction model of CNN. The optimal parameter configuration is as shown in Table 2:

Table 2. CSVM algorithm parameter configuration.

Name of parameter	Value of parameter
Number of convolution kernel	128
Convolution kernel size	5 * 64
Number of candidate category	10
Sequence length	600
Character vector dimension	64
Pooling layer	1-max pooling (1 * 1)
Hidden layer	128
Reserved node probability	0.5
Batch size	64
Number of iterations	10
Learning rate	1e−3

Selection of the number of iterations and learning rate during neural network training has a great influence on network performance. Therefore, this paper selects optimization of these two parameters.

(1) Select the number of iterations: In order to prevent over-fitting in process of network learning, we chosen the "early stopping" method to find the optimal number of iterations in neural network [14]. Most commonly used method of network training is Cross-validation, which divides all sample set into three parts, namely training set (training network), validation set (detection function) and test set (evaluation of network generalization ability). On training set and verification set, the performance of network prediction model is evaluated once for each training process of training set. If performance of network prediction model is improving, training will continue. On the contrary, if the performance of network prediction model declines on verification set, over-fitting phenomenon will occur, and generalization ability of prediction model will begin to deteriorate. Then training will be stopped in time, and select the weight s at this time to test performance of prediction model on test set. This method is simple and effective, and training time is short.

(2) Selection of learning rate: Correct selection of learning rate is conducive to network model that quickly converges to optimal weight. Although high learning rate takes less time to converge on model for optimal weight, high learning rate may

Table 3. AdaMax algorithm pseudo code.

AdaMax: Adaptive moment estimation algorithm based on Adam deformation

---

Input: α step size(learning rate)(default 0.001)

$\beta_1, \beta_2 \in [0,1)$ exponential decay rate of method of moments (The default is 0.9 and 0.99)

$f(\theta)$ random objective function with parameter θ (θ need to initialize)

ε a constant used for numerical stability (default 10^{-8})

Procedure: Initialize first-order and second-order matrix variables $s_t = 0, r_t = 0$

Initialize time step $t = 0$

While stop condition is not met **do**

$t \leftarrow t+1$ update time step

$g_t \leftarrow \nabla_\theta f_t(\theta_{t-1})$ computing the gradient

$s_t \leftarrow \beta_1 \cdot s_{t-1} + (1-\beta_1) \cdot g_t$ update partial first order method of moment

$r_t \leftarrow \max(\beta_2 \cdot r_{t-1}, |g_t|)$ update exponential weighted infinite norm

$\theta_t \leftarrow \theta_{t-1} - (\alpha/(1-\beta_1^t)) \cdot s_t / r_t$ update parameter θ

end while

Output: return parameter values θ_t

---

lead to a leap of weight renewal that is too large to precisely reach optimal point. Therefore, in this paper, AdaMax adaptive learning rate algorithm [15], which has small memory requirements and adapted to large data sets and high-dimensional space, is adopted to select appropriate learning rate. Different learning rates are tested on constructed network model, and appropriate learning rate is finally selected.

AdaMax is a distortion of Adam's (Adaptive Moment Estimation) algorithm. Update rule based on norm L^2 is generalized into update rule of norm L^p, and extremely stable and simple AdaMax algorithm is obtained when p approaching and infinity, and its pseudo-code is shown in Table 3:

As can be seen from Table 2, a text is composed of 600 characters, and dimension of character vector is 64, then the text is represented by a matrix with length 600 and width 64. In the process of feature extraction of CNN, window size of convolution kernel is 3 * 64, 4 * 64 and 5 * 64. Because there are a total of 128 convolution cores, each text can be represented by 128 feature vectors after convolution and pooling, finally, 384 features were obtained through the fully connect layer [16]. Thus, the problem of high feature vector dimensions and sparse data when traditional TF-IDF represents text information is solved effectively.

Taking a text data as an example, when CNN is used to extract text features, the structure of CSVM classification model is shown in Fig. 2:

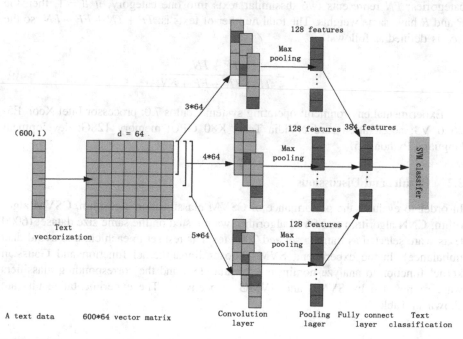

Fig. 2. Chinese text classification flow chart: CSVM, which integrating CNN and SVM into a Chinese text classifier.

3 Experiment

3.1 Experimental Introduction

In order to verify the effectiveness and stability of CSVM classification algorithm, we compared the performance of traditional SVM and CNN classification algorithm with CSVM classification algorithm. The dataset selected during the experiment is from the THUCNews, which contains 10 candidate categorization categories. The language of algorithm was python. Aiming at the traditional SVM classification algorithm, the text was segmented by the segmentation module of Jieba, and the stop words was deleted, and the text was vectorization by the combination TF-IDF and VSM. Aiming at the CNN and CSVM classification algorithm, the experiment used the Tensorflow framework to construct the CNN to extract high-level features.

The performance of SVM, CNN and CSVM classification models was compared by the experiment results, F measure (F) [17] and accuracy (Acc) ware selected to evaluate the classification effect. The F measure is the harmonic mean of precision rate P and recall rate R. The definitions of P, R and F metrics are as follows:

$$P = \frac{TP}{TP+FP} \quad R = \frac{TP}{TP+FN} \quad F_\beta = \frac{(\beta^2+1)PR}{\beta^2 P + R} \quad (\beta^2 \in [0, +\infty]) \qquad (5)$$

Among them, TP represents two similar texts into one category; TN represents two dissimilar texts into different categories; FP represents two similar texts into different categories; FN represents two dissimilar texts into one category. if $\beta = 1$, then the P and R have same weights. The total number of texts is: $TP + TN + FP + FN$, so the Acc is defined as follows:

$$Acc = \frac{TP+TN}{TP+TN+FP+FN} \qquad (6)$$

Experimental environment: operating system Centos 7.0; processor Intel Xeon E5-2620 V3; acceleration card NVidia Tesla K80 GPU; memory 128G; development language Python 3.5.

3.2 Results and Discussions

In order to evaluate the performance of CSVM classification algorithm, CSVM algorithm, CNN algorithm and SVM algorithm ware tested on the same size dataset (6000 texts ware selected as training set and 2000 texts as test set in each class to avoid data imbalance). In the experiment, SVM chooses linear kernel function and Gaussian kernel function to analyze nonlinear text data [18], and the corresponding classifiers ware represented by SVML and SVMG respectively. The experimental results are shown in Table 4.

Table 4. F measure and Acc of the four algorithms.

Dataset	SVML		SVMG		CNN		CSVM	
	F	Acc	F	Acc	F	Acc	F	Acc
Education	0.73	0.89	0.86	0.91	0.92	0.95	0.93	0.97
Entertainment	0.93	0.91	0.96	0.93	0.97	0.95	0.98	0.96
Fashion	0.68	0.90	0.76	0.86	0.96	0.95	0.98	0.99
Finance	0.93	0.85	0.95	0.91	0.97	0.96	1.00	1.00
Game	0.95	0.93	0.96	0.95	0.97	0.97	0.97	0.98
Home_furnishing	0.79	0.76	0.83	0.89	0.93	0.95	0.95	0.97
House_property	0.93	0.94	0.95	0.95	0.99	0.99	1.00	1.00
Politics	0.78	0.82	0.82	0.92	0.94	0.94	0.94	0.96
Science_technology	0.94	0.91	0.94	0.93	0.95	0.94	0.96	0.97
Sport	0.96	0.95	0.97	0.99	1.00	1.00	1.00	1.00
Average value	0.86	0.88	0.90	0.92	0.96	0.96	0.97	0.99

Table 4 shows the test result, which the CSVM, CNN and SVM algorithms on the test set ware counted. The size of the test set is 20000 texts, each class of which accounts for 2000 text data. Table 4 also shows that SVML algorithm is the worst for text categorization, but CNN algorithm and CSVM algorithm for text categorization have little difference. The reason is that convolution neural network extracts the morphological features and SVM multi-classifier solves the nonlinear problem while avoiding the dimensional disaster. In this paper, the comparison of the average F measure and the average accuracy of the four algorithms are drawn with the help of MATLAB software, as shown in Fig. 3.

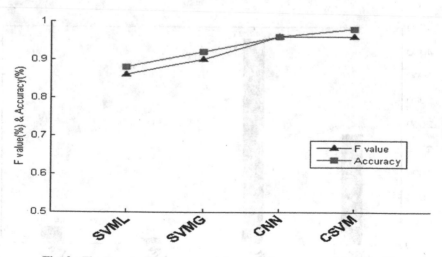

Fig. 3. The average F measure and the average accuracy of the classifier

Figure 3 shows that the average F measure and average accuracy of the CNN and CSVM classification model are all above 95% in the test set, and the CSVM classification model has the highest accuracy, the average accuracy is 99%.

In order to further verify the efficiency of the CSVM classification algorithm, the running time of SVM, CNN and CSVM algorithms ware statistically analyzed on different datasets (each time extracted different amounts of samples from different types of text as training sets and test sets). The statistical results are shown in Table 5.

Table 5. Training time of four classification algorithms on different datasets

Dataset size	SVML	SVMG	CNN	CSVM
	T(s)	T(s)	T(s)	T(s)
50000	1258.25	2325.21	64.67	194.46
80000	1587.26	2916.89	87.13	243.27
100000	1703.47	3486.78	91.23	268.63
150000	2458.77	4076.29	120.42	348.26
200000	4987.18	8405.67	231.68	639.38
Average value	2278.79	4242.17	119.03	338.80

Table 5 shows that the CNN algorithm has the shortest train time. It is often believed that deep models are slow to train the network model. However, we have to emphasize those deep architecture, like all other neural networks models, are extremely parallelization, with dramatically reduces the training time when graphics processing unit (GPU) [19]. Meanwhile, SVM multi classification model needs a large number of weights and is extremely less parallel, so the calculation is time-consuming. With the help of MATLAB software, drawing a histogram of the time consumed by four classification algorithms in training the model on datasets of 8×10^4 size as shown in Fig. 4.

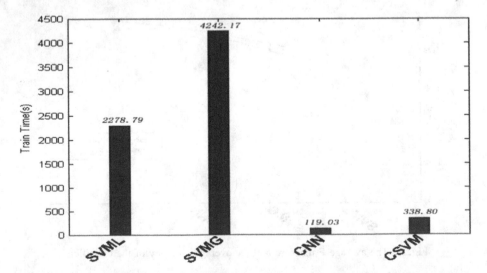

Fig. 4. Mean training time corresponding to the four classification algorithms

It is obvious that Fig. 4 that SVM classification algorithm is time-consuming, CNN algorithm and CSVM algorithm are relatively short time-consuming. According to the comparison of F, Acc and training time, CSVM algorithm is the best.

4 Conclusion and Outlook

In this paper, Char-level neural network was used to extract the high-level features of text, and the dataset was vectorization by prescribing an alphabet. Then we have used Python Scikit-learn library [20] to process the SVM classifications. The results show that the CSVM prediction model has a good performance in Chinese text classification. It was not only improves significantly the test accuracy when compared with both original systems but also reduce the training time when compared with the original SVM classifier.

However, the classification prediction model constructed by traditional machine learning methods will not improve the prediction accuracy with increase of datasets. But the classification prediction model constructed by ensemble learning will improve the performance of the model by learning and extracting high-level features. Although some progress has been made in the study of Chinese text categorization, it still needs to be further studied. Our next research focuses on the following two aspects:

1. How to construct a convolution neural network model which can flexibly adjust the size of convolution window according to the length of text is worth further study.
2. With the development of parallel technology, the text classification model can be implemented in parallel under multi-GPU, thus reducing power consumption and cost while ensuring accuracy.

Acknowledgements. This research is financially supported by National Natural Science Foundation of China (Grant No. 61672470) and the National Key Research and Development Plant (Grant No. 2016YFE0100300 and 2016YFE0100600). It is also partially supported by National Natural Science Foundation of China (Grant No. 61802350), the project of the International Cooperation of Henan Province of China (Grant No. 162102410076), the Technology Tackling Key Project of Henan (Grant No. 162102310578) and the Key Scientific Research Projects of Universities in Henan (Grant No. 17A520064).

References

1. Li, J., Cao, Y., Wang, Y., et al.: Online learning algorithms for double-weighted least squares twin bounded support vector machines. Neural Process. Lett. **45**(1), 1–21 (2016)
2. Vapnik, V.N.: Statistical Learning Theory. Wiley, Hoboken (1998)
3. Wang, S., Manning, C.D.: Baselines and bigrams: simple, good sentiment and topic classification. In: Meeting of the Association for Computational Linguistics: Short Papers, pp. 90–94. Association for Computational Linguistics (2012)
4. Silva, J., Coheur, L., Mendes, A.C., et al.: From symbolic to sub-symbolic information in question classification. Artif. Intell. Rev. **35**(2), 137–154 (2011)

5. Ji, Y.L., Dernoncourt, F.: Sequential short-text classification with recurrent and convolutional neural networks, pp. 515–520 (2016)
6. Chatterjee, R., Negri, M., Turchi, M., et al.: Guiding neural machine translation decoding with external knowledge. In: Conference on Machine Translation, pp. 157–168 (2017)
7. Zhang, X., Zhao, J., Lecun, Y.: Character-level convolutional networks for text classification, pp. 649–657 (2015)
8. Li, J., Sun, M.: Scalable term selection for text categorization. In: Proceedings of the 2007 Joint Conference on Empirical Methods in Natural Language Processing and Computational Natural Language Learning (EMNLP-CoNLL), Prague, Czech Republic, pp. 774–782 (2015)
9. Kowalski, M., Naruniec, J., Trzcinski, T.: Deep alignment network: a convolutional neural network for robust face alignment, pp. 2034–2043 (2017)
10. Simonyan, K., Zisserman, A.: Very deep convolutional networks for large-scale image recognition. Comput. Sci. (2014)
11. He, K., Zhang, X., Ren, S., et al.: Deep residual learning for image recognition, pp. 770–778 (2015)
12. Kim, Y.: Convolutional neural networks for sentence classification. Eprint Arxiv (2014)
13. Tomar, D., Agarwal, S.: A comparison on multi-class classification methods based on least squares twin support vector machine. Knowl.-Based Syst. **81**(C), 131–147 (2015)
14. Kingma, D.P., Ba, J.: Adam: a method for stochastic optimization. Comput. Sci. **28**(12) (2014)
15. Dong, Y., Wu, Y.: Adaptive cascade deep convolutional neural networks for face alignment. Comput. Stand. Interfaces **42**(3), 105–112 (2015)
16. Srivastava, N., Hinton, G., Krizhevsky, A., et al.: Dropout: a simple way to prevent neural networks from overfitting. J. Mach. Learn. Res. **15**(1), 1929–1958 (2014)
17. Carrera-Trejo, V., Sidorov, G., Miranda-Jiménez, S., et al.: Latent Dirichlet Allocation complement in the vector space model for Multi-Label Text Classification. Cancer Biol. Ther. **7**(7), 1095–1097 (2015)
18. Chanda, S., Pal, S., Pal, U.: Word-wise Sinhala Tamil and English script identification using Gaussian kernel SVM. In: International Conference on Pattern Recognition, pp. 1–4. IEEE (2008)
19. Gibson, E., Li, W., Sudre, C., et al.: NiftyNet: a deep-learning platform for medical imaging. Comput. Methods Programs Biomed. **158**, 113 (2018)
20. Pedregosa, F., Gramfort, A., Michel, V., et al.: Scikit-learn: machine learning in Python. J. Mach. Learn. Res. **12**(10), 2825–2830 (2012)

Malay-Corpus-Enhanced Indonesian-Chinese Neural Machine Translation

Wuying Liu[1,2] and Lin Wang[3(✉)]

[1] Laboratory of Language Engineering and Computing,
Guangdong University of Foreign Studies,
Guangzhou 510420, Guangdong, China
wyliu@gdufs.edu.cn
[2] School of Information Science and Technology, Jiujiang University,
Jiujiang 332005, Jiangxi, China
[3] Xianda College of Economics and Humanities,
Shanghai International Studies University, Shanghai 200083, China
lwang@xdsisu.edu.cn

Abstract. Due to the lack of structured language resources, low-resource language machine translation often faces difficulties in cross-language semantic paraphrasing. In order to solve the problem of low-resource machine translation from Indonesian to Chinese, a cognate-parallel-corpus-based expanding method of language resources is proposed, and an improved neural machine translation model is trained by the Malay-corpus-enhanced corpus. The improved model can achieve a comparable result as that of Google in the experiment of Indonesian-Chinese machine translation. The experimental results also show that the morphological similarity and semantic equivalence between the languages are very effective computational features to improve the performance of neural machine translation for low-resource languages.

Keywords: Corpus enhancement · Neural machine translation ·
Morphological overlap ratio · Corpus transfer ratio · Low-resource language

1 Introduction

With the support of big parallel corpus between foreign language and Chinese, neural machine translation (NMT) based on deep learning has a fairly good effect [1], whose performance can meet most of requirements of limited machine translation [2]. But due to the lack of big parallel corpus, low-resource language machine translation still faces difficulties. Nowadays, more than 7,000 non-universal languages in the world are facing the dilemma of lacking parallel corpus in different degrees. Consequently, machine translation study on low-resource languages to Chinese has become a challenging research focus [3].

As one of the most important countries in Southeast Asia, Indonesia has frequent exchanges and cooperation with China promoted by the "Global Ocean Fulcrum" strategy and the "One Belt One Road" initiative. Indonesian (Bahasa Indonesia) is the official language of Indonesia. At present the number of native speakers of modern

© Springer Nature Singapore Pte Ltd. 2019
H. Peng et al. (Eds.): ISICA 2018, CCIS 986, pp. 239–248, 2019.
https://doi.org/10.1007/978-981-13-6473-0_21

Indonesian is 45 million around, while that of L2 speakers is over 160 million in the world. But the Indonesian-Chinese parallel corpus is still very scarce compared with the common languages. To serve the China-Indonesia exchange and cooperation efficiently, we try to improve the Indonesian-Chinese machine translation from the perspective of language resource construction.

Morphological similarity between languages can be used to relieve the lack of language resources. Previous investigations have shown that there is not only a very strong morphological similarity between British English and American English, but also a lot of overlap words within European languages. Our study has also found that there are over 60% overlap words shared in oriental languages of Chinese, Japanese, Korean and Vietnamese [4]. Due to the influence of language homology and cross-language communication, similar forms often form equivalent semantics, which is more obvious among cognate languages. Malay and Indonesian belongs to the same Malay-Polynesian language branch of the Austronesian language family, so we want to use Malay corpus to enhance Indonesian corpus, and to train an improved model of Indonesian-Chinese NMT by the mixed parallel corpus.

2 Related Work

International research has been carried out earlier. Back in 1998, the Defense Advanced Research Projects Agency (DARPA) launched the TIDES project [5], which aims to automatically discover, extract, abstract and translate multilingual information. Then, at the end of 2006, DARPA launched the GALE project [6]. It developed computer software and hardware from voice transcription, translation and filtering to collect, analyze and interpret massive multilingual text and voice information, to improve the efficiency of language translation and text analysis, and to provide timely high-value filtered letters for decision makers. Interest. Since then, DARPA has launched MADCAT projects for optical image text analysis and translation, RATS projects for speech recognition and text transcription, and TRANSTAC practical systems for oral communication and translation. The above projects are jointly completed by the Stanford Research Institute (SRI), IBM, BBN and other research institutions.

Overseas research during this period focused mainly on the specific low-resource languages such as Arabic, Pashtun and Chinese, using the systematic top-level architecture and standard data link ports, linking the research projects to each other, supporting the rapid establishment of a foreign language to English machine translation system, serving military intelligence and national security. The study of machine translation for specific languages has gradually changed from rule-based approach to statistical approach [7], and finally established the dominant position of statistical machine translation [8]. At the same time, it has led to the development of language resources engineering, which has made the LDC of the University of Pennsylvania become an international language resources organization. The original rule-based machine translation is mainly based on formal language theory, around the context-free grammar transformation generation translation. The mainstream statistical machine translation (SMT) is based on Bayes conditional probability theory, which indirectly changes machine translation into the probability calculation of translation model and language model.

With the advent of the big data era, in early 2012, the U.S. government launched a $200 million big data research and development initiative to promote the use of large language data in artificial intelligence. Then, in late 2012, DARPA and the U.S. Air Force Research Laboratory launched the DEFT project [9] to infer semantics, explore relationships, detect text anomalies, and assist analysts to efficiently process large multilingual text data. Then in 2014, DARPA launched the LORELEI project [10], which aims to develop a language-wide system that allows military personnel to acquire critical information about topics, names, events, emotions, relationships, etc. in a short time. In April 2017, DARPA launched the AIDA project, which aims to fuse multi-source, multi-modal, potentially conflicting and deceptive linguistic information to generate schematic interpretations of real-world events, current situations and trends. The project upgrades the Language Resource Engineering to a Semantic Knowledge Engineering, which integrates contextual fragments to achieve holographic cognition of events and trends to assist decision-making. The projects were jointly studied by Stanford, Carnegie Mellon and Raytheon BBN. In 2012, the Intelligence Advanced Research Projects Activity (IARPA) officially launched the BABEL project research [11], aimed at limited corpus and very short time conditions, to achieve cross-language keyword search for any new language speech recognition. Then, in early 2017, IARPA launched the MATERIAL project for English-language information retrieval, aiming at cross-language information retrieval of documents in more than 7,000 languages worldwide. The above projects are mainly undertaken by Johns Hopkins University, the University of Southern California and Columbia University.

Recently, the object of machine translation research is no longer satisfied with several specific languages, but attempts to cover all languages by using Internet language big data. At the same time, deep learning method [12] has replaced the dominant position of statistical methods, and has made a significant breakthrough in machine translation [13]. Deep learning method is also a kind of statistical learning method. According to the theory of neural network, it directly trains translation model by using vector computing components and large-scale corpus. So far, a series of excellent algorithms, such as Sequence to Sequence NMT, Pure Attention NMT [14] and Unsupervised NMT [15], have been proposed. However, the effectiveness of the deep learning NMT algorithm largely depends on the number and quality of parallel corpus [16]. Although deep learning has achieved great success in rich-resource languages, its effect on low-resource languages is limited [17].

Now, most of the researches on machine translation in China focus on NMT [18]. The exploration of low resource language machine translation has led to the formation of "large-scale language resource construction" and "advanced machine learning algorithm development". Our existing research mainly centers on Russian, Japanese, Korean, Vietnamese, Indonesian and Malay, and has achieved remarkable results [19]. Similar to foreign research, to a certain extent, limited by the scarcity of relevant language experts, low-resource language machine translation research in China is still in the preliminary stage of exploration, Indonesian-Chinese machine translation research results are very rare.

3   Language Resource Enhancement

3.1   Architecture

To train a model to implement Indonesian-Chinese machine translation efficiently, we design a layered architecture to support efficient enhancement of language resources shown in Fig. 1, which mainly includes three layers of model training, parallel corpus construction and similarity analysis of cognate languages. In model training, according to the results of cognate similarity analysis, various machine translation models can be trained by mixing the generated corpus of Indonesian-Chinese parallel sentence bank (PSB) and Malay-Chinese PSB. In the parallel corpus construction part, we propose two construction methods based on comparable corpus and interlanguage bridging respectively. In the similarity analysis part of cognate languages, we quantitatively analyze the morphological overlap ratio and corpus transfer ratio from Malay to Indonesian.

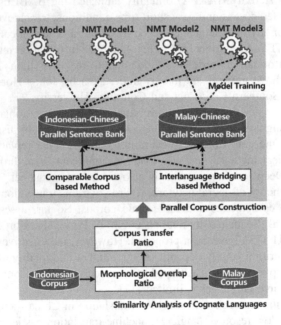

Fig. 1. Layered architecture

3.2   Parallel Corpus Construction

To build PSBs of Indonesian-Chinese and Malay-Chinese, we design two novel methods. The first method is comparable-corpus-based sentence pair extraction. We believe that the cognitive function of human brain determines the semantic equivalence of natural languages. When there are comparable corpus from Indonesian (or Malay) to Chinese, supported by a bilingual dictionary, a sentence pair with equivalent semantic can be extracted according to the semantic fixed points such as punctuations, Arabic numerals, and so on. We implement the first method from our collected comparable corpus of domestic Indonesian (and Malay) teaching textbooks and bilingual news online. The second method is interlanguage-bridging-based sentence pair extraction. We think there is not only the semantic equivalence among natural languages, but also the transitivity of the equivalent relation among languages in different morphological representations. When there are large-scale PSBs from Indonesian (or Malay) to an interlanguage and from the interlanguage to Chinese, we can use the morphological transitivity to calculate the similarity of two interlanguage sentences, and bridge an Indonesian (or Malay) sentence to its corresponding Chinese sentence to form a sentence pair. We implement the second method by using English as the interlanguage. At last, we build out an Indonesian-Chinese PSB containing 2,489,442 sentence pairs, and a Malay-Chinese PSB with 761,373 sentence pairs. Partial examples of Indonesian-Chinese parallel sentence bank are shown in Table 1.

Table 1. Partial examples of Indonesian-Chinese parallel sentence bank

Indonesian	Chinese
Acara ini sampai jam berapa?	这个表演到几点呢？
Aku berharap suatu hari aku bisa melakukan hal yang benar.	我只希望有一天我能处理好一切。
Anak perempuan ini bekerja sebagai pembantusebelum datang ke sekolah.	这个女孩在来上学之前是做女佣的。
Apakah kita sendirian di alam semesta?	我们是宇宙中唯一的文明吗？
Bali Masih Aman Untuk Dikunjungi!	巴厘岛对游客来说还是安全的！
Berapa yang kau butuhkan?	拍摄这部影片需要多少钱？
Dan permainan dimulai.	游戏就此开始。
Frekuensi serangan semakin meningkat.	频繁的袭击不断增加。
Indonesia adalah komunitas ekonomi yang terbesar di Asia Tenggara.	印尼是东南亚最大经济体。
Jika modul itu sudah mendarat, kau tak akan mau memindahkannya.	等飞船着陆后，就不方便移动了。
Kau harus kembali ke tempat dudukmu.	请你回到座位去。
Kerja keras dan dukungan para orang tua merupakan kunci kesuksesan mereka saat ini.	他们的成功离不开家长的辛勤培育和支持。
Kita berevolusi bersama peralatan, dan peralatan berevolusi bersama kita.	人类发明了工具，工具也影响着人类。
Lain kali ingin berbicara, lakukan itu sebelumnya.	下次你演讲之前，提前做到这几项。
Lebih baik tulis nama anda di bawah, suoaya penerima tahu Fax nya dari siapa.	最好在下面写上您的名字，收取人好知道传真是谁发的。
Lingkaran biru itu lebih kecil daripada lingkaran merah itu.	那个蓝色的圆比那个红色的圆小。
MasyarakatBali terkenal ramah dan penuh senyum.	巴厘人以友好善良和微笑而著名。
Saya bangun di dalam sel penjara, diborgol, dan mata disekap.	我发现自己在监狱里，带着手铐，被蒙住眼睛。
Tapi para murid kalah dari simpanse.	这些优等生们却做不到。
Tiongkok mendesak negara tetangga untuk meningkatkan upaya dalam Memerangi Ekstremisme.	中国敦促邻国加大极端主义打击力度。

3.3 Similarity Analysis of Cognate Languages

According to the statistics, there are more than 80 million native speakers of modern Malay (Bahasa Melayu), mainly in Brunei, Indonesia, Malaysia, Singapore and other places, while the global Malay language users are over 300 million. In a broad sense, Malay language includes Indonesian language. Malay and Indonesian, similarly as Mandarin and Singaporean Mandarin, British English and American English, have a strong homology of the same language family, and make it very similar in pronunciation, vocabulary, grammar and so on. Their Latin morphological alphabets are exactly the same, just as the English alphabet. Therefore, morphological similarity among cognate languages can be used to enhance language resource. But how much is the morphological similarity between Indonesian and Malay? We will give a further quantitative analysis through morphological overlap examination.

We use the Wikipedia 20180501 version as the source of statistical analysis, which contains 439.3 MB bz2 package about Indonesian articles and 173.8 MB bz2 package about Malay articles. The number of de-duplicated word-level N-gram token has counted in Indonesian texts and Malay texts respectively, and the detailed results are shown in Table 2. The results of the 1-gram token show that all Indonesian texts are composed of 657,409 distinct Indonesian words, and all Malay texts are only composed of 395,365 distinct Malay words. And the number of co-occurrence words both in the two corpus is as many as 211,453.

Table 2. Number of word-level N-gram token

N-gram	Indonesian (MOR)	Malay (MOR)	Overlap
1-gram	**657,409** (32.16%)	**395,365** (53.48%)	**211,453**
2-gram	**8,035,771** (15.36%)	**3,994,868** (30.89%)	**1,233,931**
3-gram	**19,614,857** (6.51%)	**8,756,914** (14.58%)	**1,276,456**
4-gram	**23,038,089** (2.84%)	**9,708,373** (6.73%)	**653,356**
5-gram	**20,797,228** (1.66%)	**8,658,728** (4.00%)	**345,955**

The number of morphological overlap tokens between two languages has different effectiveness to each language. We define the directive N-gram morphological overlap ratio from language A to language B $\left(MOR_{N-gram}^{A \to B}\right)$ as the percentage of the number of co-occurrence N-gram tokens both in the language A and the language B divided by the total number of N-gram tokens in the language B. The value of $MOR_{N-gram}^{A \to B}$ reflects the effective degree of N-gram morphological learning from the language A corpus to the language B. By calculating the 1-gram morphological overlap ratio, we can obtain $MOR_{1-gram}^{M \to I} = 32.16\%$ from Malay (M) to Indonesian (I).

According to the formula of above $MOR_{N-gram}^{A \to B}$, we further define the corpus transfer ratio $\left(CTR_N^{A \to B}\right)$ from language A to language B as $\sum_{i=1}^{N} \alpha_i MOR_{i-gram}^{A \to B}$, in which the coefficient α_i indicates the percentage of the number of i-gram tokens divided by the total number of all N-gram tokens without de-duplication in the language A corpus. Because the long-range correlation in all languages is often relatively weak, it is usually only necessary to simplify the $CTR_N^{A \to B}$ calculating as its value when the $N = 5$ to represent enhancement degree from the A language corpus to the B language corpus. The corpus transfer ratio from Malay to Indonesian based on the morphological overlap ratio can support our idea of enhancing Indonesian-Chinese PSB with Malay-Chinese PSB.

4 Machine Translation Experiment

To verify the enhancement effect of the Malay-Chinese PSB on Indonesian-Chinese machine translation, we design the following experiment.

The experimental corpus is divided into three sets of training, verification and testing, where there are 20,000 Indonesian-Chinese sentence pairs in the verification set and the test set respectively, which are extracted from the 2,489,442 sentence pairs in the Indonesian-Chinese PSB by random sampling without replacement. We briefly record the Indonesian-Chinese PSB as IdChSens, and abbreviate the partial bank of the remaining 2,449,442 sentence pairs as IdChSens-P, which is the rest out of the verification set and the test set. We briefly name the 761,373 sentence pairs in the Malay-Chinese PSB as MsChSens. Then we calculate the 1-gram morphological overlap (OverlapWordSet) of Malay and Indonesian in the MsChSens and the IdChSens, and scan each Malay sentence in the MsChSens. If every word in the Malay sentence is contained in the OverlapWordSet, the Malay-Chinese sentence pair containing the Malay sentence is added into the Malay-Chinese partial bank MsChSens-P. It can be seen that the MsChSens-P is a subset of the MsChSens. In actual scanning result, the MsChSens-P contains 696,840 pairs, which can be regarded as Indonesian corpus from Malay corpus.

The experimental machine translation models consist of three NMT models and a statistical machine translation (SMT) model for comparison. The SMT model is trained by the open source Moses [20] with the default optimized parameters on the IdChSens-P dataset. The three NMT models, sequence to sequence models [21, 22], are trained by the open source TensorFlow NMT Tutorial on their respective datasets. The experimental results of the four machine translation models are shown in Table 3. We find that when the training corpus is less than 2.5 million pairs, the effect of the NMT model (BLEU4 = 17.13) is less than that of SMT model (BLEU4 = 19.58); when the Malay-corpus-enhanced training corpus increases to more than 3 million pairs, the BLEU4 score of the NMT model increases from 17.13 to 20.30 significantly; the enhancement to Indonesian-Chinese NMT lies in the morphological overlap of the Malay corpus according to the same BLEU4 score of NMT2 and NMT3.

Table 3. Experimental results of machine translation

Model	Train set	Validation set	Test set	BLEU4
SMT	IdChSens-P **2,449,442**	**20,000**	**20,000**	**19.58**
NMT1	IdChSens-P **2,449,442**	**20,000**	**20,000**	**17.13**
NMT2	IdChSens-P + MsChSens **3,210,815**	**20,000**	**20,000**	**20.30**
NMT3	IdChSens-P + MsChSens-P **3,146,282**	**20,000**	**20,000**	**20.30**

To further evaluate the effect of the NMT3 model, we randomly selected 20 sentence pairs from the above test set and submitted the Indonesian sentences to the Google and Microsoft Bing machine translation systems. Indonesian experts score the Chinese reference translation, our NMT translation, Google and Microsoft Bing translations by contrasting the Indonesian source sentence. According to the faithfulness between source and translation, four ranks of 4, 3, 2, or 1 point will be scored, where the larger the score is, the higher the translation quality is.

Table 4. Manual evaluation of Indonesian-Chinese machine translation.

Indonesian Source Sentence	Chinese Reference Translation	Our NMT Translation	Google Translation	Microsoft Bing Translation
Indonesian Sentence 1	1	1	3	4
Indonesian Sentence 2	2	4	4	3
Indonesian Sentence 3	1	4	2	3
Indonesian Sentence 4	4	4	3	2
Indonesian Sentence 5	2	3	3	4
Indonesian Sentence 6	2	3	1	1
Indonesian Sentence 7	3	4	2	2
Indonesian Sentence 8	3	2	2	2
Indonesian Sentence 9	3	1	4	2
Indonesian Sentence 10	4	1	1	3
Indonesian Sentence 11	1	3	3	2
Indonesian Sentence 12	2	3	4	1
Indonesian Sentence 13	4	4	3	3
Indonesian Sentence 14	1	1	4	4
Indonesian Sentence 15	1	4	1	1
Indonesian Sentence 16	3	4	1	1
Indonesian Sentence 17	2	3	3	3
Indonesian Sentence 18	4	3	4	1
Indonesian Sentence 19	1	2	3	1
Indonesian Sentence 20	1	2	3	4
Total Points	45	56	54	47

Table 4 shows the detailed scores, where there are four background colors to represent the 4, 3, 2, and 1 point from dark to light. In Table 4, our NMT translation has won the best 56 total points, followed by the 54 points of Google translation, the 47 points of Microsoft Bing translation, and the 45 points of Chinese reference. The performance of our NMT is better than that of Microsoft Bing obviously, and is even comparable to that of the best Google. It can be found that: (1) The comparable-corpus-based sentence pair extraction and the interlanguage-bridging-based sentence pair extraction are two effective methods of parallel corpus construction for low-resource languages. (2) The morphological similarity and semantic equivalence between the cognate Malay and Indonesian support the effective enhancement of Malay corpus to the Indonesian-Chinese NMT. (3) Although the quality of the Chinese reference in the

Indonesian-Chinese PSB is not very high, the NMT can learn a more optimal model than the reference from a low quality corpus, which is mainly due to the deep learning method to fully refine learning features, to make full use of big training data, and to parallel compute in a large number of vector processors.

5 Conclusion

In order to deal with the challenging NMT issue from low-resource Indonesian to Chinese, we have designed a layered architecture, statistically analyzed the morphological overlap ratio and the corpus transfer ratio from Malay to Indonesian, and presented a corpus enhancement for NMT based on cognate parallel corpus built by two kinds of construction methods. And our NMT model trained by the Malay-corpus-enhanced parallel corpus has achieved the best performance in the Indonesian-Chinese machine translation experiment. The mixed corpus can improve the NMT effectively depends on the morphological similarity and semantic equivalence between the cognate languages.

At present, 5 million and 10 million sentence pairs are starting point of training corpus requirement for experimental NMT system and practical NMT system, respectively. Further construction study of PSB will more focus on the scale advantage of monolingual resources, and generate sentence pairs through efficient machine translation algorithms. At last, more other language families will be considered, and more effective NMT from non-universal languages to Chinese will be implemented to verify the computing universality of corpus transferring between cognate languages.

Acknowledgements. The research is supported by the Key Project of State Language Commission of China (No. ZDI135-26), the Natural Science Foundation of Guangdong Province (No. 2018A030313672), the Featured Innovation Project of Guangdong Province (No. 2015KTSCX035), the Bidding Project of Guangdong Provincial Key Laboratory of Philosophy and Social Sciences (No. LEC2017WTKT002), and the Key Project of Guangzhou Key Research Base of Humanities and Social Sciences: Guangzhou Center for Innovative Communication in International Cities (No. 2017-IC-02).

References

1. Liu, Y.: Recent advances in neural machine translation. J. Comput. Res. Dev. **54**(6), 1144–1149 (2017)
2. Liu, W., Wang, L., Zhang, X.: Fast-syntax-matching-based Japanese-Chinese limited machine translation. In: Gelbukh, A. (ed.) CICLing 2016. LNCS, vol. 9624, pp. 63–73. Springer, Cham (2018). https://doi.org/10.1007/978-3-319-75487-1_6
3. King, B.P.: Practical Natural Language Processing for Low-Resource Languages. Doctoral dissertation, University of Michigan (2015)
4. Liu, W.: supervised ensemble learning for vietnamese tokenization. Int. J. Uncertainty, Fuzziness Knowl.-Based Syst. **25**(2), 285–299 (2017)

5. Cieri, C., Liberman, M.: TIDES language resources: a resource map for translingual information access. In: Proceedings of the 3rd International Conference on Language Resources and Evaluation (LREC), pp. 1334–1339. ELRA (2002)
6. Olive, J., Christianson, C., McCary, J.: Handbook of Natural Language Processing and Machine Translation: DARPA Global Autonomous Language Exploitation. Springer, New york (2011). ISBN 9781441977120
7. Nakov, P., Ng, H.T.: Improving statistical machine translation for a resource-poor language using related resource-rich languages. J. Artif. Intell. Res. **44**, 179–222 (2012)
8. Koehn, P.: Statistical Machine Translation. Cambridge University Press, Cambridge (2009). ISBN 9780521874151
9. Bies, A., et al.: A comparison of event representations in DEFT. In: Coreference, and Representation Proceedings of the 4th Workshop on Events: Definition, Detection, pp. 27–36. ACL (2016)
10. Cieri, C., Maxwell, M., Strassel, S., Tracey, J.: Selection criteria for low resource language programs. In: Proceedings of the 10th International Conference on Language Resources and Evaluation (LREC), pp. 4543–4549. ELRA (2016)
11. Knill, K.M., Gales, M.J.F., Ragni, A., Rath, S.P.: Language independent and unsupervised acoustic models for speech recognition and keyword spotting. In: Proceedings the 15th Annual Conference of the International Speech Communication Association (INTER-SPEECH), pp. 16–20. ISCA (2014)
12. LeCun, Y., Bengio, Y., Hinton, G.: Deep learning. Nature **521**, 436–444 (2015)
13. Hirschberg, J., Manning, C.D.: Advances in natural language processing. Science **349** (6245), 261–266 (2015)
14. Vaswani, A., et al.: Attention Is All You Need. arXiv:1706.03762v5 (2017)
15. Artetxe, M., Labaka, G., Agirre, E., Cho, K.: Unsupervised Neural Machine Translation. arXiv:1710.11041v1 (2017)
16. Wu, Y.: Google's Neural Machine Translation System: Bridging the Gap between Human and Machine Translation. arXiv:1609.08144v2 (2016)
17. Manning, C.D.: Last words: computational linguistics and deep learning. Comput. Linguist. **41**(4), 701–707 (2015)
18. Zhang, J., Zong, C.: Deep neural networks in machine translation: an overview. IEEE Intell. Syst. **30**(5), 16–25 (2015)
19. Liu, W., Lin, L.: Probabilistic ensemble learning for vietnamese word segmentation. In: Proceedings of the 37th Annual International ACM SIGIR Conference on Research and Development in Information Retrieval (SIGIR), pp. 931–934. ACM (2014)
20. Koehn, P., Hoang, H., Birch, A., et al.: Moses: open source toolkit for statistical machine translation. In: Annual Meeting of the Association for Computational Linguistics (ACL), Demonstration Session, Prague, Czech Republic, June 2007
21. Sutskever, I., Vinyals, O., Le, Q.V.: Sequence to sequence learning with neural networks. In: Proceedings of the 28th Annual Conference on Neural Information Processing Systems (NIPS), pp. 3104–3112. Curran Associates (2014)
22. Neubig, G.: Neural Machine Translation and Sequence-to-sequence Models: A Tutorial. arXiv:1703.01619v1 (2017)

Combining Transformation and Classification for Recognizing Textual Entailment

Han Ren[1], Jing Wan[2(✉)], and Xiaomei Chen[3]

[1] Laboratory of Language Engineering and Computing,
Guangdong University of Foreign Studies, Guangzhou 510420, China
hanren@gdufs.edu.cn
[2] Center for Lexicographical Studies, Guangdong University of Foreign Studies,
Guangzhou 510420, China
jingwan@whu.edu.cn
[3] School of Information Science and Technology,
Guangdong University of Foreign Studies, Guangzhou 510420, China

Abstract. This paper introduces an approach combining transformation and classification methods for recognizing textual entailment. In transformation model, directional and undirected inference relations are recognized, and text fragments having such relations in text are replaced by the counterparts in hypothesis. In classification model, a hybrid kernel-based approach is introduced, and three kinds of features are employed for classifying entailment. Experimental results show that the combination approach achieves a better performance in comparison with the single classification system.

1 Introduction

Current research on natural language learning focuses on semantic analysis and inference for understanding meaning of texts. Being one of the main topics in the research area of textual inference, recognizing textual entailment (RTE) aims to detect entailment relations between two texts by making a judgment whether one can be inferred from another. For example, given a text (so-called T) *A land rover is being driven across a river* and a hypothesis (so-called H) *A vehicle is crossing a river*, it is easy to find that the meaning of the hypothesis can be inferred from the text, or the text entails the hypothesis. As a general framework of textual inference, RTE can be widely used in many natural language processing applications, such as reading comprehension, question answering and document summarization [1].

There are, generally, two main strategies for RTE. The first one treats RTE as a classification issue, that is, to classify a text pair (T, H) into entailment or non-entailment. More specifically, the text pair is expected to be classified as entailment if T entails H, or non-entailment if not. However, such approach is difficult to express those text pairs that hold complex relations that need to be inferred by multi steps. The other strategy views RTE as a transformation process, that is, to find text fragments between T and H having inference relations. For example, as shown in the text pair (T, H) in the previous paragraph, *land rover* entails *vehicle*, and *being driven across* entails *crossing*. Although this strategy is more precise to describe inference relations between two

© Springer Nature Singapore Pte Ltd. 2019
H. Peng et al. (Eds.): ISICA 2018, CCIS 986, pp. 249–256, 2019.
https://doi.org/10.1007/978-981-13-6473-0_22

texts, how to find out inferable relations in a text pair (T, H) and which relations can be transformed from T and H still remain an important issue.

This paper introduces an approach combing such two strategies to recognize textual entailment. The idea is that, since the transformation-based approach contributes to identify local inference relations, while the classification-based one helps classify entailment in a global view, combing such two approaches may benefits recognition of textual entailment in multiple layers. Our approach runs as follows: for lexical inference, a transformation approach is utilized, that is, if a word, phrase or named entity in H can be inferred from a counterpart in T, it replaces the counterpart in T; for overall entailment judgment, a classification approach is employed, that is, to judge the entailment relation between text pairs after replacement. Experimental results show that the combination approach achieves a better performance in comparison with those systems leveraging transformation or classification respectively.

The rest of this paper is organized as follows. Section 2 discuss the transformation model. Section 3 gives a detailed description on a hybrid classifier and its features. Experimental results and discussion are given in Sects. 4 and 5 gives a conclusion.

2   Transformation for RTE

Transformation is one of the major strategies for entailment recognition [2, 3]. Essentially, transformation is to search for a sequence of rule sets, which turns a text to another that can be inferred from it.

For detecting transformable pairs in text pairs, rich inference knowledge is required. Since there is little of structural or logical transformation knowledge in Chinese, we focus on word-level transformation knowledge in our model. On the other hand, such transformation process is prior to the classification model. More specifically, each text fragment in T and H are extracted to match transformable pairs in knowledge bases; if so, such text fragments in T are replaced by the counterparts in H. Finally, those transformed texts, i.e., regenerated Ts, are treated as inputs for training and prediction of classification model.

There are two types of inference transformation. The first one is undirected inference transformation, which is synonymous alternation between words and named entities with same meaning. For example, *illness* is the synonym of the word *sickness*, while *the Imperial Palace* is also called *the Forbidden City*, which is located in China. In this case, text fragments with same meaning can be interchanged without any semantic variation. The other one is directed inference transformation, which refers to hypernymous replacement between words and named entities with semantic containment relations. For example, *flower* is the hypernym of the word *rose*, while *Los Angeles* belongs to *California*. Such transformation process is based on the idea that, a word has richer information than its hypernym; in other words, a word semantically entails its hypernym. If every part of T entails counterparts in H, it is reasonable to assume that T entails H.

2.1   Undirected Transformation

There are two types of text fragments with same meaning that are considered in synonymous alternation: common synonyms and OOVs.

Common synonym includes synonymous words that always appear in lexicons or dictionaries, like *illness* and *sickness*. Since our training and test set is a Chinese data collection, we use an online resource, Baidu Hanyu[1], which is a Chinese lexicon that offers rich synonyms and antonyms. The process is simple: for each word in T, search synonyms from the lexicon to find all its synonyms; if a word in H does also appear in the synonym set, use the word in T to replace the word in H.

Another type of synonyms is OOVs, that is, two words having the same meaning do not appear in lexicons or dictionaries, like *the Imperial Palace* and *the Forbidden City*. In this case, a knowledge base called Zhishi.me[2] is employed to extract synonymous entity pairs. Such resource is a knowledge graph collecting semantically equivalent entities from online encyclopedia websites such as Wikipedia and Baidupedia. Based on it, we extract entity pairs in (T, H) that have same meaning, then use each entity in H to replace the counterpart in H.

2.2   Directed Transformation

Directed transformation is essentially asymmetric meaning replacement from T to H. More specifically, a word in T is replaced by another word in H if the meaning of the former one semantically contains the latter one.

There are also two types such words: common hypernyms and OOVs. For extracting common hypernyms, we employ Tongyici Cilin[3], which is a Chinese WordNet lexicon including over 70,000 items. We also create a constraint that each word and its hypernym should be direct hypernym-hyponym relation, in order to avoid semantic drifting. For extracting OOVs, we use another knowledge base named CN-Probase[4], which is a concept knowledge graph including over 27 million concepts as well as 33 million is a relations. The transformation process is as same as the method for undirected transformation.

2.3   Transformation Decision

Transformation contributes to narrowing the semantic gap between T and H, but how to find the counterpart in H corresponding to such word or phrase in T still remains a problem. For example, if there is a word *rose* in T, and two words *flower* in H, the transformation model should choose the correct counterpart before the replacement. As a matter of fact, if such two words lie in the same syntactic position in T and H, it may transformable. The reason is that, syntactic position represents semantic relation

---

[1] http://dict.baidu.com

[2] http://zhishi.me

[3] http://www.ltp-cloud.com

[4] http://kw.fudan.edu.cn/apis/cnprobase

between a word and other parts in a sentence, hence changing such word does probably not influence semantic relations between such word and other parts.

Table 1. Features for transformation decision.

	Description
f_1	Judges if the two words right to the transformable words in T and H are same
f_2	Judges if the two words left to the transformable words in T and H are same
f_3	Judges if the POS of the two words right to the transformable words in T and H are same
f_4	Judges if the POS of the two words left to the transformable words in T and H are same
f_5	Judges if the parents of the transformable words in T and H are same
f_6	Judges if the POS of the parents of the transformable words in T and H are same
f_7	Judges if the path lengths of the transformable words in T and H to ROOT are same
f_8	The overlapping degree of the children of the transformable words in T and H

Based on that idea, a decision tree model is adopted, to judge if a word or entity in H can be replaced by the counterpart in T. We use C4.5 algorithm to create the tree. Table 1 shows the features used in the model.

3   Entailment Classification

After transformation process, each regenerated T and H are paired to be classified.

3.1   The Classifier

RTE systems often employ SVM as their classifiers, most of which adopt polynomial kernel as the kernel function. However, it is not appropriate to describe the structure of text. More specifically, even if two sentences have a high similarity of syntactic representations, they could be featured as two vectors with very low similarity, which may lead to data sparse.

In this paper, a tree kernel-based SVM is utilized. In comparison with the polynomial kernel, the tree kernel is more appropriate to describe structural similarity. However, the tree kernel-based SVM achieves low performances when classifying text pairs having complex semantic relations and low structural similarity. Instead, the polynomial kernel-based SVM achieves better performances. Therefore, we introduce a hybrid kernel approach for RTE, that is, we joint tree kernel and polynomial kernel as one kernel function, and define entailment features for classification. The hybrid kernel is defined as follows:

$$K_{hybrid} = \alpha K_{poly} + (1 - \alpha)K_{tree} \tag{1}$$

where $0 < \alpha < 1$ is the hybrid coefficient. Since kernel functions are closed under arithmetic operation, the hybrid kernel is also satisfied with Mercer's condition.

3.2   Features

Two types of feature are employed for classification. The first one is string features, which consider string overlap or similarity between T and H. Such features are also employed in most classification-based systems in RTE [4–7] and RITE [8–12] series challenges, showing that they are effective for entailment classification. The second one is structure features, which take syntactic and semantic similarity of T and H into account by measuring ratio of their same subtrees. Table 2 lists the features for entailment classification. Note that T in Table 2 represents regenerated texts after transformation.

Table 2. Features for entailment classification.

Name	Description
N-gram overlap	N-gram overlap ratio of T and H
Word overlap	Word overlap ratio of T and H
Matching coefficient	$|words(T) \cap words(H)|$
LCS similarity	Ratio of longest common substring overlap of T and H
Levenshtein distance	Edit distance of T and H
Jaro-Winkler distance	Jaro-Winkler distance [13] of T and H
Subtree overlap	Ratio of complete same subtrees of T and H
Partial subtree overlap	Ratio of partial same subtrees (at least one branches are same) of T and H
Predicate-argument overlap	Ratio of same predicate-argument pairs of T and H

4   Experiments

The evaluation data collection in this paper comes from NTCIR-11 RITE-3 challenge. The data collection includes 581 pairs of training data and 1200 pairs of test data, each of which contains a text T, a hypothesis H and a label showing the entailment relation between T and H. The training data includes 370 entailment pairs and 211 non-entailment pairs, while the test data includes 600 entailment and non-entailment pairs, respectively.

The purpose of the first experiment is to explore the impact of the combination model against the single classification one. To this end, two systems are set: the first one (T+C) uses both the transformation model and the classification model, while the second one (C) only uses the classification model. The metrics in this experiments are precision, recall, F1-score and MacroF1. Table 3 shows the experimental results, where E denotes entailment relation, N denotes non-entailment relation, P denotes the ratio of the amount of those entailment/non-entailment pairs that are judged correctly and the amount of the pairs that are judged as entailment/non-entailment relations, and R denotes the ratio of the amount of those entailment/non-entailment pairs that are judged correctly and the amount of the pairs with entailment/non-entailment relations in gold standard.

Table 3. Experimental result of RTE.

	T+C	C
MacroF1	0.5563	0.4905
E_F1	0.6059	0.5307
E_P	0.6485	0.6122
E_R	0.5750	0.4683
N_F1	0.5032	0.4504
N_P	0.4775	0.4076
N_R	0.5317	0.5033

It can be seen from Table 3 that, the first system outperforms the second one in every metric. More specifically, for entailment relation, the first system achieves an increasing 3.62% performance of precision, an increasing 10.67% performance of recall and an increasing 7.86% performance of F1 score in comparison with the second one; for non-entailment relation, the first system achieves an increasing 7% performance of precision, an increasing 2.83% performance of recall and an increasing 5.27% performance of F1 score in comparison with the second one. As an overall performance, the first system achieves an increasing 6.58% performance of macro F1 in comparison with the second one. Apparently, transforming or aligning inferable text fragments contributes to recognizing entailment in texts.

It can be also seen that, the increasing performance of E_F1 is higher than that of N_F1, which indicates that transformation-based approach benefits the judgment of entailment than that of non-entailment. And the reason is obvious, since two texts are more similar after replacing synonyms or hypernyms.

The second experiment aims to measure the impact of each type of transformation process, that is, undirected transformation and directed one. We set two systems for this experiment: the first one(-undirected) removes undirected transformation process, while the second one(-directed) removes directed one. The first system in the experiment is set as the baseline. Table 4 shows the experimental result. Metrics in this experiment are same with the first experiment.

Table 4. Performance of each transformation process.

	Baseline	-undirected	-directed
MacroF1	0.5563	0.5195	0.5215
E_F1	0.6059	0.5659	0.5732
E_P	0.6485	0.6330	0.6265
E_R	0.5750	0.5117	0.5283
N_F1	0.5032	0.4730	0.4699
N_P	0.4775	0.4350	0.4380
N_R	0.5317	0.5183	0.5067

Table 4 shows that, when removing undirected transformation process, the system achieves a decreasing 1.55% performance of precision, a decreasing 6.33% performance of recall and a decreasing 4.36% performance of F1 score in comparison with the baseline; for non-entailment relation, the first system achieves a decreasing 4.26% performance of precision, a decreasing 1.33% performance of recall and a decreasing 3.02% performance of F1 score in comparison with the baseline. When removing directed transformation process, the system achieves a decreasing 2.2% performance of precision, a decreasing 4.67% performance of recall and a decreasing 3.63% performance of F1 score in comparison with the baseline; for non-entailment relation, the first system achieves a decreasing 3.95% performance of precision, a decreasing 2.5% performance of recall and a decreasing 3.33% performance of F1 score in comparison with the baseline. It indicate that: (1) undirected and directed transformation process help to improve the performance of entailment recognition, since the F1 performance decrease over 3% when removing either of them; (2) undirected transformation is more important than directed one, since the MacroF1 decrease of the system removing undirected transformation is higher than that of the system removing directed one. It also indicates that the amount of undirected entailment pairs is higher than that of directed ones. For a better performance, undirected entailment relations, such as synonyms and semantically equivalent entities, should have more concern.

5 Conclusion

In this paper, we introduce an approach combining transformation and classification method for recognizing textual entailment. Depending on the transformation model, words and entities with directed and undirected entailment relations are replaced to regenerate texts. In classification model, a hybrid kernel-based approach is introduced, and two types of features are employed for classifying entailment. Experimental results show that the combination approach achieves a better performance in comparison with the single classification system.

Acknowledgements. This work is supported by Natural Science Foundation of Hainan (618MS086), Special innovation project of Guangdong Education Department (2017KTSCX064), Natural Science Foundation of China (61702121) and Bidding Project of GDUFS Laboratory of Language Engineering and Computing (LEC2016ZBKT001, LEC2016ZBKT002).

References

1. Dagan, I., Dolan, B.: Recognizing textual entailment: rational, evaluation and approaches. Nat. Lang. Eng. **15**(4), i–xvii (2009)
2. Bar-Haim, R., Berant, J., Dagan, I., Greental, I., Mirkin, S., Shnarch, E., et al.: Efficient semantic deduction and approximate matching over compact parse forests. In: Proceedings of the Fourth PASCAL Challenges Workshop on Recognizing Textual Entailment, Gaithersburg, Maryland, USA (2008)

3. Watanabe, Y., Miyao, Y., Mizuno, J., Shibata, T., Kanayama, H., Lee, C.-W., et al.: Overview of the recognizing inference in text (RITE-2) at the NTCIR-10 workshop. In: Proceedings of the 10th NTCIR Workshop, Tokyo, Japan (2013)
4. Agichtein, E., Askew, W., Liu, Y.: Combining lexical, syntactic, and semantic evidence for textual entailment classification. In: Proceedings of the Fourth PASCAL Challenges Workshop on Recognizing Textual Entailment, Gaithersburg, Maryland, USA (2008)
5. Galanis, D., Malakasiotis, P.: AUEB at TAC 2008. In: Proceedings of the Fourth PASCAL Challenges Workshop on Recognizing Textual Entailment, Gaithersburg, Maryland, USA (2008)
6. Ren, H., Ji, D., Wan, J.: WHU at TAC 2009: a tri-categorization approach to textual entailment recognition. In: Proceedings of the Fifth PASCAL Challenges Workshop on Recognizing Textual Entailment, Gaithersburg, Maryland, USA (2009)
7. Wang, R., Neumann, G.: A divide-and-conquer strategy for recognizing textual entailment. In: Proceedings of the Fourth PASCAL Challenges Workshop on Recognizing Textual Entailment, Gaithersburg, Maryland, USA (2008)
8. Pham, Q.N.M., Nguyen, L.M., Shimazu, A.: A machine learning based textual entailment recognition system of JAIST team for NTCIR9 RITE. In: Proceedings of the 9th NTCIR Workshop, Tokyo, Japan (2011)
9. Ren, H., Ji, D., Wan, J.: The WHUTE system in NTCIR-9 RITE task. In: Proceedings of the 8th NTCIR Workshop Meeting, Tokyo, Japan (2011)
10. Akiba, Y., Taira, H., Fujita, S.: NTTCS textual entailment recognition system for NTCIR-9 RITE. In: Proceedings of the 9th NTCIR Workshop, Tokyo, Japan (2011)
11. Huang, H.-H., Chang, K.-C., Haver II, J.M., Chen, H.-H.: NTU textual entailment system for NTCIR 9 RITE task. In: Proceedings of the 9th NTCIR Workshop, Tokyo, Japan (2011)
12. Pakray, P., Neogi, S., Bandyopadhyay, S., Gelbukh, A.: A textual entailment system using web based machine translation system. In: Proceedings of the 9th NTCIR Workshop, Tokyo, Japan (2011)
13. Winkler, W.E.: String comparator metrics and enhanced decision rules in the Fellegi-Sunter model of record linkage. In: Proceedings of the Section on Survey Research Methods, pp. 354–359, American Statistical Association (1990)

Knowledge-Based Artificial Intelligence

Research on the Construction of Three Level Customer Service Knowledge Graph in Electric Marketing

Zelin Wang[✉], Zhengqi Zhou, and Muyan Zhou

School of Computer Science and Technology,
Nantong University, Nantong, China
whwzl@whu.edu.cn

Abstract. With the advent of the information explosion era, more and more enterprises realize that knowledge management and application requirements are the key points that enterprises attach importance to. This paper solved existing problems by building customer service of power industry marketing and relevant theories of Knowledge Graph, and explored the three-level customer Knowledge Graph framework of power system marketing. Neo4j was used to realize knowledge reasoning, and relatively good results were obtained in practice.

Keywords: Electricity marketing · Customer service · Knowledge graph · Neo4j

1 Introduction

Power system marketing usually refers to the production, sale and transportation of power products, transmission and sale of electric power products, and to meet the economic, Usually this series of activities are considered as a means to improve the economic efficiency of power system related enterprises. In the power system, power supply enterprises develop differentiated marketing strategies, including service, price, package, activity, brand value, etc., through which they can increase their share in the power system industry. Now the power industry marketing strategy has a very significant role. We need to provide the power supply users' Knowledge Graph while modeling the electricity customer behavior. Currently, the Knowledge Graph related to power industry marketing is not found in the open database [2].

However, in China's power grid industry, its research and application still need to be promoted [3].

The significance of studying Power enterprise customer service knowledge graph are as follows [4]:

- Quickly find the right answer. A keyword may represent multiple meanings; knowledge graph will show the most comprehensive information to make customer service staff find the best meaning, such as searching "Nantong", Nantong power supply business information, Nantong power outage information, Nantong weather

© Springer Nature Singapore Pte Ltd. 2019
H. Peng et al. (Eds.): ISICA 2018, CCIS 986, pp. 259–268, 2019.
https://doi.org/10.1007/978-981-13-6473-0_23

information etc. are showed as graph, which guides the customers service staff to click on the needed information.

- Best summary. Knowledge graph make the customer service better understands the search information and summarizes the relevant content and theme. Such as customer service staff searching "Hangjiang road power outage", not only he can get Hongjiang Road near the new station area line outage information (including planned outage, power failure, temporary power outages), but also obtain the region power outage maintenance information, the cause of outage, complex information, the number of people who search power outage information and the contents of dealing with power outage and the handling of the case, and the relevant information about the caller's information links etc., which make customer service staff processing approximate or repetitive work orders rapidly.
- Depth query. Based on the knowledge graph search or query, not only provide the corresponding text or image information, and the key words in the text will also be expressed with hyperlinks. For example, when customer service staff query one work order, he can get the work order related to the power supply company, user information, user address, types of business through linked information; or by keyword link in the accept content jump to more detail, to help customer service fast, in-depth understand business knowledge and the accepted case. Similarly, query customer service related to a variety of systems, processes, specifications etc.

2   Related Works

2.1   Current Status of Knowledge Graph Research

In the first half of 2012, Google put forward the concept of knowledge atlas and applied it to the next generation search engine only [5]. The published and applied knowledge graph is shown in Table 1.

Table 1. Knowledge Graph that has been applied

	Content
Baidu knowledge graph [6]	When we use baidu to search, input keywords such as place name, plant name, animal name, etc., corresponding data will appear
Sogou cube [7]	The first IT search company to use knowledge map in search engine industry in China
Fudan university GDM knowledge graph [8]	In 2013, Shanghai daily reported that Fudan university was the first university in China to use Chinese knowledge map to analyze news websites and to dig deeply
Google knowledge graph [9]	Knowledge systematization is a major feature of Google knowledge map, and its purpose is to let users acquire information and knowledge more intuitively

2.2   Related Concepts of Knowledge Graph

Semantic Web

Semantic Web represents the development and trend of the next generation of Web. Semantic Web will introduce meaningful web content into a semantic structure to create an environment and provide information resources more specific and complete semantic, which makes the computer distinguish and identify the semantic information, so as to understand the Web resources [10].

Ontology

Domain term set. Ontology knowledge graph is the most abstract, simple, which is a concept, this concept set can describe all things of common characteristics of one specific domain, and then there is a certain relationship between concepts, all constitute a hierarchical feature structure [11]. Ontology and schema basically do not separate in the Semantic Web, so there is the ontology/schema alignment, OAEI challenge.

Knowledge Base

First thinking the data by mining, which can be directly used by the semi structure, and the scale is generally larger [12]. With the development of semantic web, the knowledge base in the network world has the tendency to express the RDF data model.

Knowledge Graph

A graph of a set of related knowledge. Knowledge Graph is a relatively new argument, which expresses visually the semantic web knowledge base. Focus on the extraction of relationships, it is easy to show the high correlation and structured result. Semantic Web is to understand the meaning of human being for computer, the graph structure provides a good support for the construction of knowledge graph, the construction of knowledge graph is based on semantic web.

Graph Base

The realization of semantic web is a kind of knowledge base. The relational database used to store relational data is not good, the query is complex, slow, more than expected, and the unique design of the graphics database is to make up for this defect [13]. Figure 1 shows the relationship between related concepts

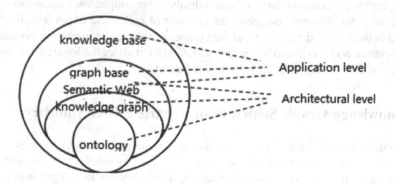

Fig. 1. Relationships between related concepts

From the above figure we can see that the foundation of the construction of the knowledge system is: "ontology", and the bridge in the middle is the "semantic web". The quality of ontological knowledge map has a great influence on the quality of graph database and knowledge base.

2.3   Neo4j

Neo4j is a high-performance NOSQL graph database that stores structured data on the network rather than in tables. Programmers work in an object oriented and flexible network structure, rather than strictly and static table–but they can enjoy all the benefits with the complete transaction characteristics and enterprise class database. Neo4j is more and more concerned because of its advantages of embedded, high performance, lightweight and so on [14].

The Neo4 structure consists of two basic data types: Nodes and Relationships. Nodes and Relationships contain attributes in the form of key/value. Nodes are connected by the Relationships defined by relationship to form a relational network structure (Fig. 2).

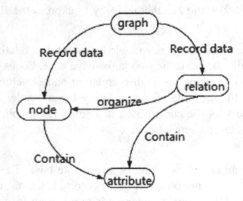

Fig. 2. Neo4j cell structure

The creation and maintenance of graph database are simple, each node corresponds to a record in the relational database, the attribute of nodes and edges is equivalent to the field in the record, the content and the number of attributes can change dynamically, edges between nodes can also be cut free which will not affect the logic of existing data structure, which is very difficult for relational databases.

3   Knowledge Graph Structure in Electric Power Industry

The construction of electric power marketing service knowledge graph is a cross disciplinary, cross organizational level, cross business processes, cross regional, cross cycle complex project. According to statistics, nearly 3 years in Jiangsu province the average annual number of orders 95598 customer service hot line received is more than 6 million, involving the main types of business consulting, fault repair, complaints, comments and suggestions, praise, service application and other power supply services and more than 300 types of seeds. Based on massive job data and power business knowledge, how to achieve knowledge, experience, problems in automatic classification of power supply service, find the optimal solution quickly by the customer service staff, find questions and answers required by the user, is an important issue to study and explore the knowledge graph for customers in service.

3.1   Knowledge Graph by Customers as Center

Knowledge graph by customers as center is an one level knowledge graph of power marketing customers service (customer ontology), which has four dimensions, and each dimension is described by the following 3 elements (as shown in Fig. 3).

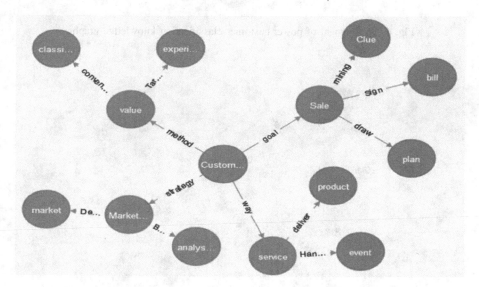

Fig. 3. Knowledge graph by customers as center

3.2   Knowledge Graph by Feature as Center

Two level knowledge graph of power marketing customer service by feature as center (feature ontology) is the quantification of each element in the four dimensions of the first level knowledge graph (Figs. 4 and 5).

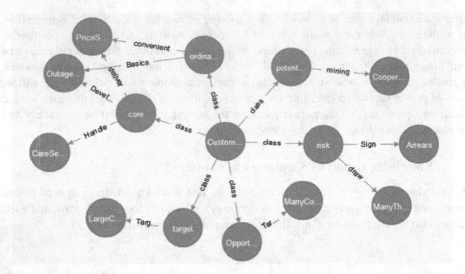

Fig. 4. Refinement of power customer classification knowledge graph

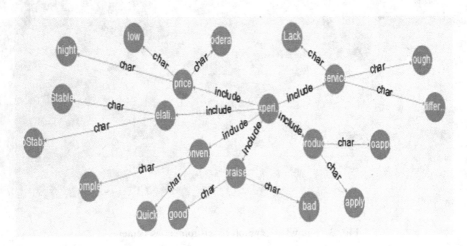

Fig. 5. Refinement of user experience knowledge graph

3.3 Knowledge Graph by Data as Center

Knowledge graph by data as center is the third level knowledge graph of power marketing customer service (data ontology), and also is known as data knowledge graph (Fig. 6).

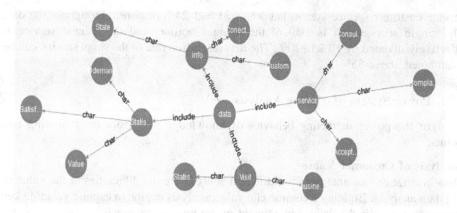

Fig. 6. Description of knowledge graph by data as center

4   Power System Marketing Knowledge Graph Architecture

4.1   Self-service Customer Service Architecture

The self-service service system architecture shown in Fig. 7 can perform context correlation, related problem recommendation. The functional scenarios mainly include business processing, multiple candidate outputs, sensitive word filtering, input intelligent prompts, voice input recognition, context correlation, and customer care. The self-

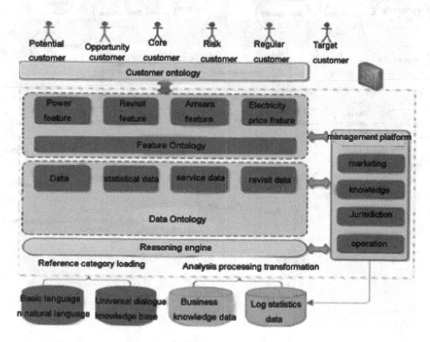

Fig. 7. Self-help customer service

service customer service system has low cost and 24 h response throughout the day. The single service cost is 1/50 of the manual hotline, and the manual service is effectively diverted by 10% to 20%. The first resolution rate of the shunt service can be maintained above 85%.

4.2   Power System Marketing Analysis

Analyze the power marketing behavior of knowledge map from the following two points:

Analysis of Customer Value

Data integration and analysis from different sources are the difficulties in the value of big data analysis. Building a commercial value analysis engine to capture valuable key customer groups is the value embodiment of the knowledge grach.

The amount of 20% of all customers brings 75% of the company's profits, which is the most direct value and benefit impact of valuable customers on the company. In addition to the growth of the company's profits, valuable customers have a profound impact on the company (Fig. 8).

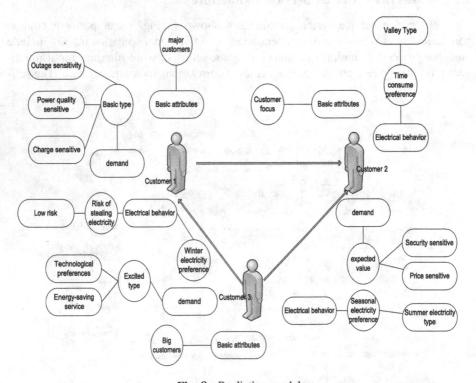

Fig. 8. Prediction model

Customer is the core of value analysis, and the knowledge map of multi-data is built through accurate source data to integrate structured knowledge. Knowledge map reasoning is not simply to capture basic customer information, but to integrate valuable information such as demand information and supply information, and to conduct knowledge map reasoning through multi-data and multi-information.

New Attribute Prediction

From the above figure, we can see that each customer has different demands. 1 customer needs energy-saving services, 2 customer needs sensitive billing, and 3 customer needs electricity model.

The self-service customer service system based on the customer service knowledge graph can also record and pre-categorize the content that cannot be answered by the current knowledge graph proposed by the user, facilitate post-human intervention, and add new user attention hotspots to the existing knowledge graph.

5 Conclusions

The research of knowledge graph mainly from three fields:

(1) Data, information, knowledge and visualization research on knowledge domain in computer science;
(2) Citation analysis visualization, Knowledge Graph and knowledge network in the field of Library and information science;
(3) Research on complex network system and social network analysis.

At present, the research direction and content of the three are moving towards integration. The time of knowledge graph proposed is not long, mostly as a tool or method to treat, most related theories are referenced simply in many disciplines, and there is no complete theoretical system, the real theoretical kernel has not formed, the application and practice of the knowledge graph lack the powerful guidance, which leads to the blindness of the application.

Acknowledgement. This work is supported by the National Natural Science Foundation of China (61171132, 61340037), the Natural Science Foundation of Nantong University (BK2014064), Nantong Research Institute for Advanced Communication Technologies (KFKT2016B06), Modern education technology research project of Jiangsu (2017-R-54131).

References

1. Kang, J.: Research on fine power marketing service management measures. Manag. Sci. **09**, 24–25 (2017)
2. Wang, G.: The Internet _ power marketing intelligent interactive service construction. China Power Enterp. Manag. **01**, 48–49 (2017)
3. Tian, X., Liu, Y., Wang, J., et al.: Application value of customer service knowledge graph construction of power grid corp. Shandong Electr. Power Technol. **42**(12), 65–69 (2015)

4. Xu, C.: Analysis of power network marketing mode under smart grid. Commun. World 03, 219–220 (2017)
5. Liu, J., Yang, L., Duan, H., et al.: Overview of knowledge graph technology. Comput. Res. Develop. 53(3), 582–600 (2016)
6. Baidu next generation search engine prototype exposure application knowledge graphing technology. Comput. Program. Skills Maintenance 19, 4 (2013)
7. Sogou cube. http://baike.sogou.com/v66616234.htm
8. Li, W., Xiao, Y., Wang, W.: Character entity recognition based on Chinese knowledge graph. Comput. Eng. 43(3), 226–234 (2017)
9. Ochs, C., Tian, T., Geller, J., et al.: Google knows who is famous today - building an ontology from search engine knowledge and DBpedia. In: Proceedings of the 5th IEEE International Conference on Semantic Computing, pp. 320–327. IEEE, Piscataway (2011)
10. Ma, L., Sun, Y., Liu, Q.: Ontology matching in semantic Web research. Comput. Appl. 34 (5), 10–18 (2017)
11. Diallo, G.: An effective method of large scale ontology matching. J. Biomed. Semant. 5, 44–63 (2014)
12. Liu, H., Jia, Y., Wang, Y., et al.: Knowledge base classification system matching method based on composite structure. Comput. Res. Dev. 54(1), 50–62 (2017)
13. Wang, R., Yang, Y., Yung, X.: Exploring the Chinese business knowledge graph based on depth learning and graph database. Books Inform. 01, 110–118 (2016)
14. Ma, Y., Wu, Z.: Modeling and analysis of large power data based on Neo4j. New Technol. Electr. Electr. Energy 35(2), 24–31 (2016)

YVONNE: A Fast and Accurate Prediction Scoring Retrieval Framework Based on MF

Yi Yang, Caixue Zhou, Guangyong Gao, Zongmin Cui$^{(\boxtimes)}$, and Feipeng Wang

School of Information Science and Technology, Jiujiang University,
Jiujiang, Jiangxi, China
cuizm01@gmail.com

Abstract. The recommendation system has many successful applications on e-commerce and social media, including Amazon, Netflix, Yelp, etc. It is a personalized recommendation system. It recommends interesting product and information to the user based on the user's interests, information, needs, etc. It is extremely important to use the known user information to get the missing information from other users. Most of previous works focus on the learning phase of the recommendation system. Only a few researches focus on the retrieval stage. In this paper, we propose a fast and accurate prediction scoring retrieval framework based on matrix factorization (MF). Our framework (Yvonne) can effectively predict the score of users' missing items. Experiments with real data show that our framework significantly outperforms other methods on the efficiency and accuracy.

Keywords: Matrix factorization · Integral approximate · SVD-transformation

1 Introduction

Recommendation system has become an extremely effective tool for recommending items that user may be interested in. Practical applications include product recommendation (Amazon), TV recommendation (Netflix) and restaurant recommendation (Yelp). One of the basic tasks of the modern recommendation system is the Top-K [15] recommendation. It means that users can score Top-K predictions in projects that he has not yet evaluated. Top-k recommendation is usually divided into two stages: learning and retrieving [3]. Specifically, consider a set of users and a set of items: each user can rate any item. In the learning stage, the missing ratings of the not-yet-rated items are estimated by machine learning, approximation theory and various heuristic methods [1]. Examples include collaborative filtering [13], user item graph model [2], regression model and matrix factorization (MF).

In this paper, we focus on MF. MF is popularizing the scoring matrix of large user projects. Let R be the $m \times n$ matrix, and there are m user ratings on

© Springer Nature Singapore Pte Ltd. 2019
H. Peng et al. (Eds.): ISICA 2018, CCIS 986, pp. 269–280, 2019.
https://doi.org/10.1007/978-981-13-6473-0_24

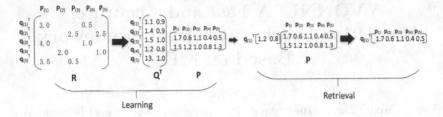

Fig. 1. Example retrieval of a recommendation system based on matrix decomposition (MF)

n elements. MF approximate decomposition of R and Calculate the factor vectors of each user and project score mapping to the d dimension which $d \ll min$. The output of the learning phase based on MF is a $Q \in R^{d \times m}$ user matrix, the i-th column is the factor vector of the i-th user, and a $P \in R^{d \times m}$ project matrix, the i-th column is the factor vector of the i-th project. Given a user vector q and a project vector p, their inner product $q^T p$ is the corresponding user's prediction score for the corresponding project. Higher inner product means that users are more likely to be satisfied with the project. MF's performance has been confirmed in the Netflix award [4].

In addition to its superior performance, MF has another advantage. It is widely used in addition to existing ratings and can easily integrate other information into the model to further improve its accuracy. This information includes social network data [10], location of users and project department [11] and visual phenomena [7]. Considering the output of the learning phase, the task of the retrieval phase is to generate a prediction scoring list for any target user. For H Li, they proposed the Urldl (user rating list dimension is large) problem [9]. This task is very challenging, as the number of n items is usually very large (e.g., millions). Actually, it is not feasible [6] to externalizing the entire rating list for all users. Thus, reducing the cost of predictive list retrieval becomes critical. In particular, designing a large recommendation system can process tens of thousands of queries per second in the real world. Most previous work has focused on the learning phase of the recommendation system. Only a few researches focus on the retrieval stage. So in the search phase, we present a fast and accurate predictive scoring search framework (Yvonne).

The contributions of this paper are as follows: Yvonne takes a single user vector q as input to a portion of the project's score. And it predicts the user's rating of all items. First, we use SVD transformation to reduce the initial large dimension project scoring matrix. Then the integer approximation is used to convert the floating-point numbers into integers in the matrix. It can make the operation more efficient.

1. SVD Transformation: We apply a lossless SVD transformation to P. And this produces a new matrix $\bar{P}$, Given a query vector q, we convert q to $\bar{q}$, such that $\bar{q}^T P = \bar{q}\bar{P}$. This transformation introduces the scalar skew of Q, So that the absolute value of each dimension is greater than the next high

probability value. For a given $\bar{q}\bar{P}$, skew result in a large amount of inner product after only handling a few dimensions, skew will lead to a large part of inner product. This creates a tight upper bound that allows us to prune conveniently without calculating the whole product.

2. Integral Approximate: Arithmetic operations on integers are much faster than floating-point numbers. If the scalar in a vector is an integer rather than a floating-point number, it cost of retrieval will be significantly reduced. The application of SVD decomposed $\bar{P}$ and $\bar{q}$ to scale the integer approximation. It can make the operation more convenient and fast. And the prediction score list of input users will be efficiently obtained.

After integrating all the above technologies into the recommendation system framework, for a given user vector Q command, Yvonne provides faster efficiency in predicting user ratings for other projects. It can show by extensive experimentation on real datasets.

In the next section, we explain why you need to use Yvonne to optimize your current recommendation system and how it is done. In the third section, we explain how Yvonne uses SVD transformation to greatly reduce the dimension to improve the efficiency of the recommendation system. We are clearly explain in the fourth section how Yvonne can use the integer pruning without losing data precision and quickly get a list of predicted scores.

2 Related Work

In this section, we first define the problem of internal product retrieval in recommender systems and explain why it is a challenging problem. Then we add our framework (Yvonne) based on the corresponding search questions, resulting in a faster and more accurate list of forecasted project scores.

In the recommendation system, the problem of accurate internal project retrieval is to generate a prediction item scoring list for a given (target) user. This problem can be formally defined as: Given a d dimension vector q, find d dimensional vector $q \in P$. The $\bar{q}^T p$ values are the largest in $\bar{q}^T P$.

Generally speaking, project problems are difficult to solve. The scoring function $\bar{q}^T P$ is different from other commonly used similar measures for ranking. It doesn't follow the triangle inequality. Therefore, it is not possible to use it to trim the boundaries. In addition, because of the dimension's distress, the index base similarity index method can easily become worse than the simple sequential scanning method. At the learning stage, thus matrix decomposition reduces the initial high dimensional space (millions of dimensions, i.e., the number of items n) to d dimensional space (d is typically tens to hundreds in order for MF to be effective). d is still too large for index based similar searches. This allows the machine to consume too much time and memory during retrieval. This is bad for the recommendation system. For a recommender system, it's more of an application in the Internet. There is not much memory and time on the Internet for system consumption, Internet should be fast and convenient. Thus, how to solve this problem will become extremely important.

Even worse, the large inner product doesn't necessarily correspond to any metric in the vector space. So that metric space technique can not directly be used. In short, it is difficult to solve the project retrieval problem effectively without special assumption about the data. In this regard, Yvonne added SVD transformation after matrix-based decomposition, and further reduce the d-dimension space into f-dimension space (f is usually ten to dozens). And we know that the known user's score is a sparse matrix, and the SVD transformation is to map the original data into the low-dimensional space, it remove the corresponding unimportant feature values, and get a precise smaller spatial dimension. This makes f much smaller for index base similar indexes. Therefore, the space can be better reduced, thereby improving the retrieval speed of the recommendation system and reducing the consumption of the recommendation system in the retrieval phase. This will fully reflect the superiority of Yvonne.

If the scalar in each dimension is within a small range, then this integer upper bound is very loose. It is very common in recommendation system. But this seriously consumes too much cost. To make the upper bound tighter, Yvonne built an integer approximation. It extends the original scalar to a range. And then, we get a tighter integer upper bound. This method not only allows us to gain a tighter upper bound, but also make our scalars into integers. We all know to use all-integer data to retrieve, it can reduce the storage space of the recommendation system, and make the recommendation system get the user's prediction project score faster, thus improving the efficiency of the recommendation system.

The proposal for this article uses a matrix decomposition framework using the gradient descent algorithm, as shown in Fig. 1. In the next few sections, two methods will be proposed, it can improve the superiority of the prediction score in the recommendation system, so that the cost of the recommendation system is reduced and the efficiency is higher, thus forming a better recommendation system.

Table 1. The meaning of the symbols in this article

Symbol	Description
q, p, Q, P	Original vector and matrix
$\bar{q}, \bar{p}$	Applying SVD transformed vectors
$\hat{q}, \hat{p}$	Used for integer scaling vector
P_i	The i-th vector of P
p_s	The s scalar of vector $p = (p_1, p_2, ..., p_d)^T \in R^d$
m, n	Number of users/projects
d, f	The dimension of the quantity
e	Scaling parameters for integral upper bound

3 SVD Transformation

A natural question is whether we can propose a global reordering of dimensions. It can maximize the ability of incremental pruning for each query. In this case, we can reorder P in a preprocessing stage. Then coordinate scanning is performed sequentially, simply reordering Q once. An effective global reordering can make the maximum absolute value of each $p \in P$ the first. However, this method seems to be very difficult to apply to the original P. The values in the same dimension may vary depending on q and P. It is difficult to find a global ordering suitable for all vectors.

To solve this problem, we propose to use singular value decomposition (SVD) to transform matrix P. The goal of the transformation is to change the value distribution of the vector. So that the absolute value of the first dimension is higher than the latter value. This transformation only needs to be executed before any query application. Whenever query Q appears, it can be converted at a very low cost. Although, matrix P and vector Q is change. However, the result of a given query is the same as that of the original P and q. In detailed information, we apply SVD to project matrix $P \in R^{d \times n}$ to obtain three matrices U, Σ and V, such that. U is a $d \times d$ unit matrix. Σ is a $d \times n$ matrix with a non-negative real numbers on the diagonal and V is a $d \times d$ - unit matrix. Σ and V can be further divided into two parts, namely:

$$\Sigma = [\Sigma_d | O], V = [V_1 | V_2]$$

Σ_d is a $d \times d$ diagonal matrix with singular value $\sigma_1 \geq \sigma_2 \geq ... \geq \sigma_d$. O is a $d \times (n-d)$ zero matrix. V_1 and V_2 are $n \times d$ and $n \times (n-d)$ matrix, respectively. The framework transfers q and P from the original space to a new space. It can give us a closer space for incremental pruning:

Theorem 1. In the original space, the inner product of Q and P is completely preserved in a new space. The same dimension is obtained by SVD. This is that $q^T P = \bar{q}^T bar P$, among $\bar{q} = \Sigma_d U^T q$, $\bar{P} = V_1^T$. Proof: Given the definition of SVD, formula (5) and vector q, we have: $q^T P = q^T U \Sigma V^T = q^T U [\Sigma_d | O][V_1 | V_2]^T = q^T U \Sigma_d V_1^T = [\Sigma_d U^T q]^T V_1^T = \bar{q}^T \bar{P}$ Therefore, for $\bar{P} = V_1^T$ and $\bar{q} = \Sigma_d U^T q$, can convert the original target. It can get the prediction score more quickly.

When the SVD transformation is applied to P, we should consider that when P is large, the standard SVD will slow down. Although, the decomposition of $d \times n$ matrix P is much faster than the initial $m \times n$ rating matrix R decomposition in the learning phase. But because the complexity of implementing SVD on P is $O(dn^2)$ [5]. So that it's still very expensive. Fortunately, the transformation has a good attribute. It can significantly reduce complexity. It can be seen from the proof of the theorem. Only the $n \times d$ matrix V_1 is used in the final transformation, while the $n \times (n-d)$ matrix V_2 which occupies most of the V, is abandoned. Similarly, only Σ_d is needed, and most of the matrix Σ is not used. Therefore, we can execute a smaller SVD (i.e.: $P = U \Sigma_d V_1^T$) rather than a complete SVD.

In practice, if $n \gg d$, the smaller SVD is usually used. It is much faster than the original SVD. The complexity is reduced from $O(dn^2)$ to $O(d^2n)$. As the experiment proves, when dealing with a very large P, the smaller SVD is also fast.

4   Integral Approximate

Floating-point operations invoke more CPU cycles [12]. It is usually much slower than integer calculation. If the scalar in a vector is an integer rather than a floating-point number, the cost of retrieval can be significantly reduced. In addition, using integer can help us reduce the error rate of CPU caching. Compared with integer, floating point occupies more space, thus when using integers, the accessed data is more likely to be accessed. However, just cutting the floating-point numbers into integers will lead to the reduction of accuracy and potential incorrect results. In this section, we can show how to use integer approximation without losing any information in the retrieval process.

4.1   Integer Upper Bound

By only using the scalar integer part in the two vectors Q and P, that we can define an upper bound for $q^T P$:

Theorem 2. The inner product of Q and P has an integer upper bound: $IU(q,p) = \sum_{s=1}^{d}([q_s] \cdot [p_s] + |[q_s]| + |[p_s]| + 1)$, Where $[q_s]$ is the integral part of q_s(that is, the largest integer is less than or equal to q_s). $|[q_s]|$ is the absolute value of $[q_s]$. Proof: Let $[q_s]$ and $\Delta q_s = q_s - [q_s]$ denote the integral part and fractional part of scalar q respectively. Because $\Delta q_s \leq 1$, We have:

$$q^T P = \sum_{s=1}^{d} q_s p_s = \sum_{s=1}^{d}([q_s] + \Delta q_s)([p_s] + \Delta p_s)$$

$$= \sum_{s=1}^{d}([q_s][p_s] + \Delta q_s[p_s] + \Delta p_s[q_s] + \Delta q_s \Delta p_s)$$

$$\leq \sum_{s=1}^{d}([q_s][p_s] + |[q_s]| + |[p_s]| + 1)$$

If the scalar in each dimension is in a small range, that this integer upper bound can be very loose. It is very common in the recommendation system. It can be explained by the principle of low rank matrix factorization [14]. In the learning phase, it tries to minimize the root mean ($RMSE = \sqrt{\frac{1}{mn}\Sigma_{r_{ij} \in R}(r_{ij} - q_{(i)}^T p_{(j)})^2}$) between the real ($r_{ij}$) and the predicted ($q_{(i)}^T p_{(j)}$). Since the largest rating is usually much smaller than the D dimension, after the iterative optimization, the values of q_s and p_s are often located near the range of value 0. It can minimize the RMSE. Another reason is the regularization item. It is usually used to decompose a low rank matrix, thus punishing large parameters (e.g., q_s and p_s), It can avoid over fitting in training.

The following table is shown by Table 2, how to tighten the integer upper bound on a scaler containing such a narrow range of values. q and p are two instances of random vectors. For simplicity, only the values of the first 5 dimensions are shown. The inner product ($q^T p$) is 0.603, and the integer upper bound is IU(q, p) = 12($\gg$0.603). When considering all dimensions, the integer upper bound is still very loose.

Table 2. An example of an integer upper bound

q^T	1.21	0.85	-1.2	0.2	-1.1
p^T	0.25	1.13	0.42	-0.23	0.1

$$q^T P = 0.603$$

$[q] + \Delta q$	1+0.21	0+0.85	-2+0.8	0+0.2	-2+0.9
$[p] + \Delta p$	0+0.25	1+0.13	0+0.42	-1+0.77	0+0.1

$$q^T P \leq IU(q,p) = 12$$

4.2 Proportional Integer Upper Bound

In order to make the upper boundary tighter, extend the original scalar (floating-point number) to a range $[-e, e]$. First, scale each scalar p_s and divide each scalar a by the largest absolute value max_p in the scalar of P. Then we multiply it by e. As shown by the formula as follow.

$$\hat{p}^T = (\frac{e \cdot p_1}{max_p}, ..., \frac{e \cdot p_d}{max_p}), \hat{q}^T = (\frac{e \cdot q_1}{max_q}, ..., \frac{e \cdot q_d}{max_q})$$

In retrospect, P is known in advance. Therefore, the maximum absolute value (expressed by max_p) of P can be obtained in the preprocessing stage. For Q, the largest absolute value max_q is very fast on the network. The transformation of a vector made up of an equation, and it preserves the order of the query results of any query Q. Because:

$$\hat{p}^T \hat{q}^T = \sum_{s=1}^{d} \frac{e^2 \cdot q_s \cdot p_s}{max_q \cdot max_p} = \frac{e^2}{max_q \cdot max_p} q^T p$$

As shown in the example of Table 3 in the following table. For the same vector as Table 2 and e = 100, extension can lead to a closer integer upper bound [8]. The ratio of new upper bound ($IU = (\hat{q}, \hat{p})$) to the exact IP value (5,206.28) on the scaled vectors is only 1.1, while the ratio before scaling is 19.9 (=12/0.603).

Table 3. The extended upper limit of integers

q^T	1.21	0.85	-1.2	0.2	-1.1
p^T	0.25	1.13	0.42	-0.23	0.1

$$q^T P = 0.603$$

$\hat{q}^T$	100	70.25	-99.17	16.5	-90.91
$\hat{p}^T$	0.25	1.13	0.42	-0.23	0.1

$$\hat{q}^T \hat{p} = 5206.28$$

$[\hat{q}] + \Delta\hat{q}$	100+0	70+0.25	-100+0.83	16+0.53	-91+0.09
$[\hat{p}] + \Delta\hat{p}$	22+0.12	100+0	37+0.17	-21+0.65	0+0.09

$$\hat{q}^T \hat{p} \leq IU(\hat{q}, \hat{p})5726$$

5   Comprehensive Integration

In this section we will demonstrate, how to use these technologies for quick retrieval in recommender systems. And get the user's accurate prediction score list, so as to extract user preferences.

Yvonne is described by the following Algorithm 1. The algorithm input a user part of the project score (q) and outputs the predicted score of all items of the user (L). This can enable us to achieve the purpose of our framework- get the prediction score of the user missing item.

Give a project score matrix $R_{m \times n}$ (first lines). We use gradient descent method to decompose it into matrix. We use gradient descent method to decompose it into matrix. This can decompose two matrices (second lines) of $Q_{m \times d}^T$ and $P_{d \times n}$. This reduces the dimension of a large dimension matrix into two smaller dimensional matrices. But this is still not enough. We need to further reduce the dimension of the $P_{d \times n}$ matrix. Yvonne apply a lossless SVD conversion to P. This produces a new matrix $\bar{P}$. For a given network query vector, q is converted to $\bar{q}$ (line 3–6). In this way, a large dimension matrix can be dimensionally reduced to a smaller dimension. This can greatly increase efficiency and reduce consumption of resources. Yvonne then prunes the integers and converts the floating point operations into integer operations (lines 7–8). But consider that if it is simply truncated, turn it into integers. It can change the authenticity of data and affect the validity of data. So it is extended to a certain range, As shown in Tables 1 and 2. This will keep the transformed data well and effectively. Finally, we return to the L (line 9) of the user prediction project.

Algorithm 1. Framework of ensemble learning for our system.

Require: q
Ensure: L
1: procedure PREPROCESS(R);
2: The P,Q matrix is obtained by gradient descent;
3: $U, \Sigma_d, V_1 \leftarrow SVD(P)$;
4: Enter user item q;
5: $\bar{q}\Sigma_d U^T q$;
6: $\bar{P} = V_1^T$;
7: Calculate$max_{\bar{p}}, max_{\bar{p}}$;
8: Calculate$\hat{q}, \hat{p}$;
9: **return** L=$\hat{q}^T \hat{p}$;

6   Experiment

This recommendation system is an MF-based recommendation system. All methods are implemented in C++ using the standard library and O3 optimization flags. In order to achieve a smaller SVD, we use Armadillo, a C++ linear algebra library. These experiments were conducted on an Intel(R) Core(TM) CPUi5-6300HQ@2.30 GHz machine running Visual Studio 2015 with 8 GB of main memory.

Experiment setup:
By entering different user item score matrix R and entering different user rating items q, we can get a list of prediction scores for all of your projects. This can push the high score items of interest to the user in the recommendation system. Using random numbers to assign values to matrices, we run two versions of the prediction system. For the existing Urdll problem, we compare the framework of GDMD's use of matrix decomposition alone, and Yvonne combine matrix decomposition and SVD transformation, the time consumed for different dimensions.

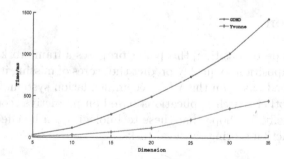

Fig. 2. Gradient descent matrix decomposition and SVD decomposition time

Figure 2 shows the time it takes for the two frames to decompose. By comparison, we can draw, in the same dimension, Yvonne has better efficiency and can get the required data list more quickly. And as the dimension increases, the rate of GDMD decomposition consumption time will be much greater than the rate of Yvonne decomposition. So for a multi-million-dimensional user project scoring matrix, Yvonne can faster and more efficient. This is greatly increase the speed of the recommendation system and reduce its computing costs.

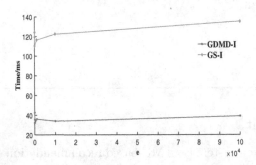

Fig. 3. Shows how the value of e affects performance

Note that when e equals 100, the time consumed is minimal. Therefore, $e = 100$ is set to achieve good performance while expanding the value to a relatively small integer (this requires less space). This shows that by using the SIMD (Single Instruction Multiple Data) instruction set. Our framework can benefit more from the computing power of modern hardware architectures. Small-range integer approximations (eg, $[-128, 127]$) can be loaded into small integer types (eg, int8), registers can hold more data and the pruning function remains the same when using large integer types. Therefore, performance can be further improved by processing multiple integer products in parallel. We plan to explore further accelerated development directions in future work.

7   Conclusion

Based on matrix decomposition, this paper proposes a framework Yvonne based on matrix decomposition to quickly predict the scores of missing items. Although Yvonne is designed based on the MF's recommendation system. This technique can be used by other search applications based on predictive scoring. Now let's talk about it briefly. We hope that these technologies can be effectively utilized for general prediction scoring retrieval tasks.

1. In this paper, we propose the SVD transformation to introduce the skew of vectors. So that after calculating some of their internal products and applying incremental pruning. It is easier to delete project vectors. However, there is a problem. If the difference between the eigenvalues is very small, SVD can not give too much acceleration. For example, if P has a high entropy value

(the distribution of the median value in P is almost the same). Then the singular value (the square root of the eigenvalue) is approximately the same. Our SVD transformation is not valid.

2. We propose an integer approximation to extend the scalar vector as an integer. This method is effective when the duty is in a small range. This is very common in a MF based recommendation system. If these values change greatly, we do not think this technology will be very effective. Integer operations are usually much faster than floating-point operations.

In the future, we plan to study the effectiveness of our framework in other predictive scoring calculations. The transformation we propose can also be used by other retrieval methods. We also plan to explore the direction of input that will be transformed as an alternative to increase their efficiency.

Acknowledgment. This research was supported by the National Natural Science Foundation of China (Nos. 61762055, 61662039 and 61462048); and the Jiangxi Provincial Natural Science Foundation of China (Nos. 20161BAB202036, 20171BAB202004 and 20181BAB202014).

References

1. Adomavicius, G., Tuzhilin, A.: Toward the next generation of recommender systems: a survey of the state-of-the-art and possible extensions. IEEE Trans. knowl. Data Eng. **17**(6), 734–749 (2005)
2. Aggarwal, C.C., Wolf, J.L., Wu, K.L., Yu, P.S.: Horting hatches an egg: a new graph-theoretic approach to collaborative filtering, pp. 201–212 (1999)
3. Bachrach, Y., et al.: Speeding up the Xbox recommender system using a euclidean transformation for inner-product spaces. In: Proceedings of the 8th ACM Conference on Recommender systems, pp. 257–264. ACM (2014)
4. Bell, R.M., Koren, Y.: Lessons from the Netflix prize challenge. ACM SIGKDD Explor. Newsl. **9**(2), 75–79 (2007)
5. Brand, M.: Fast low-rank modifications of the thin singular value decomposition. Linear Algebra Appl. **415**, 20–30 (2006)
6. Fraccaro, M., Paquet, U., Winther, O.: Indexable probabilistic matrix factorization for maximum inner product search, pp. 1554–1560 (2016)
7. He, R., McAuley, J.: Ups and downs: modeling the visual evolution of fashion trends with one-class collaborative filtering. In: proceedings of the 25th International Conference on World Wide Web. pp. 507–517. International World Wide Web Conferences Steering Committee (2016)
8. Kaltofen, E., May, J.P., Yang, Z., Zhi, L.: Approximate factorization of multivariate polynomials using singular value decomposition. J. Symbolic Comput. **43**, 359–376 (2008)
9. Li, H., Chan, T.N., Man, L.Y., Mamoulis, N.: FEXIPRO: fast and exact inner product retrieval in recommender systems. In: ACM International Conference on Management of Data, pp. 835–850 (2017)
10. Li, H., Wu, D., Tang, W., Mamoulis, N.: Overlapping community regularization for rating prediction in social recommender systems, pp. 27–34 (2015)

11. Lian, D., Zhao, C., Xie, X., Sun, G., Chen, E., Rui, Y.: GeoMF: joint geographical modeling and matrix factorization for point-of-interest recommendation. In: Proceedings of the 20th ACM SIGKDD International Conference on Knowledge Discovery and Data Mining, pp. 831–840. ACM (2014)
12. Nawrocki, E.P., Kolbe, D.L., Eddy, S.R.: Infernal 1.0: inference of RNA alignments. Bioinformatics **25**(10), 1335 (2009)
13. Sarwar, B., Karypis, G., Konstan, J., Riedl, J.: Item-based collaborative filtering recommendation algorithms, pp. 285–295 (2001)
14. Yuan, X., Yang, J.: Sparse and low-rank matrix decomposition via alternating direction methods, vol. 12, p. 2 (2009)
15. Zhu, S., Wu, J., Xiong, H., Xia, G.: Scaling up top-k cosine similarity search. Data Knowl. Eng. **70**, 60–83 (2011)

Authentication Mechanism for IoT Device in Micro Grid Environments

Jeong-Cheol Yeom, Qing Zhou, In-A Song, Young-Seok Lee[✉],
and In-ho Ra

Kunsan National University, 558 Daehak-ro,
Kunsan, Jeollabuk-do, South Korea
{yjc41471,leeys}@kunsan.ac.kr

Abstract. Recently there is much interest in how to implement IoT/IoE-based Micro Grids (MG). But, privacy and security concerns inhibit the fast adaption of IoT technology for many applications. A number of authentication protocols that address these concerns have been proposed but real-world solutions that are secure, maintain low communication cost. We present a novel authentication protocol, which offers a high level of security through the combination of a random key scheme with a strong cryptography. The protocol is applicable to resource, power and computationally constraint platforms such as IoT devices. Our investigation shows that it can provide mutual authentication, untraceability, forward and backward security as well as resistance to replay, denial-of-service and man-in-the-middle attacks, while retaining a competitive communication cost. The protocol has been integrated into the device authentication protocol, which assures low implementation cost.

Keywords: Microgrid device · Access server · Mutual authentication schemel

1 Introduction

There have been many efforts to apply the Internet of Things (IoT) technology in micro grid environments. A unique definition of Internet of Things does not exist yet. Several research groups around the world defined it differently. However, some common concept can be drawn from their works. First of all, the interaction between people and objects to deploy smart applications in smart environments. The first design of Internet was human-centric. In this approach data was created by people. But actually, entities connected to the Internet are not necessarily humans. Different "objects" or "things" can be connected too. Thus, human-centric approach cannot be applied anymore. The Internet of Things paradigm is one of the most thrilling innovations of the recent years. The exploitation of the IPv6 addressing space, along with the miniaturization of electronic and transceiver devices opened the way to provide each object on Earth with an Internet address and the technological support to transform it in a communicating object. Once each object possesses communication capabilities, the number of possible applications becomes potentially infinite. This good news is counterbalanced by the consideration that also the number of possible attacks to persons and objects security will grow exponentially [1].

© Springer Nature Singapore Pte Ltd. 2019
H. Peng et al. (Eds.): ISICA 2018, CCIS 986, pp. 281–291, 2019.
https://doi.org/10.1007/978-981-13-6473-0_25

Therefore, a new paradigm of trust, security and privacy is required to face these future issues in the IOT. In [2] authors describe a systemic and cognitive approach for IOT security. In their work, they consider three main axes: effective security for tiny embedded networks, context-aware and user centric privacy, and the systemic and cognitive approach for IoT security.

In this paper, a new authentication protocol will be suggested and verified to provide mutual identification between IoT device and gateway, solving the problem of the previously suggested authentication protocols. In Sect. 2, the research on trends of the previous authentication protocols will be examined. In Sect. 3, the protocol suggested in this study will be described. In Sect. 4, comparison between the performance of the previously suggested authentication protocols and the protocol suggested in this study will be conducted. And the efficiency of the suggested protocol will be also looked into. In Sect. 5, the conclusion and the future research direction will be suggested.

2   Related Studies

2.1   Authentication System Configuration

The system consists of 3 structural elements such as the gateway, IoT device, and access server as Fig. 1. Gateway receives data from IoT devices in same domain. We assume that access server has the pre-shared secret keys of IoT device to authenticate that device sending data. And, access server has also he pre-shared secret key of gateway in multiple domain.

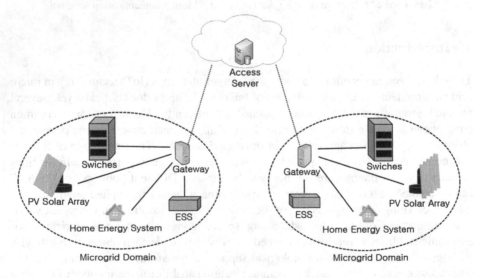

Fig. 1. System architecture

2.2 Previous Authentication Scheme

It is assumed that k, the safe session key, is set between access server and gateway in advance, and that k, the secret key of IoT device is registered in the access server. Table 1 shows the parameters used in this paper. Figure 2 shows the structure and process of performance, and the authentication process is conducted through the following 5 steps [3–5].

Table 1. Protocol parameters

Symbol	Meaning
Access server	IoT access server with private key
Gateway	IoT gateway
Device	IoT device
ID_G	IoT gateway identification
ID_D	IoT device identification
k	Secret key
$E_k()$	Encryption with secret key k
h()	Hash function
prng()	Pseudo random number generator
r	Gateway random number
t	Device random number
$\oplus$	Exclusive-OR
‖	Concatenation operation

Because the IoT device in the previous authentication protocol doesn't authenticate the gateway at all, the attacker can succeed the attack by disguising as the gateway. Moreover, suppose that a certain attacker wiretapped and possessed ID_D sent by the device in the former step (2). Because ID_D is sent through open communication channel, the attacker can obtain it easily. Then, that attacker can succeed the location tracking attack by disguising as the gateway in random session. In addition, assuming there is the gateway with a malicious purpose of attaining the secret key k for a certain IoT device, that gateway conducts the leaking attack as follows, and can conduct attacks like spoofing to that tag easily after obtaining the secret key k of the IoT device.

(1) The IoT device receiving query from the gateway sends its ID_D to the gateway.
(2) The gateway encrypts ID_D of the IoT device using posed session key k and the access server, and sends $E_{gk}(ID_D)$ to the access server.
(3) After the access server decrypts $E_{gk}(ID_D)$ received from the gateway using the session key k, it sends $E_{gk}(k, ID_D)$ to the gateway by encrypting the secret key k of ID_D IoT device into the session key k.
(4) By decrypting $E_{gk}(k, ID_D)$ received from the access server, the gateway stores the secret key k of the IoT device and sends the random value r to the IoT device.
(5) Using received random value r and its secret key k, the tag calculates $h(r \oplus k)$ and sends it to the gateway. The gateway calculates $h(r \oplus k)$ and compares its identity with received $h(r \oplus k)$. The IoT device is authenticated if the two values are same, and, if not, the authentication is discontinued

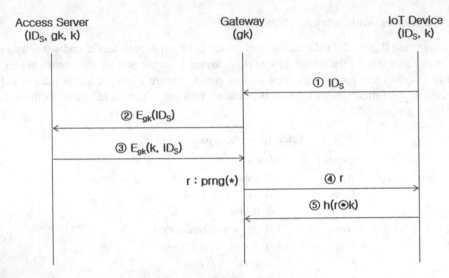

Fig. 2. Previous authentication scheme

2.3   Enhanced Authentication Scheme

It was verified that authentication method presented in unit B is weak to key leaking attack, spoofing attack, and location tracking attack, and an enhanced authentication scheme was suggested [6]. However, a contradiction against key leaking attack is found in the process of verifying the weakness and there is a problem that the enhanced authentication scheme is still weak to spoofing attack.

Like the enhanced authentication scheme, it is assumed that the safe session key k is set between access server and the gateway in advance, and that the secret key k of each IoT device is registered in the access server. Figure 3 shows the structure and the operation process of the enhanced authentication scheme, and it conducts the authentication process through following 5 steps [7].

(1) After the gateway creates the random value r, it sends r to the IoT device with ID_D.

(2) After the IoT device creates the random value t, it calculates the random hash value $h(ID_D\|k\|r\|t)$ using r received from the gateway, its ID_D, and the secret key k, and then sends $h(ID_D\|k\|r\|t)$ and t to the gateway.

(3) The gateway sends $h(ID_D\|k\|r\|t)$ and t received from the IoT device, by using the access server and posed session key k, and E_{gk} $(h(ID_D\|k\|r\|t)$, r, t) after encrypting r created by itself, to the access server.

(4) After the access server decrypts E_{gk} $(h(ID_D\|k\|r\|t)$, r, t) received from the gateway by using the session key k, and calculates $h(ID_D\|k\|r\|t)$, r, t), it searches the pairs of ID and key in accordance with each other, comparing the calculated value of h $(ID_D\|k\|r\|t)$, r, t) with $h(ID_D\|k\|r\|t)$, r, t) value received from the gateway, using all the pairs of the IoT device ID and the secret key stored in its access server, through following verification function. If an accorded value is not searched, an error message is sent to the gateway. If an accorded value is searched, the access

server authenticates the IoT device and sends the gateway $E_{gk}(r)$ encrypting the accorded value into the session key k with the random value r created by the gateway.

(5) If the value received from the access server is an error, the gateway will quit the communication with the IoT device. From the normally authenticated case, r is obtained by decryption of $E_{gk}(r)$ received from the access server. For mutual authentication, decrypted r is verified about the accordance with the random value r created by itself. If r is in accordance, the gateway conducts the expected operation to the IoT device.

Because the IoT device doesn't authenticate the gateway in the improved authentication protocol as well, disguising as a malicious gateway is possible. In case of a readable and writable IoT device, an attacker can charge the fee directly and deliver wrongful order to the IoT device by ignoring the authentic process using the malicious gateway [8].

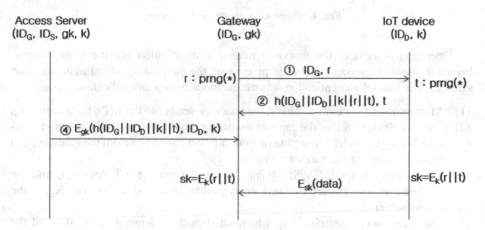

Fig. 3. Enhanced authentication scheme

3   Mutual Authentication Scheme Proposition

3.1   Proposed Authentication Scheme

Solving the problem of the previously suggested authentication scheme, I suggest a new mutual authentication scheme which provides mutual authentication between the gateway and the IoT device. Before this scheme is conducted, it is assumed that an ID and a secret key of the IoT device are registered safely in the access server, and the IoT device and the access server only know it. In addition, it is assumed that the gateway and the access server share the session key in advance and use a safe communication channel.

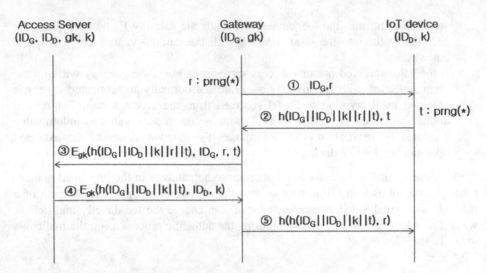

Fig. 4. Proposed authentication scheme.

Operation process of the proposed mutual authentication scheme is as follows. Figure 4 shows a message exchange process of the suggested mutual authentication scheme. The mutual authentication scheme includes 5-step authentication process

(1) After creating the random value r, the gateway sends r to the IoT device with ID_G.
(2) The IoT device creates the random number r, calculates the authentication message $h(ID_G\|ID_D\|k\|r\|t)$ using the random number r received from the gateway, and sends its value to the gateway with t.
(3) The gateway sends $h(ID_G\|ID_D\|k\|r\|t)$ received from the IoT device, t, and the random number r created by itself, encrypted by using the session key K_R, to the access server.
(4) The access server searches ID_D which satisfies the following, using ID is of the IoT devices stored by decrypting $E_{KR}(h(ID_G\|ID_D\|k\|r\|t), ID_G, r, t)$. In case that there is no accorded value, authentication failure message is sent. If any, it authenticates the IoT device, creates $E_{gk}(h(ID_G\|ID_D\|k\|t), ID_D)$, and sends it to the gateway.
(5) The gateway decrypts $E_{gk}(h(ID_G\|ID_D\|k\|t), ID_D)$ received from the database, authenticates validity of the IoT device, calculates $h(h(ID_G\|ID_D\|k\|t), r)$, and then sends the IoT device its value. The IoT device checks the accordance of received value from the gateway with its own secret key k by calculating $h(h(ID_G\|ID_D\|k\|t), r)$. In case of accordance, it is authenticated as the valid gateway. If not, communication is discontinued

3.2   Safety Analysis of Proposed Authentication Scheme

The safety of the suggested authentication protocol is analyzed.

(1) Replay attack: An authentication message used in suggested protocol includes the random numbers created by the gateway and the IoT device in every session. Therefore, if an attacker wiretaps and replays this authentication message, it can be detected by the access server. So the suggested protocol is safe from replay attack.

(2) Spoofing attack: Spoofing attack occurs when the attacker is disguised as the IoT device by obtaining the secret key of the IoT device or as the malicious gateway in the case that mutual authentication between the gateway and the IoT device isn't conducted. As for the former case, in the suggested protocol, the secret key of the IoT device is protected because the secret key k of the IoT device is sent as the value transformed by safe hash function. For the latter, the disguise of the attacker as the malicious gateway is impossible because the mutual authentication between the gateway and the IoT device is provided by verifying m1 and m3. So the suggested protocol is safe from spoofing attack.

(3) Anonymity of the IoT device: In the suggested protocol, since the access server and the IoT device only know the ID of the IoT device, and the result value hashing the ID of the IoT device is sent with the random number t and r created respectively by the gateway and the IoT device at the time of sending ID of the IoT device, anonymity of the IoT device can be guaranteed.

(4) Location tracking attack by collusion of the malicious gateway: In spite of obtaining an authentication message for the IoT device by collusion of malicious gateways, the malicious gateways can't confirm whether two different messages are the authentication messages for the identical IoT device because the authentication message is information which is changeable in every session by the random number t created by the IoT device [9].

4   Performance Evaluation

A simulation was conducted to analyze the efficiency of the suggested authentication protocol and the previous authentication protocols. The simulation compares the protocols of the previous method, the improved method, and the suggested method in two aspects of memory usage amount and communication amount in RFID system environment. The simulation was conducted by using NS-2, with 1 Mbps of IoT device data rate supposed and 11 Mbps of gateway data rate supposed. Each protocol is composed of two stages of the initialization stage and authentication one.

The initialization stage as the one of obtaining information of the IoT device in the pure state, by changing the information the IoT device has or storing other adding values, is the stage storing authenticated information for authentication protocol process. Authentication stage is the stage that the IoT device state is changed and brings authenticated information for that, and authenticates it actually.

The gateway, with the authentication information obtained from the IoT device, transforms the authentication information into encryption and non-identifiable value and sends it to the access server. After that, the server decrypts and transforms the authentication information into the identifiable value in order to certify it. If the authentication information identifiable by the server itself is sent rightly, it quits the authentication and provides the data, or sends data by encrypting it again. The gateway checking it certifies the fact that the authentication is made through the data or a certain response.

The noticeable points in performance evaluation are as follows: Checking that when gateway interrogates, what kind of information provision it needs, checking that it verifies the value by requisition of the access server or received from the access server exactly, and checking that it interrogates the stored value at the time of update. That is, it is necessary to compare the process of conducting authentication of gateway at the stage of certifying the current value of the IoT device and until the stage before updating the IoT device after certifying.

The contents of performance comparison graph are as follows. The contents of memory usage amount of each protocol are represented by comparison graph. It was assumed that, compared to others, the suggested protocol needs additional data such as the gateway ID to store additionally and the session key, that storage amount of the suggested protocol shown in the graph is proportional to the IoT device number n of X axis, and that the data like the gateway ID or the session key are registered with 10 gateways.

The memory usage amount, here, was represented in a graph divided by the composition. Figure 5, the graph about memory usage amount of the gateway, shows fixed memory usage amount regardless of the IoT device number n. Although the memory usage amount of the previous protocol is the smallest and that of the suggested protocol is the biggest, it shows the narrow margin of memory usage amount.

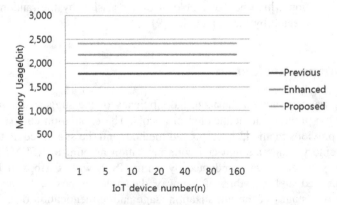

Fig. 5. Proposed authentication scheme.

In Fig. 6, the suggested protocol needing additional storage amount in the access server has the biggest memory usage amount around 5 GB, and it shows the quite narrow margin to that of the improved protocol. It was found that the memory usage amount of the previous protocol is low due to the simple process of authentication. The storage amount of the suggested protocol in order to store around 160 of the IoT device is about 5B, and it is seen that the improved protocol also needs around 5 GB. Memory usage amount of the access server is relatively big, but about 5B of storage amount is needed when the number of the IoT device is 160, if they are stored in the access server. Although the number of registered gateway is 10, they need just 0.2B, so totally 5B of storage amount is needed. However, around 5B of storage amount is unproblematic in current access server system technology. The comparison graph for storage amount was represented as the section of the IoT device and gateway and the section of gateway and the access server.

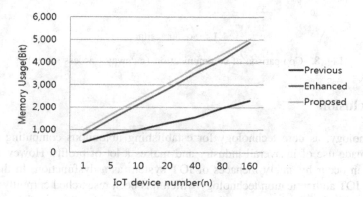

Fig. 6. Comparison of memory usage for access server

As Fig. 7 shows, the communication amount between the IoT device and the gateway is almost same with that of the suggested protocol. As for the communication amount between the gateway and the access server, when the access server storing 160

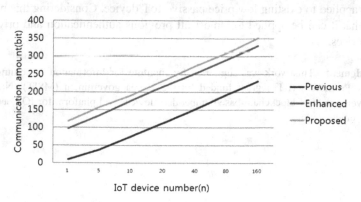

Fig. 7. Comparison of communication (IoT device - gateway)

numbers of IoT device are used like Fig. 8, the previous protocol needs 12,561 bits of communication amount and the improved protocol needs around 13,000 bits of communication amount. The suggested protocol needs only 13,400 bits of communication amount. Almost same amount is needed as shown in the graph.

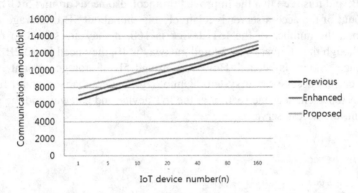

Fig. 8. Comparison of communication (gateway - access server)

5   Conclusion

IOT technology, as core technology for establishing ubiquitous computing environment, is made use of in overall industry and makes a lot of profits. However, bigger damage can occur by safety menaces of IOT system as a dysfunction. In this study, analyzing IOT authentication technology which has been researched currently for safer IOT system, authentication protocol providing mutual authentication for safer communication was suggested.

The suggested authentication protocol can prevent disguise as the malicious gateway or the illegal IoT device, and protect the secret key of the IoT device from the damaged gateway, by providing mutual authentication between the gateway and the IoT device. The suggested authentication protocol is the light-weighed protocol, so it is able to be applied to existing low price passive IoT device. Considering this point, it is expected that it can be applied to almost all previous authentication and privacy protecting services.

Acknowledgment. This work was supported by Institute for Information & communications Technology Promotion (IITP) grant funded by the Korea government (MSIT) (No. 2018-0-00508, Development of blockchain-based embedded devices and platform for IOT security and operational efficiency).

References

1. Savry, O., Vacherand, F.: Security and privacy protection of contactless devices. The Internet of Things, pp. 409–419. Springer, New York (2010). https://doi.org/10.1007/978-1-4419-1674-7_40

2. Seo, H., et al.: IOT security technical trend. Korean Inst. Electromagn. Eng. Soc. **24**(4), 27–35 (2013)

3. de Leusse, P., Periorellis, P., Dimitrakos, T., Nair, S.K.: Self managed security cell, a security model for the internet of things and services. In: 2009 First International Conference on Advances in Future Internet, pp. 47–52 (2009)

4. Hong, D., et al.: HIGHT: a new block cipher suitable for low-resource device. In: Goubin, L., Matsui, M. (eds.) Proceedings of the International Conference on Cryptographic Hardware and Embedded Systems (CHES 2006). LNCS, vol. 4249, pp. 46–59. Springer, Heidelberg. https://doi.org/10.1007/11894063_4, http://www.springer.com/lncs. Accessed 21 Nov 2016

5. Shin, J., Park, Y.: An authentication protocol using the EXOR and the hash function in RFID/USN. In: Korea Society of Industrial Information Systems, vol. 12, no. 2, pp. 24–29, June 2007

6. Ahn, H.-S., Bu, K.-D.: Improved authentication protocol for RFID/USN environment. Inst. Electron. Inf. Eng. **46**(CI-1), 1–10 (2009)

7. Savry, O., Vacherand, F.: Security and privacy protection of contactless devices. The Internet of Things, pp. 409–419. Springer, New York (2010). https://doi.org/10.1007/978-1-4419-1674-7_40

8. Engels, D., Saarinen, M.-J.O., Schweitzer, P., Smith, E.M.: The hummingbird-2 lightweight authenticated encryption algorithm. In: Juels, A., Paar, C. (eds.) RFIDSec 2011. LNCS, vol. 7055, pp. 19–31. Springer, Heidelberg (2012). https://doi.org/10.1007/978-3-642-25286-0_2

9. Eom, T., Yi, J.-H.: Performance evaluation of authentication protocol for mobile RFID privacy. Korean Inst. Commun. Inf. Sci. **36**(6), 618–630 (2011)

Event Relation Identification Based on Dependency and Co-occurrence

Junhui Yang[1,2(✉)], Zongtian Liu[1(✉)], and Wei Liu[1(✉)]

[1] School of Computer Engineering and Science, Shanghai University,
Shanghai 200072, China
jwcjhy@126.com, Zongtian@126.com, Weiliu@126.com
[2] School of Computer Science and Engineering,
Jiangxi University of Science and Technology, Ganzhou 341000, Jiangxi, China

Abstract. Event relation identification is an important branch of event research. This paper proposes a new event relation identification method from the semantic point of view between events. Use the dependency between events and the co-occurrence of the event elements in the text, and then construct a set of semantic event clues. Then use the improved AP algorithm to cluster the event set with the related thread. Experimental results show that using the six semantic elements of events can more accurately calculate the dependency between candidate related events and the correlation between candidate related event elements, it could find more candidate related events and improve the recognition ability of event relations.

Keywords: Event · Event element · Dependency co-occurrence · Algorithm · Relation identification

1 Introduction

Event is a reflection of the objective facts, which reflects the description of some characters participating and showing some action characteristics in a certain time and environment. Everything in the world is interrelated, and the occurrence and development of events are often related to other external events. Textual events refer to the pragmatic forms of describing objective events through text, which often appear in news reports, comments or blog text.

The event correlation is indicated whether there is a correlation between the two events. For example, the events between the "Watergate incident" and the "Asian Pacific stock market", the "Russian airliner crash" and the "Egyptian tourism industry hit" event, some seemingly unrelated events contain some special relationship. Therefore, only the two events of the text representation cannot determine whether them relevancy or not, it need to mining out more external information, and make full use of external information to support the identification of events related. The relation between events is a rather complex issue, analyzing the relation between events, finding the "correlated" and "uncorrelated" events can better understand the content of the text organization, mining important event information, help to grasp the trend of events,

© Springer Nature Singapore Pte Ltd. 2019
H. Peng et al. (Eds.): ISICA 2018, CCIS 986, pp. 292–305, 2019.
https://doi.org/10.1007/978-981-13-6473-0_26

especially for emergency treatment. Thus the discovery of relations between events has become a new hotspot in the research of scholars both at home and abroad.

Zelenko [1] using shallow syntactic analysis results, connecting the smallest common subtree of entity twins characterized the event relation instance, to computing the kernel function between the two subtrees, training SVM classify, at the smaller news corpus made better event relation extraction results. Pekar [2] proposed a method of using event attribute information to identify the event relation. The method has a strict definition of the trigger word which has implication relation, it can improved recognition accuracy for events relation. Lin [3] proposed an unsupervised method combining the Harris distribution assumption and the establishment of a dependency tree. The algorithm constructs all the events in the form of dependency tree. Each path in the tree represents an event, and the path node represents the words of the event. Determine whether the two paths are exactly the same, so as to identify the events represented by the two paths of the same or related. Mani [4] uses the extended rule set to train the maximum entropy classifier to achieve the semi supervised event relation classification; the experimental results show the higher accuracy. Davidov et al. [5] use the Google search engine, automatic mining and the specific concepts of the related entities and semantic relations. Rosenfeld et al. [6] found that the effective combination the feature relation and entity feature can greatly improve the accuracy of the relation extraction, and use the hierarchical clustering algorithm to cluster the related events. Hashimoto et al. [7] propose a supervised method of extracting event causalities. Exacerbate desertification from the web using semantic relation, context, and association features. To "predicted" the future event sequence in a sense.

Domestic research on event relation detection is still in its early stage. Ma [8] proposes an event relation reorganization method based on event dependency cue to detect latent semantic relation between events: whether events hold logical relation or not. Zhong [9] proposes the event influence factor to depict the strong and weak of interaction between events, and introduces a method of computing the event influence factor. Then ERM (Event Relation Map) is then constructed to describe domain event relations. Zhou et al. [10] use the entity to the shortest path tree, add the semantic relation of the different level features, and consider the predicate context information, the use of the convolution tree kernel function method, effectively improve the performance of event relation extraction.

The research can be seen that the research of the traditional event detection is mostly concentrated on the pattern matching and rule reasoning, and some scholars pay attention to the structure characteristics and the semantic components of the event itself. However, in the event relation identification these scholars only from the event of the trigger word as a factor in the identification of the relation, less consideration of other information related to the incident, such as subject, object and other information. Although there are some scholars as Ma [8] proposed a method based on semantic dependency, and considers the event dependency information. The experimental results are also good, but the semantic relation between the events is not considered, at the same time, the default information processing of the text is not deeply studied; this will affect the effect of the experiment.

2 Definitions of Event and Event Related

Definition 1. (*Event*) *Occurring in a particular time and environment with some characters involved, it refers to something which shows some movement features* [11].

Event E can be defined as a 6-tuple formalize E: = def <A, O, T, V, P, L> in which the elements are called event elements, representing action (A), objects (O), time (T), environment (V), assertions (P) and language.

*(**Event Class**) Event Class means a set of events with common characteristics, define as follows:*

$$EC = (E, C_1, C_2, \ldots, C_6) \tag{1}$$

Where E is the event set, defined as extension of event class. <A, O, T, V, P, L> are known as connotation of the event class. It denotes the set with common characteristics of corresponding factors in each event of E.

Definition 2 (Relation event). *For the same theme text events collection $EC = D(e_1, e_2, \ldots, e_i, e_j, \ldots, e_t)$, if any of the two events e_i, e_j elements collection of the sets EC satisfy $\bigcup_{\varepsilon=1}^{6} e_i \cap \bigcup_{\varepsilon=1}^{6} e_j \neq \varnothing, \varepsilon = (O, A, T, V, P, L)$ where $e_i, e_j \subset EC$, then the two events are related. Sign $e_i \overset{\lambda}{\leftrightarrow} e_j, 0 \leq \lambda \leq 1$, where λ is the degree of the relation.*

Definition 3. *(Event similarity) it indicates the degree of the similarity of the events, usually expresses by the value of [0, 1] interval.*

Suppose an event set contains two events e_i and e_j, event similarity can be calculated according to the similarity corresponding to event elements, $SIM(e_i, e_j)$ define as follows:

$$SIM(e_i, e_j) = \sum_{k=1}^{6} w_k s(e_{ik}, e_{jk}), k = (o, a, t, v, p, l), w_1 = 0.5, w_2 = 0.3, w_{3,4,5,6} = 0.1 \tag{2}$$

Where $SIM(e_i, e_j)$ refers to the similarity between e_i and e_j, e_{ik} indicates the k elements of event e_i and e_{jk} indicates the k elements of event e_j, w_k indicates the weight of the events for calculation event similarity, denoted as $\sum w_k = 1$, the weight of the event similarity between e_i and e_j is [0, 1]. Obviously, the similarity between e_i and e_j is [0, 1], that is to say, two events could be exactly the same, otherwise they may have nothing to do with each other. The "0" (less than a certain defined threshold) expresses no similarity between two events whereas "1" expresses two events exactly the same, namely, the same event. Through the experiment, when the event similarity $Sim(e_i, e_j) \geq 0.7$, e_i and e_j could be assumed to be similar.

3   Event Elements Identification and Fill

3.1   Event Extract and Event Elements Identification

In order to identify the relation between events, the event source is required to be obtained from the text. In the laboratory research work, this text combines the text with the context feature, the trigger word, the word which is similar to the trigger word, the part of speech, the position information, dependency relation and so on as a whole to consider, fusion of these features to identify events. The event recognition problem as a classification problem, using text classification thought, judgment contains the trigger word sentence is classified to a class of events. Using SVM (Support Vector Machine) machine learning algorithm for event recognition, at the same time in the process of recognition of each event element adopts the following method of six factors of events were filled, and provide the basis for the follow-up work.

3.2   Event Elements Fill

Event elements fill refers to the six elements of any event need to display in the text. Considering that the Chinese text description events often omit part of sentence composition, thus some event elements could not be clearly expressed, for example, "A semi-trailer collided with a minibus waiting for clearance and burst into flames". Three event trigger words "collided", "fire", "flame" involved, but the text only describe the event trigger essential factors of "collision", other essential factors of events trigger "fire" and "flame" did not describe the six elements, only describe the action essential factor. Therefore, it need fill up completion all event elements, could be compare relations between events and calculation similarity of events.

Event elements fill algorithm describes:

1. Word segmentation and tagging available elements of events in text, at the same time determine which events elements need to fill;
2. In the event of default elements E as the center, and to search for adjacent events and to determine whether the two event to meet the non-classification relation between the, If it is satisfied, the candidate event elements are identified as the default event elements, and the event elements are selected as the default elements of the default elements. Otherwise, the search for a non-taxonomic relation event element, until the default event elements fill the complete end.

4   Determination the Degree of Dependence Between the Events

4.1   Discover Event Chain Dependent Relations

Definition 4. (Event chain) it defined as a series of events occurring in a certain probability lead by an events, which is called the event chain. Event chain has the characteristics of the system, which is the interaction between the event elements, the interaction of the event nodes, and the interaction of the whole behavior. Event chain is new events continuous production which is driven by event elements under a certain situation. Formal representation for: $EL = \{e_1(\varepsilon_1) \rightarrow e_2(\varepsilon_2)\ldots e_m(\varepsilon_m)\ldots \rightarrow e_n(\varepsilon_n)\}$, where e_m means of action element of the number m event, and ε_m, $\varepsilon = (o, t, v, p, l)$ means of other element of the number m event.

From the event definition can be seen the six elements of the basic expressions to indicate that the event, but text description is often omitted certain elements. Therefore, before the text events chain dependency parsing, the elements of event needs complement (the matrix sparse problem of co-occurrence can be solving). And with the help of Harbin Institute of LTP platform to realize the text in the events of dependency parsing, the words which connected by the dependency parsing result and the root node is seem to be the central event. Such as the "Russian airliner crash" reported, the effect of the dependence parsing as shown in Fig. 1.

Fig. 1. Dependency parsing instance

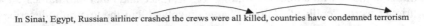

In Sinai, Egypt, Russian airliner crashed the crews were all killed, countries have condemned terrorism

Fig. 2. Event chain instance

In the preceding example can be seen the dependencies relation of the events (crash, the victims, condemned) can structured the relation similar to the chain of events (see in Fig. 2). For a given event chain. If there is a dependency between the event e_i and the event e_j, the event e_i and the event e_j is considered as a candidate for the relation event twins, at the same time, the dependency arc between the event e_i and the event e_j is recorded as a dependent step k (the max of k is 5, if dependency arc outstrip 5, then consider no dependencies relation between events). Otherwise consider no relation between the event e_i and the event e_j. As the dependency grammar is to reveal the syntactic structure of the components in the language unit, the semantic information of the text is not considered. Therefore, the semantic information of the text should be adjusted according to the semantic information of the event.

4.2 Event Dependency Calculation

Assuming that the text of the sentence window S contains N $(e_{i1}, e_{i2}, \ldots, e_{ik}, \ldots, e_{im}, e_{in})$ events, exit event e_{ik} similar to the target topic event e_i. If all of the events N can be connected by dependency arcs, the event $e_{im}(m \in n)$ is considered to be a dependent candidate event. Then event e_{ik} and event e_{im} is event twins that have a dependency on the arc of the event, thus forming a set of candidate events $se(km) = [d(e_{i1}, e_{k1}), d(e_{i2}, e_{k2}), \ldots, d(e_{im}, e_{km})]$, and the mutual information of each dependent event can be obtained.

Because the mutual information method has no consideration the frequency of the characteristic occurrence in the text, the mutual information is likelihood ratio of the probability of two P (Xi, XJ) and the probability of two separate words product P (XI) * P (XJ), it will appear that the two tuple of mutual information which composition by low frequency words more than high frequency words, which obviously cannot accept, for this, this paper uses the improved to calculate the event information, $PMI'(e_{ik}, e_{im})$ define as follows:

$$PMI'(e_{ik}, e_{im}) = \log[\frac{P(e_{ik}, e_{im})}{P(e_{ik}) \times P(e_{im})}] \ / \ \log[\frac{2}{P(e_{ik}) + P(e_{im})}] \tag{3}$$

Where $P(e_{ik}, e_{im})$ indicate the probability of the co-occurrence for e_{ik}, e_{im}, $P(e_{ik})$ indicate probability distribute of e_{ik}, $P(e_{im})$ indicate probability distribute of e_{im}, if $P(e_{ik}, e_{im}) < P(e_{ik}) * P(e_{im})$ and assume $P(e_{ik}, e_{im}) = P(e_{ik}) * P(e_{im})$, then it exist $0 \le PMI'(e_{ik}, e_{im}) \le 1$, the improved $PMI'(e_{ik}, e_{im})$ can effectively change problem of the two tuple of mutual information which composition by low frequency words more than high frequency, to a certain extent it weakened due to the sparse data on the final correlation of quantitative value.

Then it can calculate the dependence degree of event e_{im} and event e_i, $dep(e_i, e_{im})$ define as follows:

$$dep(e_i, e_{im}) = Sim(e_i, e_{ik}) \frac{1}{n} \max PMI'(e_{ik}, e_{im}) \tag{4}$$

Where $sim(e_i, e_{ik})$ indicate semantic similarity of the event e_{ik} and e_i as a ratio of error penalty for e_{ik}, n indicate the dependency arcs length of the event e_{ik} and event e_{im}, the greater the N, the more weak the two event dependency relation, and vice versa. $PMI'(e_{ik}, e_{im})$ indicate the dependency of the event e_{ik} and event e_{im} depends on the mutual information value of the collection.

4.3   Event (Elements) Co-occurrence and Relation Judgment

Definition 5. *Event (elements) co-occurrence: it defined in the same unit window events e_i (elements) and events e_j (elements), which are common occurrences (elements). The ratio of events (elements) co-occurrence is events (elements) are common occurrences in the same unit window. It is the joint probability of event (element) in the text collection in the unit window.*

The overlap co-occurrence of event elements is an important reference index to measure the degree of event relations. Therefore, it can be used to mine the relation between events in the text. Assume that the text of the sentence window S contains the N dependent candidate events set $Se \supseteq (e_{i1}, e_{i2}, \ldots, e_{ik}, \ldots, e_{im}, e_{in})$, and if there is a correlation factor λ satisfied $Se \overset{\lambda}{\leftrightarrow} e_i, 0 \le \lambda \le 1$, where the greater value of λ indicate the greater value of relevancy between the target event e_i and set of the dependent candidate event Se.

From the definition of event knows the trigger of event is an important component of the event status, and the event's trigger word is expressed as an event action, so the correlation coefficient between the action elements of the events λ_{ia} and the other factors of the events $\lambda_{i\varepsilon}$ can be calculated respectively when calculating the correlation coefficient of the event λ_m, define as follows:

$$\lambda_m = \alpha\lambda_{ia} + (1 - \alpha)\lambda_{i\varepsilon} \tag{5}$$

Where λ_{ia} indicate the correlation coefficient between the target event e_i and the action element of the dependent event e_{im}, where $\lambda_{i\varepsilon}$ indicate the correlation coefficient between the target event e_i and the other elements of the dependent event e_{im}, and α indicate weighted coefficient.

When calculating the value of the action elements of the dependent candidate event λ_{ia}, the overlap co-occurrences of the elements of the action elements set corresponding to the set of dependent candidate events e_i and e_{im} are calculated respectively, λ_{ia} define as follows:

$$\lambda_{ia} = \frac{|S_{eia} \cap S_{eima}|}{Min(|S_{eia}|, |S_{eima}|)} \tag{6}$$

Where S_{eia} indicate the set of action elements of the target events e_i, and S_{eima} indicate the action elements of the candidate events e_{im}.

While correlation coefficient $\lambda_{i\varepsilon}$ for the other factors of the dependent candidate event is calculated, the co-occurrences overlap ratio of the other elements set corresponding to the every trigger events of the dependent candidate events e_i and e_{im} are calculated respectively. $\lambda_{i\varepsilon}$ define as follows:

$$\lambda_{i\varepsilon} = \sum_{\varepsilon=1}^{5}\sum_{\varepsilon=1}^{5} \frac{|S_{ei\varepsilon} \cap S_{eim\varepsilon}|}{Min(|S_{ei\varepsilon}|, |S_{eim\varepsilon}|)}, \varepsilon = (o, t, v, p, l) \tag{7}$$

Where $\varepsilon = (o, t, v, p, l)$ indicate other elements of events which divide trigger element, and $S_{ei\varepsilon}$ indicate the set of other elements of target events $e_{i\varepsilon}$ which divide action element, $S_{eim\varepsilon}$ indicate the set of other elements of dependency candidate events $e_{i\varepsilon}$ which divide action element.

Next, the last correlation degree between the dependency candidate event e_{im} and destination theme event e_i can weighted average by the dependence degree $dep(e_i, e_{im})$ and the correlation degree λ_m which calculate from above-mentioned methods, $r(e_i, e_{im})$ define as follows:

$$r(e_i, e_{im}) = Max(sim(e_i, e_{ik})|(\lambda_m + dep(e_i, e_{im}))/2) \tag{8}$$

Thus the two-tuples can be expressed as the form of the correlation degree of r_{im} and each dependent candidate event in the collection, r_{eim} define as follows:

$$r_{eim} = \{(e_{i1}, r(e_i, e_{i1})), \ldots, (e_{im}, r(e_i, e_{im})), (e_{in}, r(e_i, e_{in}))\} \qquad (9)$$

5 Events Iterated and Relation Identification

5.1 Iteration of Candidate Related Events

Emergency report mainly based on short text, and the less event information contained in the text, so in a single text can only build a limited number of candidates. Such as determining the correlated of target event of "Russian airliner crash" and "the Egyptian tourism industry decrease", in the sentence of "a Russian airliner crashed shortly after the Sinai Peninsula in Egypt, 224 passengers and crew were all killed, extremist groups claimed responsibility for the crash", "the Russian airliner crash" can be used as a target event candidate, but it can only get the candidate related event set "the aircraft crashed in Egypt", "Sinai, the crew were killed" and "the extreme organization responsible for the crash". it is not any assistance for judgment relation with target event "Egypt's tourism industry is decreased", which needs to get more related information of the target event of damage to the Egyptian tourism industry from other texts, such as another text "due to security reasons, many countries announced the suspension of tourists to Egypt Tourism and Egypt believes that this will impact the Egyptian tourism industry". This sentence mention the events of "suspension of tourists to Egypt Tourism", it can mining the correlation coefficient event "the impact of the Egyptian tourism industry".

To this end, the following steps can be achieved in the iterative expansion of the correlated candidate events:

Step 1: in the corpus to find the target text event $e_{i(j)}$ with the highest similarity of event as the target candidate event $e_{i(j)k}(k \in (1, n))$.

Step 2: constructs a candidate event chain $Se'_{i(j)}$ by means of a dependency method use candidate event $e_{i(j)k}$ (except for the candidate event), and calculate the corresponding dependency and correlation degree between the $e_{i(j)m}$ and the $e_{i(j)}$.

Step 3: For any candidate event within the sentence window as a new target event, and the set of new candidate $e'_{i(j)}$ related events which extended by new target event add to the collection of candidate related events $e_{i(j)}$.

Step 4: returns the Step 1, until the corpus is not satisfied with the iterative conditions.

5.2 Candidate Related Events Cluster and Identification

In order to recognition of the event correlation in the text event set $Ds \supseteq (e_1, e_2, \ldots, e_i, e_j, \ldots, e_t)$, based on the given target "event", correlation degree between the candidate event set which build from one of the target event and the other target event are calculated, which is used as a basis for determining the relevance of the target event, and clustering of text semantic event set, the events in the same cluster is judged to be pairwise correlation events.

APCcluster clustering algorithm as this paper algorithm, APCcluster clustering algorithm [12], later some scholars use APCcluster clustering algorithm for text clustering [13], sample the similarity between samples as input, the output is the cluster center and the relation between the sample and the cluster center, and the clustering of text as a measure of the relevance of the text.

Therefore, the interdependent candidate events set $e_{im}(i \in (1,k), m \in (1,n))$ and the correlation degree r_{im} construct from $e_{i(j)}$ in Sect. 4.1 can transformation superset composed two set of tuples, then use the cosine similarity to calculated the similarity values, instead of used Euclidean distance as the similarity measure at APCcluster clustering algorithm to improve clustering quality [14]. When the attractor propagation algorithm convergence that the same clustering events as the pairwise correlation events, otherwise event does not exist logical relation.

The algorithm is described as follows:

Input: similarity matrix Se.

Output: class representative events and the relation between the sample and the class representative events.

Step 1. The interdependent candidate events set $Se_{im}(i \in (1,k), m \in (1,n))$ and the correlation degree r_{im} construct from $e_{i(j)}$ in this Sect. 4.1 conversion to a superset of T number of two consisting of a set of tuples.

$$D = \left\{ \begin{array}{l} \{<e_{11}, r_{11}>\}, \{<e_{12}, r_{22}>\}, \ldots, <e_{1m}, r_{1m}>, \{<e_{1n}, r_{1n}>\}, \ldots \\ \{<e_{i1}, r_{i1}>\}, \{<e_{i2}, r_{22}>\}, \ldots, <e_{im}, r_{im}>, \{<e_{in}, r_{in}>\}, \\ \{<e_{j1}, r_{j1}>\}, \{<e_{j2}, r_{j2}>\}, \ldots, <e_{jm}, r_{jm}>, \{<e_{jn}, r_{jn}>\}, \\ \{<e_{t1}, r_{t1}>\}, \{<e_{t2}, r_{t2}>\}, \ldots, \{<e_{tm}, r_{tm}>\}, \{<e_{tn}, r_{tn}>\} \end{array} \right\} \quad (10)$$

Where $<e_{im}, r_{im}>$ indicate set the of dependence candidate e_{im} with the sample event e_i corresponding to the correlation value r_{im} formed by the two tuple.

Step 2. The similarity of the sample set of samples D is calculated by cosine similarity.

Step 3. Calculate self-similarity

$$s(e_i, e_i) = \varphi \sum_{i,j=1; i \neq j}^{K} s(e_i, e_i) \ / \ n(n-1) \quad (11)$$

where φ as the adjustment factor.

Step 4. Initialization matrix A,

$$a(e_i, e_j) = 0, j \neq j' \quad (12)$$

Step 5. Update the following formula A, R, where $\partial = 0.5$.

$$r(e_i, e_j) = s(e_i, e_j) - \max_{j \neq j'} \{s(e_i, e_j') + a(e_i, e_j')\} \quad (13)$$

$$a(e_i, e_j) = \begin{cases} \min\{0, r(k,k) + \sum_{i \neq i', j} \max\{0, r(e_{i'}, e_j)\}\}, i \neq j \\ \sum_{i \neq i', j} \max\{0, r(e_{i'}, e_j)\}, i = j \end{cases} \tag{14}$$

$$r(e_i, e_j)^{(t+1)} = \partial \bullet r(e_i, e_j)^{(t)} + (1 - \partial) \bullet r(e_i, e_j)^{(t-1)}$$
$$a(e_i, e_j)^{(t+1)} = \partial \bullet r(e_i, e_j)^{(t)} + (1 - \partial) \bullet a(e_i, e_j)^{(t-1)} \tag{15}$$

Step 6. Identify the candidate cluster centers for each sample e_i, i.e. $\arg\max_j(a(e_i, e_j) + r(e_i, e_j))$

Repeat Step 5–step 6 until the clustering center of all samples is no longer changed or reached the maximum number of iterations, the algorithm ends.

At last, the correlation degree is calculated by the following formula of the event e_i and event e_j, and the threshold value is set. As shown below.

$$R(e_i, e_j) = Max(sim(e_{im}, e_j) | r(e_i, e_{im})) \tag{16}$$

Where $R(e_i, e_j)$ indicate the correlation degree of e_i, e_j, $sim(e_{im}, e_j)$ indicate similarity of the candidate event e_{im} and event e_j, $r(e_i, e_{im})$ as the correlation degree of the dependent candidate related event e_{im} and the event e_i, if the high similarity between the candidate events e_{im} and e_j, the correlation degree of the two events e_i, e_j can be replaced by the dependence degree of between the dependent candidate events e_{im} and the sample events e_i.

6 Experimental Results and Analysis

6.1 Experimental Backgrounds

In order to validate the feasibility of the method of event relation identification, need corresponding corpus to train and test. The previous research work in the laboratory [15], collect 332 articles about the earthquake, fire, traffic accidents, food poisoning, terrorist attacks and other 5 kinds of emergency news reports as raw corpus (Corpus CEC) from the internet, the corpus after clauses, part of speech tagging, event extraction elements, remove the negative events, event elements complement and marking whether there is a relation between the event are preprocessed. At relation marking (annotation) between the events, the annotators were divided into two groups, respectively for all corpus annotation. And through the HIT LEP tool for dependency analysis and the correction of events between dependency relation, at the same time staff will be based on the events on the trigger word to identify whether the relation between events. For the relation event of a dispute, the two parties participated in the vote.

In fact, at the time of the manual annotation of the relation between the events and two groups of annotators on some controversial relation between each airs his own views, in 5 kinds of documents were randomly selected in each of the 10 document according to the above method for tagging repeat annotation. In the same document, in the identification of the relation, the two groups of the number of labels are not the same, respectively, 1210 (the first group), 1216 (second), after the discussion of the relation between the number of 1208. At last, in a given 332 documents of the corpus, the number of events per class, and the number of events associated with the correlated (uncorrelated) relations are shown in Table 1.

Table 1. CEC corpus data

Corpus	Doc	Events	Sentences	Events twins	
				Correlated	Uncorrelated
Traffic accident	85	1802	514	97	173
Earth quake	62	1002	401	88	159
Fire disaster	75	1216	433	87	147
Bromatoxism	61	1111	392	59	119
Terrorist attack	49	823	324	56	93
Total	332	5954	2064	387	691

6.2   Experimental Results and Evaluation

In order to verify the validity of the proposed method in this paper, we select the recent domestic and foreign scholars to study the relation between the method and the method of this paper.

In the first experiment, the value of the weighted coefficient values α is determined, and it is needed to adjust the training data to make it in [0, 1]. To this end, the random sample training 100 of the events twins as a reference from 60 document, based on the artificial judge whether exist the correlation between events, and the use of formula (1) calculated on the basis of constantly adjust the weighted coefficient values α, so that the results of the calculation with the artificial judgment (as shown in Fig. 3). Then the optimal value is applied to the test set, and the weighted coefficient is: $\alpha = 0.7$. In fact, events trigger is the core of the event, it play a more important role to judgment whether event twins exist correlation.

The number of iterations has a certain effect on the performance of the system. To this end, the training set data is used as the sample data and test used for the selection of the number of iterations. As shown in Fig. 4, the number of iterations and the results of the calculation are 6 more appropriate.

In this experiment, we randomly selected 30 of the five kind's events from the CEC corpus, and the method was validated by a total of 150 text data. The experimental results were as the same as the general evaluation method in the field of text retrieval, and the R, F and P three indexes were calculated. Experimental results are shown in Table 2.

First, Yang et al. [16] as Baseline1, it uses the same topic under the core words and entities of the distribution characteristics of the event, for the same topic under the event relation identification task, proposed a method based on the core word and entity of the event relation identification method.

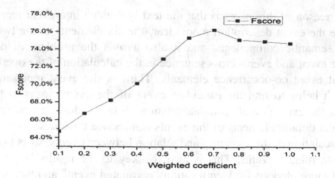

Fig. 3. Weighting factor α and F-measure contrast

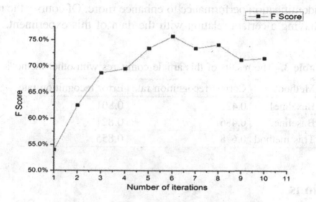

Fig. 4. Iteration number and F-measure contrast

Followed by Kolya et al. [17] as Baseline2, Anup et al. proposed a method based on CRF, which uses supervised machine learning technology, conditional random fields to identify the relation between the events.

Table 2. The results of this article compares with other methods

Method	Experimental result		
	P	R	F
Baseline1	0.689	0.675	0.682
Baseline2	0.729	0.664	0.695
This method	0.754	0.704	0.729

From Table 2 can see, the relation identification results between the different methods use same corpus can be seen in the comparison of the results, the method proposed in this paper is slightly higher than other types of recall rate, accuracy rate and harmonic mean value.

The main reason of this paper is that the text is divided into event representation, one can make the event description more clear, the six elements of the two elements have certain semantic components, and it also avoids the problem of dependency relation of the event and events cross sentence in the calculation of the overlap ratio of the dependent event co-occurrence elements. Third is the event representation text method, which helps to find the candidate event of the event, so as to lay a good foundation for the extraction of candidate relation. In fact, before determine candidate, the complement default elements of the events can reduce the sparsely of elements to impact the calculation of the similarity and relation between events, so as to construct a more candidate related events. This is also the key to the results better than other methods. It is more obvious for identification "correlated event" and the "uncorrelated event", as shown in Table 3. The results show that the default elements of the event after complement can greatly enriched the candidate related clues, in the relation of the "event" of the identification performance to enhance more. Of course, the results of this paper may be having a certain relation with the data of this experiment.

Table 3. The results of this article compares with other methods

Method	Correct recognition rate	Error recognition rate
Baseline1	0.425	0.801
Baseline2	0.486	0.821
This method	0.678	0.855

7 Conclusions

The relation between the events is the inherent property of the event, and whether it has a logical relation can be helpful to infer the dynamic development of the event, especially the emergency. At present, the research on the emergency relation between the texts is still in the primary stage. This paper proposed a method for identifying the event relation based on the dependency and co-occurrences of the text events. This method divided the text into event representation, identify events and events role, to determine the correlation degree for events by computing the semantic role of the event (the six elements), mining set of the correlation events for target event in set of corpus. On the basis of this, we construct semantic dependency analysis, and then construct the reasoning clue of event relation identification through dependency relation of the events and the phenomenon of event elements co-occurrences, and realize the event relation based on the improved APCcluster clustering algorithm. The experimental results show that the method proposed in this paper can greatly enrich the reasoning clues, and then can better identify the event relation. But it is only in the study of whether there is a logical relation between the events, the specific relation between the event (such as causal, follow, etc.) has not been thoroughly discussed, which is the need to continue to study and solve.

Acknowledgements. This research was partially supported by the Natural Science Foundation of China (No. 61273328, 61305053) and Innovation Program of Shanghai Municipal Education Commission (No. 14YZ151).

References

1. Zelenko, D., Aone, C., Richardella, A.: Kernel methods for relation extraction. J. Mach. Learn. Res. **3**, 1083–1106 (2003)
2. Pekar, V.: Acquisition of verb entailment from text. In: Proceedings of the Human Language Technology Conference of the NAACL, New York, USA, pp. 49–56 (2006)
3. Lin, D., Pantel, P.: Discovery of inference rules from text. In: Proceeding of the 7th ACM SIGKDD, San Francisco, California, USA, pp. 323–328 (2001)
4. Mani, I., Wellner, B., Verhagen, M., et al.: Machine learning of temporal relations. In: Proceedings of the 44th Annual Meeting of the Association for Computational Linguistics, Sydney, Australia, pp. 753–760 (2006)
5. Davidov, D., Rappoport, A., Koppel, M.: Fully unsupervised discovery of concept-specific relations by web mining. In: Proceedings of the 45th Annual Meeting of the Association of Computational Linguistics. pp. 232–239 (2007)
6. Rosenfeld, B., Feldman, R.: Clustering for unsupervised relation identification. In: Proceedings of the 16th ACM Conference on Information and Knowledge Management, pp. 411–418. ACM (2007)
7. Hashimoto, C., Torisawa, K., Kloetzer, J., et al.: Toward future scenario generation: extracting event causality exploiting semantic relation, context, and association features. In: Proceedings of the 52nd Annual Meeting of the Association for Computational Linguistics, vol. 1. Association for Computational Linguistics (2014)
8. Ma, B., Hong, Y., Yang, X., et al.: Using event dependency cue inference to recognize event relation. Acta Sci. Natur. Univ. **49**(1), 109–116 (2013)
9. Zhong, Z., Liu, Z., Zhou, W.: The model of event relation representation. J. Chinese Inf. Process. **23**(6), 56–60 (2009)
10. Zhou, G.D., Zhang, M., Ji, D.H., et al.: Tree kernel-based relation extraction with context-sensitive structured parse tree information. In: Proceedings of the 2007 Joint Conference on Empirical Methods in Natural Language Processing and Computational Natural Language Learning, pp. 728–736 (2007)
11. Liu, Z., Huang, M., Zhou, W., et al.: Research on event-oriented ontology model. Comput. Sci. **36**(11), 189–192, 199 (2009)
12. Frey, B.J., Dueck, D.: Clustering by passing messages between data points. Science **315**, 972–976 (2007)
13. Guan, R., Pei, Z., Shi, X., et al.: Weight affinity propagation and its application to text clustering. J. Comput. Res. Dev. **47**(10), 1733–1740 (2010)
14. Ahmad, W., Narayanan, A.: Feature weighing for efficient clustering. In: 6th International Conference on Advanced Information Management and Service, Seoul, pp. 236–242 (2010)
15. Fu, J., Liu, W., Liu, Z.: A study of Chinese event taggability. In: Proceedings of the 2nd International Conference on Communication Software and Networks, Singapore, pp. 400–404 (2010)
16. Yang, X., Hong, Y., et al.: Event relation recognition by event term and entity inference. J. Chinese Inf. Process. **28**(2), 100–108 (2014)
17. Kolya, A.K., Ekbal, A., Bandyopadhyay, S.: Event-event relation identification a CRF based approach. In: Proceedings of the 6th International Conference on Natural Language Processing and Knowledge Engineering, NLP-KE, pp. 1–8 (2010)

Adaptively Calling Selection Based on Distance Sorting in CoBiDE

Zhe Chen[1,2]([✉]) and Chengjun Li[1,2]

[1] School of Computer Science, China University of Geosciences,
No. 388 Lumo Road, Wuhan 430074, Hubei, China
chenzhe@cug.edu.cn, cuglicj@126.com
[2] Hubei Key Laboratory of Intelligent Geo-Information Processing,
China University of Geosciences, No. 388 Lumo Road, Wuhan 430074, Hubei, China

Abstract. Differential Evolution is fit for solving continuous optimization problems. So far, the imbalance between exploration and exploitation in DE runs often leads to the failure to obtain good solutions. In this paper, we propose selection based on distance sorting. In such selection, the individual has the best fitness among parents and offspring is selected firstly. Then, the genotype distance from another individual to it, the distance in their chromosome structure, decides whether the former individual is selected. Under the control of a adaptive scheme proposed by us, we use it replace the original selection of the CoBiDE in runs from time to time. Experimental results show that, for many among the twenty-five CEC 2005 benchmark functions, which have the similar changing trend of diversity and fitness in runs, our adaptive scheme for calling selection based on distance sorting brings improvement on solutions.

Keywords: Exploration and exploitation balance ·
Secondary selection · Stagnation · Premature convergence · CoBiDE

1 Introduction

Differential Evolution (DE) originating from [15] is fit for solving continuous optimization problems, such as multi-objective, constrained, dynamic, large-scale, and multimodal optimization ones [9]. So far, the imbalance between exploration and exploitation in DE runs often leads to the failure to obtain good solutions. As a type of Evolutionary Algorithms (EAs), DE is also based on a series of population composed of individuals. In the gth generation, the chromosome of each individual is represented by a target vector, $\boldsymbol{x}_{i,g} = (x_{i,1,g}, x_{i,2,g}, \ldots, x_{i,d,g})(i \in 1, 2, \ldots, NP)$. In every generation, for each target vector, a mutant vector $\boldsymbol{v}_{i,g} = (v_{i,1,g}, v_{i,2,g}, \ldots, v_{i,d,g})(i \in 1, 2, \ldots, NP)$ is generated by mutation. Then, crossover is implemented on each target vector and its mutant vector to produce a trial vector, $\boldsymbol{u}_{i,g} = (u_{i,1,g}, u_{i,2,g}, \ldots, u_{i,d,g})$.

© Springer Nature Singapore Pte Ltd. 2019
H. Peng et al. (Eds.): ISICA 2018, CCIS 986, pp. 306–316, 2019.
https://doi.org/10.1007/978-981-13-6473-0_27

In DE, crossover and mutation together are called trial vector generation strategy. Selection of DE is based on a one-to-one competition between a target vector and its trial vector.

In the field of DE, a balance between exploration and exploitation is still difficult to achieve on many occasions. Premature convergence, which means that all trial vectors converge to a non-optimal solution, or stagnation, which means that more befitting individuals can be hardly found any more although convergence does not come, occurs in many runs. Thus, further work is needed to be done. Therefore, DE is constantly improved at least four aspects. Recently, the four aspects are improving the trial vector generation strategy [7, 12–14, 18, 22–24], adapting the control parameter setting [2, 6, 7, 13, 16–18], hybridizing with other techniques [3, 5, 7, 8, 10] and integrating multiple trial vector generation strategies with multiple control parameter settings [1, 6, 11, 16, 17, 19, 20]. Some of these contributions are general schemes for different DE algorithms, such as [5, 12, 14, 16, 22], while others are special improvements based on a particular DE algorithm.

The motivation of this paper is as below. The imbalance between exploration and exploitation always leads to the failure to obtain good solutions [4]. Although the combination of operators, settings and chromosome representation in some DE variants leads to a good ratio of exploration and exploitation in runs, such a ratio cannot be fit for fitness landscapes of all functions. The balance between exploration and exploitation is hardly achieved in runs for the functions with complicated fitness landscapes. Consequently, the optimal cannot be obtained or even approximated. In this situation, a methods for maintaining the balance based on fitness landscapes of the current task are conducive to improve solutions. In practice, diversity that refers to differences among individuals is used to reflect the state of exploration and exploitation. Compared with other aspects, changing selection strategy is not a focus of improving DE. Nevertheless, selection is the most standard step among all operators in DE. Therefore, a scheme implemented in selection may be useful in different DE algorithms.

In this paper, we propose selection based on distance sorting. In such selection, the individual has the best fitness among parents and offspring, the elite, is selected firstly. Then, the genotype distance, distance in chromosome structure, from another individual to the elite decides whether the former individual is selected. In detail, individuals longer in the distance are all selected, while others are all eliminated. Under the control of a adaptive scheme proposed by us, we use our selection replace the original selection of the CoBiDE, a state-of-the-art DE algorithm, in some generations. Experimental results show that, for many among the 25 CEC 2005 benchmark functions, which have the similar changing trend of diversity and fitness in runs, our adaptive scheme for calling the proposed selection brings significant improvement on solutions.

The rest of this paper is organized as follows. Section 2 introduces related works. In Sect. 3, our proposed selection is presented and analyzed. The experiments go in Sect. 4. Finally, a conclusion and a prospect are dealt with in Sect. 5.

2   Related Works

Our work devotes to improving selection of EA. Nevertheless, we focuses on DE in this paper. Therefore, the contributions on selection of DE is regarded as related works and listed below. In addition, the DE algorithm employed in our experiment is introduced.

2.1   Methods Implemented in Selection of DE for the Exploration and Exploitation Balance

Yi et al. [21] proposed a novel differential evolution algorithm based on $p$best roulette wheel selection and retention mechanism. According to the proposed selection, the generated offspring with better fitness function value indicates that the $p$best vector of current individual is suitable for exploitation. In this case, the $p$best vector should be retained into the next generation. If this top vector can achieve better trial vector, it can survive into the next generation, even it may not be included in the top vectors anymore. This modification is used to avoid the individual gather around the $p$best vector, thus diversify the population. The performance of the proposed algorithm is extensively evaluated both on the benchmark test functions developed for the 2005 Congress on Evolutionary Computation and four real-world application problems. Experimental results and statistical analyses show that the proposed algorithm is highly competitive when compared with other state-of-the-art differential evolution algorithms.

Tian et al. [17] proposed a differential evolution algorithm to improve search efficiency by employing information of individuals to set the parameters and update population in an adaptive manner. Firstly, a combined mutation strategy was developed by mix two mutation strategies with a prescribed probability. Secondly, fitness values are used to guide the parameter setting. Finally, a diversity-based selection strategy is designed by assembling greedy selection strategy and defining weighted fitness. In detail, weighted fitness of vector v_i is defined as follow.

$$f_w(v_i) = \alpha \frac{f(v_i) - f_{min}}{f_{max} - f_{min}} + (1 - \alpha) \frac{dis_{max} - dis(v_i, v_{best})}{dis_{max} + dis(v_i, v_{best})}) \qquad (1)$$

In Eq. 1, $\alpha \in [0, 1]$ is a weighted factor, $f(v_i)$ is the fitness of v_i. f_{max} and f_{min} are the maximum and minimum fitness value, respectively. dis_{max} is the maximum Euclidean distance from the best vector v_{best} to another vector, while $dis(v_i, v_{best})$ represents the Euclidean distance between v_i and v_{best}. The proposed algorithm compares with eight existing algorithms on CEC 2005 and 2014 contest test instances, and is applied to solve the Spread Spectrum Radar Polly Code Design. Experimental results show that the proposed algorithm is very competitive.

2.2   CoBiDE

In CoBiDE, not only the covariance matrix learning based coordinate system, but also the bimodal distributing parameter setting are presented as measures for giving the good ratio of exploration and exploitation. In [18], CoBiDE was tested on the 25 CEC 2005 benchmark functions, as well as a variety of real-world optimization problems taken from diverse fields. The experimental results demonstrated the effectiveness of CoBiDE. Compared with some other DE variants and other state-of-the-art evolutionary algorithms, CoBiDE showed overall better performance. The pseudo code of CoBiDE is given with our modification in the next section.

3   The Proposed Selection

In EAs, every selection scheme includes two aspects, selecting model and selecting criterion. In general, fitness is regarded as selecting criterion directly. However, diversity-based factor also can be considered at the same time. Anyhow, existing selection schemes always afford more opportunities for individuals having better fitness.

Selection based on distance sorting is proposed by us. The flow of it is as Algorithm 1. It can be seen that the rank-based selecting model, which is very common, is employed. On the other hand, a very unusual selecting criteria, which even has nothing to do with fitness, is used.

Algorithm 1. The flow of selection based on distance sorting

Input:
　　SM: the selecting model used in the main selection
　　CS_t: $P_t \cup P'_t$, the candidate set for P_{t+1}
Output:
　　P_{t+1}: the $(t+1)$th generation population
　1: Find BI in CS_t
　2: Give BI the highest rank
　3: Calculate genotype distance from BI to every other individual
　4: Select individuals with higher rank and eliminate others

In this selection, individuals more different in gene with the best one among parents and offspring are selected. In this way, the provided ratio of exploration and exploitation is changed. As a result, genotype diversity is improved. On one hand, individuals of the new population are still selected from candidates. On the other hand, the elite is remained to the new population. Therefore, excessive genetic drift does not occur when our selection is executed. Nevertheless, such selection, which always gives the individuals much different with the best one an surviving chance, hardly drives a population toward the regions of highly fit individuals just as traditional methods. It must be used with traditional selection in an EA and replace the latter only at right moments. In fact, finding right moments for calling our selection is more difficult than proposing it since the right moments may be relevant to particular EAs or tasks.

4   Experiments

In this section, firstly, we run the original CoBiDE for all CEC 2005 benchmark functions. According to results, for each function, we draw a figure reflecting the changing trend of both diversity and fitness during runs. We find that a group of functions have common points in their figure. Thus, we propose a adaptive scheme for calling selection based on distance sorting to improve solutions for these functions. Then, we run the CoBiDE with our scheme for these functions and compare its results to the results of the original algorithm.

4.1   Experiment on the Original CoBiDE

In this experiment, we run the CoBiDE thirty times for each CEC 2005 benchmark function, respectively. In runs, diversity and the best fitness are recorded at each interval. Settings for the CoBiDE in our experiments are shown in Table 1. These settings are decided based on [18]. Nevertheless, maximum generations are set much larger than before. Table 2 reports the average error and the standard deviation of solutions for each function. In addition, the value of average diversity of the final population is also reported in the table.

Table 1. Settings for the CoBiDE

Function dimension	30
Population size	60
pb	0.40
ps	0.50
Terminal criterion	50000 generations done

It can be seen from Table 2 that the original CoBiDE can obtain the optimal at 100% only for F1 and F9. In fact, the average error in solutions to the optimal of some functions is very large. For example, that of F12 even reaches 3.78E+03. Therefore, solutions of these functions require be improved further. On the other hand, only for F1 and F6, the average final diversity goes to zero. Further, average result of F6 not zero shows that runs for F6 are trapped into premature convergence.

The Figs. 1, 2 and 3 shows that, runs of ten functions show similarity in the changing trend of diversity and fitness. These functions are F11–F14, F16–F20 and F22. The detailed features of the similarity are given as follow. Both the changing trend of diversity and that of fitness begins with a decrease period and finally goes to a flat one. However, the former trend may have more than one decrease periods and flat periods. Besides, the decrease of fitness is always much sharper than that of diversity. In short, for the ten functions, individuals becomes better rapidly when diversity is still high but changes little when that goes below a value.

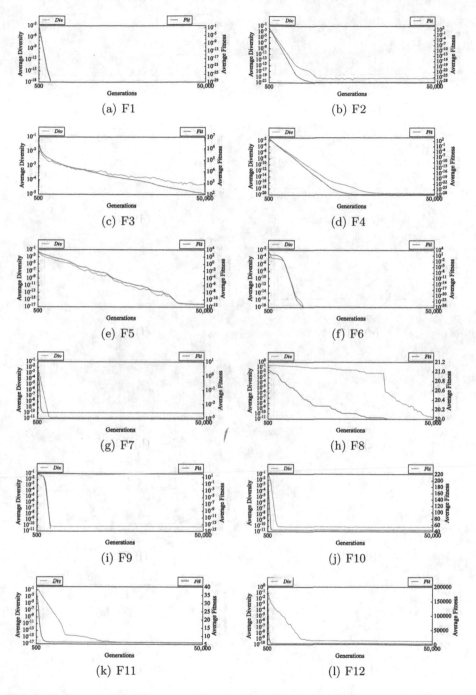

Fig. 1. The average of diversity and that of the best fitness during runs of the original CoBiDE (part 1)

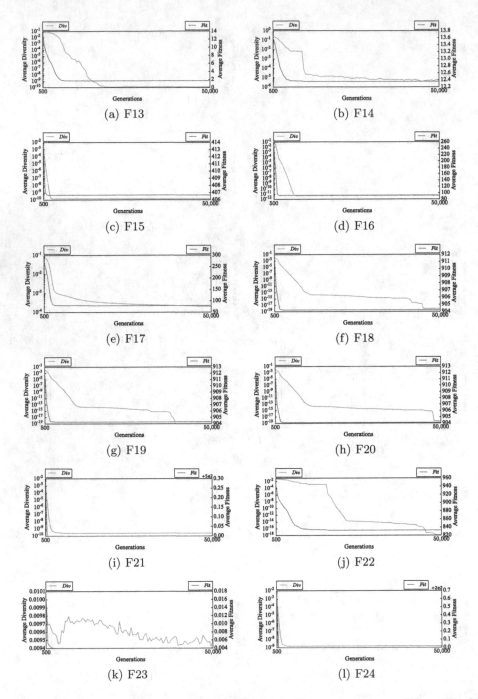

Fig. 2. The average of diversity and that of the best fitness during runs of the original CoBiDE (part 2)

Table 2. Results of the original CoBiDE

Function	Average (standard deviation)	Average final diversity
F1	0.0000E+00 (0.00E+00)	0.00E+00
F2	1.9390E−28 (1.42E−28)	2.63E−20
F3	1.1434E+02 (1.60E+02)	4.92E−05
F4	2.0600E−28 (1.27E−28)	2.65E−20
F5	7.0031E−12 (9.30E−13)	5.30E−17
F6	1.3829E−26 (3.11E−26)	0.00E+00
F7	2.5449E−03 (5.39E−03)	1.38E−11
F8	2.0001E+01 (2.88E−03)	2.39E−11
F9	0.0000E+00 (0.00E+00)	6.67E−11
F10	4.4942E+01 (1.51E+01)	6.64E−11
F11	6.1589E+00 (3.08E+00)	2.92E−17
F12	3.7778E+03 (4.28E+03)	4.44E−10
F13	1.6766E+00 (4.12E−01)	1.27E−10
F14	1.2356E+01 (4.32E−01)	4.81E−06
F15	4.0667E+02 (5.83E+01)	1.49E−10
F16	9.2541E+01 (6.78E+01)	5.01E−12
F17	7.9355E+01 (2.75E+01)	2.00E−04
F18	9.0423E+02 (8.80E−01)	8.38E−19
F19	9.0429E+02 (1.10E+00)	4.45E−19
F20	9.0411E+02 (5.82E−01)	4.62E−19
F21	5.0000E+02 (0.00E+00)	2.49E−10
F22	8.3259E+02 (2.20E+01)	1.28E−18
F23	5.3416E+02 (1.83E−04)	9.50E−03
F24	2.0000E+02 (0.00E+00)	1.52E−09
F25	2.0962E+02 (5.22E−01)	1.35E−01

4.2 Our Proposed Adaptive Scheme for Calling Selection Based on Distance Sorting in CoBiDE

In Algorithm 2, we propose a adaptive scheme for calling our selection based on the finding in the previous subsection. According to the scheme, genotype diversity is calculated at each interval. If genotype diversity at an interval is lower than the threshold set by us, our selection replaces the original selection in all followed generations till next interval comes. Otherwise, the original selection is carried out. Our purpose is always maintaining diversity in a high level to further improve solutions.

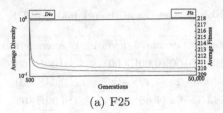

(a) F25

Fig. 3. The average of diversity and that of the best fitness during runs of the original CoBiDE (last part)

Algorithm 2. The scheme for calling our selection

Input:

    i: the interval of generations;

    t: the threshold of genotype diversity;

1: $flag = 0$

2: Execute other steps for initialization

3: **for** $g = 0 : MAX\_GEN$ **do**

4:    Execute evolutionary steps other than selection

5:    **if** $g\%i = 0$ **then**

6:        Compute current genotype diversity, gd

7:        **if** $gd < t$ **then**

8:            $flag = 1$

9:        **else**

10:           $flag = 0$

11:        **end if**

12:        Apply the original selection in this generation

13:    **else**

14:        **if** $flag = 1$ **then**

15:           Apply the selection based on distance sorting in this generation

16:        **else**

17:           Apply the original selection in this generation

18:        **end if**

19:    **end if**

20: **end for**

4.3 Experiment on CoBiDE with Our Proposed Adaptive Scheme

In this experiment, we set the interval of generations $i = 500$. Moreover, the threshold of genotype diversity $t = 1E - a$ is set differently to different functions. In Table 3, we give the results improved by our scheme with the original result. In the table, a is given for each function, respectively. It can be seen that our scheme can significantly improve solutions of eight functions. At the same time, standard deviation of solutions is decreased in majority cases. In fact, provided that a can be set a real number, significant improvement may occur in more cases.

Table 3. The significate improvement in terms of Wilcoxons rank sum test at a 0.05 significance level by our adaptive scheme

Function/a	Average (standard deviation)	
	Original CoBiDE	CoBiDE with our scheme
F10/7	4.4942E+01 (1.51E+01)	3.6213E+01 (1.01E+01)
F11/12	6.1589E+00 (3.08E+00)	4.5444E+00 (1.97E+00)
F12/6	3.7778E+03 (4.28E+03)	1.5699E+03 (3.04E+03)
F14/5	1.2356E+01 (4.32E−01)	1.1689E+01 (4.79E−01)
F16/11	9.2541E+01 (6.78E+01)	6.1980E+01 (1.34E+01)
F18/9	9.0423E+02 (8.80E−01)	9.0380E+02 (3.43E−01)
F20/9	9.0429E+02 (1.10E+00)	9.0383E+02 (3.08E−01)
F22/8	8.3259E+02 (2.20E+01)	8.0974E+02 (1.73E+01)

5   Conclusion

CoBiDE is a state-of-the-art DE algorithm and shows well performance in comparisons. However, for some complicated functions, this DE algorithm still cannot obtain an optimal. In this paper, we propose selection based on distance sorting and employ it in CoBiDE based on our proposed adaptive scheme. Results show that our scheme can improve solutions for some functions.

In fact, our selection can be used in more DE algorithms or even more EAs because it does not depend on chromosome representation, operators or settings. Nevertheless, to use our selection in more DE algorithms or even more EAs, adaptive schemes for call it should be designed based on the features in runs. We will focus on this direction in the future.

References

1. Ali, M.Z., Awad, N.H., Suganthan, P.N., Reynolds, R.G.: An adaptive multipopulation differential evolution with dynamic population reduction. IEEE Trans. Cybern. **47**(9), 2768–2779 (2017)
2. Awad, N.H., Ali, M.Z., Suganthan, P.N., Reynolds, R.G.: An ensemble sinusoidal parameter adaptation incorporated with L-shade for solving CEC2014 benchmark problems. In: 2016 IEEE Congress on Evolutionary Computation (CEC), pp. 2958–2965. IEEE (2016)
3. Awad, N.H., Ali, M.Z., Suganthan, P.N., Reynolds, R.G.: CADE: a hybridization of cultural algorithm and differential evolution for numerical optimization. Inf. Sci. **378**, 215–241 (2017)
4. Črepinšek, M., Liu, S.H., Mernik, M.: Exploration and exploitation in evolutionary algorithms: a survey. ACM Comput. Surv. (CSUR) **45**(3), 35 (2013)
5. Du, W., Leung, S.Y.S., Tang, Y., Vasilakos, A.V.: Differential evolution with event-triggered impulsive control. IEEE Trans. Cybern. **47**(1), 244–257 (2017)

6. Fan, Q., Yan, X.: Self-adaptive differential evolution algorithm with zoning evolution of control parameters and adaptive mutation strategies. IEEE Trans. Cybern. **46**(1), 219–232 (2016)

7. Fu, C., Jiang, C., Chen, G., Liu, Q.: An adaptive differential evolution algorithm with an aging leader and challengers mechanism. Appl. Soft Comput. **57**, 60–73 (2017)

8. Guo, Z., Liu, G., Li, D., Wang, S.: Self-adaptive differential evolution with global neighborhood search. Soft Comput. **21**(13), 3759–3768 (2017)

9. Islam, S.M., Das, S., Ghosh, S., Roy, S., Suganthan, P.N.: An adaptive differential evolution algorithm with novel mutation and crossover strategies for global numerical optimization. IEEE Trans. Syst. Man Cybern. Part B (Cybern.) **42**(2), 482–500 (2012)

10. Jadon, S.S., Tiwari, R., Sharma, H., Bansal, J.C.: Hybrid artificial bee colony algorithm with differential evolution. Appl. Soft Comput. **58**, 11–24 (2017)

11. Li, G., et al.: A novel hybrid differential evolution algorithm with modified CoDE and JADE. Appl. Soft Comput. **47**, 577–599 (2016)

12. Liao, J., Cai, Y., Wang, T., Tian, H., Chen, Y.: Cellular direction information based differential evolution for numerical optimization: an empirical study. Soft Comput. **20**(7), 2801–2827 (2016)

13. Mohamed, A.W., Suganthan, P.N.: Real-parameter unconstrained optimization based on enhanced fitness-adaptive differential evolution algorithm with novel mutation. Soft Comput. 1–21 (2017)

14. Qiu, X., Tan, K.C., Xu, J.X.: Multiple exponential recombination for differential evolution. IEEE Trans. Cybern. **47**(4), 995–1006 (2017)

15. Storn, R., Price, K.: Differential evolution-a simple and efficient heuristic for global optimization over continuous spaces. J. Global Optim. **11**(4), 341–359 (1997)

16. Tatsis, V.A., Parsopoulos, K.E.: Differential evolution with grid-based parameter adaptation. Soft Comput. **21**(8), 2105–2127 (2017)

17. Tian, M., Gao, X., Dai, C.: Differential evolution with improved individual-based parameter setting and selection strategy. Appl. Soft Comput. **56**, 286–297 (2017)

18. Wang, Y., Li, H.X., Huang, T., Li, L.: Differential evolution based on covariance matrix learning and bimodal distribution parameter setting. Appl. Soft Comput. **18**, 232–247 (2014)

19. Wu, G., Mallipeddi, R., Suganthan, P.N., Wang, R., Chen, H.: Differential evolution with multi-population based ensemble of mutation strategies. Inf. Sci. **329**, 329–345 (2016)

20. Wu, G., Shen, X., Li, H., Chen, H., Lin, A., Suganthan, P.: Ensemble of differential evolution variants. Inf. Sci. **423**, 172–186 (2018)

21. Yi, W., Zhou, Y., Gao, L., Li, X., Mou, J.: An improved adaptive differential evolution algorithm for continuous optimization. Expert Syst. Appl. **44**, 1–12 (2016)

22. Zheng, L.M., Liu, L., Zhang, S.X., Zheng, S.Y.: Enhancing differential evolution with interactive information. Soft Comput. 1–20 (2017)

23. Zheng, L.M., Zhang, S.X., Tang, K.S., Zheng, S.Y.: Differential evolution powered by collective information. Inf. Sci. **399**, 13–29 (2017)

24. Zhou, Y.Z., Yi, W.C., Gao, L., Li, X.Y.: Adaptive differential evolution with sorting crossover rate for continuous optimization problems. IEEE Trans. Cybern. **47**(9), 2742–2753 (2017)

Predictive Data Mining

Outlier Detection Based on Cluster Outlier Factor and Mutual Density

Zhongping Zhang[1,2](✉), Mengfan Zhu[1](✉), Jingyang Qiu[1],
Cong Liu[1], Debin Zhang[3], and Jie Qi[4]

[1] School of Information Science and Engineering, Yanshan University,
Qinhuangdao 066004, Hebei, China
zpzhang@ysu.edu.cn, 1101031686@qq.com
[2] The Key Laboratory for Computer Virtual Technology and System Integration
of Hebei Province, Qinhuangdao 066004, Hebei, China
[3] Hebei Education Examinations Authority, Shijiazhuang 050000, Hebei, China
[4] The First Middle School of Qian An Country, Qian'an 131400, Jilin, China

Abstract. Outlier detection is an important task in data mining with numerous applications. Recent years, the study on outlier detection is very active, many algorithms were proposed including that based on clustering. However, most outlier detection algorithms based on clustering often need parameters, and it is very difficult to select a suitable parameter for different data set. In order to solve this problem, an outlier detection algorithm called outlier detection based on cluster outlier factor and mutual density is proposed in this paper which combining the natural neighbor search algorithm of the Natural Outlier Factor (NOF) algorithm and based on the Density and Distance Cluster (DDC) algorithm. The mutual density and γ density is used to construct decision graph. The data points with γ density anomalously large in decision graph are treated as cluster centers. This algorithm detect the boundary of outlier cluster using cluster outlier factor called Cluster Outlier Factor (COF), it can automatic find the parameter. This method can achieve good performance in clustering and outlier detection which be shown in the experiments.

Keywords: Data mining · Outlier · Mutual density · γ density ·
Cluster outlier factor

1 Introduction

Outlier detection, as an important branch of data mining [1], has been applied in many fields. Such as information security [2], financial fraud detection [3], medical and public health detection [4, 5], the weather forecast [6]. The core idea is that outlier detection, first create a normal pattern in the data, then the degree of deviation from the normal mode to impart a outlier factor for each point [7], which is the focal point data that deviates from the normal excavation mode data points, and then dig out more valuable information.

It is precisely because outlier detection has such a wide range of applications that domestic and foreign scholars have been active in this field. Many excellent algorithms

© Springer Nature Singapore Pte Ltd. 2019
H. Peng et al. (Eds.): ISICA 2018, CCIS 986, pp. 319–329, 2019.
https://doi.org/10.1007/978-981-13-6473-0_28

have been proposed. The research methods can be roughly divided into five types: distribution-based, depth-based, distance-based, density-based and cluster-based [8]. Each type of outlier detection algorithm has its own advantages and disadvantages.

Points in the distribution-based algorithm that deviate from the normal distribution or probability model are outliers [9], excavate outliers quickly and efficiently with known data set distribution. However, this algorithm is not suitable for high-dimensional data sets and data sets whose distribution is unknown; Based on the distance [10] method, if the data set has more than pct% of the data object distance from the target point is greater than dmin, then the target point is considered to be outliers. The distance-based method is widely used because of its simplicity and efficiency, but the algorithm can only detect global outliers and cannot detect local outliers. The method based on density [11] solves the problems of the above method well, such as LOF [12], INS [13], INFLO [14]. However, these methods require parameters and the accuracy of outlier detection is limited by the parameters. In order to solve the problems of the density-based method, a method based on clustering [15] was proposed. This type of method can filter the original data set and only calculate the degree of outliers of data at the boundary of the cluster. This type of algorithm has high efficiency, but cluster-based outlier detection methods usually need to introduce new parameters.

In order to solve the above problems, an outlier detection algorithm called outlier detection based on cluster outlier factor and mutual density (COF) is proposed in this paper. The algorithm does not require manual input parameters. Firstly, the mutual neighbor search method in the NOF algorithm [16] is introduced to obtain the number of neighbors of the data points adaptively. Then the mutual density defined in this paper is calculated based on the mutual neighbors of the data points. The mutual density and the γ density defined in this paper are used to construct the decision graph. Depending on the γ density anomaly, the number of cluster centers and the number of clusters are determined, and the remaining data sets are assigned to clusters where the density is greater than the nearest neighbor of the clusters, and the clustering is completed in one step. After the clustering is completed, the number of outlier clusters is much smaller than the normal cluster detection outliers.

The advantage of this algorithm over DDC algorithm [17] lies in that the mutual density can be used to better characterize the local density of data points, thereby effectively reducing the decision graph fraud [18] and improving the clustering reliability of the clustering algorithm; the algorithm of this paper solves the problem. The adaptive problem requires no manual input of parameters and can automatically obtain parameters according to different data sets. When detecting outliers, the sparse clustering of data is treated as outlier clustering, which increases the outlier detection algorithm to process data and improves the efficiency of outlier detection.

2   Related Work

This section briefly introduces the mutual neighbor search algorithm and DDC algorithm of the NOF algorithm. In this section, D is used to represent a data set. p, q, o are data points in data set D, k is a positive integer, and $d(p, q)$ represents the Euclidean distance between p and q points.

2.1   Mutual Neighbor Search Algorithm Based on NOF Algorithm

Definition 1. K_distance [16]. The k-distance of the p-point is the Euclidean distance between the point p and the point o, denoted by kdis(p), where point o satisfies the following conditions:

(1) There are at least k data points $o' \in D$ such that $d(p, o') <= d(p, o)$
(2) There are at most $(k-1)$ data points $o' \in D$ such that $d(p, o') <= d(p, o)$

Definition 2. K_near Neighbor [16]. The k-nearest neighbor of p-point is represented by $NN_k(p)$ and is a set of data points X. X satisfies $d(p, X) <= $ kdis(p), $NN_k(p) = X \in D|$ $d(p, X) <= $ kdis(p)}.

Definition 3. Mutual Neighbor [16]. With the same value of k, if p is a neighbor of q and q is a neighbor of p, then p and q are a pair of mutual neighbors.

With the same k-value, there are more neighbors in dense data points, and there are fewer neighbors in sparse regions in the data set. Sparse and dense are a pair of relative concepts. As shown in Fig. 1, when $k = 2$, there are 4 mutual neighbors at point A in the dense area, and there are only 2 mutual neighbors at point B in the sparse area, and the number of neighbors at point C is 0, so the number of the mutual neighbors can show the outlier properties of the data points, and the data points whose neighbors are 0 are located far from the dense area.

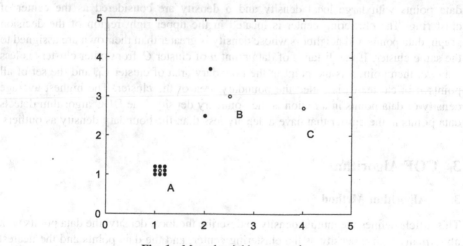

Fig. 1. Mutual neighbor example

2.2   DDC Algorithm

The DDC algorithm considers that the center of clustering in the data set has the greatest density in the same cluster, and the centers of different clusters are separated from each other. Therefore, if the data points have a high density and are distant from the centers of other clusters, then take this data point as the center of its clustering.

Definition 4. Local Density. The local density of data point p is defined as Eq. (1):

$$\rho(p) = \sum_q \chi(d_{pq} - d_c) \qquad (1)$$

Where d_{pq} is the Euclidean distance between the p and q points, d_c is the clipping distance, Its value needs to be set manually. χ is the activation function, where $\chi(x) = 1$ if $x < 0$ and $\chi(x) = 0$.

Definition 5. Delta-density Of $p.\delta(p)$ density describes the minimum distance between a data point p and a data point whose local density is greater than its own, defined as Eq. (2):

$$\delta(p) = \underset{q:\rho(q) > \rho(p)}{\text{Min}} (d(p,q)) \qquad (2)$$

Among $\rho(q) > \rho(p)$, for data points with the largest local density in the data set, the distance between the δ density and the point q farthest from itself can be expressed as $\max(d(p, q))$.

When the local density and δ density of objects in the dataset are determined, the data points with large local density and δ density are considered as the center of clustering. The clustering center is located in the upper right region of the decision graph, data points and neighbors whose density is greater than their own are assigned to the same cluster. If the distance of data point p of cluster C_i from other clusters is less than d_c, then point p is the point in the boundary area of cluster C_i, and the set of all points p in cluster C_i is called the boundary area of the cluster. The highest average density of data points in a region is the boundary density. The DDC algorithm detects data points in the cluster that have a density less than the boundary density as outliers.

3   COF Algorithm

3.1   Algorithm Method

This article defines the mutual density to describe the local density, the data points with abnormally high γ density as the clustering center, and the data points and the nearest neighbors whose density is greater than itself are assigned to the same cluster. The γ density of two kinds of data objects is abnormally large. One is an outlier and the other is a true clustering center. When real clustering centers are used as clustering centers for clustering, since the actual clustering centers are in dense data areas, the number of data points in clusters is large; clustering centers are used as clustering centers. When the outliers are in data sparse regions, the mutual density is very small, so the number of data points in the cluster is very small, so outlier clustering can be detected according to the number of data points in the cluster.

3.2   Related Definitions

This section describes the COF algorithm and related definitions in detail. Use D to represent the data set. p and q are the objects in data set D, and k is a positive integer to represent the number of neighbors of the data object.

Definition 6. Mutual Density. The mutual density is used to describe the degree of closeness between data points and surrounding data points. It is defined as Eq. (3):

$$md(p) = \sum_{i \in MuN(p)} e^{-d(p,i)} \tag{3}$$

In Eq. (3), $MuN(p)$ is a set of mutual neighbors of p-points. The number of neighbors in dense-area data points in the data set is large, the distance between data points and neighbors is small, and the mutual density of data points is large. By the same token, sparse regions have a small mutual density.

Definition 7. Gamma-density Of p. $\gamma(p)$ describes the minimum distance between the data point p and the data points whose mutual density is greater than their own, defined as Eq. (4):

$$\gamma(p) = \underset{q:md(q) > md(p)}{\text{Min}} (d(p,q)) \tag{4}$$

Among $md(q) > md(p)$, for data points with the largest local density in the data set, the distance between the γ density and the point q farthest from itself can be expressed as $\max(d(p, q))$.

Definition 8. Cluster Outlier Factor. Assuming that the cluster set $C = \{C_1, C_2, \ldots, C_n\}$ is sorted according to $|C1| <= |C2| <= \ldots <= |Cn|$, then the outlier factor of the cluster is defined as Eq. (5):

$$COF(C_i) = 1 - e^{-\frac{|C_{i+1}|}{|C_i|^2}}, i = 1, 2, \ldots, n \tag{5}$$

COF(C_i) describes the fluctuation of the number of data points between the clusters C_{i+1} and C_i, The value range is (0, 1). The larger the value is, the more likely C_1, C_2... C_i become outlier clusters. As shown in Fig. 2. The four clusters C_1, C_2, C_3, and C_4 have 3, 3, 300 and 1000 data points, COF(C_1) = 0.6321, and COF (C_2) = 1, COF (C_3) = 0.0328, COF(C_2) has a maximum value of 1, and C_1 and C_2 are outlier clusters.

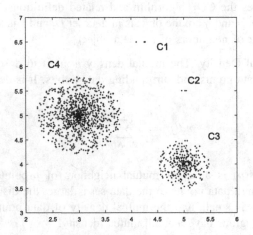

Fig. 2. Normal clustering and outlier cluster samples

Definition 9. Cluster Boundary of Outlier. If COF(C_b) = max{COF(C_i)}, C_1, $C_2, \ldots, C_b$ is the outlier clustering and b is the boundary of outlier clustering.

3.3   COF Algorithm Description

The number of mutual neighbors in different density regions is different, and mutual density is not the same; even if the number of neighbors is the same, the mutual density is not necessarily the same. Therefore, mutual density can better describe the closeness of data points and surrounding data, effectively suppressing The role of decision-making fraud increases the accuracy of clustering. The data in the data set where the outliers are located is very sparse, and the number of outlier clustering data points is much smaller than that of normal clusters. The COF describes the fluctuation of the number of data points between clusters, so the outlier clustering can be well found. And normal clustering boundaries.

The outlier detection algorithm COF based on the clustering outlier factor and mutual density can be obtained according to the above. The algorithm is described as follows:

input: Dataset D
output: Outlier clustering OC=$\{C_1,C_2,...,C_b\}$
COF(D)
BEGIN
(1) initialization: Clusters=Φ, templist=Φ, C_i=Φ, OC=Φ
(2) Run the MuN-Searching algorithm to calculate the mutual neighbors of each data point
(3) For each data point $p \in D$
(4) Calculate md(p) according to equation (3)
(5) End For
(6) For each data point $q \in D$
(7) Calculate the γ density of q according to equation (4)
(8) End For
(9) Constructing decision graphs using mutual densities and γ densities
(10) Determines m_i that the point of high γ density in decision graph as the center of clustering
(11) $C_i = C_i \cup m_i$, i=1,2,...,k
(12) For any data points $p \in D$
(13) If visited(p)$\neq$true
(14)   templist=templist$\cup p$
(15)   finding the nearest neighbor q with a density greater than p
(16)   If $q=m_i \| q \in C_i$
(17) $C_i = C_i \cup$ templist
(18)   templist=Φ
(19)   Else
(20)   templist=templist$\cup q$
(21)   visited(q)=true
(22) $p=q$
(23)   goto step(15)
(24)   End If
(25) End If
(26) End For
(27) Sort $C_1,C_i,...,C_k$ in ascending order by number of data points
(28) According to COF(C_b)=max$\{$COF(C_i)$\}$
       Finding the boundary of the outlier cluster b
(29) OC=OC$\cup C_i$, i=1,2,...,b
(30) output OC
(31) END

In the pseudo code, C_i is the i-th cluster, m_i is the center of the cluster, and templist stores the temporary cluster where p-point is located. The output OC of the algorithm is the union of outlier clusters. The points in the outlier cluster are outlier points.

4 Evaluation

In order to test the performance of the COF algorithm, experiments were conducted under simulated data and real data. The UCI data set was used in the experiment. In the experiment, the proposed algorithm was compared with the DDC to verify the self-adaptation of parameters and the accuracy of outlier detection. Experimental hardware environment: CPU is Inter Core 3.90 GHz, memory is 8 GB; software environment: the operating system is Windows7, the experimental program is written in Java, the development environment is MyEclipse10.0, and the experimental results make MATLAB perform visual processing.

4.1 Experimental Index

In order to evaluate the performance of outlier detection, two indexes are used, Recall and Precision, represented by Re and Pr respectively. Use TP to represent the actual number of outliers detected by the algorithm. Use PN to represent the number of outliers contained in the data set. Use FP as the algorithm to incorrectly detect the actual data as the number of outliers. Then the definitions of Re and Pr are Eqs. (6) and (7):

$$Re = \frac{TP}{PN} \tag{6}$$

$$Pr = \frac{TP}{TP + FP} \tag{7}$$

The maximum value of Re and Pr is 1 and the minimum value is 0. The larger the values of Re and Pr, the better the performance of the algorithm.

4.2 Simulation Data Set Experiment

In order to test the clustering performance of the COF algorithm proposed in this paper, cluster shape, density, and number of different test data sets are used. The effect of clustering is compared with the DDC algorithm. The parameter dc of the DDC algorithm is recommended by the literature [18]. This article uses the Fraction of Covered referred to as FoC, that is, how many specific data points are clustered, FoC is defined as Eq. (8):

$$FoC = \frac{|alldatas| - |outliers|}{|alldatas|} \tag{8}$$

The data set used in this experiment is as follows:

Flame data set [19] contains 2 clusters, 246 data points, including 6 outliers; R15 data set [20] contains 15 clusters, 613 data points, including 19 outliers;

The Circle data set [18] contains 4 clusters, 1310 data points, of which two small clusters each have only 5 data points, taking two small clusters as outlier clusters;

For ease of observation, the clustering of the COF algorithm and the DDC algorithm in different data sets is drawn into a data table. As shown in Table 1, with the increase of the number of clusters and the size of the data set, the decision fraud of the DDC algorithm increases. The more obvious, the FoC of the algorithm is far lower than the COF algorithm of this paper, so the clustering performance of this algorithm is more stable than the DDC algorithm, and the outliers can be detected more accurately. Moreover, the proposed algorithm does not require manual input parameters.

Table 1. Comparing the performance of two algorithm of simulation data set

DataSet	DDC					COF				
	$TP + FP$	FoC	TP	Re	Pr	$TP + FP$	FoC	TP	Re	Pr
Flame	67	0.27	5	0.83	0.07	7	0.96	5	0.83	0.71
Circle	0	1	0	0	0	10	0.99	10	1	1
R15	117	0.22	4	0.26	0.04	21	0.97	19	1	0.95

4.3 Real Data Set Experiment

The real data set of this article uses the iris, wine, and iris data sets. There are three clusters, namely, the "mountain tails", "the variegated irises," and the "Virginia tails". The first two clusters of the iris data set are: As a normal point, 10 outliers in the third cluster are randomly selected, and 110 data points in the data set; 15 points in the third cluster are randomly selected as outliers in the wine dataset. Data. The experimental results of the COF algorithm and DDC algorithm are shown in Table 2.

Table 2. Comparing the performance of two algorithm of real data set

DataSet	COF			DDC		
	TP	Re	Pr	TP	Re	Pr
Wine	13	0.86	0.86	12	0.80	0.26
Iris	10	1	1	10	1	0.40

It can be seen from Table 2 that under the wine data set, the Re of the DDC algorithm is 0.80 which is slightly lower than the COF of this paper 0.86. However, the Pr of the COF algorithm in this paper is 0.86 which is much higher than the 0.26 of the DDC algorithm and the experimental results of the iris data set. It has a similar situation with the wine data set, which verifies that this algorithm can detect outliers completely and accurately.

5 Conclusions

In this paper, we propose an outlier detection algorithm COF based on clustering outlier factor and mutual density by combining the mutual neighbor search algorithm and DDC algorithm. This algorithm uses the mutual density to describe the local density of the data, and uses the mutual density and γ density builds a decision graph, clusters the data points with large γ density as the center of the cluster, and detects outlier clusters based on the clustering outlier factors. This paper applies to most non-uniformly distributed data sets, because for a uniformly distributed data set, the local densities of the data points are the same, and the γ density is 0 at this time and cannot be used to find cluster centers. Experiments in both simulated data sets and real data sets have shown that the algorithm has good outlier recognition ability, and the algorithm does not require manual input parameters.

The algorithm of this paper does not have a quantitative index to measure the abnormal γ density when determining the center of a cluster based on γ density. This requires further study.

References

1. Han, J., Kamber, M.: Data Mining: Concepts and Techniques. Morgan Kaufmann, Burlington (2001). 5(4):394–395 (2006, in Chinese)
2. Denning, D.E.: An intrusion-detection model. IEEE Trans. Softw. Eng. **SE-13**(2), 222–232 (2006)
3. Bolton, R.J., David, J.H.: Unsupervised profiling methods for fraud detection. In: Proceedings of Credit Scoring & Credit Control VII, pp. 5–7 (2001)
4. Laurikkala, J., Juhola, M., Kentala, E.: Informal identification of outliers in medical data. In: Intelligent Data Analysis in Medicine & Pharmacology (2000)
5. Lin, J., Keogh, E., Fu, A., et al.: Approximations to magic: finding unusual medical time series. In: 2005 Proceedings of IEEE Symposium on Computer-Based Medical Systems, pp. 329–334. IEEE (2005)
6. Zhao, J., Lu, C.T., Kou, Y.: Detecting region outliers in meteorological data, pp. 49–55 (2003)
7. Bhattacharya, G., Ghosh, K., Chowdhury, A.S.: Outlier detection using neighborhood rank difference, pp. 24–31. Elsevier Science Inc. (2015)
8. Xue, A.-R., Ju, S.-G., He, W.-H., et al.: Study on algorithms for local outlier detection. Chinese J. Comput. **30**(8), 1455–1463 (2007)
9. Wang, Y., Zhang, J.-F., Zhao, X.-J.: Contextual outlier mining algorithm based on particle swarm optimization. J. Taiyuan Univ. Sci. Technol. **36**(5), 327–332 (2015)
10. Hawkins, D.M.: Identification of outliers. Biometrics **37**(4), 860 (1980)
11. Xu, X., Liu, J.-W., Luo, X.-L.: Research on outlier mining. Appl. Res. Comput. **26**(1), 34–40 (2009). (in Chinese)
12. Breunig, M.M., Kriegel, H.P., Ng, R.T., et al.: LOF: identifying density-based local outliers. ACM SIGMOD Rec. **29**(2), 93–104 (2000)
13. Ha, J., Seok, S., Lee, J.S.: Robust outlier detection using the instability factor. Knowl.-Based Syst. **63**(2), 15–23 (2014)
14. Jin, W., Tung, A.K.H., Han, J., Wang, W.: Ranking outliers using symmetric neighborhood relationship. In: Ng, W.K., Kitsuregawa, M., Li, J., Chang, K. (eds.) Advances in Knowledge Discovery and Data Mining. LNCS, vol. 3918, pp. 577–593. Springer, Heidelberg (2006). https://doi.org/10.1007/11731139_68
15. Tao, J.: Clustering-based and density outlier detection method. Master dissertation of South China University of Technology, pp. 1–56 (2014, in Chinese)

16. Huang, J., Zhu, Q., Yang, L., et al.: A non-parameter outlier detection algorithm based on Natural Neighbor. Knowl.-Based Syst. **92**(C), 71–77 (2016)
17. Rodriguez, A., Laio, A.: Machine learning. Clustering by fast search and find of density peaks. Science **344**(6191), 1492 (2014)
18. Huang, J., Zhu, Q., Yang, L., et al.: A novel outlier cluster detection algorithm without top-n parameter. Knowl.-Based Syst. **121**, 32–40 (2017)
19. Veenman, C.J., Reinders, M.J.T., Backer, E.: A maximum variance cluster algorithm. IEEE Trans. Pattern Anal. Mach. Intell. **24**(9), 1273–1280 (2002)
20. Fu, L., Medico, E.: FLAME, a novel fuzzy clustering method for the analysis of DNA microarray data. BMC Bioinform. **8**(1), 3 (2007)

Local Outlier Detection Algorithm Based on Gaussian Kernel Density Function

Zhongping Zhang[1,2(✉)], Jiaojiao Liu[1], and Chuangye Miao[1]

[1] School of Information Science and Engineering, Yanshan University,
Qinhuangdao 066004, Hebei, China
zpzhang@ysu.edu.cn
[2] The Key Laboratory for Computer Virtual Technology and
System Integration of Hebei Province, Qinhuangdao 066004, Hebei, China

Abstract. With the rapid development of information technology, the structure of data resources is becoming more and more complex, and outlier mining is attracting more and more attention. Based on Gaussian kernel function, this paper considers three neighbors: k nearest neighbors, reverse k neighbors and shared nearest neighbors. A local outlier detection algorithm based on Gaussian kernel function is proposed. Firstly, the algorithm stores the nearest neighbors of each data object through kNN maps, including k-nearest neighbors, reverse k-nearest neighbors, and shared nearest neighbors, forming a kernel neighbor set S. Secondly, Estimating density of data objects through kernel density estimation KDE method. Finally, the relative density outlier factor RDOF is used to estimate the degree of data objects deviating from the neighborhood, and then determines whether the data objects are outliers, and the validity of the algorithm is proved on the real and synthetic data sets.

Keywords: Data mining · Outliers · Gaussian kernel function ·
Kernel density · Kernel neighbor

1 Introduction

With the rapid development of the Internet, the amount of data generated by the modern society is getting larger and larger, and the useful information hidden in it is of great value. Outliers are data that deviate from the vast majority of records in the target data set, so that people suspect that the deviations from these data are not due to random factors, but rather result from completely different mechanisms from other records. Outlier data mining has a very wide range of applications in real life. For example, predicting diseases in medical tests, predicting fraud in the financial sector, selecting seeds in the agricultural sector, etc. [1]. The existing outlier data detection algorithms still have problems such as low detection accuracy and low efficiency. Therefore, how to improve the accuracy and efficiency of outlier detection is a hot topic of research [2].

In order to solve the problem that the accuracy of excavating outlier data is not high, many outlier data mining algorithms have been proposed. In density-based algorithms, outliers can be detected when the local density is different from its

© Springer Nature Singapore Pte Ltd. 2019
H. Peng et al. (Eds.): ISICA 2018, CCIS 986, pp. 330–343, 2019.
https://doi.org/10.1007/978-981-13-6473-0_29

neighborhood. For example, the local outlier factor LOF (Local Outlier Factor) represents the abnormal score that represents the distribution difference between the object and its reachable neighborhood. Studies have shown that the greater the abnormality factor, the more likely the object is outlier data [3]. Based on this, the researchers proposed several improvements of LOF. For example, M. Hutter and other people proposed a distance-based outlier mining algorithm LDOF (Local Distance Based Outlier Factor), which uses the relative distances from other data objects to perform outlier detection on discrete data sets through INFLO (Influenced Oulierness) estimates the anomaly scores of data objects and considers neighbors and indirect neighbors when estimating the relative density distribution [4]. Taking into account the basic model of data, Tang and others proposed a connection-based outlier factor COF (Connectivity based Oulier Factor) solutions [5]. The LOF algorithm calculates the relative density of data objects firstly, and then uses the relative density outliers to estimate the degree of outliers of the data points. Based on this idea, a more accurate density estimation method can be used to estimate the data density and improve the accuracy of outlier data mining.

2 Related Work

2.1 Outlier Mining Algorithms

Outlier mining algorithms have the following five types:

2.1.1 Statistical Outlier Mining Algorithm

The statistics-based algorithm is the earliest proposed mining algorithm. The main idea of the algorithm is to assume that the data space D obeys a distribution model, and then determine whether the object is an outlier by the dissimilarity between the data. It is assumed that the data set D is subject to the distribution model F, where the object o_i is a certain data object in the distribution model F. If the data object o_i has no significant influence on the distribution model F, the determination object o_i is not an outlier, whereas if the data object o_i has a significant influence on the distribution of the model F, the determination object o_i is an outlier [6, 7]. The algorithm is often based on the detection of single-dimensional data. Nowadays, most of the data are high-dimensional data, so the algorithm is not suitable for outlier detection in high-dimensional datasets. Therefore, for most databases, the outlier detection algorithm based on statistics can not achieve better detection results.

2.1.2 Depth-Based Outlier Mining Algorithms

The depth-based algorithm is a refinement of t he statistically-based detection algorithm, which is suitable for cases where the data set does not obey a certain distribution [8]. The main idea of this algorithm is: Firstly, the data points in the data space are mapped one by one into the k-dimensional space. Secondly, the depth value of each data point is calculated according to the depth definition. Thirdly, the data points are organized according to the depth value. Data points with larger depth values are placed deeper, data points with smaller depth values are placed in shallow layers, and finally, detection points are detected in shallow layers. Due to the skipping of deeper layers, the efficiency of the detection is greatly improved, among which there is a DEEPLOC (DEEP LOCation) algorithm [9]. The algorithm can be detected on high-dimensional data sets, but the time complexity of the algorithm increases exponentially with the increase of the number of data objects and dimensions, which leads to the algorithm can not achieve better results in massive data sets.

2.1.3 Distance-Based Outlier Mining Algorithm
For the defects based on statistics and depth algorithms, researchers have proposed a new detection algorithm, a distance-based outlier detection algorithm. Knorr and Ng proposed the concept of distance-based outliers firstly. In data set D, given the parameters pct and d_{min}, for data object o in D, if there is at least a pct object to o distance greater than d_{min}, then it is considered that the object o is an outlier when the parameters pct and d_{min} are used. That is, for the object o, there are not enough neighbors around it to prove that it is not an outlier [10].

In addition, Ramasmawy extends the definition of distance-based outliers: For data point o, the distance between object o and its nearest k objects is calculated, after which the calculated distance and descending order are arranged in the front of the m object as the outlier.

2.1.4 Clustering-Based Outlier Mining Algorithm
The core idea of this type of algorithm is to aggregate the data containing the same characteristics in the entire data space into a cluster [11, 12]. Conversely, there are many different characteristics or differences between data points in different clusters. In the clustering algorithm, if the dataset is split after applying a different clustering method and some objects are not in any cluster, then these data are outliers [13]. Classical clustering algorithms can be divided into three categories, which are divided-based, model-based, and grid-based subspace clustering algorithms [11]. In the clustering of subspaces, these classical algorithms all have good results, and the accuracy is also high when mining clusters. However, since the clustering-based algorithm is mainly used to cluster the subspace, the detection accuracy of the clustering algorithm is not high when the outlier mining of data is carried out.

2.1.5 Density-Based Outlier Mining Algorithm
The algorithm based on statistics and distance based detection is to determine whether a data point is a outlier from a global point of view. It often requires that the distribution of the data set is uniform and the outliers are based on the global. However, for many datasets, there are easily overlooked but more valuable outliers—local outliers, which are outliers relative to their local neighborhoods. Therefore, they are considered as is a local outlier [14]. So, the researchers proposed a density-based detection algorithm [15]. This kind of algorithm describes the outlier degree of the object by introducing the outlier factor. It does not simply distinguish whether the data object is the outlier, but gives the outlier factor of each object, and determines which data object is the outlier point by the user. Among them, the most representative is the LOF algorithm.

2.2 LOF Algorithm and Its Analysis

Although, the LOF algorithm can effectively detect local outliers, but the time complexity of the algorithm is high when detecting massive data sets, which results in the algorithm can not effectively detect massive data sets. In addition, the mining results of the algorithm are easily affected by the k value. Since the k value is given by the expert, the algorithm is often affected by human factors. If the value of k is set to be relatively small and the outliers are relatively close, these outliers will be treated as a cluster and judged as a normal point set; if the value of k is set too large, it will be close to the normal cluster. Outliers are judged as normal data points. The above situation will cause the situation of missed outliers. Therefore, in order to obtain the desired result, it is necessary to set the value of k differently several times until a stable result is detected. However, since the k-value is set several times, the neighborhood needs to be constructed again, which will result in high space-time overhead. In addition, the LOF algorithm cannot accurately mine outliers in sequential and low-density data sets. In order to solve the above problems, the researchers proposed many solutions, for example, the classic COF algorithm, this algorithm has a better detection effect for sequential data sets, INFLO algorithm achieves ideal detection results in complex data sets [16].

The distribution density of data points is one of the basic problems of probability statistics. To solve this problem, there are parameter estimation and non parameter estimation.

In parameter estimation, firstly, assuming that the data obeys a certain distribution, such as linear and exponential distributions, etc., then find the appropriate unknown parameters in the objective function family. However, for the case of abnormal data distribution, the estimation of the neighborhood density of data objects by these methods is still not very accurate, which leads to the case of missing outliers in the data set [17]. Theoretical and experimental results show that there is a big difference between this assumption and the actual model, and the ideal result is often not obtained. In response to this problem, the researchers proposed a non-parametric estimation method, namely KDE (Kernel Density Estimation). This method does not rely on any assumptions. Relative parameter estimation is more suitable for estimating the distribution density of various types of data [18]. Based on the Gauss kernel density function, a local outlier detection algorithm based on Gauss kernel density function is proposed to estimate the density of data objects by considering the three nearest neighbors of the data object which are k-nearest neighbors, reverse k-nearest neighbors and shared nearest neighbors.

3 GLOD Algorithm

3.1 Algorithm Ideas

Local Outlier Detection Algorithm Based on Gaussian Kernel Density Function (GLOD) is proposed based on the LOF algorithm and kernel density estimation. For local outlier mining problems, density-based algorithms can achieve efficiently mine. Among them, there are many methods for estimating the local density of data points based on the density-based algorithm. Based on knowledge of probability theory, this paper selects the kernel density with Gaussian kernel density function as the core to estimate the local density of data points. In order to improve the mining accuracy of outlier data, the reverse neighbors and shared nearest neighbors are introduced to partition the data neighbors into core neighbors, thereby effectively expressing the data distribution information. Finally, according to the idea of LOF algorithm, we can obtain the Relative Density based Outlier Factor (RDOF) of data points, which can effectively improves the accuracy and efficiency of outlier mining.

3.2   GLOD Algorithm Related Concepts

Definition 1. The kernel density estimate for a given data set $D = \{x_1, x_2, x_3, \ldots, x_n\}$, and the kernel density estimate function for the data point object xi is p(xi), then the kernel density estimate at this point is defined as formula (1).

$$p(x_i) = \frac{1}{h} \sum_{i=1}^{m} \frac{1}{h^d} K\left(\frac{x - x_i}{h}\right) \tag{1}$$

Among them, h represents the window width; d represents the dimension of the data set, among them the nuclear function K usually chooses the Gaussian kernel function, expresses like formula (2).

$$K\left(\frac{x - x_i}{h}\right)_{Gaussian} = \frac{1}{(2\pi)^{2/d}} exp\left(-\frac{\|x - x_i\|^2}{2h^2}\right) \tag{2}$$

Where, it represents the Euclidean distance between the objects x and x_i.

Definition 2. k nearest neighbor given data set $D = \{x_1, x_2, x_3, \ldots, x_n\}$, the k nearest neighbor of the data point object x_i is a set of data points in the data set whose distance is not greater than the k-th point and its distance. Defined by Eq. (3).

$$S_{KNN}(x_i) = \{o \in D | dist(o, x_i) \leq dist(x_p, x_i)\} \tag{3}$$

Where dist(o, x_i) represents the distance between data points o and x_i.

Definition 3. Reverse nearest neighbor given data set $D = \{x_1, x_2, x_3, \ldots, x_n\}$, reverse nearest neighbor is the set of objects x_i as their k nearest neighbors, denoted as S_{RNN} (x_i), defined As shown in formula (4).

$$S_{RNN}(x_i) = \{o | \neg \exists o' \in D \wedge (dist(o, o') < dist(o, x_i))\} \tag{4}$$

Definition 4. Share nearest neighbor given data set $D = \{x_1, x_2, x_3, \ldots, x_n\}$, shared nearest neighbor is a set of one or more objects shared with the data object x_i, denoted as $S_{SNN}(x_i)$, defined As shown in formula (5).

$$S_{SNN}(x_i) = \{o \in D | S_{KNN}(o) = S_{KNN}(x_i)\} \tag{5}$$

Definition 5. Core neighbor given data set $D = \{x_1, x_2, x_3, \ldots, x_n\}$, k-nearest neighbors, reverse k-nearest neighbors, and shared nearest neighbors combined to form an extended local neighborhood are the core neighbors of the object x_i, denoted as $S(x_i)$, is defined as Formula (6).

$$S(x_i) = \{o | o \in (S_{KNN}(x_i) \cup S_{RNN}(x_i) \cup S_{SNN}(x_i))\} \tag{6}$$

In order to estimate the density at the position of the object x_i, only the neighbors of xi are used instead of all the objects in the data set, and there are two reasons. First, many complex actual data sets usually have multiple clusters or components, which are the inherent mode of data. Density estimation using full datasets may lose local differences in density without detecting local outliers. Second, outlier detection will calculate the score for each object. Using complete datasets will result in higher computational costs and complexity. $O(N^2)$, where N is the total number of objects in the dataset.

Definition 6. Relative density outliers Given data set $D = \{x_1, x_2, x_3, \ldots, x_n\}$, the ratio of the average of the nuclear density of the core neighbor of the object x_i to its nuclear density is called the relative density outlier factor of the object x_i. Let RDOF be expressed as (7).

$$RDOF(x_i) = \frac{\sum_{x_i \in S(x_i)} P(x_i)}{|S(x_i)|} / P(x_i) \tag{7}$$

RDOF is the ratio of the average neighborhood density to the core density of the data object x_i. If RDOF(xi) is much greater than 1, the object x_i will be outside the dense cluster, indicating that x_i will be an outlier. If RDOF(x_i) is equal to or less than 1, the data object x_i will be surrounded by the same dense neighbor, indicating that x_i is not an outlier. According to the definition of kernel density estimation, when the neighborhood distribution of data object x_i is sparse, its nuclear density value is smaller, which means that the distance between data point and surrounding data points is larger. When the average neighborhood density of the object x_i is much larger than the average neighborhood density of the object x_i, the object x_i is more likely to be outliers. Conversely, when the average neighborhood density of the object x_i is less than the average neighborhood density of the object x_i, The possibility that the object x_i is an outlier is very small. Therefore, the proposed local outlier detection algorithm GLOD based on Gaussian kernel density function has a good universality.

3.3   The Implementation of GLOD Algorithm

In the GLOD algorithm, these parameters need to be input in the algorithm: the parameters k of the data object k neighbors, the window width h (usually h is a positive number), the dimension d, the threshold T, and the outlier mining using the GLOD algorithm Proceed as follows.

Traverse the entire data set D, calculate the distance between data objects, then calculate the neighbor relationship of each data object according to the distance between data objects, and then construct the kNN map according to the neighbor relationship between the objects.

For each data object, the k nearest neighbors are read sequentially, and through the k nearest neighbors of each object, we can obtain k nearest neighbor sets for each point. Then read the kNN map again. According to the definition of the reverse nearest neighbor, calculate the reverse nearest neighbor of each data point by formula (4), and then obtain the reverse k-nearest neighbor set of each data point.

Traversing the data set, sharing the definition of the nearest neighbor, using formula (5) to determine the neighbor relationship of the data point, calculating the shared nearest neighbor of the data object, so as to obtain the shared nearest neighbor set. Then read the k-nearest neighbor set, reverse k-nearest neighbor set of each data point according to formula (3), and share the nearest neighbor set to obtain the core neighbor set S of the object.

Then use the formula (1) to calculate the core density of the data object, and obtain the neighborhood density of each data object with the core impact point set S as a neighbor.

Finally, using formula (2), calculate the neighborhood density of the core set S of data objects, and calculate the average value. Using the formula (7) to calculate the relative density outlier factor RDOF of the object to calculate the relative density outlier factor of each record, the degree of outlier of each data is obtained.

The RDOF value is compared with the threshold T. If it is greater than the threshold T, it is determined as an outlier.

From the kNN graph we can see that an object will have k out-degree edges, and there is no one or more in-degree edges. By reading the kNN graph, we calculate the k-nearest neighbor set, reverse nearest neighbor set and shared nearest neighbor set of the data object, and obtain the core neighbor set S of each piece of data. We estimate the neighborhood density of the object based on the kernel density. Finally, the relative density outlier factor RDOF is calculated based on the neighborhood density of the object, and the RDOF value is compared with the threshold T. If the threshold is greater than the threshold T, the outlier is determined. The specific description of the GLOD algorithm is shown in Algorithm 1.

Algorithm 1: Local outlier detection algorithm based on Gaussian kernel density function.

Input: data set D, parameter k, dimension d, kernel width h, threshold T

Output: outlier data points

GLOD(D, h, d, k, T)

 BEGIN

(1)For $x_i \in D$

(2)Calculate the minimum value dist and the maximum distance maxdist of the sample

(3)If (dist<maxdist)

(4)Take this sample as the k-nearest neighbor of the object

(5)End if

(6)End For

(7)Constructing kNN maps based on calculated neighborhoods of data space

(8)For $x_i \in kNN$

(9) $S_{KNN}(x_i) = \{o \in D \mid dist(o, \ x_i) \le dist(x_p, \ x_i)\}$

(10) $S_{RNN}(x_i) = \{o \mid \neg \exists o' \in D \wedge (dist(o,o') < dist(o,x_i))\}$

(11) $S_{SNN}(x_i) = \{o \in D \mid S_{KNN}(o) = S_{KNN}(x_i)\}$

(12) $S(x_i) = \{o \mid o \in (S_{KNN}(x_i) \cup S_{RNN}(x_i) \cup S_{SNN}(x_i))\}$

(13) $p(x_i) = \dfrac{1}{h} \sum_{i=1}^{m} \dfrac{1}{h^d} K(\dfrac{x - x_i}{h})$

(14) $RDOF(x_i) = \dfrac{\sum_{x_i \in S(x_i)} P(x_i)}{|S(x_i)|} / P(x_i)$

(15) END For

(16) For $x_i \in kNN$

(17) If $RDOF(x_i) > T$

(18) outputs xi

(19) End If

(20)End For

END

3.4 Analysis of GLOD Algorithms

3.4.1 Correctness Analysis

In the GLOD analyses, firstly, KNN graphs are constructed that based on the spatial relationships between data objects. Each data object is a vertex, and the outbound direction is connected to the k nearest neighbors. The KNN graph is an accurate graph that based on the data structure. Then, by traversing the KNN map, the k-nearest neighbors and the reverse nearest neighbors of each object in the data are calculated, resulting in k-nearest neighbors and the nearest reversing neighbor for each object.

Then calculating the shared nearest neighbors for each object can obtain the core neighbors. The nearest neighbor is obtained by reading the KNN map and therefore is accurate. Reversing the nearest neighbor and sharing the nearest neighbor can provide effective local data distribution information and are used successfully for clustering and outlier detection. At the same time, the algorithm uses Gaussian kernel density function to estimate the density of data objects, and the relative density outlier factor to detect the degree of outliers for data objects. To sum up, it is correct to estimate the degree of outliers for data objects.

3.4.2   Analysis of Time Complexity

In the GLOD algorithm, it is mainly divided into two parts: KNN map storage data and outlier mining of data objects. The KNN graph can well represent the set of neighbors of the data object. In solving the KNN graph, the time complexity is O $(N\log N^2)$, according to the storage structure of the index structure. In the outlier mining part of the data object, the k-nearest neighbor set of the object, the reverse k-nearest neighbor set, the nearest neighbor set are calculated for each object, and the core neighbor set S of each data object is calculated; The kernel density of the data object is calculated by using the core neighbor neighborhood partition method and the kernel density estimation method with the Gaussian kernel density function as the kernel. The time complexity of the outlier mining stage is O (N^2). Therefore, the total time complexity of the GLOD algorithm is O (N^2).

4   Experimental Results and Performance Analysis

In this section, the proposed algorithm is verified on UCI real datasets and synthetic datasets, and compared with existing algorithms and results analysis to verify the effectiveness of the algorithm.

4.1   Experimental Environment

The algorithm in this paper is mainly implemented on the My Eclipse platform. The experimental environment configuration of the algorithm consists of two parts: hardware environment configuration and software environment configuration.

Hardware environment configuration: Xeon CPU E5-2603, clocked at 1.80 GHz, memory capacity of 8.00 GB, hard disk capacity of 1 TB.

Software environment configuration: The development tool used is Eclipse; the compilation environment is jdk1.6.0; the experimental test environment is configured as 64-bit Windows 8.

4.2   Sources of Experimental Data

In order to verify the accuracy and efficiency of the LDOD algorithm, UCI real data set and synthetic data set were compared with the comparison algorithm for experimental comparison and result analysis. UCI real datasets are from reference [19] and synthetic datasets reference from literature [20]. Among them, the three UCI real data sets are the

Glass data set, the Ionosphere data set, and the Pen Digits data set. The number of data bars and the number of outliers contained in the real data set is shown in Table 1. In the composite data set, each data set contains a different number of records, and the number of data records varies from several hundred to ten thousand. At the same time, there is a certain gap between the numbers of outliers. In the composite dataset, the number of datasets contained in the dataset is 500, 1000, and 5,000, respectively. The number of datasets in the composite dataset and the number of outliers is shown in Table 2.

Table 1. Real data set information list

Data set name	Records	Outliers
Glass	214	14
Ionosphere	224	12
Pen digits	10164	110

Table 2. Synthetic data set information list

Data set name	Records	Outliers
KDD-100	500	9
KDD-1000	1000	50
KDD-5000	5000	100

4.3   Performance Analysis

4.3.1   Analysis of Algorithm Execution Accuracy

In order to verify the accuracy of the GLOD algorithm, experiments and analysis were performed on UCI real data sets and synthetic data sets. Figures 1 and 2 respectively show the experimental results detected on the UCI real data set and the synthesized data set. Figure 1 shows that each piece of data onto the target data set is on the real data set, and they are respectively tested for the GLOD algorithm and the LOF algorithm. Figure 2 shows the results of the GLOD algorithm and the LOF algorithm for each record of the dataset on the composite dataset. In order to compare the accuracy of the GLOD algorithm and the LOF algorithm to mine outliers on the data set, AUC (Area under the ROC) is used to measure the accuracy of the algorithm to mine outliers on the target data set. Under normal circumstances, AUC can describe the level of algorithm performance well, so using AUC can better estimate the merits of the algorithm. The smaller the AUC value, the lower the precision of the outlier mining algorithm. On the contrary, the larger the AUC value, the higher the accuracy of the outlier mining algorithm. Therefore, the accuracy of the algorithm is performed using the AUC curve, and the effectiveness of the algorithm is compared by the respective running time.

Figures 1 and 2 are the results of the comparison about the ALG values between the GLOD algorithm and the LOF algorithm proposed in this paper. We can observe from Fig. 1, in the real data set, due to the complex structure of the target data set and the difference number of data records, in the Glass data set, the AUC value of the GLOD algorithm and the AUC value of the LOF algorithm is not much different. But in the

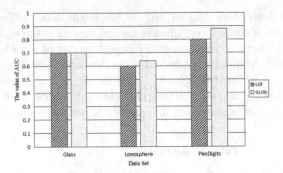

Fig. 1. AUC values of GLOD and LOF algorithm on real data sets

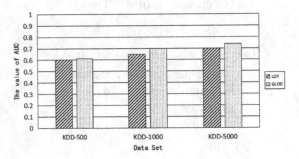

Fig. 2. AUC values of GLOD and LOF algorithm on synthetic data sets

Ionosphere, when the dataset and the Pen Digits dataset are detected, it can be seen that the AUC value of the GLOD algorithm is larger than the value of the LOF algorithm. This means that when the GLOD algorithm uses a kernel density function of a Gaussian kernel density function as the kernel, the data points are estimated. After the neighborhood density is estimated, the accuracy of the algorithm is higher than that of the LOF algorithm. In other words, the kernel density estimate is more accurate than the neighbor density estimated by the LOF algorithm, so the accuracy of excavation outliers is relatively high. Therefore, it can be seen that in real detection, the GLOD algorithm is more accurate than the LOF algorithm. In the composite data set, since the number of data contained in the target data set is different, when the data set has less records, it can be seen from Fig. 2 that the value of the AUC of the GLOD algorithm is similar to that of the LOF algorithm, that is, the data composition. In the uncomplicated case, the GLOD algorithm and the LOF algorithm are not very different in estimating the neighborhood density of data points. Both algorithms can effectively detect outliers, but they are accompanied by the number of records of the target data set. The GLOD algorithm is more and more obvious than the AUC value of the LOF algorithm. When the data record is 5000, it can be seen that the AUC value of the GLOD algorithm has far exceeded the AUC value of the LOF algorithm, which means that when the data set is more complex, compared with the LOF algorithm, the GLOD algorithm can more accurately describe the density of the neighborhood of the data points, thereby more effectively tap outliers. Therefore, the accuracy of the GLOD algorithm is better than the LOF algorithm.

4.3.2   Analysis of Algorithm Time Complexity

Figures 3 and 4 are schematic diagrams of the comparison results of the GLOD algorithm and the LOF algorithm when they run. From Figs. 3 and 4, we can clearly see that the running time of the GLOD algorithm under the same data is less than the running time of the LOF algorithm in the real data set. In the synthesized data set, the conclusion is more obvious. In the composite data set, the number of records contained in the data set is different, from a few hundred to a few thousand. As we can see from Fig. 4, the running time of the GLOD algorithm increases slowly with the number of bars, indicating that the GLOD algorithm has good scalability. Therefore, experiments show that the GLOD algorithm is effective.

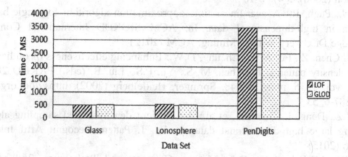

Fig. 3.   The time that GLOD and LOF algorithms run on real data set

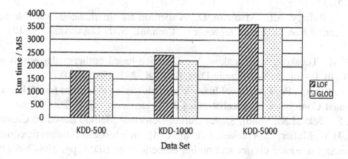

Fig. 4.   The time that GLOD and LOF algorithms run on synthetic data set

5   Summary

Outlier mining is a hot topic in the era of big data. Aiming at the low efficiency of outlier mining, this paper proposes a local outlier detection algorithm GLOD based on Gaussian kernel density function. The algorithm uses relative density outliers to measure the degree of outliers of data objects. The density distribution of data points is not only described by k-nearest neighbor, but includes reverse k-nearest neighbors and shared nearest neighbors to estimate the data density distribution. Effectively characterizes the density distribution of the data. The validity of GLOD algorithm is verified by real data sets and synthetic data sets.

References

1. Aggarwal, C.: Outlier Analysis, pp. 75–99. Springer, Germany (2015). https://doi.org/10.1007/978-1-4614-6396-2_3
2. Braun, T.D., Siegal, H.J., Beck, N., et al.: A comparison study of static mapping heuristics for a class of meta-tasks on heterogeneous computing systems. In: Eighth Heterogeneous Computing Workshop. IEEE Computer Society (1999)
3. Han, J., Kamber, M., Pei, J.: Data Mining: Concepts and Techniques. Morgan Kaufmann, Burlington (2006). 5(4), 1–18
4. Pham, N., Pagh, R.: A near-linear time approximation algorithm for angle-based outlier detection in high-dimensional data. In: ACM SIGKDD International Conference on Knowledge Discovery & Data Mining. ACM (2012)
5. Tang, J., Chen, Z., Fu, A.W., Cheung, D.W.: Enhancing effectiveness of outlier detections for low density patterns. In: Chen, M.-S., Yu, P.S., Liu, B. (eds.) PAKDD 2002. LNCS (LNAI), vol. 2336, pp. 535–548. Springer, Heidelberg (2002). https://doi.org/10.1007/3-540-47887-6_53
6. Qian, X.Z., Deng, J., Qian, H., et al.: An efficient density biased sampling algorithm for clustering large high-dimensional datasets. Int. J. Pattern Recognit Artif Intell. 29(08), 1550026 (2015)
7. Han, J.W., Micheline, K.: Data Mining: Concepts and Techniques, 2nd edn. Morgan Kaufmann Publishers, San Francisco (2006)
8. Muller, E., Sanchez, P.I., Mulle, Y., et al.: Ranking outlier nodes in subspaces of attributed graphs (2013)
9. Hoeting, J., Raftery, A.E., Madigan, D.: A method for simultaneous variable selection and outlier identification in linear regression. Comput. Stat. Data Anal. 54(12), 3181–3193 (1996)
10. Knorr, E.M., Tucakov, V., Tucakov, V.: Distance-based outliers: algorithms and applications. VLDB J.—Int. J. Very Large Data Bases 8, 237–253 (2000)
11. Zhang, H., Wu, Q., Pu, J.: A novel fuzzy kernel clustering algorithm for outlier detection. In: International Conference on Mechatronics & Automation. IEEE (2007)
12. Pamula, R., Deka, J.K., Nandi, S.: An Outlier Detection Method Based on Clustering (2011)
13. Nguyen, H.V., Müller, E., Vreeken, J., et al.: CMI: an information-theoretic contrast measure for enhancing subspace cluster and outlier detection. In: SDM, pp. 198–206 (2013)
14. Zhou, S., Zhao, Y., Guan, J., Huang, J.: A neighborhood-based clustering algorithm. In: Ho, T.B., Cheung, D., Liu, H. (eds.) PAKDD 2005. LNCS (LNAI), vol. 3518, pp. 361–371. Springer, Heidelberg (2005). https://doi.org/10.1007/11430919_43
15. Wu, S., Wang, S.: Information-theoretic outlier detection for large-scale categorical data. IEEE Trans. Knowl. Data Eng. 25(3), 589–602 (2013)
16. Sun, P., Chawla, S., Arunasalam, B.: Mining for outliers in sequential databases. In: Proceedings of the Sixth SIAM International Conference on Data Mining, Bethesda, pp. 94–105 (2006)

17. Lazarus, D., Weinkauf, M., Diver, P.: Pacman profiling: a simple procedure to identify stratigraphic outliers in high-density deep-sea microfossil data. Paleobiology **38**(1), 144–161 (2012)
18. Zhang, K., Hutter, M., Jin, H.: A new local distance-based outlier detection approach for scattered real-world data. In: Theeramunkong, T., Kijsirikul, B., Cercone, N., Ho, T.-B. (eds.) PAKDD 2009. LNCS (LNAI), vol. 5476, pp. 813–822. Springer, Heidelberg (2009). https://doi.org/10.1007/978-3-642-01307-2_84
19. Bache, K., Lichman, M.: UCI machine learning repository (2013). http://archive.ics.uci.edu. html
20. Hettich, S., Bay, S., Musster, K., Winner, J.: KDD CUP (1999). http://kdd.isc.uci.edu/databases/kddcpu99/kddcpu99.html. Accessed 01 Sept 2011

The Research of Data Blood Relationship Analysis on Metadata

Fenfen Guan[1,2], Yongping Gao[1(✉)], Congcong Cai[3], and Jun Zhang[1]

[1] Jiangxi Engineering Laboratory on Radioactive Geoscience
and Big Data Technology, East China University of Technology,
Nanchang 330013, Jiangxi, China
ypgaoypgao@163.com
[2] School of Foreign Language, East China University of Technology,
Shanghai, China
[3] Teradata, San Diego, USA

Abstract. In the process of continuous expansion of data and continuous expansion of the system, various data relations and data forms form crisscross connections, forming an extremely complex network diagram. If there is an error in the data, how do we quickly lock the cause of the problem? How do we find out which entities are affected by the implications or changes of the problem? These issues create challenges and pressures for large-scale, enterprise-level data platforms. The paper proposes to use data blood analysis to solve the relationship among tens of millions of tables. To get this kind of more underlying blood information, we need to add embedded parts to the execution engine, which will be fed into the blood relationship collection system using push mode when the job is executed. The paper is to implement field level blood relationship analysis in the data warehouse of China Commercial bank on the architecture of Teradata, and separated it from the ETL process and made it into a single part. By parsing multiple ETL jobs, we get a number of mapping relationship of atoms, and atoms and relationships make up the molecules that form the blood relationship network we need. This experimental scheme can be simply embedded into the data platform by eliminating the complexity of the system and achieving a separate component structure. The blood relationship can be conducted any time and temporary scripts and error logic of related data will have no data pollution on the data blood relationship.

Keywords: Network diagram of data relations · Quickly lock ·
Enterprise-level data · Data blood analysis · Blood relationship network

1 Introduction

At present, the scale of enterprise big data systems is usually very large, with the capacity of terabytes, petabytes and the development to EB level. Some systems even increase the data volume of terabytes overnight. In the process of continuous expansion of data and continuous expansion of the system, various data relations and data forms form crisscross connections, forming an extremely complex network diagram. If there is an error in the data, how do we quickly lock the cause of the problem? How do we

© Springer Nature Singapore Pte Ltd. 2019
H. Peng et al. (Eds.): ISICA 2018, CCIS 986, pp. 344–351, 2019.
https://doi.org/10.1007/978-981-13-6473-0_30

find out which entities are affected by the implications or changes of the problem? These issues create challenges and pressures for large-scale, enterprise-level data platforms.

In 2016, Google proposed the concept of data blood relationship analysis and collected blood relationship to solve the architecture from ETL log, which solved the relationship between tens of millions of tables in Google. Whether domestic or international, however, at present big manufacturers did not provide data blood relationship analysis tools, and do not support field level of traceability, but have the corresponding theoretical support, only staying in the relationship between the table and table. However, the link between the field levels still stays in theoretical phase, and there will be more investment in the field level than in table level, thus leading to enterprise input-output ratio imbalance [1]. It is almost impossible to obtain blood relationship between fields with the current reverse-engineering approach of getting information from logs. To get this kind of more underlying blood information, we need to add embedded parts to the execution engine, which will be fed into the blood relationship collection system by using push mode when the job is executed. In the Hive execution hook, for example, you can collect blood relationships between fields (see cloudera navigator). But for data processing systems where the source in the execution engine is not open or the embedded architecture is not flexible, it is very difficult to get this level of kinship. The paper is to implement field level blood relationship analysis in the data warehouse of China Commercial bank on the architecture of Teradata, and separated it from the ETL process and made it into a single part.

2 The Problems of Data Blood Relationship

Now suppose a data development engineer who needs to generate a table in order to meet a business need. From the point of view of program logic clarity or performance optimization, he will need to use many tables and produce many intermediate tables through MR, Spark or Hive. After some time, the business engineer feels that a field in the data provided is always not right, even suspects that something is wrong with the data, and needs the data development engineer to trace the source of the field. How does he do this work?

In a real data warehouse implementation, the data can be derived not only by a fixed set of operators or algebraic attributes. In most cases, data are transformed through a complex programming process which means sometimes the conversion will reach as many as 60 or more. Transformation is sometimes very complex, because sometimes some transformation logic is customized and manually coded, and may not adhere to any formal transformation defined [2]. When data passes through different transformations, even where an exception may occur somewhere in the transformation process, the trajectory that wants to trace back to the data source becomes blurred. It is very difficult to find these anomalies in the absence of data blood relationship analysis.

3   The Necessity of Data Blood Relationship Analysis

Supporting blood relationship tracking in a data warehouse environment brings several benefits, some of which are listed below:

Deep data analysis: for some applications where data generated in a data warehouse is used for legitimate purposes, an important requirement is data traceability. Support for blood relationship tracing can be traced back to the origin of data, sometimes even necessary for in-depth data analysis.

Anomaly survey: sometimes data in a data warehouse can look abnormal. An analyst might ask, "Where are these data coming from?" And he may need to explain how it is derived. Answering this question would be difficult and expensive without data on blood relations analysis [3].

Debugging: data blood relationship analysis can be used to investigate source data programs that produce abnormal data. It is possible to report source-to-target mappings and view transformation descriptions (i.e., derivations, operators), which is an important aspect of data warehouse maintenance.

Impact analysis: different forces or influences may impose changes on the transformation process or even the data warehouse pattern. Enterprise development, internal and external requirements may change over time. The impact of these changes on the data warehouse can be analyzed before the implementation of the data lineage. Impact analysis identifies which tables, columns, and processes are affected by the change [4]. In addition, blood relationship information allows users to track the impact of fault source data or derived concentrators.

Facilitating data mining and discovery: understanding data sources can enhance the process of data mining and discovery. It can also improve the consistency of the data used for data mining.

Ensuring correct data in the operating system: data blood analysis can be traced back to cleaned data and can be used as a feedback loop to correct data in the operating system.

4   How to Conduct Data Blood Relationship Analysis on Metadata

Data acquisition and integration is an important process in data warehouse. The data in the data warehouse enter through a cleansing and integration process. The fusion data come from heterogeneous and different data. Source is a major challenge (for example, given naming, domain definition, identification number, etc.), and the data integration process is extremely complex and error-prone. The original source tends to be vague, because the data in the data warehouse is usually integrated from multiple sources and transformed through complex processes.

Data acquisition and integration is usually a part of extraction, transformation, and loading, or ETL. Often referred to as data transformation, ETL is a well-known process cycle inherent in the warehouse environment. The typical end result of an ETL process in a warehouse environment is data stored in a multidimensional schema. ETL typically contains transformation programs that perform data cleansing, integration, and aggregation tasks on source data before loading it into the warehouse, and finally apply to a variety of applications (see Fig. 1).

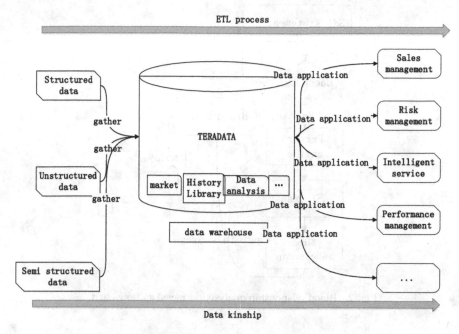

Fig. 1. ETL data processing flow chart

ETL jobs run through the entire data stream. To obtain data consanguinity and influence analysis, we can start from ETL jobs. As shown in 2, the ETL job is parsed to extract the SQL statement, which is then passed to the built Parser parsing engine for the syntactic analysis tree (AST tree) [5].

Then how do we build the Parser engine? The concept of grammar is known in the principles of compilation, which describes a programming language and how to implement its compiler by using the Backus paradigm. Here we recommend you use a gadget –antlr.

ANTLR (full name: ANother Tool for Language Recognition) is a parser generator based on the LL(*) algorithm, using the top-down recursive descent LL profiler method. Currently, both Hibernate and WebLogic use ANTLR for parsing HQL. See Fig. 2.

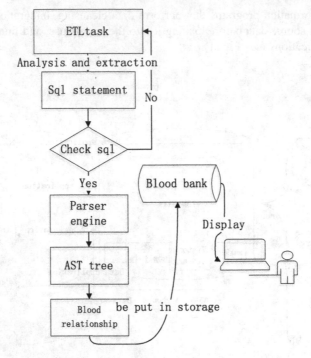

Fig. 2. Blood relationship analysis on metadata flow chart

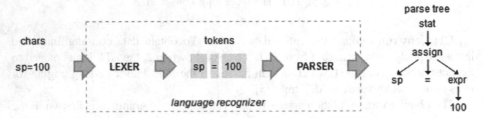

Fig. 3. The basic data flow diagram of Antlr language recognizer

Programs that recognize languages are called parsers. To make it easier to implement a language-recognition program, we usually break the parsing of the language into two similar but different tasks or stages [6].

The first stage of forming characters into words or tokens is called lexical analysis or simple markup. We call the program for marking input a lexical analyzer. When a lexical analyzer cares only about types, it makes lexical symbols into types, instead of individual tokens. A token contains at least two pieces of information: the token type (determines the lexical structure) and the text that matches the token.

The second stage is the real parser, which uses these tokens to identify sentence structures. In Fig. 3, the real parser uses tokens to identify assignment statements [7].

By default, the parser generated by ANTLR builds a data structure called a parse tree or syntax tree, which records how the parser recognizes the structure of the input sentence and its component phrases.

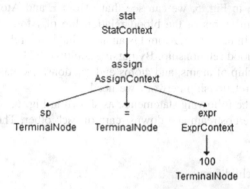

Fig. 4. The AST tree graph

After the grammar corresponding to SQL is built, we get the syntax analysis tree (AST tree). Take sp = 100 as an example. As shown in Fig. 4, after the AST tree is built, it can be analyzed through the familiar languages such as Java, python, and c++.

By analyzing the AST tree, we obtained the atomic graph, which can represent the library, table and field, etc. After the analysis, the blood relationship of the atom can be recorded. Now we obtained the single molecule composed of the atom by analyzing the smallest single ETL job. In a single ETL job, we got the following atoms and the mappings between the atoms, by which we can connect the atoms with related ones. See Fig. 5.

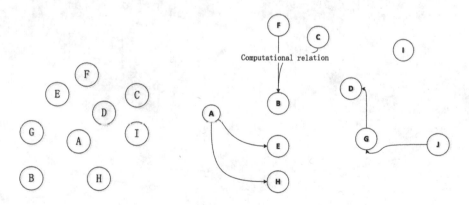

Fig. 5. Atoms and their connection diagrams

The atoms represented by this diagram can be libraries, tables, fields, and so on, and of course the calculation and transformation relationship only exists with the atoms represented by the fields. Calculation relationship can count equations with data from the origin to the application. For example, in the equations of a + b = c, and c/d = e, we can get the equation of (a + b)/d = e by atomic mapping, thus the e field is computed, and the single ETL job also recorded the interactional relationship between atoms. For example, in Fig. 5, we can see that, Atom E and Atom H are the corresponding downstream atoms of the blood relationship of Atom A, while Atom J is affected by Atom G. In the figure, Atom I is an atom that is not related with other atoms and cannot form a blood relationship. By parsing multiple ETL jobs, we get a number of mapping relationship of atoms, and atoms and relationships make up the molecules that form the blood relationship network we need.

When we parse the following statements, as shown in Fig. 6, we can clearly know which roles affect the upstream and downstream of each other. The child is from Dad +Mon.

```
select Dad+Mon as child from
(
        select Dad+mon as Dad from home1
        union all
        select Dad+mon as Mon from home2
);
```

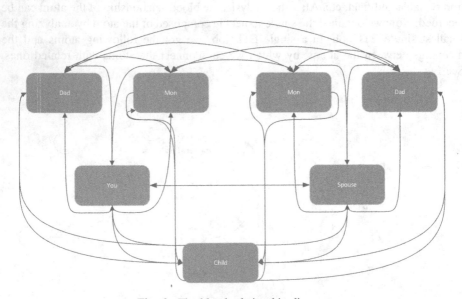

Fig. 6. The blood relationship diagram

5   Conclusion

This experimental scheme can be simply embedded into the data platform by eliminating the complexity of the system and achieving a separate component structure [8]. It has the following advantages. The blood relationship can be conducted any time and temporary scripts and error logic of related data will not affect the data blood relationship. Due to the complexity of the SQL syntax, many people had tried but failed to produce successful parser. We have developed a parser that successfully reduces the difficulty of decoding SQL syntax. Vendors keep releasing new versions of databases, and it is easy to maintain native SQL parsers. However, it also has its disadvantages. It is difficult to update the blood relationship which had dependence before and now has no dependence.

Acknowledgment. The paper is sponsored by fund (fund id: JELRGBDT201707, National Natural Science Foundation of China 61662002, 61463003 & 11865002). Fenfen Guan, Yongping Gao & Jun Zhang are the corresponding authors.

References

1. Chen, X.-J.: Research and realization of the college scientific research management system based on SSH frame. Electron. Des. Eng. **8**, 8–12 (2011)
2. Liang, L., Yi, C., Yang, X., et al.: Computer Applications and Software, vol. 29, p. 283 (2012)
3. Sankaradass, V., Arputharaj, K.: An intelligent recommendation system for web user personalization with fuzzy temporal association rules. Eur. J. Sci. Res. **51**(1), 88–96 (2011). ISSN 1450-216X
4. Zhang, Y., Liu, X.: Application of "consanguinity analysis" technology in information system of commercial banks. Inf. Technol. Inf. **6**, 147–149 (2017)
5. Heng, X.: Research and practice of metadata management system in electric power enterprises. Autom. Instrum. **4**, 101–107 (2017)
6. Huang, B., Peng, Y.: An efficient scalable metadata management method in cloud computing. Comput. Eng. Des. **9**, 1147–1154 (2014)
7. Pesic, M., Schonenberg, M.H., Van der Aalst, W.M.P.: Declare: full support for loosely-structured processes. In: Proceedings of the 11th IEEE International Enterprise Distributed Object Computing Conference, pp. 287–298. IEEE Computer Society, Washington, D.C. (2007)
8. Peng, J.: Research on deep aggregation of characteristic resources based on metadata ontology. Libr. J. **11**, 82–89 (2016)

Detection of Pedestrians Based on the Fusion of Human Characteristics and Kernel Density Estimation

Shi Cheng[1], Muyan Zhou[1], Chunhong Lu[1], Yuanjin Li[2(✉)], and Zelin Wang[1]

[1] School of Computer Science and Technology,
Nantong University, Nantong, China
whwzl@whu.edu.cn
[2] School of Computer and Information Engineering,
Chuzhou University, Chuzhou, China
liyuanjin11@126.com

Abstract. The kernel density estimate does not need to have the characteristic distribution hypothesis to the background, it also does not require the estimation parameter, and it can deal with the moving target detection under the complex background, but the kernel function bandwidth choice uniformly puzzles the algorithm application. To solve this problem, this paper proposes a fusion method of human body characteristics and kernel density estimation for pedestrian detection. Firstly, the kernel function bandwidth is chosen by the prior information of moving target, then the foreground (moving target) is extracted based on kernel density estimation, finally, using human features to detect video pedestrians. The experimental results show that the calculation of kernel density estimation is reduced by comparing introduction of prior information with traditional methods, and the pedestrian and no pedestrian can be detected accurately by the interference of light variation and noise.

Keywords: Moving target · Priori information · Kernel density estimation · Pedestrians

1 Introduction

Moving target detection is an important subject in video processing, in order to find the moving target, and then extract the information such as size, position and speed of the target, and provide support for the deeper image analysis, image understanding and motion tracking. In the research of moving object detection, many systems and algorithms are put forward by the domestic and foreign scholars. The United States DARRA project developed a video surveillance system VSAM (Video Surveillance And Monitoring) [1] can implement monitoring the future of some of the world's complex scenes through the user's operation. First, the background image is initialized regularly, and then the feature region is extracted by the background subtraction method and matched with the corresponding background image to find the moving target. For aerial video, VSAM is to use three frame difference subtractions to

© Springer Nature Singapore Pte Ltd. 2019
H. Peng et al. (Eds.): ISICA 2018, CCIS 986, pp. 352–364, 2019.
https://doi.org/10.1007/978-981-13-6473-0_31

find the moving object in the image after motion compensation. IBM company developed W4 (what, where, when, who) system [2] and smart Surveillance [3] are mainly used for pedestrian feature extraction and movement trend tracking. EPSRC (UK Engineering and Physical Sciences Research Council) project VISPATH (vision based Internet software platform for the smart factory™ tracking of humans) is supported by an imaging team in the University of London, the aim of this project is to achieve efficient, non-intrusive and real-time tracking of pedestrians. The nonparametric density estimation method is proposed for the deficiency of the parameter density estimation by Elgarmnal [4] and some other persons, which is used to estimate the density of the background kernel, which mainly utilizes the gray information of the image. Without the assumption of the background feature distribution and the estimation parameters, the robustness of the algorithm is greatly improved, and the multimode background is preserved in the background modeling, so that the algorithm can deal with the video in the complex background.

Many universities and institutes in China have put a lot of effort into the research of sports target detection and achieved some results. The Chinese Academy of Sciences has studied the analysis of behavior and events in traffic scenes and the pattern recognition algorithm for pedestrian movement [5]. Tsinghua University has developed a long distance pedestrian recognition system [6]. Zhang [7] is blocking the movement of human body, it uses 3-D position information of human body to avoid the effect of occlusion on the detection and tracking of human motion. Sun [8] and some other persons use the background subtraction method and the histogram method to determine the center position and the detection of the human target, and the particle swarm optimization algorithm and the Parzen particle filter are used to track. Sun [9] and some other persons use the method of extracting key frames to realize background modeling, which improves the real-time effect of target detection greatly. Xu [10] use the approximate calculation of kernel function index in kernel density estimation, the algorithm is optimized, but because the new parameters are introduced and the parameters cannot be adaptively, the robustness of kernel density estimation algorithm is affected. Jin [11] uses the less samples for kernel density estimation directly, in order to overcome the loss of information, it is combined with the background motion compensation method to improve the real-time detection effect, and the disadvantage is to restrain the advantage of using kernel density estimation method to deal with complex background.

In view of the insufficiency of the above method, a kernel density estimation method is proposed, which can reduce the computation amount of kernel density estimation by means of human body feature prior information selection and function bandwidth. The experimental results show that the real-time performance is greatly improved while the pedestrian detection effect is ensured.

2 Method for Estimating Kernel Density

In the nonparametric density estimation method, the Histogram method is the most commonly used one, but because the histogram method mainly estimates the number or probability of the sample points in each region, the estimation accuracy is not high.

However, kernel density estimation is much more accurate than histogram method, and kernel density estimation method has become a perfect nonparametric density estimation method.

The kernel density estimation method is a very effective nonparametric density estimation method proposed in the middle of 20th century, which is also called Parzen window estimation, which is defined as follows:

Sample $\{x_1, x_2, \ldots, x_n\}$ is a set of independent distributions with a probability density function of $f(x)$. Suppose that the region R (centered in X, H is the side length), contains a K-sample in the region R. The kernel function k (λ) defined in the sample data process in the estimation area R is:

$$K(\lambda) = \begin{cases} 1, & |\lambda_j| < 0.5, j = 1, \ldots, D \\ 0, & Otherwise \end{cases} \tag{1}$$

where D is a hypercube of space dimensions. When the total number of samples in the R region is:

$$m = \sum_{i=1}^{n} K(\frac{x - x_i}{h}) \tag{2}$$

When and only when $K(\frac{x-x_i}{h})$ (i = 1, 2, ..., n) falls into the region R, its function value is 1.

The general formula from nonparametric probability density can be:

$$\hat{f}(x) = \frac{1}{nh} \sum_{i=1}^{n} K(\frac{x - x_i}{h}) \tag{3}$$

where x is the measured sample point.

The formula (2–1) shows that the kernel density estimation has two drawbacks in practical application:

(1) Discontinuous

Since the sample point used is discontinuous, it does not take into account the distance from the measured sample x.

In order to overcome the discontinuity of estimation, the kernel function satisfying the condition $\int_{R^D} K(x)dx = 1$ can be adopted, thus the estimation is continuous.

(2) Equal weights

The sample points used in the above kernel density estimates are equal weights, because the distances between each sample point and the measured sample are different, so it is bound to affect the estimated result.

This shortcoming can be solved by assigning weights to each sample point, which is satisfied by the distance weight α_i between the sample x_i and the measured sample x. α_i satisfied by $\sum_i \alpha_i = 1$.

In principle, the kernel function can choose any probability density function, but also can not choose the density function, but in the practical application, the kernel function's choice is related to the estimated function, if the estimated function is the density function, then the kernel function best also chooses the density function. When estimating the probability density function f(x), the kernel function K(x) generally chooses the radial symmetric single-mode density function, the most commonly used function is the Gaussian density function Gaussian with multi-variable, and its expression is shown in the formula (2–2):

$$K(x) = \frac{1}{(2\pi)^{D/2}} \exp(-\frac{1}{2}x^T x) \tag{4}$$

where D is dimension of space.

Although the Gaussian function is often used as kernel function in kernel density estimation, the Gaussian function is different from the sample distribution of Gaussian function model. The Gaussian function is chosen as the kernel function, and the purpose is to assign weights to the sample points. Moreover, the mixed result of the local function is different from that of the simple maximum likelihood, and it is obviously different from the mixed Gaussian model, the biggest advantage of kernel density estimation is that it can estimate the density function of any shape.

Choosing a reasonable window width h is critical for kernel density estimation, and the expectation of a probability function estimate function can be expressed as a formula (2–3):

$$E[\hat{f}(x)] = \frac{1}{h^D} \int K(\frac{x - x_i}{h}) dx \tag{5}$$

Among them, where $i = 1, 2, ..., n$.

In the formula (2–3), we assume that x_i is the satisfied probability density which is an independent and distributed sample of f(x). In this way, the expected probability density $\hat{f}(x)$ is estimated to be true probability density f(x) and kernel function convolution. The bandwidth h of the kernel function can be regarded as the smoothing parameter, and if the smoothing function is wider, the estimated probability density function $\hat{f}(x)$ is smoother. When h is approaching 0, the $\hat{f}(x)$ is closer to the real probability density function f(x). However, in reality, the sample data is limited by the amount of computation, so the choice of h cannot be arbitrarily small.

h over the small edge will appear burr, h too large edge is too smooth, resulting in no guarantee that the estimated result is unbiased, so, the kernel density estimation of the bandwidth h selection is critical.

The best choice of bandwidth should be obtained from the sample, and the size of the bandwidth is related to the number of samples, the larger the number of samples, the smaller the bandwidth. If the number of samples is severely limited to the use of a wider kernel function and larger bandwidth, and the sample number can be appropriately increased when the use of a narrower kernel function and smaller bandwidth. Generally, the minimum value (MISE) of the mean integral squared error value is taken as the measurement standard of h.

$$MISE = E\left\{\int[\hat{f}(x) - f(x)]^2 dx\right\} = \int E[\hat{f}(x) - f(x)]^2 dx \qquad (6)$$

3 Moving Target Detection Based on Kernel Density Estimation with Prior Knowledge

The system diagram of moving target detection using kernel density estimation method is shown in Fig. 1:

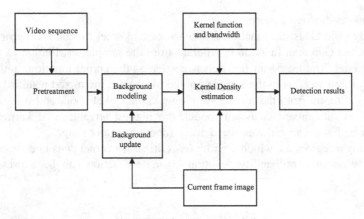

Fig. 1. System block diagram of moving object detection based on kernel density estimation.

3.1 Background Modeling

In the research of video, the pixel value of each frame image in video sequence can be used as a stochastic process, but the outdoor environment is more complex and the background of image cannot be static. The background model of a single-mode state cannot completely touch the real background element, and the density function of the background model is generally unknown. The characteristic of kernel density estimation is that it can simulate any unknown density distribution function, which makes the kernel density estimation method very suitable for computer vision analysis. Set $x_1, x_2, \ldots, x_n$ is a pixel in the video image of a pixel (i, j) in the feature space of the pixels of the characteristics of the N sample value, then the use of kernel density estimation at the t-moment pixel value of x_t the probability density is:

$$\hat{f}(x_t) = \frac{1}{n}\sum_{i=1}^{n} K(x_t - x_i) \qquad (7)$$

Where K(x) is the kernel function, here the Gaussian function is chosen as the kernel function:

$$\hat{f}(x_t) = \frac{1}{n}\sum_{i=1}^{n}\frac{1}{(2\pi)^{d/2}|\Sigma|^{0.5}}e^{\varphi(x_i-x_t)} \qquad (8)$$

Among them,

$$\varphi(x_i - x_t) = -\frac{1}{2}(x_t - x_i)^T\Sigma^{-1}(x_t - x_i) \qquad (9)$$

If the video is visible, we choose the gray value of the image as the characteristic space, and use the gray difference between the background and the target to estimate the kernel density. For the application of kernel density estimation to other practices, it is possible to select the most suitable feature by analyzing each feature. Because the size of the choice of n against noise interference ability has a direct impact, if n select too small, the ability to resist noise is very poor, n too large and will affect the estimation of nuclear density of the operational speed, so we must consider comprehensively, both to ensure the anti-interference ability and does not affect the computational speed.

3.2   Selecting Kernel Function Bandwidth

In the kernel density estimation of the background modeling, the meaning of the bandwidth h reflects the local change of the pixel grayscale caused by the blurred image, not the jump-type change of the gray value. If the optimal bandwidth value obtained by the formula (2–4), we must know some prior knowledge of the real probability density function f(x). From this principle, the bandwidth of pedestrian detection can be obtained by Super Pixel.

Super Pixel is a kind of segmentation processing technology for image [12]. In the field of machine vision research, people tend to extract the image features in a certain size pixel block, for example, the Harr block is used as a template for face recognition. Compared with pixel based algorithm, Super pixel not only saves time, but also retains the structure information of image, and greatly reduces the influence of image noise point. However, in practical applications, if you randomly select a number of pixel blocks or a fixed pixel size directly, it often appears in the same pixel block with multiple target pixel points. Using the pedestrian movement prior knowledge to determine the super pixel is the thought of this paper. The key prior knowledge for determining the super Pixel includes:

(1)   The width-height ratio >0.25, that is, the height is at least 4 times of the width;
(2)   The speed is non-uniform, because the person and the vehicle ratio, belongs to the non rigid body, the rigid body each part movement velocity is the uniform;
(3)   The lower part has upper and lower movements, that is, the backward lift.

According to these prior knowledge, the moving object is divided into $(x_1, x_2, \ldots, x_n)$ super pixel. Typically, adjacent mega-pixel pairs (x_i, x_{i+1}) obey the same distribution in the local context.

Assume x_i, x_{i+1}, the Gaussian distribution of $N(\mu, \sigma^2)$ is obeyed, and the difference $(x_i - x_{i+1})$ is subject to $N(0, 2\sigma^2)$ distribution, which is defined by the median number of the sample and the symmetry of the Gaussian distribution, and the median m of the absolute value of $(x_i - x_{i+1})$ satisfies the formula:

$$\int_{-\infty}^{m} \frac{1}{\sqrt{2\pi h^2}} e^{-\frac{u}{2h^2}} du = 0.25 \tag{10}$$

From the standard normal distribution table can be found, the upper side of the 0.25-digit $\varphi(\mu_{0.25})$ is 0.68, then the following form:

$$m = 0 + u_{0.25}(\sqrt{2}h) = 0.68\sqrt{2}h \tag{11}$$

The obtained bandwidth: $h = m/0.68\sqrt{2}$.

3.3 Moving Target Detection and Background Update

Since the characteristic frame sample is multi-mode, it can not be done by using the simple background subtraction method to detect the real-time image, and the kernel density estimate of the current pixel value $\hat{f}(x_t)$ is obtained by the formula (2–5). It represents the probability that the pixel value is the background point, so you can use the comparison between $\hat{f}(x_t)$ and the threshold th to detect the moving target, if $\hat{f}(x_t)$ is less than the threshold th, then the pixel is the moving target, the current image pixel value is assigned to M_t, otherwise the background point, M_t value is 0.

$$M_t = \begin{cases} x_t, & \hat{f}(x_t) < th \\ 0, & \hat{f}(x_t) > th \end{cases} \tag{12}$$

Where x_t is the pixel value of the current image, Thresholds th can be obtained through multiple experiments.

In the process of video image processing, the background is always changing, so the background model should be updated with the change of the scene, and the background update in kernel Density estimation will be realized by the update of the sample. The update of the sample can be advanced first out of the method, first the sample of the first K frame removed, and then the video processing of the later K-frame into the sample.

3.4 Experimental Analysis

There are two sets of video experiments, video sequences from the Internet video sharing data, and video Test1 image format for bmp (640 × 480) in the indoor video, video length 887 frames. Experimental parameters: k = 10, th = 0.008.

Figure 2 for the experimental results, a1, a2, a3 and a4 are the 31st frame, 38th frame, 44th frame and 82nd frame in the original video Test1 image. The people in the picture are motion, the image is the color image, and the video image is preprocessed in the detection, including the color image to the gray image. b1, b2, b3 and b4 are the results of a kernel density estimator with a sample value of 30. In other words, b1 is based on the 1st–30th frame image in the video image; b2 is based on the video image of the 7th–37th frame image as a sample, and so on. c1, c2, c3, and c4 are the results of super pixels computation. The time of detection is show as Table 1.

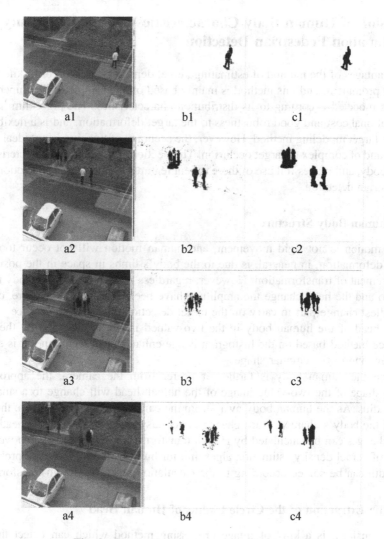

Fig. 2. Test1 video sequence experiment results

It can be seen from Fig. 2 and Table 1 that the detection effect is better and the anti-interference ability is strong with the kernel density estimation of prior knowledge in moving target detection. However, the effect of occlusion and shadow processing is poor, which is detrimental to the following target tracking and behavioral analysis.

Table 1. Test1 estimated time/s

Method	31st frame	38th frame	44th frame	82nd frame
Traditional method	4.23	4.40	4.21	4.30
Method in this paper	3.10	3.01	2.99	2.00

4   Fusion of Human Body Characteristics of Nuclear Density Estimation Pedestrian Detection

The advantages of the method of estimating kernel densities based on prior knowledge are very prominent, and this method is mainly based on the sample of the Super Pixel, which is modeled according to its distribution characteristics. The algorithm has low computational cost and good robustness to the target deformation, and is a flexible and effective target modeling method. However, the accuracy of tracking is not ideal for the background of complex or target occlusion. This section combines the characteristics of human body, and makes full use of these salient features to improve the detection effect in pedestrian detection.

4.1   Human Body Structure

Human motion is not rigid movement, and human motion will not occur too exaggerated deformation, in general, is due to the body's limbs in space in the position of the movement of transformation. However, regardless of how the human body moves, the torso and the head change the amplitude have been very small, therefore, can use the smallest change part to carry on the target detection characteristic choice.

The head of the human body in the two-valued image is extracted by the frame difference method based on the histogram image enhancement technique; it is a graph approximating to the circular shape.

When the human body is farther or nearer from the camera, the approximate circular shape of the two-value image of the human head will change to a smaller or larger radius. As the human body away from the camera or near the camera, the other parts of the body's characteristics change is not easy to calculate, but the head of the image changes can be calculated by Hough transformation. Therefore, when we detect the use of kernel density estimation algorithm for human motion, the fixed problem of bandwidth can be solved according to the calculation result of Hough transform.

4.2   The Extraction of the Circle Radius of Human Head

Hough transform is a kind of image processing method which can detect the geometrical shape of straight line, circle, Ellipse and so on in the image. Its basic principle is based on the dual characteristics of point and line, which transforms the given curve in the original image space into a corresponding point in the parametric space with the curve expression form. In this way, we can detect the given curve in the original image by looking for the corresponding peak value in the image parameter space. For example, the detection of the original image of the circle, line, ellipse and so on.

The Hough transform can detect a circle with a known radius, or a circle with an unknown radius. When the human body is extracted, the radius of the circle of the head in the binary image of the human body is unknown as the movement of the human body changes, so here we focus on how the Hough transform detects the circle of unknown radius. An x-y planar image to determine an unknown radius of the circle, you need to determine three elements, that is, the radius of the circle and the dots are in the y-axis and x-axis coordinates. The radius and origin

For any given set$\{(x_i, y_i)\}$, a c coordinates of each circle in the image can be detected by Hough transform.

Suppose the equation of an x − y plane circle is a formula (7).

$$(x_i - a)^2 + (y_i - b)^2 = r^2 \tag{13}$$

Among them, x_i, $y_i (i = 1, 2, ..., n)$ is a collection of points on the circle to be predicted in the two-valued image. a, b is the center coordinate, r is the radius; It can be seen from the formula (3–1) that any definite point in the original image corresponds to a three-dimensional cone in the parameter space, and the equation of the cone is:

$$(a - x_i)^2 + (b - y_i)^2 = r^2$$

Conical cluster composed of these three-dimensional cones is shown in Fig. 3:

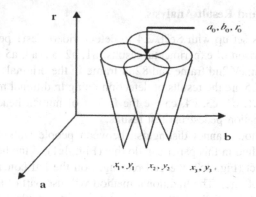

Fig. 3. Hough transformation of a circle

In Fig. 3, if the points a_0, b_0, c_0 within a set are in a circle, then in parametric space these cones intersect at the point a_0, b_0, c_0, and this corresponds to the radius and center coordinates of the circle in the original image plane. The radius of the center coordinate and the circle is the intersection point of a cluster of cones that are mapped to the parameter space in the two-value image space of the head. Using a three-dimensional cumulative array P(a, B, r) = P (A, B, r) + 1 to denote the center and radius, In the image plane, we find the maximal value of the dot in the corresponding P (a, b, r), then this maximum gives the parameter of the circle and radius.

4.3 Fusion of Human Head Characteristics by Nuclear Density Estimation Pedestrian Detection

For pedestrian detection, select the rectangular window as the detection window (According to the human body painting common sense: the height is 7 times of the head diameter, the width is twice times of the head diameter, if in such rectangular window, the pixel connected area does not reach the rectangular window edge, then takes the connecting area diameter as the quasi), so when the choice of bandwidth changes, You can assume that the trace bandwidth in the previous frame is $hx_i(i = 1, 2, \ldots, n)$, $hy_i(i = 1, 2, .., n)$, the following time bandwidth for the trace window is:

$$hx_{i+1} = hx_i \times k, \; hy_{i+1} = hy_i \times k \tag{14}$$

K is the ratio of the circle radius of the moment to the circle radius of the previous moment, that is:

$$k = \frac{r_{i+1}}{r_i} \tag{15}$$

The above algorithm can be used to zoom the detection window, avoid the disadvantage of fixed bandwidth of kernel density estimation algorithm and make the target detection more ideal.

4.4 Experiment and Result Analysis

The experiment was set up with Sect. 3.4 to detect video Test1 pedestrian detection, Fig. 4 is the comparison of experimental results. a1, a2, a3, a4, a5 are the 31st frame, 38th frame, 44th frame\62nd frame and 82nd frame in the original video Test1 image. b1, b2, b3, b4, and b5 are the results of detection using traditional methods (connected region diameters). c1, c2, c3, c4, c5 are the fusion of human head characteristics of kernel density estimation pedestrian test results.

Traditional methods cannot distinguish between people walking together (Fig. 4 b1, b2, b3), the method in this paper can do this (Fig. 4c1), if the head is blocked, this method cannot detect (Fig. 4c3, the 2nd rectangle on the left contains two of people, with less detection of one); The traditional method will use part of the body as a target (Fig. 4b4, two rectangles on the left), because it does not consider the characteristics of the human body, this will affect the accuracy of detection, will mistakenly put other moving targets as human targets, figure c4 detection effect is more ideal: In addition, the method of this paper can avoid the body movement abnormality and affect the detection, as shown in Fig. 4c4's left 1th target, arm stretched out, but not as part of the human body or as an independent human body: The distinction between human body and non human body, the advantage of the method in this paper is obvious (Fig. 4c5).

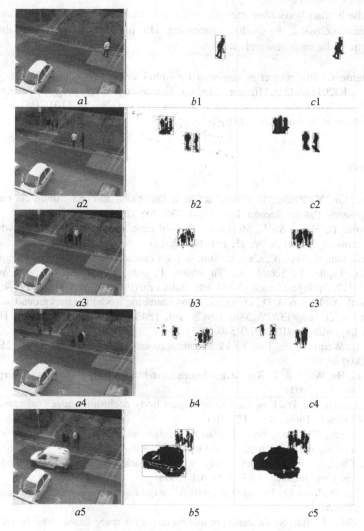

Fig. 4. Comparison of pedestrian test results

5 Conclusions

Pedestrian detection has wide application prospect and research value. The kernel density estimation method has become a perfect method for moving target detection, but the kernel function bandwidth is difficult to be chosen. A pedestrian detection method for fusion of human body characteristics and kernel density estimation is proposed.

Firstly, the super Pixel is constructed based on the prior knowledge of pedestrians, as the sample point of distribution, and the bandwidth should be determined adaptively according to the Super pixel. The experiments show that the detection effect of pedestrian is good, the anti-interference ability is strong and the efficiency is high.

Then, the human body characteristic and the kernel density estimate fusion, solves the pedestrian occlusion, the shadow processing. But for the head occlusion, there is no good way; it is the next research work.

Acknowledgment. This project is supported by Anhui University Natural Science Research Project (No. KJ2018A0431), Jiangsu Modern Educational Technology Research Project (No. 2017-R-54131), Nantong Science and Technology Project (No. MS12016036), Research on Teaching Reform at Nantong University (No. 2018043).

References

1. Shao, L., Liu, Y., Zhang, J.: Human action segmentation and recognition via motion and shape analysis. Pattern Recogn. Lett. **33**(4), 438–445 (2012)
2. Matsubara, T., Hyon, S.-H., Morimoto, J.: Real-time stylistic prediction for whole-body human motions. Neural Netw. **25**, 191–199 (2012)
3. Chen, D., Ren, S., Wei, Y., Cao, X., Sun, J.: Joint cascade face detection and alignment. In: Fleet, D., Pajdla, T., Schiele, B., Tuytelaars, T. (eds.) ECCV 2014. LNCS, vol. 8694, pp. 109–122. Springer, Cham (2014). https://doi.org/10.1007/978-3-319-10599-4_8
4. Elgammal, A., Harwood, D., Davis, L.: Non-parametric model for background subtraction. In: Vernon, D. (ed.) ECCV 2000. LNCS, vol. 1843, pp. 751–767. Springer, Heidelberg (2000). https://doi.org/10.1007/3-540-45053-X_48
5. Wang, L., Weiming, H., Tan, T.: Identification based on gait. J. Comput. Sci. **26**(3), 353–360 (2003)
6. Wang, L., Hu, W., Tan, T.: Recent developments in human motion analysis. Pattern Recogn. **36**(3), 585–601 (2003)
7. Zhang, L., Yu, H.: Tracking method of human body occlusion under dual camera. Chin. J. Graph. Graph. **16**(4), 606–612 (2011)
8. Sun, Y., Weng, P.: Study on pedestrian recognition and tracking based on particle swarm optimization algorithm. Comput. Eng. Des. **32**(3), 988–994 (2011)
9. Sun, J., Chen, Y., Ji, Z.: Kernel density estimation background modeling method based on key frames. Opt. Technol. **34**(5), 699–701 (2008)
10. Yu, J., Xu, D., Liao, Q.: Research progress of image fog technology. Chin. J. Graph. **16**(9), 1561–1576 (2011)
11. Jin, T., Zhou, F., Bai, X.: Detection of motion target for space-based video based on kernel density estimation. Infrared Laser Eng. **40**(1), 153–157 (2011)
12. Liu, Y.: Research on algorithm of moving target detection and tracking based on super pixel. Master's degree thesis of China University of Science and Technology, Hefei (2013)
13. Rui, L., Lei, Z.: Design of syntactic parsing unit for structural pattern recognition system based on relational algebra. J. Dalian Jiaotong Univ. **33**(3), 59–63 (2012)
14. Chen, F., Shui, A., Li, L.: Small sample pattern recognition method for pipeline plugging in storage and transportation process. Comput. Appl. Res. **31**(7), 2031–2034 (2014)
15. Peng, D.: Research on brain activity of paired association learning in visual haptic cross pattern. Doctoral dissertations of East China Normal University, Shanghai (2015)
16. Cheng, X.: Research on pattern recognition framework APRF based on multi agent. Doctoral dissertations of Nanjing University of Science and Technology, Nanjing (2006)
17. Di, J., Yin, J.: Application of Wavelet Analysis. Science Press, Beijing (2017)
18. Haken, H. (Yang Jia-ben translated): Work with Computer and Cognitive - Top-Down Method of Neural Network. Tsinghua University Press, Beijing (1994)

Entropy Isolation Forest Based on Dimension Entropy for Anomaly Detection

Liefa Liao and Bin Luo[✉]

Jiangxi University of Science and Technology, Ganzhou 341000, China
luobin_poom@foxmail.com

Abstract. Anomaly detection, as an important basic research task in the field of data mining, has been concerned by both industry and academia. Among many anomaly detection methods, iForest (isolation Forest) has low time complexity and good detection effect. It has better adaptability in the face of high-capacity and high-dimensional data. However, iForest is not suitable for the special high-dimensional data, is not stable enough, and is not so robust to the noise features. In view of these problems, this paper proposes an improved anomaly detection method E-iForest (entropy-isolation forest) based on dimension entropy. By introducing the dimension entropy as the basis for selecting the isolation attribute and the isolation point during the training process, the method uses three isolation strategies and adjust the path length calculation. The experiments show that the E-iForest has better detection effect, has better speed in high-capacity datasets, is more stable than iForest and is more robust to the noise features.

Keywords: Anomaly detection · Dimension entropy · Isolation strategies · Robustness

1 Introduction

Anomaly detection is an important basic research task in the field of data mining. Its main goal is to find the data objects which are different, abnormal and inconsistent with most data [1]. Various anomaly detection technologies have been widely used in various application fields, such as credit card fraud detection, network intrusion detection, medical diagnosis, environmental monitoring and gene sequence research [2].

In recent years, the increase of capacity and dimension in dataset has posed new challenges to traditional data mining and analysis technologies, including anomaly detection [3]. How to find a small number of outliers in a larger and more complex dataset more quickly has become an important research direction for anomaly detection [4]. High-capacity and high-dimensional features usually make computational complexity higher for most traditional methods. It will prevent the methods from producing results in a meaningful time. On the other hand, the possible irrelevant attributes in high-dimensional data have higher requirements on the robustness of the methods. Therefore, anomaly detection methods for high-dimensional and large-capacity data require both excellent computational efficiency and strong robustness to noise features.

Among many anomaly detection methods, the isolation-based detection method has better adaptability in the face of large capacity and high-dimensional dataset [5]. The

© Springer Nature Singapore Pte Ltd. 2019
H. Peng et al. (Eds.): ISICA 2018, CCIS 986, pp. 365–376, 2019.
https://doi.org/10.1007/978-981-13-6473-0_32

representative method is iForest which makes use of the property that the outliers are easier to be isolated to quickly separate outliers. IForest has linear time complexity and good detection result [6, 7]. However, the method has poor stability with a greater randomness result, and also does not apply to particularly high-dimensional datasets, especially in high-dimensional space with large number of noise features. In order to make iForest more sensitive to local anomalies, Aryal proposes to use a local ranking measure based on relative mass to replace the global ranking measure [8]. SCiForest can randomly generate cutting planes of various angles, which is suitable for more complex anomalies, but it has higher computational complexity [9]. LSHiForest is a generic framework for measures, data types, and data spaces that can be extended to any distance [10].

The problem of poor stability and robustness of iForest has not been solved among various improved methods. To solve this problem, this paper proposes E-iForest that is an improved anomaly detection based on iForest and entropy. The proposed method builds a list of EiTrees for anomaly detection of data. Each EiTree is trained by selecting isolation attributes and isolation points according to the information entropy of each attribute of random samples. Similarly, the calculation of path length has also made corresponding improvements. The experimental results show that the E-iForest has faster running speed in the large-capacity dataset and better detection effect. The obtained result is more stable and robust to noise features than result of iForest.

The rest of this paper is organized as follows. In the next section, iForest is introduced briefly. E-iForest is elaborated in Sect. 3. Section 4 shows the experimental results. Section 5 contains the conclusions and summary.

2　Isolation Forest

There are only two parameters in iForest: the sample size (s) and the number of isolation trees (t). The training process is to construct iForest composed of a list of isolation trees (iTree for short). The process of constructing an iTree is as follows [6, 7]:

I. From a m-variate dataset D containing n instances, a training sample $D_i = \{d_1, d_2, \ldots, d_s\}$ of an iTree is obtained by sampling randomly.
II. Within the range from the minimum value to the maximum value of the random feature A, a cutting value P_a is obtained randomly.
III. Two subsamples of left and right subtrees are obtained by cutting the sample D_i according to P_a.
IV. In this way, the left and right subtrees are constructed repeatedly on the left and right datasets until the training data only contains same samples or the height of the tree reaches the defined height $log_2 s$.

Finally, repeat the above training process and construct t iTrees to get iForest. It is judged by the anomaly score that whether the instance X in D is an outlier. The anomaly score of X is calculated by the statistics of the average path length in the iForest.

The path length of X can be normalized by Formula (1). In the formula, $H(k) = lnk + \gamma$, and γ is Euler constant. The average of path length is indicated as $c(s)$ when the sample size is s.

$$c(s) = 2H(s-1) - 2(s-1)/s \tag{1}$$

The detailed calculation of anomaly score is as follows:

$$score(x, s) = 2^{-\frac{E(pathL(x))}{c(s)}} \tag{2}$$

In this formula, $E(pathL(x))$ represents the average of the path length $pathL(x)$ of instance X in forest. Because the outliers are easier to be isolated, they all have shorter average path lengths which will make their anomaly scores closer to 1.

3 Entropy-Isolation Forest

E-iForest uses the information entropy of each attribute to feed back the uniformity of the distribution of sample data in each attribute. The more inhomogeneous the attribute is, the more likely it will be selected to cut the data samples every time. Compared to the randomly cut ways of iForest, this method can make the outliers and normal clusters separated earlier. Corresponding to this change of cutting method, the calculation of the final path length has also been improved. In order to improve the efficiency of the method, the repetitive calculation part of the path lengths is eliminated by storing the path lengths in the nodes for direct extraction. As the upper and lower limit of the path length has not changed, the anomaly score is still calculated by formulas (1) and (2).

3.1 Computation Dimension Entropy

By projecting the data sample D with capacity size of b to attribute i, a set of projection D_i is obtained. Projection D_i is cut into bin segments by equal distance, which is used to get a set of probability $p_j = b_j/b$. The variable b_j ($0 \leq j \leq b$) is the statistical value of the data number on each segment. Then the formula for calculating entropy [11] on this attribute can be obtained as follows:

$$ent_i = -\sum_{j=1}^{bin} p_j ln p_j \tag{3}$$

This method can eliminate the influence of different attribute scale on dimension entropy. It can be deduced from Formula (3) that the entropy is the maximum when $p_j = 1/b$.

$$ent_{max} = -bin \cdot \left(\frac{1}{bin} \cdot ln\left(\frac{1}{bin}\right) \right) = -ln\left(\frac{1}{bin}\right). \tag{4}$$

From the calculation method of dimension entropy, it can be known that the dimension entropy can feed back the uniformity of sample distribution in a certain dimension to a certain degree. When outliers and normal clusters coexist, it is likely that the projections on some dimensions are more unevenly distributed with a smaller dimension entropy. On the other hand, since the ent_{max} is only related to the setting of *bin*, a critical entropy coefficient α can be set as the critical value of entropy to judge whether the dimension entropy is small or not. The dimension entropy is small enough if $0 < ent_i < \alpha \cdot ent_{max}$. By the way, α can't be too small or too large because it should be able to distinguish the list of dimension entropy. The default α is suggested to be set to 0.8 for general purpose. Therefore, the isolation strategy can be formulated by using this distribution fed back by dimension entropy to improve the effectiveness of each cutting.

3.2   Three Isolation Strategies

For a training data sample, the first step is to calculate the list of dimension information entropy $\{ent_1, ent_2, \ldots, ent_m\}$ by projection for each attribute. If there are abnormal points or normal clusters in the training samples, the projections on some attributes may have large blank areas. It means that This means that the projection distribution is uneven with the smaller dimension entropy. In this case, the outliers and different clusters in the sample can be separated earlier by choosing these attributes to cut the sample. In summary, the first isolation strategies is given as follows:

Isolation Strategy 1: The attributes with dimension entropy smaller than critical value are preferred.

If a certain dimension entropy is smaller than the given threshold, the projection distribution of the data samples in this dimension is uneven with great possibility of big blank areas. For this attribute, it is possible that there are lonely outliers or multiple normal clusters. In either case, it can isolate the outliers or isolate multiple normal clusters as a good isolation result by selecting the middle point of the max blank on this attribute as a split value. Because all the attributes whose dimension of entropy is less than the given critical value may be effective, an eligible attribute selected randomly is used to split the samples. Based on the above analysis, the second isolation strategy can be described as follows.

Isolation Strategy 2: If the list of dimension entropy exists, an attribute can be selected randomly to separate the samples. The split point is the middle value of the biggest gap which is searched on this attribute.

On the other hand, if all dimension entropy is greater than the threshold value or even approximate to the maximum value, the samples are more orderly in all dimensions. It will not work to search the biggest gap on a certain attribute. Due to similarity of the dimension entropy, it is no longer meaningful to choose an attribute according to dimension entropy. Under the circumstances, it may be a good strategy that dividing the sample into two nearly equal subsets with the midpoint of a random attribute. In this way, it is possible that the dimension entropy of the subset may be smaller than the set threshold value. Therefore, the isolation strategy 3 is obtained.

Isolation Strategy 3: If all dimension entropy is greater than the set threshold value, the sample should be divided into two relatively balanced parts as the left and right subsets. The split point is the middle value of a random attribute.

The above three strategies of the training stage can be used to construct an EiTree with that the instances in normal clusters having large probability to be isolated at a late time.

3.3 Calculation of Path Length

Because E-iForest uses isolation strategy as isolation basis, the effectiveness of each cut is different. It means that the path length between different nodes should be different in order to ensuring the validity of the final anomaly scores. Therefore, it is necessary to adjust the calculation of the path length according to the strategy. When using isolation strategy 2, the larger the ratio of the maximum distance to the projection length, the easier the data will be cut. Therefore, the path length of these nodes should be small. The formula of the path length for step i using strategy 2 is as follows:

$$pathL_i = 1 - \frac{length(blank)}{length(data)} \tag{5}$$

On the other hand, when isolation strategy 3 is adopted, the data can't be separated easily as the random selection from attributes expects next effective cut. Therefore, the path length of step i should be the largest value as $pathL_i = 1$.

And the path length of instance x on the EiTree j is as follows:

$$PathL_j(x) = \sum pathL_i \tag{6}$$

The path length of instance x in EiForest can be obtained by averaging:

$$PathL(x) = \frac{1}{t} \sum_{j=1}^{t} PathL_j(x) \tag{7}$$

Because of the size of training model is fixed, it can improve the efficiency of the method to store the path lengths on nodes instead of to calculate them repeatedly.

3.4 E-iForest Process

As mentioned above, the proposed method E-iForest contains two main steps: the training stage of EiForest construction and prediction stage for each instance. For given a dataset D consisting of n instances with m-variate attribute, the EiForest contains t EiTrees. The EiTree i corresponds to a random sample as $D_i = \{d_1, d_2, \ldots, d_s\}$. In the training part, EiTree is constructed by iteratively cut sample according to the three isolation strategies. Details of the training stage are as shown in Algorithms 1 and 2.

Algorithm 1: EiForest (D, t, s, bin, α)

---

inputs: D, t, s, bin, α
output: A set of EiTree
  1.   Initialize EiForest;
  2.   Set parameters: $l = ceiling(\log_2 s)$ $bin = 10$ $\alpha = 0.8$
  3.   For $i = 1$ to t
  4. $D_i \leftarrow sample(D, s)$;
  5.   EiTreeList $\leftarrow$ EiTree(D_i, l, bin, α);
  6.   End for
  7.   Return EiForest

There are four input parameters in Algorithm 1. The first parameter is the number of EiTrees t. The path length usually become stable before $t = 100$. Therefore, t is suggested to be set to 100. The sampling size s is the size of random subsample for construction of each EiTree. Empirically, it can provide a good detection effect in a wide range of datasets that setting s to 256. The parameter bin is, as mentioned in 3.1, the number of segments that cut projection into. The default value of bin is set to 10. The last one, critical entropy coefficient α, as mentioned before, is the threshold for deciding which strategy to choose. We find that in most data, $\alpha = 0.8$ is a general preferably choice.

Algorithm 2: EiTree $(D_i, e, l, bin, pathL, \alpha)$

---

inputs: $D_i, e, l, pathL, \alpha$
output: An EiTree
  1.   If $e \geq l$ or $|D_i| \leq 1$ then
  2.   Return exNode;
  3.   Else
  4.   Calculate $\{ent_1, ent_2, ..., ent_m\}$;
  5.   End if;
  6.   If $0 < ent_i < \alpha \cdot ent_{max}$ then record the attribute i into $\{ch_1, ch_2, ...,$
      $ch_{chnum}\}$;
  7.   If $\{ch_1, ch_2, ..., ch_{chnum}\}$ is not empty then
  8.   Isolation strategy $2 \rightarrow D_{left}$ and D_{right};
  9.   Return inNode {
        $pathL = pathL + pathL_i$;
        left$\leftarrow$ EiTree(D_{left});
        right$\leftarrow$ EiTree(D_{right}); }
 10. Else
 11.   Isolation strategy $3 \rightarrow D_{left}$ and D_{right};
 12.   Return inNode {
        $pathL = pathL+1$;
        left$\leftarrow$ EiTree(D_{left});
        right$\leftarrow$ EiTree(D_{right}); }
 13. End if

As a function, Algorithm 2 will be called by giving input data D_i and the other four parameters. The first one is the current height e of the current node. The limited height l is a constant initialized as $log_2 s$. The parameter *pathL* is short for path length. The last α is the critical entropy coefficient.

In the prediction phase, every instance in dataset D traverses the EiForest in order to get their path lengths. At last, the anomaly scores are calculated by formulas (1) and (2).

Table 1. Briefly descriptions of the datasets

Dataset	m	d	Ratio
Creditcard	284807	29	0.17%
Covertype	286048	10	0.96%
Shuttle	49097	9	7.15%
Satellite	6435	36	31.64%
Wdbc	569	30	37.26%
Ionsphere	351	34	35.90%

4 Experimental Evaluation

4.1 Datasets

The experiment adopted six real-world datasets from the UCI Machine Learning Repository and Kaggle Competition. The datasets from UCI are Shuttle, Wdbc, Satellite, Ionosphere and Covertype [12]. The dataset from Kaggle is Creditcard [13].

These datasets are briefly described in Table 1, where n is the number of instances, d is the number of dimensions, and *ratio* is the proportion of outliers. Creditcard contains 28,4807 transactions of the European credit card holders during 2 days in September 2013. The 492 fraudulent transactions accounting for about 0.17% in the dataset are marked as outliers. Covertype is the actual forest cover type data from US Forest Service (USFS). From the seven classes in this dataset, we selected the smallest class 4 as outliers and the largest class 2 as normal points. The proportion of outliers is about 0.96%. Shuttle, as the statistical data of the space shuttle, contains seven classes of which class 1 accounts for 80%. The smaller classes 2, 3, 5, 6 and 7 are labeled as outliers accounting for about 7.15%. Satellite is the classification data of satellite images. The dataset contains seven classes of which the class 6 has no instance. The smaller class 2, 4 and 5 are labeled as outliers, accounting for about 31.64%. For the Wdbc (Wisconsin Diagnostic Breast Cancer) dataset, we regard the data points of which the diagnostic results are *Malignant* as outliers. Ionosphere is a dataset of classification of radar returns from the ionosphere. The samples are classified as *bad* and *good*. The points in *bad* class are used as outliers, accounting for 35.90%.

4.2   Experimental Setup and Evaluation Indicators

The experiment consists of two parts. One part is to compare E-iForest with iForest [7], LOF [14], DWOF [15], SOD [16] and ParallelKNNWeight (PKNNW) [17] in terms of AUC and processing time. LOF and DWOF are based on density. SOD is based on subspace. PKNNW is based on distance. These four methods are implemented from ELKI [18]. The other part is to compare E-iForest with iForest in terms of stability and robustness.

For E-iForest parameters were set as $treeNum = 100$, $subSize = 256$, $bin = 10$, $\alpha = 0.8$. In the other methods default or regular setting were adopted in the experiment. For E-iForest, the parameters were assigned as default values ($treeNum = 100$, $subSize = 256$) mentioned by the author. For LOF and PKNNW, a commonly used setting of $k = 20$ were adopted. Similar situation to DWOFW where $k = 20$, $\delta = 1.5$. And at last, l $= 20$, $k = 20$, $\alpha = 0.8$ in SOD.

In order to evaluate the performance of the method, the AUC (area under curve) under the ROC curve is used as the performance measure [19]. The AUC value is in the range of [0, 1]. The closer the value is to 1, the better the detection effect is. For E-iForest and iForest, the AUC value is the average of 10 results. We use the coefficient of variation of AUC values from ten running results to compare the stability of iForest and E-iForest. The range of variation coefficient is [0, 1). The smaller the variation coefficient is, the more stable the method is. The variation coefficient is calculated on the basis of 10 experiments. For comparing the robustness of iForest and E-iForest, the variation trend of their AUC is obtained by adding noise features to the datasets. The noise features are randomly generated, independent of each other and obeyed Gauss distribution.

4.3   Experimental Result

4.3.1   Comparation in Terms of AUC and Processing Time

The first part of the experiments is to compare E-iForest with iForest, LOF, DWOF, SOD and PKNNW in terms of AUC and processing time.

Table 2. Running time of the all methods on each dataset (in seconds)

Dataset	E-iForest	iForest	LOF	DWOF	SOD	PKNNW
Creditcard	**2.11**	3.21	3010.63	17410.66	17952.58	1313.38
Covertype	**1.89**	2.71	1202.55	62944.17	8088.99	745.66
Shuttle	**0.38**	0.41	43.30	75635.31	634.94	22.86
Satellite	0.19	**0.09**	1.63	16.29	7.85	0.73
Wdbc	0.13	0.03	**0.02**	0.19	0.11	**0.02**
Ionsphere	0.14	0.03	**0.01**	0.16	0.07	**0.01**

The running time of each method in different datasets is shown in Table 2. The bold parts in the table is the shortest running time for each dataset. As Satellite, Wdbc and Ionosphere contain few instances, the performance of all methods is almost the same. However, in the other three larger datasets Creditcard, Covertype and Shuttle, the differences in the running time of different methods become obvious. In these three datasets, E-iForest best and iForest performs better than the others. On the other hand, with the increase of number of instances, the running time of LOF, DWOF, SOD and PKNNW increases much faster than iForest and E-iForest. By the way, the performance of E-iForest is the best or close to the best in all datasets.

The AUC statistics of each method in different datasets are shown in Table 3. For each dataset, the two largest AUC values are highlighted in bold as a good performance. From the results, it can observe that E-iForest performs outstanding in all datasets except Wdbc, where SOD and PKNNW performs better. Especially, on the three larger datasets, E-iForest has an AUC close to 1. PKNNW also achieves larger AUC on four datasets. LOF and DWOF performs not bad on Ionsphere but really bad on the other five datasets. The performance of iForest and SOD is in the middle. E-iForest has larger AUC than iForest on five datasets and close AUC to iForest on Satellite. The results in this table shows that the three isolation strategies and the calculation of path length can achieve a good anomaly detection effect particularly on large datasets.

Table 3. The AUC of the all methods on each dataset

Dataset	E-iForest	iForest	LOF	DWOF	SOD	PKNNW
Creditcard	**0.95**	0.92	0.47	0.50	0.94	**0.96**
Covertype	**0.97**	0.79	0.59	0.54	0.65	**0.80**
Shuttle	**0.99**	**0.94**	0.52	0.48	0.67	0.66
Satellite	**0.73**	**0.75**	0.54	0.33	0.61	0.68
Wdbc	0.74	0.68	0.56	0.52	**0.79**	**0.89**
Ionsphere	**0.94**	0.72	0.89	0.89	0.90	**0.93**

4.3.2 Comparation in Terms of Stability and Robustness

The second part of the experiments is to compare E-iForest with iForest in terms of stability and robustness.

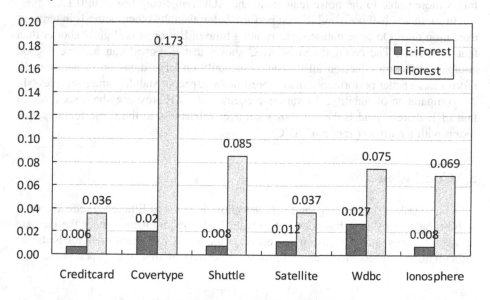

Fig. 1. Variation coefficient of AUC

In order to compare the stability of E-iForest and iForest, their variation coefficients of AUC on each dataset are calculated in Fig. 1. For each variation coefficient, it is calculated form the AUC of a method running 10 times on a dataset. Obviously, the variation coefficients of E-iForest are much smaller than those of iForest. On average, the variation coefficients of iForest are about 5 times larger than that of E-iForest.

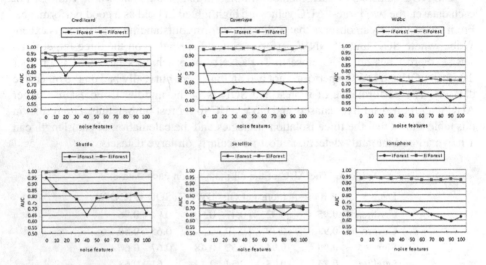

Fig. 2. AUC tends of E-iForest and iForest for the datasets with increasing the noise features

The resistance of iForest and E-iForest to the noise features is highlighted in Fig. 2, where the trend of AUC with increasing noise features in each dataset are shown. For iForest, the AUC decreases obviously on all datasets, especially on Covertype and Shuttle where the fluctuation range exceeds 0.4. Compared to iForest, E-iForest performs more stable to the noise features as the AUC range stay less than 0.1.

In summary, E-iForest and iForest perform better than the other methods in terms of execution time. On large datasets, the running time of E-iForest is slightly shorter than that of iForest. The comparation of AUC shows that E-iForest can achieve a good anomaly detection effect on all datasets, especially on large datasets. In addition, E-iForest has a better performance than iForest in the aspect of stability and robustness. In the comparison of stability, the variation coefficients of iForest are about six times of that of E-iForest. And E-iForest shows stronger robustness to the noise features than iForst with a narrower range of AUC.

5   Conclusion

As a basic task of data mining, anomaly detection, in terms of Efficiency, effectiveness, stability and robustness, has been put forward higher requirements under the increase of data capacity and dimension in recent years. However, traditional methods are difficult to take account of all these aspects. Aiming at this, this paper proposes a